PRAGMATICS FOR LANGUAGE EDUCATORS

Making pragmatics accessible to a wide range of students and instructors without dumbing down the content of the field, this text for language professionals:

- raises awareness and increases knowledge and understanding of how human beings use language in real situations to engage in social action;
- fosters the ability to think critically about language data and use; and
- helps readers develop the ability to "do pragmatics".

The book features careful explanations of topics and concepts that are often difficult for uninitiated readers; a wealth of examples, mostly of natural speech from collected data sources; and attention to the needs of readers who are nonnative speakers of English, with non-Western perspectives offered when possible. Suggested Readings, Tasks, Discussion Questions, and Data Analysis sections involve readers in extending and applying what they are reading. The exercises push readers to recall and synthesize the content, elicit relevant personal experiences and other sources of information, and engage in changing their own interactional strategies. The activities go beyond a predictable framework to invite readers to carry out real-life observations and experiment to make doing pragmatics a nonjudgmental everyday practice.

Virginia LoCastro has worked in the United States, Canada, Japan, Slovakia, and Mexico as a teacher and researcher in the fields of sociolinguistics and language education, most recently as Associate Professor of Linguistics and Director of the Academic Spoken English and Academic Written English Programs, University of Florida, and has published widely on ESL/EFL pedagogy and teacher development.

ESL & Applied Linguistics Professional Series
Eli Hinkel, Series Editor

Vandergrift/Goh	*Teaching and Learning Second Language Listening Metacognition in Action*
LoCastro	*Pragmatics for Language Educators: A Sociolinguistic Perspective*
Nelson	*Intelligibility in World Englishes: Theory and Practice*
Nation/Macalister, Eds.	*Case Studies in Language Curriculum Design*
Johnson/Golombek, Eds.	*Research on Second Language Teacher Education: A Sociocultural Perspective on Professional Development*
Hinkel, Ed.	*Handbook of Research in Second Language Teaching and Learning, Volume II*
Nassaji/Fotos	*Teaching Grammar in Second Language Classrooms: Integrating Form-Focused Instruction in Communicative Context*
Murray/Christison	*What English Language Teachers Need to Know Volume I: Understanding Learning*
Murray/Christison	*What English Language Teachers Need to Know Volume II: Facilitating Learning*
Wong/Waring	*Conversation Analysis and Second Language Pedagogy: A Guide for ESL/EFL Teachers*
Nunan/Choi, Eds.	*Language and Culture: Reflective Narratives and the Emergence of Identity*
Braine	*Nonnative Speaker English Teachers: Research, Pedagogy, and Professional Growth*
Burns	*Doing Action Research in English Language Teaching: A Guide for Practitioners*
Nation/Macalister	*Language Curriculum Design*
Birch	*The English Language Teacher and Global Civil Society*
Johnson	*Second Language Teacher Education: A Sociocultural Perspective*
Nation	*Teaching ESL/EFL Reading and Writing*
Nation/Newton	*Teaching ESL/EFL Listening and Speaking*
Kachru/Smith	*Cultures, Contexts, and World Englishes*
McKay/Bokhosrt-Heng	*International English in its Sociolinguistic Contexts: Towards a Socially Sensitive EIL Pedagogy*
Christison/Murray, Eds.	*Leadership in English Language Education: Theoretical Foundations and Practical Skills for Changing Times*
McCafferty/Stam, Eds.	*Gesture: Second Language Acquisition and Classroom Research*
Liu	*Idioms: Description, Comprehension, Acquisition, and Pedagogy*
Chapelle/Enright/Jamison, Eds.	*Building a Validity Argument for the Text of English as a Foreign Language*™
Kondo-Brown/Brown, Eds.	*Teaching Chinese, Japanese, and Korean Heritage Students: Curriculum Needs, Materials, and Assessments*
Youmans	*Chicano-Anglo Conversations: Truth, Honesty, and Politeness*
Birch	*English L2 Reading: Getting to the Bottom, Second Edition*
Luk/Lin	*Classroom Interactions as Cross-cultural Encounters: Native Speakers in EFL Lessons*
Levy/Stockwell	*CALL Dimensions: Issues and Options in Computer Assisted Language Learning*
Nero, Ed.	*Dialects, Englishes, Creoles, and Education*
Basturkmen	*Ideas and Options in English for Specific Purposes*
Kumaravadivelu	*Understanding Language Teaching: From Method to Postmethod*

McKay	*Researching Second Language Classrooms*
Egbert/Petrie, Eds.	*CALL Research Perspectives*
Canagarajah, Ed.	*Reclaiming the Local in Language Policy and Practice*
Adamson	*Language Minority Students in American Schools: An Education in English*
Fotos/Browne, Eds.	*New Perspectives on CALL for Second Language Classrooms*
Hinkel	*Teaching Academic ESL Writing: Practical Techniques in Vocabulary and Grammar*
Hinkel/Fotos, Eds.	*New Perspectives on Grammar Teaching in Second Language Classrooms*
Hinkel	*Second Language Writers' Text: Linguistic and Rhetorical Features*

Visit **www.routledge.com/education** for additional information on titles in the ESL & Applied Linguistics Professional Series

PRAGMATICS FOR LANGUAGE EDUCATORS

A Sociolinguistic Perspective

Virginia LoCastro

Routledge
Taylor & Francis Group

NEW YORK AND LONDON

First published 2012
by Routledge
711 Third Avenue, New York, NY 10017

Simultaneously published in the UK
by Routledge
2 Park Square, Milton Park, Abingdon, Oxon OX14 4RN

Routledge is an imprint of the Taylor & Francis Group, an informa business

© 2012 Taylor & Francis

The right of Virginia LoCastro to be identified as author of this work has been asserted by her in accordance with sections 77 and 78 of the Copyright, Designs and Patents Act 1988.

All rights reserved. No part of this book may be reprinted or reproduced or utilized in any form or by any electronic, mechanical, or other means, now known or hereafter invented, including photocopying and recording, or in any information storage or retrieval system, without permission in writing from the publishers.

Trademark notice: Product or corporate names may be trademarks or registered trademarks, and are used only for identification and explanation without intent to infringe.

Library of Congress Cataloging in Publication Data
LoCastro, Virginia, 1945-
Pragmatics for language educators: a sociolinguistic Perspective / Virginia LoCastro.
 p.cm. — (ESL & Applied Linguistics Professional Series)
 Includes bibliographical references and index.
 1.Pragmatics. 2. Language and languages—Study and teaching. 3. Sociolinguistics.
 4. Teacher-student relationships. I. Title.
P99.4.P72L67 2011
401'.45—dc22   2011009583

ISBN: 978-0-415-80115-7 (hbk)
ISBN: 978-0-415-80116-4 (pbk)
ISBN: 978-0-203-85094-7 (ebk)

Typeset in Bembo
by RefineCatch Limited, Bungay, Suffolk, UK

Printed and bound in the United States of America on acid-free paper by Edwards Brothers, Inc.

To all my third culture friends, colleagues, and former students who understand

CONTENTS

Preface xi
Acknowledgments xvi
List of Transcription Conventions xvii

PART I
What is Pragmatics?   **1**

1 Defining the Territory   3

2 Principles of Pragmatic Meaning   18

3 Sociolinguistic Theories of Pragmatic Meaning   46

PART II
Core Areas of Pragmatics   **77**

4 Cross-cultural Pragmatics   79

5 Interlanguage Pragmatics   111

6 Politeness   136

7 Interactional Construction of Identity   159

8 Institutional Talk   184

9	Language, Gender, and Power	210
10	Classroom Pragmatic Development	234

PART III
Research in Sociopragmatics — 265

11	Guidelines for Small Sociopragmatics Projects	267
12	Ideas for Research Projects in Sociopragmatics	291

PART IV
Conclusion — 303

13	Pragmatic Competence in Our Diverse World	305

Note — *310*
References — *311*
Index — *327*

PREFACE

The goal of *Pragmatics for Language Educators: A Sociolinguistic Perspective* is to help both novices and experienced researchers in the field of pragmatics to expand their awareness of the social aspects of language in use. Intended to be accessible to all readers, this book facilitates understanding through a host of multilingual examples and studies. Language educators, sociolinguists, and applied linguistic professionals can benefit from an understanding of this established and highly important field of linguistics.

In this volume I adopt an inclusive view of pragmatics. A problem with pragmatics has been what to include in the field. Formerly, pragmatics focused on the speaker only in discussions of meaning and in general comprehension and production of pragmatic meaning. Crystal, in his 1985 definition of pragmatics, did include the need to "study language from the point of view of users ... and the effects their use of language has on other participants in the act of communication" (1985: 240). However, it was my own research and that of other scholars such as Clark (2007) that expanded the perspective and took on board the simple notion that since speakers become hearers, and hearers become speakers, it seems obvious that all language use is "joint action," to use Clark's term. This perspective is where we must start to achieve greater understanding of interactions. Understanding of pragmatic meaning requires an interweaving of linguistic analysis, local contextual information, and sociolinguistic dimensions such as sociocultural and historical information. Language use is always complex, multidimensional, and inherently interactive.

Clark compares the role of participants in interactional discourse to those of jazz musicians improvising in a band. Here is another vivid metaphor inspired by a passage from the program of the June 28, 1997 performance of the University of Hawaii Gamelan Ensemble, "Music and Dance of Java and Bali."

> A gamelan is a unified instrumental ensemble, composed entirely of bronze percussion instruments. Gamelan ensembles do not rely on a visual conductor, but instead rely on audible drum signals to determine tempos and dynamics. In dance genres, dancers must adhere to the musical form, and at the same time, the musicians pay close attention to the initiative of the dancers. Thus there is a marvelous interplay among the performing artists which includes change, predictability, and surprise.

I see the gamelan orchestra as a poetic metaphor for human conversational interaction. Subtle cues of head movements or gaze from one individual inform other performers of their turns to contribute to the flow of the music, just as the same types of cues influence interactional moves and create pragmatic meaning.

In this book, the inclusive view of pragmatics focuses on the interface of pragmatics and sociolinguistics, where contextual features are considered to contribute essential dynamics to interpreting interactional meaning. Clearly, sociocultural aspects have an important role to play, from the micro levels where age and status of interlocutors constrain talk to macro level influences such as socioeconomic background. All these factors have direct influence on participants. In addition, this volume also includes, where appropriate, attention to cognitive dimensions in processing pragmatic meaning.

One question that could be asked about the title and subtitle of this book is how pragmatics and sociolinguistics come together. Sociolinguistics is a very broad field that comprises different ways of studying language, specifically language variation and change. Given that language is used differently in different contexts, sociolinguistics looks at patterns of language in use as well as attitudes towards variation in language. It is possible to separate sociolinguistics into two major areas, for heuristic purposes: macro and micro sociolinguistics. The macro sociolinguistics agenda is to explicate and interpret the connections between social structure and language, whereas micro sociolinguistics seeks to deal more with language use at the inter-speaker level: how individuals or groups use language and what they use it for. Pragmatics originated in the work of Austin (1962) and Searle (1969), among others, on single speech acts in sentences. These philosophers of language revolutionized thinking about language as human beings use it. Pragmatics has developed beyond those concerns into a multifaceted field that recognizes the complexities inherent in what might appear to be simple conversational interactions, such as neighbors inquiring about their day. All instances of language use are by definition interdependent and mutually constructed in the myriad of contexts of everyday life.

Another central concern of sociolinguistics is social structures, particularly in language contact environments. Pragmatics includes in its scope those macro sociological dimensions that have an effect on interactions or instances of everyday use. The chapters on language, gender, and power and institutional talk, in particular, include explicit attention to connections between social structures and language use.

My Approach to Sociopragmatics

I have made efforts in this volume to include examples from non-Western languages and cultures for several reasons. First of all, while I am myself educated and hold degrees from Anglo-American universities (U.S., Canada, and U.K.), I try to avoid having an exclusively Anglo-American perspective that may constrain my thinking and my decision-making about theoretical frameworks, data collection and analysis, and interpretations of data. My intellectual and affective formation have been influenced by extensive periods of time I've spent living, working, and studying in second language/cultural contexts: France, Quebec, Japan, Slovakia, and Mexico. My experiences in those environments deeply challenged me and opened my eyes to many new aspects of my field of study, linguistics and language in use, as well as everyday life. Thus, my decision to take an inclusive perspective in the choice of content and examples in this book reflects my own journey and adventures in intercultural dimensions. Second, I have taught and trained students and worked with colleagues all over the world at the undergraduate and graduate levels in various institutions as we become members of the increasingly international community of teachers, researchers, and writers. It would be untenable for me to exclude their research, approaches to understanding pragmatics, and discoveries about language use in their cultural contexts as well as their interpretations of Anglo-American research studies and interactional patterns. Third, both the academic and the popular press inform the public of international news and developments as well as new thinking about a myriad of topics, including those of interest to pragmatics—power, culture, and ideology—consequently motivating and informing my own efforts to activate an inclusive perspective in this volume.

The need for an inclusive pragmatics, in particular on sociocultural factors, is being recognized by others in the field. The January, 2009 special issue of the *Journal of Pragmatics* is devoted to "emancipatory pragmatics," with an introduction by the three editors, Hanks, Ide, and Katagiri, that lends support to my own perspective which has developed over many years of work in the field. While this current book cannot go far in developing a more general awareness in pragmatics of this notion of emancipatory pragmatics, it moves in the direction of raising awareness of the need to challenge the dominance of the Western view of language, culture, and interactions and open the doors to reinterpreting even speech acts from non-Western, non-European perspectives.

Language Educators

This introduction to a sociolinguistic perspective on pragmatics makes this field accessible to a wide range of learners and language educators without dumbing down the content. Through careful explanations, a wealth of examples, and attention to the needs of nonnative speakers of English readers when possible, this volume contributes to fostering pragmatic competence development in second and foreign language instructed environments. Some chapters include a section on "Applications to the Classroom" and Chapter 10 addresses specifically issues related to pragmatic competence development in language classrooms. Recommendations for helping learners develop their ability to understand and produce pragmatic meaning can be found in the Suggested Readings section of Chapter 10.

Organization of the Book

This book is divided into four sections. Part I introduces terms and concepts as well as relevant theories of pragmatic meaning to readers regarding the sociolinguistic/pragmatic perspective on human communication. Part II brings core areas of pragmatics to the forefront by discussing the contributions of influential work by researchers, their empirical findings, and applications to the concerns of language educators. This part includes topics of current interest and new developments that are particularly motivating to readers in terms of demonstrating the relevance of pragmatics in the everyday world. Part III links the knowledge gained in Parts I and II to actual hands-on research projects on pragmatics topics. Part IV contains the conclusion.

In Part 1, Chapter 1, "Defining the territory," aims to describe the field of pragmatics, what kinds of studies are conducted, how they are done, and how pragmatics differs from other forms of language analysis. Chapter 2, "Principles of pragmatic meaning," provides an introduction to traditional pragmatic concepts and principles to equip readers with the basic intellectual tools needed to carry out pragmatic analysis on everyday talk. Chapter 3, "Sociolinguistic theories of pragmatic meaning," reviews theories that have been particularly influential regarding the social dimensions of pragmatic meaning: Grice's Cooperative Principle and the four maxims, preference organization, adjacency pairs, speech acts, and interactional sociolinguistics.

Part II comprises seven chapters on the following topics: cross-cultural pragmatics; interlanguage pragmatics; politeness; interactional construction of identity; institutional talk; language, gender, and power; and classroom pragmatic development. Key vocabulary and concepts from these core areas are introduced and reviewed, as is their relevance to real-life communication situations—such as in an exchange between a visa applicant and an official responsible for processing visas. The theories and interpretive frameworks are explained through examples, and illustrative studies provide evidence of practical applications of the material. Multiple examples from scholarly texts as well as popular culture support the aims of this part. All efforts have been made to avoid the use of constructed examples and to include non-Western studies.

Part III, "Research in sociopragmatics" aims to provide support for readers who may need to carry out data-based studies on pragmatics topics. It includes two chapters. The first comprises guidelines for pragmatics research by reviewing issues such as data collection, the Observer's Paradox, ethical issues, and techniques to elicit data. The second chapter provides ideas and examples of studies to spark the interest of readers. This chapter, "Ideas for research projects in sociopragmatics," is included to increase awareness of real situations, foster the critical thinking necessary to carry out research, and develop the competence to do pragmatics.

Finally, Chapter 13, the conclusion, discusses the important role that pragmatics plays in the everyday world of today, and links the book's goals of awareness raising about language in use, pragmatic meaning, and teaching and learning to be communicative competent in a chosen second/foreign language. The volume aims to foster the ability to think critically about language data and use.

Note that each chapter has a list of Suggested Readings and Tasks and Data Analysis sections. The exercises push readers to recall and synthesize the content, elicit relevant personal experiences and other sources of information, and engage in change of their own interactional strategies. The activities go beyond a predictable framework to invite readers to carry out real-life observations and experiment to make doing pragmatics a nonjudgmental everyday practice.

ACKNOWLEDGMENTS

I am very grateful to my former students and advisees, now in many parts of the world, for inspiring me to continue to make pragmatics accessible and alive for them.

I am also grateful to colleagues and students who have contributed both directly and indirectly to this book: Steve Brown, Paula Golombek, Janet Holmes, Im Hee Sung, Gabrielle Kasper, Julie Kereckes, Ewa Kusmierczyk, Celia Roberts, Joan Rubin, and Karin Zotzmann. A former colleague in Mexico, Ed Simmen, provided moral support and lots of laughter.

And needless to say, I very much appreciate the support and direction of Eli Hinkel, the Editor for the ESL & Applied Linguistics Professional Series, Naomi Silverman, Senior Editor—Education, Routledge, Donna White at RefineCatch, Ian Howe and Carrie Walker.

LIST OF TRANSCRIPTION CONVENTIONS

The following transcription symbols are used in the spoken language data that appear in this volume:

(irrecoverable)	speech that cannot be deciphered
. . .	very brief hesitations or deletions of nonrelevant talk
(.) or +	just noticeable pause
(0.1) (0.3)	estimated pause length in tenths of seconds
?	rising intonation
[ ] or // or =	overlapping talk of speakers
[silence]	comments about accompanying nonverbal behaviors
word.	full stop (period) after a word denotes the falling and end of an intonation [contour]
word?	question mark after a word depicts a rising, questioning intonation
wo:rd	a colon indicates stretching of the preceding sound
(word)	transcriber's guess at an unclear word or words
( )	unclear talk
<u>word</u>	underlined words are those which are spoken loudly
WORD	capitals indicate even louder speech

PART I
What is Pragmatics?

1
DEFINING THE TERRITORY

Introduction

What is pragmatics? How is it important to me? How would I do pragmatics? Here is an example from a conversation between two 19-year-old Japanese university students, one female (A) and one male (B). They tape recorded their conversation in a student lounge at their university in Tokyo for purposes other than for a linguistic analysis of their talk.

1 A: *demo sa nande golfubu haitta no o*
       now why did you choose the golf club?
2 B: *chisai koro golfu otosan ni tsurerarete renshuu itte tee*
       when I was a child, my father often took me to practice
3 A: *n n*
4 B: *soredesaa o-kekoo omoshiroi naa to omotte soredee ICU haitta toki nii*
       and I thought I liked it. Then when I entered ICU
5 A: *n n*
6 B: *gookku iwai to shitee*
       as a present for passing
7 A: *n n n n n n*
8 B: *setto*
       a set
9 A: *oo*
10 B: *kurabe no setto*
       a golf set
11 A: *oo hohhohho*
       o o great

12 B: *moratta no ne sorede golfu yatte miyo kanaa to omottee chyodo ore mo saa sono toki hanami hanami itta toki dee*
        I got them and I thought of playing golf, at that time I went to view the cherry blossoms
13 A: *n n*
14 B: *a golfubu sasowaretee oo chyodo tanoshi soo kana to omottee*
        I was induced to belong to the golf club and it looked interesting
15 A: *n n*
16 B: *de nanka natsu yasumi no aida ne*
        and during the summer vacation
17 A: *n n*
18 B: *nanka baitode golfuojo de hataraita no nee*
        I had a part-time job at a golf course
19 A: *n n*
20 B: *zuttoo sorede mainichi golfu renshuu shite daibu jootatsu shitakaraa sore nara ma haitte miyoo kanaa to omottee*
        I played golf every day and I got better, then I liked playing golf
21 A: *n n sokkaa*
        n n I see
22 B: *n n maa kekko tanoshiiyo*
        yeah, it's kind of fun
23 A: *n n*
24 B: *n n*
25 A: *ee demo kekko okane kakan nai*
        but it is expensive, right?
26 B: *kakaru kakaru chyoo kakaru*
        yeah, it is
27 A: *hee*
        is that so?
28 B: *datte golfu de hotondo ore no okozukai kieteru mo n*
        I spend almost all of my money on it
29 A: *honto [nii*
        really?
30 B: *[n n* (overlapping talk)

(LoCastro 1999, p. 377-378)

There are two noticeable features of their conversation from the point of view of pragmatic analysis: (1) mostly B talks while A asks just two questions (lines 1 and 25) while in most of the lines, she gives a lot of listener responses (*n n n*); (2) the content of the talk (A seems to be interviewing B) may be less important than other possible purposes or functions, such as getting to know each other or passing the time.

Pragmatics is primarily and fundamentally interested not only in the meaning of the words of the talk, but also how human beings can get from what is said in words to the communicative purpose beyond the words of any piece of talk. A question such as the following is the base that drives the thinking of researchers in pragmatics: how do we assign speaker meaning to this talk? Even though in point #1 above, where B, talks the most may appear to be a purely descriptive feature, the fact that one person, B, talks more than the other, A, helps us focus on the why, i.e. the reasons B, a man, talks more. There is a stereotype in many cultures that women, in mixed-sex dyads, talk in a way to facilitate the men's contributions. A asks B a leading question and she then utters encouraging noises (line 7) or short phrases (line 27) to signal that B should continue talking. Thus, the linguist, carrying out a formal linguistic analysis of the actual forms of A's and B's utterances, suggests a likely interpretation of the underlying purpose of the speaker's contribution to this conversation: They are discussing how he came to join the golf club. This analysis gives the semantic or propositional meaning of the conversational interaction. Once attention focuses on the meaning beyond what is said, interactively created by the two participants, it is pragmatic analysis. In this instance, A may have wanted to get to know B as a potential boyfriend, and the topic or content was irrelevant.

The following section elaborates on this icebreaker introduction and elaborates on a definition of pragmatics that informs this book and in general maps out the territory for doing pragmatics.

What is Pragmatics?

The term *pragmatics* was coined by Charles Morris, a philosopher of language, in 1938, to label "the science of the relation of signs to their interpreters," thereby locating this new field of linguistic analysis within semiotics. Within four decades, the social dimensions had become recognized as important, as Ferrara's (1985: 138) definition indicates: pragmatics is "the systematic study of the relations between the linguistic properties of utterances and their properties as social action." Social action denotes the premise that human beings engage in action whenever they use language. Asking someone to close the door, ordering a latte at the local coffee shop, and telling a story about one's grandfather are all actions from the point of view of social theory, a recognized theoretical perspective on language in use. In the early days of pragmatics, all nonlinguistic elements were excluded from this domain of linguistic pragmatics. For example, the ritual bowing behavior Japanese business people engage in as they exchange business cards would be excluded, with the focus of analysis exclusively on the formulaic language used in the interaction. Yet, anyone who has lived in Japan or exchanged business cards with Japanese business people in international hotels or conferences outside of Japan might smile at any suggestion that the nonverbal dimension is not important. Exchanging cards includes not only bowing, but also holding the extended card in a specific way and putting the card on the table in front of one. The card always has to face the person who received it, and the recipient must carefully read it and perhaps comment on the content of the card.

Thus, there has been pressure from a variety of sources, including scholars of Asian languages and cultures (see Matsumoto 1988; Gu 1990) to adopt a more inclusive view of pragmatics. The communicative functions of language in use – in particular, the speaker's intended meanings in interactions – began to be included in pragmatic analysis. Instead of asking only what linguistic forms a speaker was using, not only were nonverbal features included, but also questions concerning the perceived intended meanings, purpose of the talk, sociocultural context of the talk, social distance between the speakers, and other aspects all took on importance as potentially significant in answering the basic question: why did X say Y to Z in this context?

A pragmatic analysis clearly requires a descriptive linguistic study to answer questions such as the language being used, whether or not there are nonnative speaker or dialectical features present, whether the language or word choice is formal or informal, and whether the syntactic choices result in lots of compound or complex sentences. At the same time as the participants' minds are processing these and potentially many other linguistic features for noticeable or salient elements, the individuals are also analyzing the talk for evidence of what the speaker's intended meaning is likely to be. Pragmatics prioritizes the functional or communicative purpose of a speaker's talk as a core feature as the speaker's cognitive decisions are made on the basis of what the message intends to communicate.

The cognitive processing and decision-making about the elements, both linguistic and nonverbal, of the talk are carried out largely without awareness, as the principle of economy of effort drives the brain's functioning. Except for linguists and other specialists, rarely does the average person consider how we process the speaker meaning from what is said. Yet many scholars, teachers, public policy makers, and personnel management staff, to name only some relevant groups of people, recognize the great need to raise awareness of just how much is communicated in an unexamined way in everyday interactions. A recent *New Yorker* cartoon by Roz Chast (2010), entitled "The G.P.S. for conversations," depicts a modern man with examples of what he needs to be aware of for conversations in bubbles around him in the cartoon: "Continue talking next twelve seconds," "Prepare to change topics," "Exit conversation next right," and "Recalculating." While this social commentary is likely to be targeting people who overuse their cell phones and computers to "communicate" with others, it describes as well the subconscious cognitive processes of conversational interactions.

Thus, this more inclusive view of pragmatics has been labeled *ethnopragmatics*, or *anthropological pragmatics*. It has become an overlap field with other areas, as will be discussed below. Pragmatics has sometimes been viewed as a kind of catch-all category, where any phenomena that do not fit into another area of linguistics – phonology, morphosyntax, semantics – get viewed as pragmatic issues. Formal or theoretical linguistics pursues explanations of language competence, claimed to be located in an area of the brain. In contrast, pragmatics draws on what Chomskian linguistics calls *performance data*, the everyday talk of human life, as it places emphasis on the centrality of the functional analysis of language, what people do with language in context. This different emphasis does not mean pragmatics is not interested in building a theory of human communication. Scholars with this goal maintain that language use in context, in everyday situations, must be the basis for theory building.

Thus, distinguishing between data constructed by linguists for analysis of mental constructs and collected data that provide discourse for pragmatic analysis is important. Constructed examples may serve as illustrative texts, whereas naturally occurring data from family dinner conversations to formal business letters to classroom discourse with learners completing an information gap task can only provide the rich texts suitable for pragmatic analysis.

Within contemporary pragmatics, there are two main schools: Anglo-American and Continental. The first places pragmatics as a core area that overlaps with semantics within formal linguistics, along with syntax, morphology, phonology, and semantics. It shares the research agenda of formal linguistics and the theory-building goal. This view reflects pragmatics' origins in the philosophy of language. The Continental school includes pragmatics with sociolinguistics and discourse analysis, and emphasizes the functional perspective on language behavior. In other words, the starting point is what people want to do with language and then how they carry out their communicative goals through language. Further, the European perspective includes a critical analysis of language in use, where researchers analyze how language in use discriminates against participants such as members of minority groups.

To refocus on the definition of pragmatics that informs this book, let's revisit the view of pragmatics in the preface. Crystal (1985: 240) defines pragmatics as "the study of language from the point of view of users, especially the choices they make, the constraints they encounter in using language in social interaction and the effects their use of language has on other participants in the act of communication." This inclusive definition provides a map of the territory of contemporary pragmatics from a sociolinguistic perspective and informs this volume.

What does Pragmatics Study?

Pragmatics concerns speaker meaning, specifically deriving the intended communicative message from what is said in a particular context. For instance, the ubiquitous question of "How can I help you?" uttered by a hardware store clerk is typically a friendly icebreaker and potentially an offer to help the customer find and purchase a sought-after screwdriver. The same question uttered at home may be an offer to help a particularly busy mother by driving the children to their school for that day. At a very general level, pragmatics seeks to understand how human beings can comprehend and produce the different intended meanings. A speaker's decision-making involves word choice, syntactic structures, prosodic contours, constraints on how to address the listener in the context, and the possible effect on the listener. Scholars in pragmatics strive to describe the principles and theories that underlie how human beings achieve utterance interpretation and production.

In order to address that general concern, pragmatics engages the scholar in a wide variety of topics. One major area is speech acts. A typical everyday type of speech act is making an apology. A direct apology – "Sorry, I didn't mean to step on your toe!" – is seemingly non-problematic, if the person whose toe may be hurting is a friend. However, an apology by one nation to another for wartime actions is controversial, as any apology that engages the speaker, the apologizer, in humbling her/himself, is not an action willingly carried out at the high levels of governments in international relations forums.

Related to speech acts, there is the form/function problem: a question is not always a request for information. A greeting – "Hi, how are you?" "Are you all right?" "*Doko-e?*" – is conventionally an example of phatic communication. *Phatic* is used to refer to a function of language, specifically "establishment and maintenance of contact, one of six basic components of a communicative event, according to Jakobson (1960, cited in Levinson 1983: 41). Thus phatic communication functions as a means to break the ice, to establish co-presence. Rarely does the greeting imply the speaker wants to know details of the addressee's physical or mental state. If the speaker does, usually the intonation contour in English changes from the expected to a different stress pattern of the phrase. A marked or noticeable difference in the stress signals a different speaker meaning, in this case to a more sincere wish to learn how the addressee is. Pragmatics studies how one form can have several functions and one function can take several different forms. For instance, here are some of the many ways to thank someone in English:

Thank you
Thanks
Ta [British]

With a marked stress on *thank*, the usual *thank you* becomes a sarcastic comment to someone who has let a door slam in the face of someone with a pile of books struggling to get into a building.

Another topic that has interested researchers is the extent to which strategies for interpreting speaker meaning are universal or culture specific. For example, indirectness in making requests appears to be universal. Rather than state "Help me with this suitcase!" the request is likely to be phrased "Would you mind helping me with this suitcase? It's a bit heavy for me." Instead of the imperative verb form, a question with a modal verb and an explanation for the request are found. However, it is not clear how the indirectness of the second version is interpreted across cultures. It may be valued in some societies whereas in others it may be viewed as a waste of time. Research has shown that indirectness does require more cognitive processing. Explanations and excuses for behavior are not equally valued across ethnic, gender, and sociocultural groups.

In terms of the principles of interpretation, researchers in pragmatics have proposed cognitive processing models to account for the steps the mind takes to arrive at an appropriate interpretation of speaker meaning. For instance, one well-known theory is Sperber and Wilson's (1986) Relevance Theory (RT) that elaborates a cognitive, inferential model. It is a psycholinguistic theory on information processing that claims the primary importance of relevance of a speaker's contribution to talk. The addressee in an instance of talk seeks the most relevant possible interpretation, with the least amount of cognitive effort. RT is based on the notion that there are degrees of inferencing and thus there is always one intended meaning by a speaker that has optimal relevance. Sperber and Wilson seek to make transparent stages of inferential processing that were previously left undeveloped.

While an important contribution to pragmatic analysis, RT's explanations of contextual effects are restricted to information within cognitive structures and processes, such as new, given, and activated information. The word *context* thus has a different meaning from that found in other theories. Indeed, an issue of serious concern is the role of sociocultural dimensions in the cognitive processing. The social contextual features – such as gender, age, power, social distance/status – must be taken into consideration in assigning speaker meaning. Consequently, a socio-cognitive model is a new direction for researchers interested in the workings of the human mind regarding pragmatic meaning.

Finally, pragmatics often is viewed as being concerned solely with politeness, a ubiquitous feature of language use, arguably universal, yet controversial when comparing an average person's definition of politeness with that of scholars. The average person on the street has what is called a folk linguistic theory of what is polite and what isn't. This prescriptive view of politeness, often strongly held, involves black-and-white notions, and etiquette books, written by columnists like Emily Post, include recommendations about polite language use as well as nonverbal behaviors such as what to wear for a spring wedding. Given pragmatics includes an interest in how human beings actually use language in their daily lives, the range of topics goes far beyond a single concern regarding politeness. Much theorizing and research using natural language data has taken place in both Anglo-American parts of the world and other areas, in particular Japan, Europe, and recently China. One main issue derives from the question of how individuals are regarded – as rational, independent social actors or as members of groups or communities where their resulting social status constrains their speech. Chapter 6, Politeness, goes into more depth on the theories of (im)politeness and relevant empirical studies.

The list of questions that intrigue pragmaticists does not end here. This chapter serves only as an introduction to the issues. New topics and those already mentioned are elaborated and the knowledge base deepened throughout the book.

How does Pragmatics Study Language?

One of the distinctive features of pragmatics is that it requires data collected in the everyday, real world contexts of language in use. Ideally, researchers seek situations where speakers are unaware of how they are speaking. Their talk is unmonitored and their choices of language use are subconscious. The point is to acquire data of talk that is the most natural and closest to how people normally use language in interactions with conversational partners. Pragmatics is less interested in self-report data of how people think they speak. However, a comparison of beliefs about normative, standard language usage of participants and actual use in particular contexts can be informative. For instance, it is claimed that subject personal pronouns are not used in conversational Japanese. An introductory textbook for learners of Japanese explains this perceived usage norm. However, a study of the pronoun use in unmonitored talk in a Japanese company office results in a much different picture of where first person (*watashi*), second person (*anata*), and third person (*kanojo, kare*) forms find their way into office talk.

Nevertheless, note that although pragmatics tends to focus on conversational data, considered to be closest to the vernacular, or most natural kind of talk and thus a kind of prototype for all other forms of talk, it can be very informative to do a pragmatic analysis of other data such as scripted TV dramas, unscripted political debates, feature-length movies, courtroom trials, and written texts, in particular letters and published research articles. In sum, pragmatics works with performance data that may be full of grammatical infelicities, stops and starts, and stretches of boring talk to establish co-presence, a kind of verbal hanging out to get to know others. Yet it is only with careful, meticulous analysis of such data, the off-record, subconscious talk, that informative insights can be achieved.

In addition to collecting natural language data, pragmaticists include details about the contexts of each data sample: the gender, age, and ethnicity of each participant, aspects of the physical setting, the time of day, social status aspects, among others. Thus, pragmatics research is data-driven: naturally occurring talk provides the basis for analysis, theorizing, model building, and generalizations about communication of speaker meaning. The research methodologies are derived from the qualitative paradigm that informs anthropology, discourse analysis, and sociolinguistics. Quantitative research skills, nevertheless, are needed in studies where, for example, counting the number of times interruptions occur in a business meeting and who interrupts whom can draw attention to contextual features such as the gender roles, status within the company, and manifestations of dominance at the meeting of the speakers that a line-by-line, linguistic analysis might miss.

How does Pragmatics Differ from Semantics?

The relationship between pragmatics and semantics has been controversial, with pragmatics either subsumed within semantics or viewed as a substandard form of language study due to its emphasis on sociocultural features. Both pragmatics and semantics study meaning. The differences relate to the domains of the two areas within formal linguistics.

One position on this issue is reductionism that would abolish any distinction between the two fields; the other, the complementarist view, sees "semantics and pragmatics as complementary, although distinct disciplines of linguistics, shedding light on different aspects of meaning" (Huang 2007: 211). This second view accepts that some contributions to establishing meaning are more easily handled through a semantic analysis, whereas phenomena such as conversational implicature are more clearly a pragmatic question (see Huang 2007 for an extended explanation of this topic).

Given the definition adopted for this book, which emphasizes sociolinguistic variables, the controversy concerning the domains of semantics and pragmatics is not consequential for pragmatic analysis. There are, however, two situations where it is necessary to make a distinction. Taking a functional analysis perspective on language use, it is possible to claim that any and potentially every linguistic form carries meaning. For example, discourse markers, those interjected noises and bits of language that appear in talk as we tell a story or argue a point of view, can signal the speaker's intended meaning.

A: that was an excellent movie
B: well, . . . (0.2) I thought the cinematography was spectacular and some parts were brilliant

Well communicates hesitation and potential disagreement on the part of B in the context of A's assessment of the film. There is also a two-tenths pause, a cue likely to signal B's discomfort in disagreeing with A's comment.

In a semantic analysis, the linguistic form *well* has no denotative meaning, nor does it contribute to the truthfulness of the utterance. It is not considered relevant to establishing the speaker's intended meaning. This example illustrates the limitations of a purely semantic analysis; where semantics stops, pragmatics contributes additional information.

The second limitation of semantics involves its focus on the truthfulness of an utterance. Semantic analysis is also done on utterances such as imperatives and questions, where truthfulness is not an issue. However, as Mey (1993:14) states, it may be more interesting to ask *why* people say what they do, rather than whether or not the content of their utterance is truthful. An interest in the nitty-gritty of everyday human communication may lead to an awareness that a lot goes on in language use as social action. Here is an example of classroom talk (LoCastro and Tapper 2006):

P: yeah?
S: we're having a little problem, right when we let it go, right in this area, right here, around 30, it like has this little bump
P: yeah . . . careful . . . I wouldn't worry about that
S: it's OK?
P: yeah, it's a minor thing . . . you should get the spike . . .
S: it could be like this (points to the computer monitor)
P: yeah, it could be anything . . . I wouldn't worry that, it's very tiny, yeah, go ahead

P, the teacher Pedro, seeks to reassure his students that their lab procedures are correct; his communicative purpose, as is true of a lot of everyday talk, is to do relational work with his students. That is the stuff of pragmatics. The function or purpose – the why – is of greater interest to pragmaticists than the truthfulness of an utterance. Consequently, analysis of pragmatic meaning must comprise a functional analysis as a purely semantic analysis results in a loss of what are viewed as salient features of talk to establish speaker meaning.

What are Other Related Forms of Language Analysis?

Pragmatics overlaps with several other approaches to language analysis: sociolinguistics, conversation analysis, discourse analysis, ethnography of speaking, to name the most common. While semantics studies individual sentences, abstracted from social contexts, these other approaches use written or more typically spoken discourse or texts and include both the linguistic and nonlinguistic contextual features, viewed as vital to understanding meaning. The differences among these discourse-based forms of analysis surface depending on what one's research questions are, i.e. what one wants to learn. Sociolinguists seek generalizations that can be made at a societal level, finding correlations between a particular social group and their language use. Among members of certain ethnic groups in New York City even now, for instance, a dropped postvocalic *r* is still heard and still distinguishes speakers: those who drop their *r*'s tend to be from lower socioeconomic groups or were at an earlier period of their lives. So the phrase *fouth floo* can be heard instead of the more standard *fourth floor*.

Conversation analysis, an approach within discourse analysis, concentrates on the structure of talk and its subsystems: turn taking, adjacency pairs, repairs, and sequences, among other features. The data sets are typically extended samples of naturally occurring talk and there is little or no attention to variables outside the text, unless the participants orient or pay attention to an external feature in the talk. For example, the gender of an interlocutor is not considered to be important or relevant unless it is brought into the ongoing talk by the participants. This key concept is called *occasioning*; that is, a participant's talk provides the opportunity or occasion for the topic of gender to become relevant. There are other features of conversation analysis that are discussed in Chapter 2. Discourse analysis includes text issues beyond individual sentences or utterances, such as macrostructures of texts (for example, problem–solution, cause–effect, and the structure of narratives) as well as the microanalysis of characteristics of spoken versus written language discourse and of airport controller talk to promote safety through transparent language use internationally.

Ethnography of speaking developed as an approach to study natural language use in speech events. In addition to speech acts, Hymes (1972) proposed a higher level category, speech events, as the frame for analysis for classroom interactions, psychoanalytic consultation, or wedding ceremonies. Hymes argued that it is only within the context of a community speech event that the interpretation of meaning occurs. The local knowledge of the participants in the speech event is indispensable for making sense of the interactants' interpretation of the language use.

To summarize, sociolinguistics may study correlations between variation in speech and socioeconomic backgrounds of speakers; conversation analysis tends to restrict its analysis to text-internal features such as turn taking and adjacency pairs across multiple turns of talk; discourse analysis may zero in on question-and-answer sequences in a courtroom trial; and ethnography of speaking mostly emphasizes cultural influences and constraints on, for instance, speaking rights at a mealtime in a U.S. subculture. As a form of analysis that focuses on speaker meaning, pragmatics is a basic tool to be used within all of these fields and others, as discussed in the next chapter. Pragmatics can range from studying speech acts in a narrow linguistic perspective to the interpretation of pragmatic meaning within the framework of sociolinguistics, conversation analysis, discourse analysis, and ethnography of speaking, among others.

The boundaries between the forms of language use analysis may be fuzzy. It is useful to imagine trying to do close-up photography with a single-lens reflex camera; if one zooms in on one petal of the flower, the rest of the flower goes out of focus. Adopting this metaphor, the researcher can see all these fields as part of the fuzzy, out-of-focus background, while narrowing down to one approach will enable the analyst to study in detail one view of how language is used. The researcher's choice of analytic perspective is basically constrained by the purpose of the study. Put simply, it depends on what the analyst wants to understand. If it is the structure of a particular conversation, then CA will drive the analyst's work. However, at the micro level, the analyst is doing pragmatics. In sum, pragmatics is characterized by the following features:

- Meaning is created by interaction between speakers and hearers.
- Context includes both linguistic and nonlinguistic features.
- Choices made by the users of languages are an important concern.
- Constraints (who can say what to whom) in using language in social action are significant.
- The effects of choices on co-participants are studied.

Conclusion

Chapter 1 has addressed the main questions brought up when someone asks "Oh, what's pragmatics?" It is very much a part of linguistics, specifically sociolinguistics, and cannot be ignored in the modern world of rapid messages from diverse places and message makers. The next chapter outlines important principles of pragmatic analysis, specifically key concepts that comprise the framework to interpret speaker–hearer meaning. These principles form another tool or body of knowledge required for doing pragmatics.

Suggested Readings

This first chapter lists below some classic books on pragmatics and discourse analysis.

Brown, G. and Yule, G. (1983). *Discourse analysis.* Cambridge: Cambridge University Press.
Leech, G. N. (1983). *Principles of pragmatics.* London: Longman.
Levinson, S. C. (1983). *Pragmatics.* Cambridge: Cambridge University Press.
Mey, J. L. (1983). *Pragmatics: An introduction.* Oxford: Blackwell.
Thomas, J. (1995). *Meaning in interaction: An introduction to pragmatics.* London/New York: Longman.
Yule, G. (1996). *Pragmatics.* Oxford: Oxford University Press.

Tasks

Awareness-raising Tasks

1. Pragmatics is, put simply, about communication. Yet how do we define "communication"? Here are some examples of the word *communication* in advertisements in English in Tokyo.
   Bath communication
   Aluminication

Workout: creates comfortable sweat, communication, and mutual understanding
Security communication
Communication happens only once or twice in a lifetime
Computers, communications, and microelectronics

What do you suggest the word means in each case? Can you write one definition for *communication* that includes all of these uses? Now work with a group and share answers with students from different ethnic, gender, and cultural backgrounds.

2. Can there be different definitions of *communication*? A bilingual Japanese–English dictionary gives "communication" as the translation of *dentatsu*, a Japanese word that is defined as the transmission of a superior's order to a subordinate. Do you know words in other languages that imply a different view of communication? Might different interpretations of what communication is about influence interactions in language classrooms?
3. A basic concept of pragmatics is that human beings act in and on the world through language. Discuss this view and give examples that illustrate how you act in the world as well as on it.
4. Make a list of social factors that influence how you interact with other people. Have you ever noticed that you may have offended your conversational partner? What do you think caused you and your partner to feel uncomfortable? What did you do about it?
5. How do you figure out age differences in any languages you speak? Is age important in interactions? How so? How can you understand the importance of age by observing interactions, for example, between you and your teachers, who are usually older and have higher social status?
6. Can you predict how pragmatics can be important in a language classroom? Give examples and explain.
7. Tag questions at the ends of utterances communicate more than a speaker's effort to get agreement, as, for example, "It's time for lunch, isn't it?" Generate more examples and then the extra meaning that the speaker is conveying beyond the linguistic forms.
8. It is time to start actually practicing doing pragmatic analysis. If you watch a regular TV sitcom or talk show, start paying attention to the interactions between the conversational partners. Keep a notebook of field notes on what you notice. At first, just observe. Then focus in on how you are able to figure out speaker meaning. What elements of the context play a role, for example? You may want to record some segments so that you can listen to them several times.
9. If there are Japanese speakers in your class or in your circle of friends, talk with them about the conversation in the first part of this chapter. Have them role play the dialogue in Japanese, if possible. Discuss what you

16 What is Pragmatics?

learned by having native speakers of the language speak the dialogue aloud and their comments about this piece of talk.
10. Keep a notebook with you as you go about your daily activities and write down examples of talk with contextual details that you find interesting or unusual. Be ready to share what you have collected with classmates.
11. Compare your reactions to service encounters in restaurants you go to. What do you notice about how the staff address customers? Does their behavior influence your interest in returning to the same restaurant?
12. Collect examples of junk mail. Begin to read and analyze the language use in this form of written communication. What do you notice/learn from this exercise?
13. Summarize what you now know about pragmatics, from the reading of this chapter, class discussions, and these tasks. What questions do you now have about the field?

Data Analysis

First of all, read through the dialogue below between A, B, and C. Then, working individually or in pairs, answer the questions, for class discussion.

1. A: she talked to someone today who made her feel better that, oh he might be looking at six months to a year (.) in jail and (0.2) that would be a lot better than (.) she was thinking of seven years (.) Shawn would be grown up, going to college already or something
2. B: [simultaneous talk and laughter of A, B, and C]
3. A: so now (0.2) it won't be that long (0.3) she hired this attorney today, so (.)
4. B: is he expensive?
5. A: uh (0.2) I don't know (.) I think they all are (.) but she didn't want to take her chances with a public attorney.
6. B: really? (.03) sometimes though (.) those public defenders (.) really you know are for their clients (.) (overlapping talk) you know (.) so
7. A: yeah, it depends (.) it's like ugh the roll of the dice (.) you don't know who you're gonna get
8. B: yeah, um sure [overlap] you might get somebody who couldn't care less
9. A: (irrecoverable) Glen's lawyer was (.) really bad
10. B: the public defenders?
11. A: uhum (.) because they'd only come in, like, maybe half an hour before court is when Glen could see them (.) and they already had this deal kinda worked up in their mind and then that's when they run it past Glen so they really didn't talk to Glen or get his ideas or anything (.) and so
12. B: (0.2) huh
13. A: she thought a criminal lawyer might be different (irrecoverable)
14. B: Yeah, it might be better (.) I just hope it doesn't break them (.) they're already broke

15.	A:	(overlapping talk) they're already broke (0.3) she's ugh looking at taking her car to the to a school to get it fixed
16.	C:	that might be a good idea
17.	B:	like the high school's that (irrecoverable)
18.	A:	yeah
19.	C:	yeah
20.	B:	but isn't it cheaper (.) all they have to pay for is parts I hear
21.	A:	yeah
22.	C:	(irrecoverable) (overlapping talk of all participants) but still she'll have to car pool Sunday

Source: LoCastro 1990

1. Who's speaking? How many people are speaking? Who are they are, based on the information in the data?
2. What is the physical situation?
3. What is the context: social, cultural?
4. What is the topic – main and related topics?
5. What type of speech event is this?
6. What is the purpose of this event?
7. What is being discussed?
8. What are the rules of interaction being practiced in this event?
9. What kinds of shared background knowledge are required to interpret the speakers' meanings?
10. What gets in the way of your fully understanding this excerpt of talk?

2
PRINCIPLES OF PRAGMATIC MEANING

Introduction

This chapter reviews key concepts and principles, related to linguistic analysis, that form the basic intellectual tool kit to carry out pragmatic analysis of naturally occurring data. Chapter 2 focuses on "the basics," the concepts and assumptions that bring to light the integral, core areas of the field. It helps the reader build a knowledge base in the field. The concepts and terminology about pragmatic meaning are frequently used throughout the book and are often expanded upon in chapters 4 through 10 in the second part of the book.

Sentence and Utterance Meaning

A sentence is basically an artifact of writing, characterized by grammatical correctness, punctuation markers, and more subordinate clauses than spoken language use. Clearly, human beings don't generally speak in "sentences" (unless the speaker is an experienced speaker or lecturer); rather humans speak in "utterances" to communicate meaning to interlocutors. Sentences are well formed; they start with a capital letter and end with some form of punctuation, depending on the language. They are of interest in semantics that ascribes sentence meaning, that is, meaning in the abstract, independent of any actual realization in conversation or context. "Utterance" refers to instances of language use, from a one-word utterance ("hey") to a much longer turn at talk by individuals. From an utterance, listeners derive "utterance meaning" or "speaker meaning." By definition, pragmatic analysis focuses on the speaker's intended meaning to understand the interactionally constructed inferences that go beyond the actual words being used.

Use and Usage

Use and usage are different notions. "Use" recurs frequently in pragmatics. It denotes linguistic action that may not conform to the norms of a language and its users. It refers to what speakers do with language, where the focus is on expression of meaning rather than the form of the utterances. "Use" is essentially the function of the linguistic form in communicative interactions. In some varieties of French, for example, choice of the address form *tu* rather than *vous* can serve as a solidarity marker, recognized by members of that particular francophone community. The community norm, then, may expect use of *tu* to address each other, whereas in other Francophone communities, *vous* is the preferred form for anyone unknown to the speaker and for signaling deference to higher status addressees.

Studying use includes interest in variations in speech, such as code switching, style shifting, hesitations, repetitions, gender markings and a myriad of other features of everyday talk. Speakers ignore or break the grammar book rules of speech and thus flout the norms to express irony or sarcasm, or tell a joke. Pragmatics does not focus on performance "errors," but rather on creative language use by people as they employ speech to achieve their interactional goals.

"Usage" is not so concerned with grammaticality that governs linguistic forms, but rather more with what is usually "done" in a particular social context of language use. Widdowson (1978) defined usage as the inclusion of features of the context of an utterance that are encoded in the language itself. An example of usage occurs when features of participants, such as their social status, age, and gender, are grammaticalized in languages such as Japanese, where it is not possible to speak or write the language without signaling the relative social position of the speaker, by using sentence final particles, lexical items, or address forms. The absence of such linguistic forms is noticeable and breaks the norms of usage rules of Japanese.

In effect, usage and use are not a dichotomy; rather, they lie on a continuum, with "rule-influenced" behavior or regularities on one end (usage) and more creative use of language on the other (use). Pragmatics is concerned with explaining the regularities as well as creative, norm-ignoring uses of language in everyday life, and all the gradations between the two poles.

Usage ←---------------------------------→ Use
[Rule-influenced regularities] [Norm-ignoring language use]

Context and Action

Two central concepts of pragmatics are "context" and "action." The context of an instance of language use is composed of linguistic and non-linguistic features, including the physical and social settings, and background knowledge of the participants. The linguistic context is all of the language, before and after, the particular instance that is the subject of analysis. Here are a couple of examples:

> Yesterday, I saw *a* little girl get bitten by *a* big dog. I tried to catch *the* dog, but *it* ran away. *The* little girl was crying.
>
> Susie missed *the* bus for school this morning. She had to take *the* metro.

The linguistic context provides the information needed to understand the interplay between the indefinite and definite articles.

The non-linguistic context can be broken down into two main categories: (1) nonverbal features, such as paralinguistic cues that include voice quality, stress and intonation contours, and pragmatic markers; (2) the setting, which includes aspects of the physical environment and of the individuals involved in the interaction. A chat in a coffee shop will influence the interlocutors just as much as a tutorial in the office of a professor; the individuals are likely to vary such aspects of their speech as the tempo, level of loudness, topics, and use of careful or unmonitored word choice, depending on the context.

There have been multiple attempts to develop a taxonomy of features to account for the variables of context. Perhaps the most well-known and still valuable set of categories is Hymes' (1972) SPEAKING taxonomy. Hymes introduced the concept of communicative competence, which challenged the dominant Universal Grammar view of language that factored out any attention to the use of language in context. Hymes prioritized performance variables, that is, the sociolinguistic dimensions. He further proposed that speech has to be studied as it is used in actual speech events. A speech event is a macro category for grouping language-related activities, such as a wedding or graduation ceremony, Supreme Court hearings or a visit with a counselor. Within a macro category, there are micro categories for categorizing language use, such as giving compliments, challenging a decision by a justice, or asking for advice.

In Hymes' model, speech-event analysis involves features of the setting, the participants, and other aspects as well as the structure of the event (Hatch 1992: 152). Hymes' (1972) mnemonic exemplifies the orientation of this type of analysis and serves as a useful heuristic to inform studies.

S setting
P participants
E ends
A acts
K keys
I instrumentalities
N norms
G genre

In this taxonomy, the terms are defined as follows: setting = where and when the speech event is taking place; participants = the people involved; ends = purposes or outcomes; acts = sequences of language behavior; keys = the tone of the event, such as the use of modality in grammatical forms; instrumentalities = channels (oral, written, telegraphic, etc.) and forms of speech, that is, varieties or dialects; norms = norms of production and interpretation; genres = lectures, poetry, business negotiations, and so forth.

As for "action," the basic assumption is that when humans use language, they act both in and on the world. Human beings use language to create obligations and new social relations as well as do such things as reassure, promise, and apologize.

This insight into human language behavior derives from Austin, a philosopher of language. A collection of his lectures at Harvard University in 1955 was published in *How to Do Things with Words* in 1962. Austin contended that truth or falsehood and the logical relationship between words were inadequate to account for language use and that "the more we consider a statement not as a sentence (or proposition) but as an act of speech . . . the more we are studying the whole thing as an act" (1962: 20). From Austin's insights grew a perspective that is one of the well-recognized attempts to account for pragmatic meaning, Speech Act Theory. (Speech Act Theory is discussed in further detail in Chapter 3.) As a consequence of viewing human language use as instances of actions, the speakers are "actors" who carry out social actions. From the perspective of pragmatics, the primary function of language is to interact with other human beings.

Intentionality and Force

Two very salient concepts in pragmatics are force and intentionality. A basic issue in pragmatics is the speaker's intended meaning. Discussions may arise, for example, regarding whether or not yawning in class signals boredom with the teacher's lecture. Research has shown that people yawn for all kinds of reasons: fatigue, lack of sleep, medical conditions, tension, or an attempt to achieve a more relaxed state. Clearly, just as yawning does not always signal boredom, a possible pragmatic meaning of that action, the task of the listener in any context of speech use is to figure out the speaker's intended meaning. Intentionality is key in assigning meaning in context.

A related underlying assumption is that the only grounds for communication with another social being is that the speaker consciously or unconsciously has something to say that the speaker assumes has some value to the listener. It may be a transfer of information ("Try looking online for information on B and B's in that area."), an acknowledgment of the co-presence of a fellow human being ("Hi, how are you doing? Do you see that rain out there?!"), or an assertion of power over someone ("You need to serve coffee to the guests when they arrive.") In one sense, pragmatics is the study of how intentionality is carried out in language use; more precisely it is how social beings comprehend and produce intended pragmatic meanings.

Force is often used as a term to refer the speaker's communicative intention (Thomas 1995: 18). It involves the actual linguistic forms, the speech acts, which are used by the speaker to enact an intended meaning. If a policeman stops you, asking, "Is that your bicycle over there?" just after you locked it to a pole, you are liable to begin to feel a bit nervous. You know that "your bicycle" is used by the policeman to refer to your possession, and that "over there," especially accompanied by a pointing gesture in the direction of your possession, at a distance from both of you, but still within sight, means that your bike is being indicated. However, unless you are particularly good at understanding intonation cues, you may be at a loss to assign "force" to the question. Is he about to reprimand you for locking your bike to the pole on campus? Or is he going to warn you about the danger of its being stolen? Figuring out the speaker's intended meaning entails assigning the most likely force for the situation. It is possible to understand the "dictionary" meaning – you know all the meanings of the words he uttered – without being able to work out the full force of the policeman's words. His words perform his intended meaning.

Reference and Indexicality

Reference is traditionally defined as the use of words to refer to things in the context of the sentence or utterance. The pragmatic concept of reference, however, assigns the act of referring to speakers. That is, speakers refer by means of expressions, not the words themselves. Reference is thus an action by the speaker (Brown and Yule 1983).

Part of the task of figuring out pragmatic meaning is that the listener has to be able to determine who or what the speaker is referring to in the context of an utterance. Assigning reference can be complex. Here is an example from Yule (1997: 11):

A: the part that broke is a little plastic thing, sort of like a wing that turns all the way round
B: do we have any more of those wings?

This two-part sequence from a conversation about fixing things in the home is uninterpretable if A and B assume that "wings" is referring to those of birds or airplanes. If so, then reference cannot be assigned.

Speakers and writers use linguistic forms to enable a listener or reader to identify something or someone in the context of the utterance. It is an important pragmatic problem in that meaning cannot be established if words such as "he" and "she," prototypical examples of undetermined referential expressions, remain ambiguous. Brown and Yule (1983: 28) provide a not atypical example from spoken data:

A: my uncle's coming home from Canada on Sunday (.) *he*'s due in (.)
B: how long has *he* been away for or has *he* just been away?
A: oh no *they* lived in Canada eh *he* was married to my mother's sister (.) well, *she*'s been dead for a number of years now (.)

A's first contribution to the talk confuses B, who asks if A's uncle has been away for many years or just on a holiday in Canada. It is hard to say whether or not B became less or more confused by A's second contribution!

In the field of pragmatics, there are referential expressions in all languages that denote this connection between context and the communicative intention of the speaker. These linguistic forms are called indexicals. Indexicality is a phenomenon of language; it refers to the potential meanings that are implicitly attached to a word. For example, "I'm here now" has meaning, yet takes on a particular contextual meaning in each situation in which it is used. If a friend telephones from Grand Central Station in New York City, with the message "I'm here now," the caller and the listener on the telephone line must have agreed beforehand on what "here" and "now" mean, that is, at the information booth in the main hall at 7:00 p.m. or they may never find each other in the large train station.

Thus, indexicals are prototypical signals to create reference between the speaker and listener. They are indispensable for dealing with the indeterminacy of linguistic forms that have no clear meaning outside of an instance of use. When one son returns home without the other son, the mother might ask, "Where's Tony?" She may receive the response, "He fell down" (Green 1989: 8, 12). The indeterminacy of the words leaves the mother to assign sense or semantic meaning and reference to the utterance: where? What were the circumstances? Is he seriously hurt? In an actual context of situation, such words as "he" and "fell down" are indexed, compared against elements in the local situation so that their "value" or meaning is determined. Here is another example:

B2: so **this other** lady who was on the phone wouldn't know
A1: what colour hair did **the** girl – **the** lady with **the** telephone + did she have
B1: long brown hair
A1: brownish **sort of**

(Brown 1995: 136)

In this example, the two women are trying to index the woman on the telephone. A1 is not sure she knows who the woman is and B1 is indexing or pointing to the woman with further, finer details.

Deixis

The above example of talk illustrates how commonplace indeterminacy is in everyday language, especially with demonstratives and the definite article. These small words that point via language to items, persons, and places in the context of an utterance are examples of *deixis*, from the Greek term for "pointing." Words such as *that, now, the, you,* and *here* are deictic forms. In English, demonstrative pronouns and adjectives, first and second person pronouns, and some time and place adverbs can be used by the speaker to point. The assumption is that the speaker and listener share the same context or at least knowledge of the same context. The most basis distinction made by deixis seems to be "near the speaker" and "away from the speaker." Thus, there are both proximal – *this, here* – and distal terms – *that, those, there*.

Some languages have a three-part deictic system. In Japanese, it is possible to distinguish near the speaker (*kore*), near the addressee (*sore*) and away from both (*are*). The Spanish of Spain has three as well: *aquí* (here), *ahí* (there), and *allí* (over there). Outside of Spain, it is also possible to hear *acá* (here) and *allá* (there). Of course, it is possible in English to say "over there;" however, it is not with a single word as in Spanish and Japanese.

There are several types of deictic expressions: person, spatial, temporal, social, and discourse deixis. Many languages have a three-part system of linguistic forms for personal pronouns. In English, first person (*we*), second person (*you*), and third person (*he, she,* and *they*) can refer to the speaker, addressee, and others outside the immediate context: "*they*'re arriving tomorrow from Rio." In face-to-face conversations, the persons that *I* and *you* refer to are constantly changing, as the interactants exchange roles in the course of the talk. Note that with *we*, the speaker can include the addressee with the speaker explicitly in the talk. *We* can be inclusive or exclusive, depending on the intended meaning. Here is an excerpt from a speech given by President Reagan in 1984 (Lakoff 1990: 189).

> By beginning to rebuild **our** defenses, **we** have restored credible deterrence and can confidentially seek a secure and lasting peace, as well as a reduction of arms. As I said Wednesday night, America is back and standing tall. **We**'ve begun to restore great American values: the dignity of work, the warmth of family, the strength of neighborhood, and the nourishment of human freedom. But **our** work is not finished.

It is not clear who Reagan is referring to when he uses *we* and *our*: the government of the United States, the people, or both. It may be a strategy of language choice that functions as a subtle means to bring the American people into believing they are the U.S. government, reinforcing nationalist beliefs and values through this use (or his speech writers' use!) of deictic markers.

Note that not all uses of *you* in English or *vous* in French are deictic. When *you* is deictic, it should be possible to point out the referent, commonly the addressee. However, in other cases, such as "*You* never know what's going to happen," the pronoun has no specific referent and thus is ambiguous. Here is an example from a Mexican student's essay, written in L2 English.

> I think that if **you** are really convinced about **your** goals **you** don't need to be socially accepted, but if it occurs that **you** can't reach that desire **you** could get frustrated. **You** only have to look for the biggest goal, not for other factors that **you** can attain on the way to reaching the biggest one.
>
> *(LoCastro 2000)*

In all of the instances of use in this excerpt, the writer does not use *you* to refer to any specific addressee or reader of the essay. This type of impersonal use of *you* almost always has a generic reading.

Spatial deixis, the second category, concerns space and movement. The most obvious ones in English are *here* and *there*. Rather than limit this group of forms to a static view of spatial deixis, it is useful to consider movement away from or towards the speaker.

> Come home! (movement toward the speaker)
> Go home! (movement away from the speaker)

This distinction in English may not hold in all languages, as second language learners may experience even with verbs like *borrow* and *lend*. In English, A loans a book to B and B borrows a book from A. However, in Latin American Spanish, the verb *prestar* can mean both "to borrow" and "to lend."

Another important point with spatial deixis is that distance from the speaker or addressee may be psychological and not simply physical; it is dependent on the speaker's affective stance towards the addressee or situation. For example, psychological distance can be communicated by the speaker uttering, "I don't like *that*," referring to the behavior of a child standing right in front of the speaker. Here, the speaker uses "that" to convey an attitude of displeasure, even disgust or anger, about the child's behavior.

A third category of deixis signals temporal meanings, such as *now* and *before*. Deixis is concerned with the time of an event relative to the actual time of speaking about it. It can be complicated, as the following example shows:

> I can give you a lift home then. (A few minutes from now.)
> I was able to swim five hundred meters then. (When I was a child).
> I will meet you at noon in the plaza. See you then. (Tomorrow, over the weekend, etc.)

Interpretation of these utterances depends on knowing the utterance time, that is, when the speaker is doing the talking. If a teacher leaves a note on her office door that reads, "I'll be back in an hour. Gone to the library," students coming to visit the teacher for help cannot know when the hour is up unless they know the time the message was put on the door.

There is another type of temporal deixis that derives from present and past verb tenses in English that can signal proximal and distal deictic meanings.

> Current moment: I teach in the United States. (now)
> Distance from the current moment: I lived in Paris. (in the 1960s)
> Distance from reality: If I could live anywhere in the world ... (but I don't have such choice).

The tense system signals the event time, which may be simultaneous with the utterance time or with the time reported in the utterance

Congruent:	It's raining now.	Utterance time same as event time.
Incongruent:	By the time you read this, I will have arrived in Istanbul.	Time of intended receipt of message and event time later than utterance time.
Incongruent:	Zakia will be back in Karachi on Wednesday.	Event time later than utterance time.

The fourth category of deixis comprises linguistic resources that encode social status differences, such as the choice between *tu* and *vous* in French and *du* and *Sie* in German. *Tu* is used with friends and intimates in France, while in other francophone parts of the world it also expresses solidarity. *Vous*, in France, is employed with all nonfamiliars. Italian and varieties of Spanish have a more complex system. Two forms may be used with familiars: *tu* (taking Italian as the example) for second person singular, and *voi* for the second person plural. There are two other forms to signal social status: *lei* is the polite second person singular and *loro* the second person plural to mark the social distance with people of higher status than the speaker. Peninsular Spanish has four forms as well: *tu/vosotros*, for informal second person singular and plural, respectively; and *usted/ustedes,* the singular and plural formal forms. Another regional variation occurs in Mexican Spanish, which lacks the second-personal plural form *vosotros*: *tu, usted* and *ustedes.*

Other languages, such as Japanese, avoid use of personal pronouns in direct address despite their existence: *I – watakushi, you – anata, he – kare, she – kanejo,* with the plural forms formed by adding the suffix, *-tachi,* to the base forms.

When they are used in Japanese, in addition to the literal meanings, social and attitudinal meanings are present that are not related to the pointing or deictic function. The following example signals that the speaker has a negative attitude towards the person (*kanojo*) or her habit of being late.

Kanojo wa, itsumo osoi n desu. [Her, she's always late!]

Social deixis thus allows the speaker to express social and other contextual meanings through the choice of one deictic marker.

The final, fifth category is discourse deixis, which concerns "the encoding of reference to portions of the unfolding discourse in which the utterance (which includes the text-referring expression) is located" (Levinson 1983: 62). Here is a transparent example:

> *This* chapter will *first* define speech acts and provide a brief overview of how *this* field of discourse has been applied to second language acquisition (SLA). *Next*, research methodologies used in studying speech acts will be examined, and selected empirical studies that have appeared in recent years will be considered. *Finally*, the available studies on the teaching of speech act behavior to nonnative speakers will be reviewed, and the pedagogical implications of the findings to date will be described.
> *(Cohen 1996: 383)*

The italicized words act as signposts, whereby the writer can cue the reader about the order of information presented in the textbook. University lecturers are often evaluated on their ability to present information to students in an orderly fashion so that they can take notes and understand easily. The signposts *first*, *second*, *next*, and *finally* are important deictic markers in many contexts.

Anaphora

In addition to background knowledge to help an addressee interpret speaker meaning, listeners must be able to assign reference, that is, know who or what is being referred to in the context of an utterance. All language is regarded as referential in nature and referring expressions, such as deictic markers, are not the only means to indicate links between a speaker's talk and the surrounding world.

Common referring expressions in English are proper nouns (*Mount Fuji, China, Montreal*), noun phrases that are definite (*the book, the ocean, the stars*) or indefinite (*an Italian restaurant, a tall man*), and pronouns (*she, it, them*). The speaker makes choices of referring expressions based on assumptions as to how much information the addressee needs in order to comprehend the speaker's utterance.

> My neighbor told me not to park in front of her house.
> You know my unfriendly neighbor? She told me not to park in front of her house.

In the second sentence, the speaker adds the first part just in case the listener does not know which neighbor the speaker is concerned about.

There are two main types of reference: *exophoric* and *endophoric*. Exophoric denotes linguistic items in the text that signal some entity outside of the text itself (exo = outside), while endo (= inside) cues the listener to pay attention to what is within a piece of text. This example from a Mexican newspaper appeared the day after the French football team beat Italy in the World Cup final: "Oh, la, la!" This stereotypical French phrase is an exophoric reference to French culture in general and part of the sociocultural context of the text about football at that time.

Endophoric reference is perhaps much more common, the target of language textbook exercises where the learner is asked to find the referent for a particular form:

> **My neighbor** is a veterinarian. **She** has lots of animals at home.

Here is an example from conversational data:

A: so now (0.2) it won't be that long (0.3) she hired **this attorney** today, so
B: is **he** expensive?

This type of reference requires the listener to work backwards in the text to find the antecedent or referent. It is labeled "anaphora."

There are two other types of endophoric reference. The first is cataphora, where rather than working backwards to find the referent, it can be found further along in the text.

> It's going down quickly, the sun.
> *(Brown and Yule 1983: 193)*

Cataphora is commonly found in newspaper articles or in advertisements where the writer wants the reader or listener to engage with the text. It is a way to draw in the audience to learn more of what the speaker or writer has to say that may be of interest.

Finally, there is zero anaphora, which denotes instances where the referent is ellipted.

> I was waiting for the bus, but he drove by without stopping.
> *(Yule 1996: 131)*

Although the reader or listener does not find a specific referent for *he*, the assumption is that it can only refer to the bus driver. Zero anaphora is less common than other forms of reference; however, it tends to occur often in spoken discourse.

Reference is an important feature of language use. Establishment of reference is very much collaborative in nature as it depends on the shared knowledge of the speaker and addressee. Comprehension and production of reference is one feature of the joint actions carried out by co-participants in talk.

Entailment and Presupposition

Both entailment and presupposition involve the cognitive processing of inferencing. Entailment or a logical consequence has to do with on-record information whereas presuppositions are part of the background, invisible information that is not stated.

As a scientific term, entailment has to do with understood information derived solely from the words or sentences. For example, if a fan of the New York Yankees states "They won!" the entailment associated with the word *won* is that the Yankees scored more runs than the opposing team. It is a semantic inference, essentially the same as the dictionary definition, always assigned to the word *won*, irrespective of the context of the statement.

Note that this technical use of the word *entailment* differs from the ordinary dictionary meaning where *entail* means "to cause or involve by necessity or as a consequence" (*Random House College Dictionary* 1984). Although the basic meaning is still concerned with a logical consequence, everyday usage is not strictly associated with the meaning of individual words, but rather the situation that is described.

> The road construction around Chicago entails our having to change our route to the airport, or we'll be late for the flight.

In this example, a synonym for *entails* could be "means."

Presuppositions are of greater concern in assigning pragmatic meaning as they are part of the assumed, unstated background knowledge of interactants. While entailments logically follow from what is asserted by the linguistic forms in a proposition, presuppositions comprise the background information, such as knowledge of the world, that enable inferences to be made and meaning derived. They are part of what is communicated, but not part of what is said. Presuppositions are properties of speakers and listeners, whereas entailments are properties of sentences. An example of presuppositions becoming transparent would be as follows: a speaker utters an assessment on the food being shared at a gathering, such as "Who brought that awful *lasagna*?" This utterance suggests the speaker presupposition that the listener also thinks the pasta dish is awful, that the speaker can joke with the listener, and that someone else at the party has bad taste in pasta. The speaker takes it for granted that the listener can infer the unstated presuppositions.

A humorous example of a presupposition is that most human beings presuppose that the sun will rise tomorrow. Another is that a deity may not always be so helpful to human beings. The latter presupposition is encoded in interactions in Arabic, when native speakers of Arabic insert *insha'allah* (God willing) even into their conversations in English. Or in Mexico, one can hear *ojalá que sí* when discussing a person's plans; it also means "God willing." Note that the Spanish *ojalá* is derived from Arabic *insha'allah*, one borrowing from Arabic that resulted from historical events. According to religious and cultural practices, it is only with the "grace of God" that we will be around tomorrow. Graffiti on a notice board during final exam period at an American university communicates about such presuppositions:

> Tomorrow has been canceled due to circumstances beyond our control.
> God

Some of the presuppositions are:

There is a God.
God controls the universe.
It is possible that tomorrow is an optional event.
God makes mistakes too.
Students during final exams fantasize that tomorrow will not come, especially if they have a particularly difficult exam on that day.

To understand the humor of the graffiti, the addressee must share the presuppositions held by the speaker or writer, without articulating them. The shared presuppositions are usually not stated, due to the principle of economy regarding the cognitive processing involved in arriving at inferring the intended meaning. Speakers tend to package what they want to say to make it minimally sufficient for the addressee to understand. To do otherwise may result in the addressee feeling insulted or the joke not being understood. Here is an example where B felt insulted while she was an international student studying for a doctorate at a British university.

A: oh, do you know that there is a town, not too far away from London, where you can go watch Shakespeare plays?
B: (silence)

Since B was from the United States and had gone through the twelve-year school system when reading Shakespearian plays and learning about that period of British history was mandatory, like many students all over the world, Stratford-upon-

Avon was known to B, at least from books. Presuppositions, explicitly stated, communicate the speaker's incorrect assumption about the addressee's background knowledge. In this case, A's question was perceived as insulting by B.

Presuppositions can also become transparent in answers to questions as the responder focuses on part of the question. B may not be sure that A, a new housemate, knows about the trash collection procedures in the neighborhood.

A: did you take out the garbage?
B: uh, yeah, I did . . . I put out the non-burnable, 'cause it's Thursday

In this case, the presuppositions are that there are two categories of trash, burnable and non-burnable, which must be put out on different days of the week. B provides that information by stating the presupposed information, i.e. Thursday is the "non-burnable" day.

Presuppositions may be flouted. If A asks "Would *madame* care to dine at the local Chinese takeout?" the first half is likely to bring up images of an elegantly dressed couple off to a posh French restaurant, while the second half turns around those images to a quick drive to a local hole-in-the-wall, where one cannot actually sit down to eat.

Thus, presuppositions form part of the background knowledge that speaker and addressee must share for communication to occur and pragmatic meaning to be processed. Unless they have some background knowledge in common, interlocutors may find it difficult to even begin a conversation. Evidence of this is transparent at social events of all sorts where an astute host introduces one guest to another guest to enable interactions to proceed smoothly.

Prosody

Prosody includes a variety of language-related features in the stream of talk: pitch, accent, loudness, rhythm, tempo, stress, and intonation. Although prosodic features are usually produced at an unexamined level, they contribute very significantly, particularly as they encode attitude. How something is said is as important as or perhaps more important than what is said. President Obama is criticized for not expressing anger – in other words, not showing through his tone of voice and loudness when he is frustrated by events and people.

In fact, it is not possible to speak any language, regardless of the context, without using some features of prosody. Although we might say of someone that that person speaks in a monotone, in fact a monotone pitch range does not exist. It is rather that one person has a larger range of pitch than another person, but everyone has some changes in pitch in the process of uttering speech. In comparison to American male speech, a narrow pitch range characterizes Japanese male speech. The likely explanation is the correlation between a seemingly monotone speech style and male identity within Japanese culture.

Yet, prosody is an area of linguistic analysis that has been virtually ignored until technological advances have enabled researchers to arrive at more reliable generalizations about its role in communication. One researcher on prosody and pragmatics is Wichmann (2000). She has been exploring the value of corpus data to support studies based on naturally occurring talk. A recent work (Wichmann 2004) focused on the intonation of *please* in the context of requests. It is a very ubiquitous combination as most social actors learn in childhood that a request should be accompanied by *please*. How that word is pronounced is important to assigning speaker meaning as the intonation contour can signal friendliness, politeness, sarcasm, or coercion. Clearly, the word is used to communicate interpersonal or attitudinal meaning.

Prosody is an important aspect of language production and comprehension for many nonnative speakers of languages, who find that their foreign accents are difficult to overcome despite attempts to do so. Misunderstandings may arise from what seem to be fine distinctions in an intonation contour or stress pattern. Ramirez Verdugo and Romero Trillo (2005) found that there are discrepancies in the choice of tone and pitch accent by L1 Spanish native and L1 English native speakers that may cause misunderstanding in the pragmatic meanings associated with tag questions. A rising or falling tone on tag questions in English is used to express degrees of uncertainty by speakers. Ramirez Verdugo and Romero Trillo found that the Spanish learners in their study overgeneralized the rising tone for tags, thus signaling a pragmatic meaning that did not match their intended goal. It is likely that this mismatch, according to the authors, is a transfer of training from language instruction and textbooks. Learners probably relied on the syntactic cues and limited instruction of interpreting them as polar questions only, rather than as opportunities to communicate other meanings. Tags at the ends of questions may even lead a native speaker of a language to be unclear as to the speaker's intended meaning.

> You're going, aren't you?

As a polar question, the answer could be either "Yes, I'm going" or "No, I am not going." However, intonation and stress cues with this question can turn it into a strong suggestion that the person should definitely go. A preferred answer would be "Yes, of course," although the speaker could respond in a way that signals she doesn't really want to and it is against her will that she is going.

Stress patterns and intonation contours are particularly important in signaling new and given information. *Given* information is what the speaker regards as known to the listener, while *new* information is assumed to be unknown. The operative difference regarding this distinction is that it is the speaker's belief about the addressee's background and the extent to which assumptions about a topic are shared by both speaker and listener that contribute to marking new and given information. That belief informs the choice by the speaker to mark some information as old or new. Recipes provide examples of where, once an item is established and made relevant in the text, it is often ellipted when it next occurs:

> Slice *the onion* finely, brown * in the butter, and then place * in a small dish.
>
> *(Brown and Yule 1983: 175)*

Notice that *onion* appeared in the list of ingredients ("1 medium-sized onion") and the writer acknowledges the status of that ingredient by using a definite article to signal that it is not new information. Then, in the rest of the sentence, the author can use ellipsis to signal definitely that it is given information as it is assumed the reader of the recipe understands what to do with the onion and not the potatoes.

The following example comes from a textbook by Bradford (1988: 7) to practice listening comprehension regarding the pitch and loudness to mark new or salient information. A man is taking a picture of his girlfriend in front of a church in England and he is giving her instructions so that he can take a good photo of her.

> TURN slightly towards me ... your HEAD slightly towards me ... only SLIGHTLY towards me ... JUST a bit further to the RIGHT ... I mean to MY right ... LIKE THAT ... NOT QUITE like that ... HOW about a SMILE ... CAN you make it a more NATural smile?

Each of the capitalized words is spoken more loudly and made prominent with a higher pitch. The signals function as general cues to get the addressee to pay particular attention to the new information. In this case, the new information involves what the speaker wants to emphasize or contrast with the given. The hearer would pay more attention to those cues in the context of taking a good photo.

Stress cues can also signal presuppositions as explained by Grundy (1995: 75) using an example from Shakespeare. The following is from *Twelfth Night*:

> **If** music be the food of love, play on.

Depending on how much stress is put on *if*, either of two presuppositions can be triggered:

1. Music is not the food of love (counterfactual conditional meaning).
2. Music may or may not be the food of love (real conditional).

Another example comes from Lakoff (1971: 333; cited in Grundy 1995: 75): "John called Mary a Republican and then *she* insulted *him*." This comment presupposes that calling someone a Republican in the U.S. is an insult.

Information Structure

Social actors organize the information of spoken and written texts for two reasons: (1) there are cognitive constraints on both comprehension and production of meaning; and (2) the speaker must constantly assess the ability of the listener to disambiguate the intended meanings. Thus, one aspect of pragmatic analysis of discourse is how information is presented by the interactants. What matters is not only what is said, but also in what order. Due to physiological constraints, language is produced in a linear stream of speech sounds, and it is tempting to consider that the structure as manifested in the linguistic forms mirrors the information structure or cognitive ordering of events (Brown and Yule 1983). However, it is rather more appropriate to examine how the information in a text is given status or salience so that the listener can distinguish what is important or new from the rest of the propositional content of the text. Here is an example of the linearization of speech that helps the listener derive the pragmatic meaning (Brown and Yule 1983: 125).

1. I can't stand Sally Binns. She's tall and thin and walks like a crane.
2. I do admire Sally Binns. She's tall and thin and walks like a crane.

Whether the listener is led to conclude the speaker considers "tall and thin and walks like a crane" to be positive or negative attributes depends entirely on the verb of the first utterance.

However, speakers and writers can overcome the linearization problem by setting up the information structure of a sentence or utterance to communicate what is to be regarded as salient by staging the information. Staging is a theatre metaphor that connotes arrangement of information or props so that one element stands out prominently. It can be achieved through syntactic arrangement of linguistic elements and prosody. The topic-comment structure found in many Asian languages provides an illustration of information structure that contrasts with that of Standard English. The characteristic word order of English and most other European languages is SVO: subject, verb, and object. The subject is the theme element, typically the grammatical subject, and the most important constituent of the sentence.

> The property manager surprised a burglar in the act of breaking into an apartment.

In contrast, many Asian languages have a topic-comment structure, where the topic occurs in the first part of the utterance or sentence and is marked by a linguistic form.

> *huang   se   de   tu-di   dafeu   zui   heshi*
> The yellow soil [topic], manure is most suitable
>
> *(Li and Thompson 1976: 479, cited in Young 1982: 73)*

The topic element sets the scene, so to speak, by introducing what the utterance is "about," carrying the old or given information, with the comment constituent comprising the new (Young 1982). Note that the topic-comment structure also occurs in English.

> Hey, you know, my father, he's decided to remarry.
>
> Speaking of Tom, he's just sold a painting.

In everyday talk in English, such utterances are not uncommon. The topic-comment structure carries a pragmatic meaning of a desire on the part of the speaker to lessen the social distance between speaker and addressee, communicating friendliness and co-membership. Thus, despite the fact that the first example would be regarded as ungrammatical in standard English, the colloquial dimension with these pragmatic meanings takes precedence over concern for correctness. Structuring of information so that it is communicated transparently to listeners and readers is very much a feature of everyday talk.

Grammaticalization

In many languages, over time, devices to signal social or pragmatic meanings are encoded into linguistic forms that become a part of the lexical and syntactic resources for everyday talk. Javanese, one of the languages of Indonesia, has six levels of addressee forms and verb endings to encode different social statuses of speakers and listeners. A question like "Did you take that much rice?" can be said in six different ways (see table, in which the levels are listed in decreasing order of hierarchical status) depending on contextual variables of an interaction.

Question marker	You	take	rice	too much	
Menapa	nandalem	mundhut	sekul	semanten?	3a high
Manapa	panjenengan	mendhet	sekul	semanten?	3
Napa	sampeyan	mendhet	sekul	semonten?	2
Napa	sampeyan	nyupuk	sega	semonten?	1a
Apa	sliramu	mundhut	sega	semono?	1b
Apa	kowe	njupuk	sega	semono?	1 low

Source: Holmes 1992: 273.

In other words, a high-level addressee would require the speaker use level 3a High speech, and when asking a co-worker, for instance, the speaker would choose 1 low.

In Japanese, there has been a noticeable degree of grammaticalization or codification of social variables in the language. Here is an example where the pragmatic meaning of "social responsibility" is encoded by means of *beki* being added to a basic verb.

> *Wakai toki wa isshookenmei hataraku* **beki** *da.*
> When young, you ought to work hard.
> *(Maynard 1990: 340)*

By adding *beki* to the verb *hataraku* (to work), the addressee infers that working hard is a rule or obligation and strongly expected of young people.

Another example is the following:

> *Hachi-ji made ni Tokyo eki e* **ikanakereba narimasen***.*
> I have to be at Tokyo station by 8 o'clock.
> *(Maynard 1990: 342)*

The bolded forms express duty and obligation; the intended meaning is "if you do not do this, it is not good" or "it bothers me." Maynard (1990) explains that the difference between *beki* and *ikanakereba narimasen* is that while *beki* emphasizes social responsibility, the second verb combination is stronger and can also be found in describing how cars must drive in Japan. A Japanese worldview would expect observance of the norms regarding enactment of sociocultural variables in everyday language use.

The important point here concerning the interaction of grammar and interactional dimensions is that the role of grammar as it is traditionally interpreted by Universal Grammar theorists is problematic. On this view, a mentalist view of language that theorizes a language module in the brain holds sway where researchers have developed their premises on the basis of decontextualized or idealized language samples. Recently, from an interaction perspective on language, there has been a turn to "the question of how grammatical and lexical structure relates to society and culture by articulating ways in which linguistic structure are themselves interactional" (Schegloff, Ochs and Thompson 1996: 7). Grammar, on this view, develops in the give and take of human interactions, reflecting the social variables of everyday talk and life. This functional view of language argues that grammar evolves and changes as it is used as a tool by human beings. An example from Japanese illustrates this approach. Listener behavior in conversational interactions, the *uhum,* *yeah,* and *right* cues, occur more frequently in Japanese talk than in American English data. Some researchers argue that this phenomenon has to do with the phrasal structure of spoken Japanese in comparison to the clausal patterns found in spoken American English. LoCastro (1999) argues that a functional view would turn the argument around; the shorter phrases used in spoken Japanese have developed over time to facilitate the practice of more frequent listener behavior due to the local cultural beliefs. As Schegloff et al. (1996: 8) state,

> An anthropology of language in this sense warrants studying not only how linguistic and socio-cultural histories inform social interaction, but also how interactional processes universally and locally motivate, give meaning to, and otherwise organize language, society, and culture.

This more inclusive view of interaction dovetails with the approach of this book.

Functional View of Language

Human beings are inherently social beings, and language is arguably the primary means through which they act in the world to communicate with others and are acted upon by others (Halliday 1978). Indeed, even in dream sequences, people recount arguing with others! According to Schiffrin (1994: 20–3), there are two views of language, the formalist and the functional perspectives. Both are based on different assumptions of the nature of language, the goals of linguistic analysis and theory, and the methods of studying language. While formal linguists seek to develop a theory of language as a mental phenomenon, functionalists study language in relation to its social functions with a theoretical aim of describing universals of language use in society. In addition, formal linguistics tends to move from word to phrase to clause to sentence levels of analysis. Within the paradigm of functional linguistics, the starting point is first asking what communicative goal the speaker has in using language in a piece of data. The functional view thus takes a different starting point, of asking how the speaker's meanings are realized in linguistic forms. The example below presents a common situation in countries with outdoor markets and fruit stands.

Customer: can I have ten oranges and a kilo of bananas, please?
Vendor: yes, anything else?
Customer: no, thanks
Vendor: that'll be a dollar forty
Customer: two dollars
Vendor: sixty, eighty, two dollars, thank you.

(Hasan 1985: 54)

In this service encounter of buying and selling of goods, the function of the transaction is transparent and its realization through linguistic forms and use of turn taking is evident. Further, a functional analysis would notice the ellipsis in the second and third lines; it causes no problems of comprehension as the context of situation enables the two interactants to understand the meanings each one wants to convey. A formal analysis would indicate the second and third lines are structurally incomplete, a feature that may be irrelevant in a pragmatic analysis.

Pragmatics takes an inherently functional perspective on language by asking first how a speaker realizes an intended meaning through linguistic and non-linguistic resources available to the interactants. It asks first what is the function – i.e. to make a compliment, to express sadness, or to carry out a bank transaction – and then how it is carried out with language.

Meaning in Interactions

Meaning is the key concept within the field of pragmatics. Understanding what a speaker intends to communicate, as we do without apparent effort in our daily use of language, become a less transparent process once we ponder it. Exactly how is speaker-intended meaning in a stream of sounds understood? One way to study this process is to observe the difficulties interactants have using a second language, as in this conversation between a Japanese undergraduate student and a teacher who is a native speaker of English.

T: please tell me, what is the topic of your paper?
S: em . . . my topic is m . . . current education should change . . . should change
T: current, you mean education the way it is now? the way people are educated now in Japan should be changed?
S: yes
T: so current education
S: current?
T: current . . . world is happening now current education should =
S: = oh, I see
T: = be changed the (method of) current education should be changed OK all right?

(Mori 1996: 56)

The teacher and student are clearly having some difficulties in understanding each other. The main problem seems to center around the word *current*, which might lead the reader to conclude it is only a matter of vocabulary. However, pragmatics is also involved. It is possible the student's cultural background (Japanese) is getting in the way of asking questions of the teacher: cultural practices in Japan discourage students from asking direct questions of someone with higher social status. The student's hesitations may signal discomfort, a pragmatic meaning inferred by the teacher. Still another point is that the student's final comment, "oh I see," may signal the student does not in fact understand the meaning of *current*, and is merely saying so in order not to appear to be ignorant of what the word means. Clearly, aspects of this conversation have to do with dimensions that go beyond the meanings of the words themselves.

Beyond the basic units of meaning – of words, phrases, syntactic patterns, sentences – the meanings that concern pragmatics are essentially derived from contextual features. Contextual meaning is also called *utterance meaning*. In utterance meaning, the speaker's intended meaning or force, in the context of situation, is the focus.

The meaning of a word, its sense, may be derived solely from its dictionary definition. The word *smart* is polysemous and it has a variety of possible meanings.

> She's smart. She got perfect scores on the GREs.
>
> He's a smart guy. He figured out how to get out of losing more money on the stock market.
>
> You look really smart today. Are you going to a job interview?

It is the linguistic context of the other lexical items that enables the listener to interpret speaker meaning. In linguistic analysis, the sense of the words leads to the sentence meaning. In addition, within the framework of pragmatics, contextual meaning can be further derived if prosodic cues used by the speaker are also analyzed. Try varying the intonational contours or adding "well . . ." to these three examples to show various attitudinal stances. Pragmatic meanings are an inherent aspect of human interactions.

Inference and Implicature

Comprehension of pragmatic meaning entails inferencing, a cognitive process that underlies many human behaviors. Through inferencing, a listener can infer the speaker meaning in such utterances as "Could you pass the salsa, please?" The interrogative form here is, in its pragmatic meaning, a request for the listener to pass the salsa and not an inquiry about the listener's ability to do so, despite the use of the modal *could*. Given that pragmatics is essentially the study of the extra or implied meanings of language use in context, meaning that is not explicitly stated, the cognitive ability to infer that extra meaning must be present.

As a result of inferencing, a cognitive process, the listener may derive an implicature from an instance of talk:

A: let's go to a movie
B: well, it's such a lovely evening . . . and

A's contribution to the conversation is fairly direct: a suggestion that A and B spend the evening seeing a movie at a local theatre. B, however, does not respond with a direct answer. Rather, the first cue in B's talk that B is not really interested in going to a movie is the word *well*, a common hesitation marker that signals B feels uncomfortable about refusing A's suggestion. The rest of the utterance could be interpreted as a counter suggestion that it might be nice to be outside, going to an outdoor café or plaza to listen to some music. These meanings of B are the likely implicatures from B's words, the extra, implied meaning; in a sense, the product of these two utterances.

This example also serves to introduce the distinction between conventional and conversational implicatures. A highly frequent conventional expression in American English is "hi, how are you?" It has become conventionalized as a common way to greet others. Another example in Mexican Spanish is *"hola, qué tal?"* a conventional means to greet that does not entail having to use *tu* or *usted/es*.

The example above exemplifies conversational implicatures. B's talk is a creative choice of words to communicate hesitation with expressing a desire to do something other than to go see a movie. In other words, a conversational implicature is situated in the particular instance and would not be found in a phrase book for learners of the language. Here are other examples:

(1) A: Has the newspaper arrived yet?
    B: It's already 7 o'clock.
(2) A: I hope you brought the bread and cheese for the party
    B: Well, ah, I bought the bread . . .

In both instances, A elicits talk from B, in #1 with a question and in #2 with a statement. B's responses require extra work from A to work out the full meaning of B's utterances. In #1, B is indirectly referring to the fact that the morning newspaper arrives early, well before 7 a.m. The conversational implicature here is that it must be at the front door as it arrived a while ago. Further, B does not seem to be offering to go get it from outside! In #2, the hesitation markers – *well* and *ah* – again suggest that something is up and then B admits to having only bought bread. The conversational implicature here is that B forgot to buy cheese – and is feeling a bit guilty about it.

Cultural and Background Knowledge

An elaborate definition or discussion of the word *culture* is beyond the scope of this book. Even within the field of anthropology, which studies differences in ways of living, behaving, and talking, there is no agreement on what exactly *culture* means. Yet, pragmatics assumes that cultural features interact with language use, influencing and constraining spoken and written texts. There is culture with a small *c* and culture with a big *C*. Typically culture with a small *c* refers to aspects of everyday life, such as the food served at holiday time and the elaborate ceremonies for coming of age in Hispanic and Jewish communities. Culture with a big *C* includes art, music, literature, and architecture, among other forms. When a comedian jokes that he wants to go visit New York or St. Petersburg, Russia, he might say he "needs *culture*." He could mean both notions of culture. Even at a folk linguistic level, it is difficult to cite a clear, inclusive definition of culture.

One assumption for pragmatic analysis calls for including cultural influences on language in use. Chapter 4 looks into cross-cultural pragmatics. Included in the notion of culture is the recognition that it can refer to the practices of a variety of groupings in a community. Sociolinguistics increasingly categorizes people according to their ethnicity, the geographical area where they live, and their socioeconomic class as it has acknowledged that those three dimensions of peoples' lives have an effect on how they use language. Dialect studies comparing the North and the South in the U.S. tend to zero in on accent differences. Yet, there are other distinguishing features, such as greeting patterns, address forms, and topics of conversation that are common in the Southern states but are not found in the large urban areas in the North, on the East Coast. For instance, during a walk through a neighborhood in a Southern city, people who may not know each other still nod, say "How you doing?" and give a smile, and even pass the time of day about local concerns. This type of behavior contrasts sharply with interactions on streets in a Northern area where no eye contact is the norm. One community considers it safer to know neighbors and the other places value on privacy and avoidance of contact.

In addition to the importance attached to cultural influences on language behavior, what is called background or world knowledge plays a role as well. Experience is one part of background knowledge. An individual who lives in a suburban area of a city with a car available for transportation at all times may find it difficult to adjust to an overseas post in a city where subways, buses, and trains are used by everyone. A language use example could involve job interviews where the potential employee does not know norms of interactional discourse for that type of interaction. Chapter 8 on institutional talk considers this area of mismatches in depth. Other instances from daily life comprise background knowledge about permissible talk at rituals such as weddings, bar mitzvahs, and tea ceremonies. Dinner table talk in formal and informal meals or with Italian-American versus African-American families can demand the kind of verbal movements required of getting through an important business or political meeting. The potential exists in all of these situations for differences to arise due to idiosyncratic characteristics of each situation as well as community standards for ethnic, geographical or regional, and/or socioeconomic groupings.

Language Data

One distinguishing characteristic of research in pragmatics is the use of naturally occurring, extended samples of language in use as data. In other words, the data are not constructed by the analyst and, further, are composed of more than one utterance. Often, the samples of language are from everyday situations: dinner table talk, business negotiations, or arguments between a landlord and a drunken tenant. Further, the researcher does not ideally elicit the data; that is, the interactants are not prompted or asked questions to talk on a particular topic. Data sets that are elicited are avoided in preference to more natural, unmonitored speech samples. The ideal is conversational interactions where no researcher agenda influences or constrains the talk. As the content of this book shows, collecting such data is not always easy and at times impossible. Researchers revise the plans for their studies and use a variety of techniques to acquire other forms of data.

Another issue concerning data is obtaining spoken language samples that represent as closely as possible natural use of language. Spoken language, even more so than written texts, is viewed as performance data, riddled with all kinds of errors or infelicitous instances, such as slips of the tongue, hesitations and false starts, grammatical sloppiness, and fragmented, online processing qualities. Discourse markers and connectors tend to be limited in variety (*so, but, and*) and clauses are conjoined into compound rather than complex utterances. Hours of data could be collected without providing anything of interest for a researcher.

Researchers confront prescriptive attitudes towards what constitutes appropriate data. There may be a belief in some cultures that spoken language data are perhaps embarrassing, as they do include the performance errors noted above. In the same way that clothing regarded as socially inappropriate at a formal event may be said to reflect badly on the individuals who have worn such clothing, talk that is not viewed as appropriate for the social context will also be regarded as tantamount to airing the family's dirty laundry. One debate about emailing is to what extent casual writing, full of the characteristics of spoken language, is acceptable or not, depending on the audience. While sentence grammarians, interested in cognitive theories of the mind, consider everyday empirical data unacceptable, it is just the type of data needed to understand contextualized language as action. It is precisely data from those contexts that the researcher can use to learn how lay people use language to construct their worlds.

Conclusions

This chapter has introduced many of the key concepts needed to build background knowledge in pragmatics and prepare for the next step, the sociolinguistic theories and methodologies about language in use. Chapter 3 continues building the reader's knowledge by reviewing four major approaches to understanding pragmatic meaning.

Suggested Readings

Brown, G. (1995). *Speakers, listeners, and communication: Explorations in discourse analysis.* Cambridge: Cambridge University Press.
Erickson, F. (2004). *Talk and social theory: Ecologies of speaking and listening in everyday life.* Cambridge: Polity Press.
Gee, J. P. (2005). *An introduction to discourse analysis: Theory and method.* 2nd edition. New York/London: Routledge.
Goodwin, C. (1981). *Conversational organization: Interaction between speakers and hearers.* New York: Academic Press.
Holmes, J. (2008). *An introduction to sociolinguistics.* 3rd edition. Harlow, England: Pearson/Longman.
Ochs, E., Schgeloff, E. A. and S. A Thompson (Eds.) (1996). *Interaction and grammar.* Cambridge: Cambridge University Press.
Partridge, B. (2007). *Discourse analysis: An introduction.* London/New York: Continuum.
Stilwell Peccei, J. (1999). *Pragmatics.* London/New York: Routledge.

Discussion Questions

1. What are basic or core concepts? What is the purpose of learning these concepts?
2. What are key differences between *sentences* and *utterances*? Why is this distinction an important one for studying speaker meaning?
3. When should *use* be used to talk about language rather than *usage*? Give an example of this distinction.
4. Define *context* and *action* and give examples of each as if you had to teach a mini lesson on these concepts.
5. Intentionality is important in studies of pragmatic meaning. How so?
6. Discuss the connections among *reference*, *indexicality*, and *deixis*. Provide examples.
7. What are the different categories of deixis? Give an example of your own for each one.
8. What is *anaphora*? What are the types of anaphora discussed in the chapter? How does anaphora enter into ascribing pragmatic meaning? Example, please.
9. Compare and contrast entailment and presupposition. Which one is important in pragmatics? Explain.
10. Define *prosody*. How does it play a role in pragmatics?
11. The order of presentation of information in an utterance is another concept that can have an effect on pragmatic meaning. Explain.
12. Find examples in other languages you know of grammaticalization of pragmatic meaning.

13. Explain the functional perspective of language. Some teachers feel it is a better approach for the teaching of a second/foreign language. What do you think they mean? What do you think about adopting a functional approach?
14. Is pragmatic meaning a rare occurrence in human interactions? Explain.
15. Compare and contrast the items in the following pairs: inference and implicature; conventional and conversational implicatures. Give examples.
16. What are the roles culture and background knowledge play in figuring out speaker meaning?
17. What do you need to know about data to do pragmatic analysis?

Data Analysis

A. Read through the transcript of a conversation with two women in the U.S. Then examine the deictic markers in this excerpt of everyday talk and provide an analysis.

1.	B:	I gather (irrecoverable) was really upset about the fact that she didn't get to to have any input of when Barb's last day would be
2.	C:	huh? I knew it
3.	B:	she said she had no idea whatsoever that this was going on and she thought that was really unfair
4.	C:	that's a lie
5.	B:	oh, yes cause she knew about it
6.	C:	right
7.	B:	and then she said about um what's she gonna do with the committee now and more help she needs her to attend those meetings so Barb said that she would go to to this last meeting which is Wednesday, the 15th
8.	C:	the 15th
9.	B:	and then she would go to the Board of Health meeting and that's it . . . I said Barb you know what she's gonna make you do too
10.	C:	(irrecoverable)
11.	B:	she's gonna do the minutes and everything and she goes no way
12.	C:	yeah
13.	B:	I said you shoulda just told her no let her handle it and she said no and I said you didn't volunteer for it did you and she said no she actually told me I should

Source: LoCastro 1990

B. A mother and daughter are discussing what the daughter should do about her roommates. Read through the text and then answer the questions below.

1.	D:	you want me to just say "YOU clean it?"
2.	M:	yeah! If they say "No," just say "Why?"
3.	D:	you can't – it's not like somebody you really know you can't just say – you can't say "YOU do this and you do that"
4.	M:	go ahead and just ask them
5.	D:	well, they're not really dirty (.03) but they're not really clean it's not like with someone you really know.

Source: Hatch 1992: 273

What unstated but assumed knowledge are both mother and daughter using? How do the presuppositions they hold result in a disagreement between the two? Comment as well on any inferences important to the understanding of each other's talk.

3
SOCIOLINGUISTIC THEORIES OF PRAGMATIC MEANING

Introduction

Sociolinguistics studies language variation in the context of use to assess the effect of such features as age, status, and the relationship of the social actors on language use. Even a language like English, which has fewer explicit linguistic markers to signal age and status differences than, say, Japanese, provides evidence of those two features in conversations between older and younger people. A tone of voice, vocabulary choice, or topics of conversation communicate that the speakers are orienting or paying attention to the differences. Modern linguistics, including the philosophy of language, has been dominated by a view of language that separates it from the sociocultural environments in which it functions in the everyday life of human beings. Sociolinguistics studies language as the most significant resource for making meaning by human beings.

This chapter goes beyond the basic concepts that provide the analytical tools for carrying out pragmatic analysis of language data. Here the focus is on theories of pragmatic meaning embedded within frameworks for analysis of naturally occurring talk. In other words, a theory constitutes a type of lens that brings clarity to observations of interactions. Without a theory, human communication may appear to be chaotic and without patterns or reoccurring sequences. A theory or perspective enables the observer to "see" the patterns, the sequences, and the actions performed by utterances to then comprehend meanings beyond the words, i.e. pragmatic meanings. A theory then provides the underlying premises for methodologies for data collection, data analysis, and interpretations of the collected data. Each of the approaches or perspectives discussed in this chapter is thus both a theory as well as a methodology for studying pragmatics.

This chapter starts with a brief review of the contributions to pragmatics from H. S. Grice, a philosopher of language; followed by two approaches to the study of language in use: speech act theory and preference organization. Both of these include linguistic formal analysis and then go beyond this to assess the role of contextual features. The fourth part of the chapter introduces interactional sociolinguistics, a perspective on language in use developed by Gumperz, another major contributor to pragmatics. The first three approaches tend to limit analysis to individual utterances or relatively short samples of data. Interactional sociolinguistics requires longer excerpts of data and pays greater attention to the sociocultural features of texts, both those external and those that are manifested in the linguistic evidence in the texts. In addition, interactional sociolinguistics begins the overlap of pragmatics and the field of critical discourse analysis of interactions. Although this chapter is organized from a chronological perspective, all of the sociolinguistics theories of pragmatic meaning are still very commonly used by researchers and students, depending on the questions being asked in their studies.

Grice's Contribution to Pragmatics

No introduction to pragmatics can ignore the contribution of H. P. Grice (1975) to advancing understanding of meaning creation in interactional contexts. He was a philosopher of language and did not base his thinking on empirical data. He elaborated an inferential model of communication that is based on the notion of intention. Specifically, Grice argued that a listener is able to work out the inferred meanings in a speaker's utterances only if the listener assumes that the speaker intends to communicate something. The listener must recognize the intention to communicate.

Grice regarded conversations as rational, cooperative activities. An example illustrates Grice's approach.

A: oh no, I'm out of cash ... I forgot to go to the ATM
B: oh, don't worry ... I've got a credit card ... you can pay me back

A, looking at her wallet, is commenting about her own behavior. By means of that description, rendered aloud, she is also offering an excuse and asking for help without doing either directly, at the same time. Assuming A intended those meanings, B quickly works out the inferences and offers to pay for lunch (I have a credit card) and suggests a solution for the problem (you can pay me back). It helps that B has sociocultural knowledge regarding loaning A money and expecting to be paid back. Note that, in some cultures, the expectation would entail B offering to treat A to lunch and then A would "pay B back" by paying for lunch on another occasion.

Grice's theory of pragmatic meaning is based, as noted above, on the assumption that a speaker has something to communicate. Further, another assumption is that the speaker and listener are both rational and base their interactional behaviors on the basis of underlying principles that a society or community recognizes as the norms for human interaction. Grice (1975) theorized that there is such a principle for conversational interactions, called the Cooperative Principle (CP):

> Make your conversational contribution such as is required, at the stage at which it occurs, by the accepted purpose or direction of the talk exchange in which you are engaged.

Rather than taking a moral or judgmental stand, Grice was making a general statement about human talk behavior to explain how participants act in order for addressees to arrive at speakers' intended meaning. Grice regarded the CP as the underlying principle in all cases of interaction. He theorized that without such an underlying principle, misunderstandings arise and even chaos. A particular concern of Grice was the observation that sometimes people speak directly and say what they mean and sometimes they don't. Indirectness is frequent. Here are two fairly common examples:

#1
A: I'm going to be late for work ... could you take care of washing up the breakfast dishes for me?
B: sure, I'll take care of them for you

#2
A: I have to go or I'm going to be late for work ... I know it's my turn (looking at the unwashed breakfast dishes)
B: OK, I'll do them

In #1, A states her intended message directly and B responds in the same vein. In #2, instead, she acknowledges the rules of the household without an explicit comment about her responsibility. However, B, being a rational person according to the CP, assumes that A knows the rules and would do the dishes if time allowed.

In addition to the CP, Grice generated what are called the Four Maxims, subcategories of principles of human behavior that also guide interactants in deriving speaker intentions. Grice argues that without the assumptions that the speakers are following some basic principles, addressees cannot presume rational behavior behind what may appear to be obscure instances of talk.

Grice's Four Maxims

Quantity:
1. Make your contribution as informative as is required (for the purposes of the exchange).

2. Do not make your contribution more informative than is required.

Quality: Try to make your contribution one that is true.
1. Do not say what you believe to be false.
2. Do not say that for which you lack adequate evidence.

Relation: Be relevant.

Manner: Be perspicuous.
1. Avoid obscurity of expression.
2. Avoid ambiguity.
3. Be brief (avoid unnecessary prolixity).
4. Be orderly.

The maxim of quantity involves what is found internally in a text; the appropriate amount of information is what is required, not more and not less. The maxim of quality, that is, the truth or falsity of the speaker's utterance, is concerned with aspects that are external to the text. The maxim of manner again involves the text itself, the linguistic forms and the way in which the information is presented in the text. As for the maxim of relevance, it is claimed to be of a different order as it appears in all instances of talk and is the one most frequently flouted or not observed.

A: have you seen any of the new Swedish films, you know, about this "girl" with tattoos?
B: violence is not my thing

B's response to A's question may at first appear to lack relevance. Further cognitive processing on the part of A, however, is likely to lead to A's inferring that B may or may not have seen the films, perhaps one of them, may have read negative critical reviews about the movies, or heard another friend talking about the level of violence.

Here is another example of flouting the maxim of relevance. The listener, assuming the speaker is behaving rationally, considers what meaning the speaker intends to convey. A typical example may be found in the following:

A: So what did you think of José's dissertation?
B: Well, it was very well written …

If A and B are two professors on a doctoral student's committee, about to meet for a feedback session with José, B's comment may be interpreted by A to be a compliment or an ironical remark about other aspects of the dissertation that were not very well done. So A may be at a loss as to which inference is the correct one unless A knows that B tends to speak frankly concerning students and their work.

The next example demonstrates the role of all the maxims.

1	C:	um, I was in a smaller town, outside Tokyo, and I was there, I guess, '91 to '92
2	B:	really?
3	C:	yeah, so, I guess a little bit after you guys were there
4	B:	the suburb?
5	C:	yeah, yeah, suburb, it was between Tokyo and Chichibu I told Mona how I love the location
6	B:	really?
7	C:	'cause, 'cause I could go kind of either way to Tokyo, for city, and the other way to Chichibu, for the mountains
8	A:	that's great!
9	B:	the best of both worlds

Source: Sasaki 1995

In line 1, C provides information about her stay in Japan, to which B reacts with "really?", implying surprise. In fact, B's response is not clear in isolation; it is in line 3 that the analyst can understand how B understood line 1, that is, with surprised recognition, perhaps delight. B was not questioning the truth of C's statement, but rather recognizing that C had been in Japan after both B and A had been living there. The maxim of quality is respected. B enters again in line 4 with another clarification comment. Notice that in line 5, C assumes shared knowledge and does not give too much detail, only enough for B and A to have a general idea of where C had lived. Thus, the maxim of quantity is in operation. As regards the maxim of manner, in line 7, C again gives enough information, her contribution being brief, orderly, without ambiguity or obscurity of expression. Because all three lived near Tokyo, they shared the knowledge that the area in which C lived indeed allows one to go either direction on the train lines either to Tokyo or to the lovely Chichibu mountains. Finally, the maxim of relevance has been adhered to as well. The final comments of B and A at the end of the example are relevant to C's account of her living environment in Japan in the early 1990s.

Limitations to Grice's Model of Communication

At the time of publication of Grice's model it was a seminal contribution, supporting a breaking away from formal linguistics and the efforts of scholars and researchers to consider nonformal dimensions of human interaction. Although his work was a start, it has limitations. One of the issues relates to the meaning of the word "information" in the CP and the maxims. One approach to the meaning of "information" recognizes there is a continuum from transactional to interpersonal language functions. At one extreme, a prototypical transactional interaction constitutes selling and buying stocks. Another example where language use is minimal is exchanges between pilots and air traffic controllers to get airplanes landed safely. The information exchanged in such situations is brief, to the point, with little extra talk. At the opposite extreme, an example is interpersonal talk between romantic partners where the content of the discourse may not be as important as the sentiments expressed through tone of voice.

Content is important if visiting a travel agent or going online to find timetables of trains in Europe or India. The interpersonal function is more concerned with building and maintaining relationships through language. Thus, by chatting for hours with friends at a coffee shop, the participants are carrying out phatic communication, the mutual acknowledgement of each other's presence, feelings, and opinions about many topics. Quantity, quality, relevance, or manner features, while still important, may be less important. In the case of Grice, it is not clear if, by "information," he intended to include both of these potential meanings of that word.

Related to the issue of the meaning of Grice's terms, from an intercultural perspective, the word "information" may certainly be interpreted in different ways as well as the CP and the maxims. Speakers who do not share the same cultural background may have a very different view of how relevance, quantity, quality, and manner maxims are enacted in conversational interactions. For example, rather than tell a foreign guest at a restaurant in Thailand that a particular flavor of ice cream (coconut!) is not available, a waitress, to avoid giving bad news, may simply be silent and not take the dessert order.

Clearly, the major limitation of Grice's model derives from the lack of any explicit attention to the sociocultural context of interactions. As in the example above with two professors commenting on José's dissertation, inferring an ironic or humorous interpretation is often influenced by the relationship between the two interlocutors. For example, if B makes the comment with a particularly sarcastic tone of voice, A may be quite shocked, wondering if in fact B is suggesting that the dissertation was plagiarized or written by someone else rather than José. If B has higher status in the academic unit than A, that fact can also constrain the interpretation and leave A feeling at a loss as to how to interpret the comment. Hence, most pragmatists argue for the inclusion of sociocultural features in any analysis of data.

The role of interpersonal factors in the speech event of complimenting in Japanese is evident in the following example of older women, where A is using language to show deference and to flatter B about her garden. Undoubtedly, A is the younger woman who is making positive comments on B's garden, using very formal language. B may be a neighbor or perhaps the wife of someone important to A or her husband.

A: *maa, go-rippa na o-niwa de gozaamasu we nee, shibafu go hirobiro to shite ite, kekkoo de gozaamasu wa nee*	[my, what a splendid garden you have here – the lawn is so nice and big, it's certainly wonderful, isn't it?]
B: *iie, nan desu ka, chitto mo teire ga yukitodokimasen mono de gozaimasu kara, moo, nakanaka itsumo kirei ni shite oku wake ni wa mairiamasen no de gozaamasu yo*	[oh no, not at all, we don't take care of it at all any more, so it simply doesn't always look as nice as we would like it to]
A: *aa, sai de gozaimashoo nee, kore dake o-hirion de gozaamasu kara, hitotoori o-teire asobasu no ni datte taihen de gozaimashoo nee, demo maa, sore de mo, itsumo yoku o-teire ga yukitodoite irasshaimasu wa, itsumo honto ni o-kirei de kekkoo de gozaamasu wa*	[oh no, I don't think so at all – but since it's such a big garden, of course, it must be quite a tremendous task to take care of it all by yourself, but even so, you certainly do manage to make it look nice all the time, it certainly is nice and pretty any time one sees it]
B: *iie, chitoo mo sonna koto gozaamasen wa*	

Source: Miller 1967: 290, cited in Leech 1983: 136–7.

The information being exchanged in the talk is not the kind that traders on the floor of a stock exchange care about! The example demonstrates that the CP and the maxims may be regularly flouted out of concern for the face-saving needs of the interlocutors in the context of use.

Another limitation of Grice's theory of pragmatic meaning derives from an aspect of context that has to do with what are called activity-specific inferences. Not only cultural differences may bring the CP and the maxims into question as guides of interpretation of speaker meaning. Activities such as media interviews have their own norms that influence the processing of pragmatic meaning. According to Weizman and Blum-Kulka (1996), maxims may be suspended. In an effort to elicit an answer to a question, a newscaster interviewing a politician may not hesitate to pursue the interviewee in a hard-hitting manner. Such directness would not be tolerated – or at least it would not be a norm – in many other contexts. Thus, the CP and the maxims can be suspended in certain contexts or settings to allow for the pursuit of the goal, in this case to get genuine answers to questions of great interest to voters.

Interviewer:	How do you explain this uh collapse of the road system? roads that merely underwent a few days of rain look like ruins
Interviewee:	First of all I would like to refer to inter city roads only … and I would like to explain this …
Interviewer:	Uh I am sorry before you explain doesn't it sound a bit strange? Uh only uh a week even less of rain and it couldn't do what's expected of it? It didn't rain like it does in Switzerland not even the US!
Interviewee:	No, let me explain …

Interviewer:	I'm sorry I must ask you again on this point, it's not]
Interviewee:	[please do
Interviewer:	A certain capacity which is too small for three days of rain?
Interviewee:	Uh I would like to explain three days of rain …
Interviewer:	Is our system designed for drought, uh 360 days a year?
Interviewee:	Our system …

Source: Weizman and Blum-Kulka 1996

All of the interviewer's statements or questions push the interviewee to give an explanation, flouting the CP and the maxims, and the interviewer here appears to be impolite or rude. Yet within the context of a political interview, this linguistic behavior may be tolerated, perhaps even welcomed, depending on the cultural expectations of the television audience. With this particular example, the maxim of relevance, considered to be minimally necessary in human interactions, borders on not being adhered to by the interviewee, signaling a pragmatic inference of not wanting to address the question of the interviewer. Without awareness of the activity-related norms of the television interview, Grice's CP and maxims are not sufficient to account for the interactional behavior here.

The next section takes up an approach to the study of language in use and the socially influenced patterns that are based on naturally occurring talk. One issue that grew out of Gricean pragmatics is the nature of coherent discourse. Grice's CP and maxims provide reasons for a piece of language to be more than a string of random utterances. Human beings create discourse or talk, that is, utterances that cohere, according to Grice, because people cooperate in communication. Indeed, psychologists interpret incoherent talk to be potentially a symptom of neurological or mental illness. Coherence is the result of speakers' making relevant contributions and of addressees' processing the inferences or imposing coherence even where it is only implied through linguistic forms and prosody.

Preference Organization

Introduction

Preference organization, which rests on the assumption of coherence in discourse, draws its premises from conversation analysis (CA). It focuses on conversational structure, in particular the sequence of participants' contributions in extended samples of naturally occurring talk. The main concept of CA concerns the fact that the nature of talk, despite the chaotic appearance of a transcribed sequence of an interaction, is structured. If interactants did not enact predictable patterns, talk would be incoherent. Preference organization studies make it transparent that B's response to A's question, statement, or command is contextualized by the previous utterance and by what follows a particular line of talk. In other words, an answer to a question, for instance, is interpreted in the context of the question that was posed in the previous talk. Coherence is enacted in this manner, thus enabling the listener to interpret any pragmatic meanings from a question–answer sequence.

CA is the well-established methodology for research on preference organization and sequences in talk. The following sections look into three issues addressed in CA: (1) turn taking, (2) adjacency pairs, and (3) preferred and dispreferred responses. These three areas are regarded as "problems" in the sense that speakers and listeners have to know how to exchange turns at talk, open and close conversations, and make a response relevant to the previous speaker's contribution.

Turn Taking

An early seminal paper in the field of CA is that of Sacks, Schegloff, and Jefferson's (1978) article entitled "A simplest systematics for the organization of turn-taking for conversation." Their analysis of talk in interaction generated a list of characteristics of talk:

1. Overwhelmingly, one party talks at a time.
2. A change of speaker recurs.
3. Transitions between turns with no gap are common.
4. The order of turns is not fixed, but varies.
5. The length of turns is not fixed, but varies.
6. The length of conversation is not specified in advance.
7. What parties say is not specified in advance.
8. Relative distribution of turns is not specified in advance.
9. The number of parties can vary.
10. Talk can be continuous or discontinuous.
11. Techniques to allocate turns are used.
12. Mechanisms exist for dealing with turn-taking errors or violations.

Based on data of multiple examples of natural talk, these characteristics can be viewed as the most basic, prototypical norms of social interaction. Exchanges of turns at talk, where there is a scarce commodity called the "floor," is similar to competition on a stock market floor for buying and selling financial instruments (Yule 1996: 72–3). In interactional discourse, there is also competition for the right to speak, in other words, to take a turn, and the twelve mechanisms describe the standard procedures.

Because turn taking is a form of social action, some form of local management of talk agreed upon by interactants must be present in the interaction.

Note that human beings normally don't explicitly discuss how all of this is managed; the norms are learned through socialization in their own cultures where they are usually performed out of awareness. However, whenever another type of interaction presents itself, such as committee meetings, the individuals involved may have to negotiate a set of conventions to govern the proceedings, including the turn taking. Robert's Rules of Order and parliamentary procedures are examples of conventions that have been formalized and recognized internationally. It is also important to note that there may also be cultural differences regarding the characteristics listed above. For example, talk at departmental meetings in university settings outside of North America may be either more controlled and formalized or less so, with constant overlapping of participants' contributions. The sociocultural context of talk in interactions has to be considered.

Of the items on the list from Sacks *et al.* (1978), turn taking became one focus of attention. A model to account for speaker selection was generated on the basis of data. This is a summary of the options open to the first speaker in their model of turn taking:

The first speaker can select the next speaker by naming or alluding.
The first speaker can constrain the next utterance but not select the next speaker.
The first speaker can select neither the utterance nor the next speaker and leave others to self-select.

Essentially, the model claims that the next speaker in a conversation is either selected by the current speaker or is left to compete for the next turn without any signal from the current speaker. The advantage for the current speaker in designating the next speaker is that it allows the current speaker to have some control over the talk. The person selected by the current speaker has the right and even obligation to speak next. However, the current speaker may elect to stop talking, leaving the floor open to whoever wants to compete for a turn at talk, relinquishing any control over the floor or the talk itself.

A particular aspect of turn taking that interested Sacks *et al.* (1978) was the question of how interactants know when a speaker is about to end a turn at talk. In other words, how do co-participants avoid bumping into each other over the floor? When the current speaker makes no attempt to select the next speaker and the listeners wish to take over the floor, listeners need to predict a possible entry point, called a transition relevant place (TRP). It is the moment in the stream of speech when a possible change of speakers can take place. Both speaker and listener play a role in this situation. Listeners are constantly observing and listening to the speaker, out of awareness most of the time, for cues that may signal that the speaker is ready to relinquish the floor, usually indicated by a combination of cues:

Unfilled pauses
Turning one's head toward the listener
A drop in pitch or loudness
Relaxation of the foot or feet of the speaker
Audible inhalation
Drawling on the final syllable, and a general slowing down
Head nods, body posture
Eye contact
Intonation contour

Usually there is more than one cue present as they tend to occur in clusters that may vary according to the situation. Obviously, telephone conversations cannot depend on visual cues. Speaker and hearer engage in a dance, with constant mutual awareness and self-monitoring to carry out smooth turn taking.

Violations of the norms, often unexamined and implicit to native speakers of the language's social and cultural practices, can cause discomfort and miscommunication among the participants. Turn taking in intercultural communication may be problematic due to different assumptions about the basis of cues in the list and the resources for turn taking. For instance, members of a culture that practices direct eye contact may misinterpret co-participants from an eye-avoidance culture, assuming that they are not intending to contribute to the conversation. The lack of eye contact, a divergent intonation contour, or elongated, unfilled pauses, may be unexpected by speakers whose cues are different and thus, there may be a lot of "stumbling" in the course of the conversation.

Adjacency Pairs

The inferred linkages between utterances by speakers and listeners are called adjacency pairs. This noticeable feature of natural language use, observed by Sacks *et al.* (1978), accounts for ubiquitous two-part sequences such as this North American greeting that every learner of English studies:

A: hi, how are you?
B: fine, thank you, and you?

This is called an adjacency pair and consists of a first pair part, that is, what A says, and a second pair part, what B responds to A. The important point is that the first pair part constrains the second pair part: certain responses are preferred. If B responds with an elaborated example, the inference is that B is not a native speaker of American English and/or really wants to talk more with A about events in his life.

The first pair part constrains the way in which the second pair part is interpreted. Pragmatic meaning derives from this linguistic context. In the following example, the second pair part is interpreted as a negative answer. In other words, B's response is not expected or preferred, and a conversational implicature is present as a result of the flouting of the expectation. B may actually want to see the film, but can't due to the need to study.

A: there is a good Iranian film on at the Duke; it starts tonight
B: I've got a paper to finish for tomorrow

More analysis of talk-in-interaction leads to the awareness that not all adjacency pairs occur in such a straightforward pattern. There can be embedding of pairs within pairs.

1. A: are you coming tonight?
2. B: can I bring a guest?
3. A: male or female?
4. B: what difference does that make?
5. A: an issue of balance
6. B: female
7. A: sure
8. B: I'll be there

The question posed in #1 does not get answered until utterance 8. Other adjacency pairs are embedded within the sequence: numbers 2 and 7, 3 and 6, and 4 and 5. The following dialogue includes a request–response adjacency pair:

Jean: could you mail this letter for me?   Request
Fred: does it have a stamp on it?   Question
Jean: yeah   Answer
Fred: OK   Response

(Yule 1996: 78)

Many other types of adjacency pairs occur in natural conversational data. Whenever the expected adjacency pair pattern is not enacted, the flout is interpreted as meaningful. From a hesitation in accepting a request to outright silence in response to a greeting, all such behaviors are regarded as conveying pragmatic meaning. The next section goes into more detail on the concept of preference organization.

Preferred and Dispreferred Responses

A characteristic of talk, then, is that two-part pairs occur frequently; the first part of the pair constrains the second, in terms of the type of response and the possible pragmatic meaning. Pomerantz (1984) also drew attention to the existence of preference organization and labeled responses as preferred and dispreferred. She studied assessments. In many cultures, commenting on the state of the local weather is a common practice, even expected, while waiting for a train or bus. In Britain, one stereotype is that people always talk about the weather while in New York City people complain a lot about the buses and the subways being late. These are examples of phatic communication of those two cultures.

In the following examples, in the first dialogue, the second speaker offers a positive assessment, while in the second, B's silence communicates a negative one, as if she agreed with A's assessment of her body.

Preferred: A: Oh, the weather's lovely today, don't you think? Not too humid
B: oh definitely
Dispreferred: A: I'm getting fat – look at this flab on my abs
B: [silence]

These examples demonstrate the tendency for the first part of a pair to elicit a second part that is preferred by the speaker of the first part for reasons of social action and the need to attend to the face needs of the conversational partner. In the preferred example above, A expects B to show cooperation by giving a preferred, agreeing response to A's comments about the weather. In the second example, the silent response of B is dispreferred and implies acceptance of A's comment. The accompanying table outlines the types of preferred and dispreferred responses for some commonly occurring speech acts.

	Request	*Offer*	*Assessment*
Preferred/expected	Acceptance	Acceptance	Agreement
Dispreferred/unexpected	Refusal	Refusal	Disagreement/silence

Assessments associated with agreement and disagreement are particularly interesting to study for what they reveal about the concept of preference organization and the question of face needs. In the dispreferred example, B is in a bind because had he agreed, which is the preferred response for an assessment, A's face needs would also not have been met. The dispreferred disagreement response would have been the only acceptable assessment: "oh, naw, all that working out at the gym is doing you a lot of good." Disagreement is actually preferred in this case as well:

A: I'm so dumb, I didn't even know what was going on … [laughter]
B: no, you're not dumb

Unless they are close friends, B would be viewed as impolite.
Here is another example.

A: it's a beautiful day, isn't it?
B: yeah, it's just gorgeous

A gives her point of view on the weather, assuming that most conversational partners would just agree with her assessment. However, it is possible for a dispreferred response to arise.

B: well, yes, but I heard on the weather forecast this morning that it's going to change any day now … a cold front is coming from the north …

This is a dispreferred response, with the tell-tale "yes, but …" linguistic phrase, signaling initial agreement ("yes") and followed by a proposition expressing if not outright agreement, then some hesitation in showing complete agreement.

Disagreements are often marked by delay in responding or other distinctive features: (1) delays, in the form of pauses before delivery; (2) prefaces, such as "oh, well" or token agreements ("yes, but …"); or appreciations before disagreements ("I very much appreciate your offer …"; (3) accounts or reasons for the dispreferred alternative; and (4) mitigated or indirect forms ("well, I don't think I'll be able to come" rather than " I have no intention of coming.")

Preference organization is also noticeable in repair sequences, where self-initiated corrections are preferred to other-initiated corrections of a speaker's performance mistakes. In instances of everyday talk, participants tend to correct their own slips of the tongue or lexical inaccuracies rather than allow listeners to do so. Moreover, it also offers a general explanation for pre-requests, pre-invitations, and pre-arrangements, where a possible face threat to the speaker is avoided to prevent a dispreferred second pair part being performed. Here is an example of a pre-invitation or a pre-request.

A: are you very busy these days?
B: terribly

B's answer tells A that B is not going to be free to accept an invitation or to carry out a request and, as a result, A may decide not to make the invitation or request.

In sum, a general characteristic of conversation is preference organization. It accounts for the observed coherence in such actions as turn taking. It is the label for the regularities and expectations that are embedded in and constrain talk.

Any breaking or flouting of the expectations of preferred responses is meaningful and can generate implicatures. Moreover, preference organization is linked with the CP and maxims as well as face needs and politeness. Gricean pragmatics is clearly based on expectations of interactants carrying out talk in adherence to the CP and the maxims. They would engage in preferred responses with their conversational partners as rational members of society. Further, preferred responses would also be interpreted as behaviors that display mutual attention to face needs of the interlocutors. Dispreferred responses within the paradigm of politeness studies would be viewed as impolite.

From Speech Acts to Events and Activities

Introduction

This section reviews a well-known theory of language, speech act theory (SAT). It is both a theory, an attempt to explain phenomena, as well as a methodology for analysis of data. After an introductory explanation of SAT, limitations are discussed, followed by developments beyond speech act analysis.

Speech Act Theory

The basic notion that human beings use language to act on the world, both to create obligations and new social relations as well as do such mundane things as reassure, promise, and apologize, derives from insight by J. L. Austin, another philosopher of language. A collection of his lectures at Harvard University in 1955 was published in *How to Do Things with Words* in 1962. Austin argued that truth or falsehood and the logical relationship between words or phrases were inadequate to account for language use and that "the more we consider a statement not as a sentence (or proposition) but as an act of speech … the more we are studying the whole thing as an act" (1962: 20). From Austin's insights grew a perspective that is another seminal account of pragmatic meaning.

At first, Austin stated that actions are performed via utterances only with verbs he called performatives, the prototype speech act. A performative is a verb or verbal phrase, typically formulaic, which explicitly indicates the act the speaker is performing as it is uttered.

> I christen you Felicia.
> I bet you one million yen.
> I promise to meet you at 5 p.m. tomorrow.

The basic argument is that some utterances are not statements or questions, but rather actions. From this category of verbs, all used with the first person singular pronoun and referring to the present time only (present indicative active),

Austin generalized the notion of performing actions with language, arguing that all utterances had the underlying performative structure:

I (hereby) Vp you (that) + utterance

For example, "clean up that mess!" can be rewritten as "I hereby order you to clean up that mess in your bedroom." The imperative sentence form with the utterance functioning as a command is an explicit performative speech act. Austin called his claim the performative hypothesis. However, Austin soon realized there were limitations to his hypothesis.

First, the two versions of "clean up that mess!" are not equivalent in pragmatic meaning. Depending on the intonation contour and voice quality, the imperative form to make a command or order, although direct, can be used among friends and intimates and be considered friendly, even humorous. However, the underlying performative structure (I hereby ...), if used by an actual speaker, is likely to be heard as a very strong order, used only by someone who has recognized power over the addressee. The sergeant in *Beetle Bailey* cartoons – a famous American series about army life – would be such a person. Thus, the explicit performative and the command forms do not communicate the same implicatures.

Second, outside a list of conventional, explicit performative verbs (bet, christen, promise, wager), and the grammatical criteria for person ("I") and tense (present), it is difficult to decide which verb is appropriate for a particular function in all instances. In the course of the argumentation in his book, Austin reaches the insight that, in fact, "stating" is also a form of "doing," that is, performing an act, and consequently a special category of verbs is unnecessary, as all language use in a speech situation is "performative."

Third, Austin recognized that analysis of individual speech acts may not account for all of the aspects of language use. He concluded that a more important consideration is "the total speech act in the total speech situation" (1962: 148). Stating, betting, or christening are only three of many speech acts and are not a privileged class (Austin 1962: 148–9). Consequently, Austin shifted to a more inclusive classification of how language is used to carry out actions. He presented a three-part categorization for different features of speech acts.

Locutionary act	the literal, basic meaning of the proposition, the lexico-grammatical meaning that has truth value and sense; that is, the proposition or sentence describes a state of affairs and has determinate meaning.
Illocutionary act	the speech act or force, showing the intention of the speaker; how the act is to be understood by the addressee.

Perlocutionary act   the effect on the addressee, unpredictable, possibly nonlinguistic.

Theoretically, speech acts comprise all three levels of analysis. Note, however, that in practice pragmatics had tended to focus primarily on studying the illocutionary act or force. In particular, the third act, the perlocutionary force, is of less interest due to the fact that while some perlocutions are intended by the speaker, unpredictable ones also occur. For example, if no one laughs at the joke the speaker thinks is hilarious, this is beyond the range of pragmatics. Further, the addressee can always refuse to recognize the intended meaning: a greeting may not be reciprocated or a dirty joke may not cause laughter. To the extent that the effect is nonlinguistic, pragmatics has tended until recently to deemphasize the prelocutionary act.

Recognition of Intended Force

Putting aside the hypothesis of a performative verb, Austin realized that speech acts could be enacted directly or indirectly. The force of a speech act could be marked directly by what Austin called an illocutionary force-indicating device (IFID) that explicitly names the speech act: "I order you to see me later." Most speech acts, however, are performed indirectly; that is, the illocutionary force is not explicit and the addressee must work out the force by inference. It was also recognized that the linguistic form of an utterance (declarative, interrogative, or imperative) and accompanying intonation contours commonly correlate with particular speech acts. This is the classical approach to account for the illocutionary force (Clark 1996: 136).

You're going! (rise –fall)	Assertion
You're going? (rise)	Request for confirmation
Are you going? (rise)	Asking for information

In the following examples of speech acts in English (from Clark 1996: 136), the relation between the forms and functions is transparent:

Declarative form: assertions	I need to borrow your coat.
Imperative form: order	Please loan me your coat.
Yes/no interrogative: ask for information	Can you lend me your coat?
WH-interrogative: ask for information	When can you lend me your coat?
Exclamation: exclamation	You've lent me your coat!

However, within SAT, it is problematic to focus just on the function and the form of the utterance. There is no necessary relationship between form and illocutionary force or function of an utterance. An indirect speech act can be performed by a declarative verb to signal a request to close the window: "It's chilly in here" can be a suggestion that the addressee consider turning up the heat. The linguistic form of a speech act is a matter of the speaker's choice, depending on features of the communicative context as such as the setting, the participants, and social distance.

Felicity Conditions

To infer pragmatic meaning, the addressee has to interpret the speaker's intended force. Certain expected, contextualized features must be present for speech act recognition that differ from the more sociolinguistic variables of age, gender, and setting. These are called conditions of appropriateness or felicity conditions that are closer in nature to presuppositions; they have to be present before or as the act is being performed. Individual speech act types may have their own felicity conditions, although there are overlaps. For the category of promises, the following partial list of felicity conditions are expected to be in operation (see Grundy 1995: 90):

1. The speaker must believe that the promised action is within her/his power to do.
2. The speaker has good reasons to believe what is promised will be of some benefit to the receiver.
3. The speaker must believe that what is promised will not happen anyway.

This is only a partial list of the felicity conditions for promises, generated by Western scholars. They involve both the speaker and the addressee. One presupposition is that people always carry out their promises. Further, they are not part of any assumed background knowledge, like the time of day for lunch in Mexico (3 p.m.) or dinner in Spain (10 p.m.). The basic point is that the circumstances and the social actors, the speaker and addressee, must be in compliance with the felicity conditions in order for the speech act to "go through." For example, one can only divorce a spouse by saying "I hereby divorce you" three times in countries whose laws allow this speech act to have legal consequences. In this particular example, the felicity conditions are codified in the laws of the countries or in religious practices that have the force of law. The concept of felicity conditions is one approach to acknowledging contextual features that affect how a speech act can be interpreted. They, in effect, specify underlying norms of human communication. As all schoolchildren learn early in life, a promise is only a promise if certain conditions can be met, including the sincerity of the person doing the promising!

The Form and Function Problem

One of the unsolved problems of linguistic phenomena is the relationship between the formal features of an utterance and the situation or context that leads to an interpretation of the function or illocutionary force of the utterance. Mismatches of form and function are particularly problematic for language learners. An example from a study of a Japanese verb patterns illustrates the misunderstanding that arises in confusing form and function. In structural analyses of Japanese and in textbooks for learners of the language, it is claimed that polite requests are commonly formed by using V + -*te kudasai* (Jorden with Noda 1987, pt. 1: 93–4). However, anecdotal evidence indicates that this form is not always interpreted as signaling politeness. If a person on a bicycle runs into a jogger and only utters a phrase with V+ -*te kudasai*, the addressee, who anticipated an apology, will not view it as a polite request.

Shiraishi (1997) carried out a functional analysis of empirical uses of this form in a variety of contexts. Her results showed that V + -*te kudasai* is used for requests, orders, instructions, directions, offers, invitations, complaints, and encouragements (cited in Maynard 1990: 140).

> *Mado o akete-kudasai.*   Please open the window.
> *Tabako o suwanaide kudasai.*   Don't smoke, please.

Further, it became clear that, in situations where a speech act of polite requesting would be the most likely to occur, the form was used only 2.9 percent of the time. Shiraishi concluded that V + -*te kudasi* is most frequently used:

- when a speaker has the right to ask the listener to do the act;
- when the imposition on the hearer is not heavy; and
- when the speaker has a higher rank than the listener or the acts are beneficial to the listener.

These felicity conditions were found for the V + -*te kudasi* form. However, Shiraishi found an exception in emergency situations, where the form was used frequently. The form may function in the bicycle–jogger incident as a complaint, an order, or a suggestion to jog elsewhere. A functional analysis asks first what meaning the speaker is enacting in the context of utterance and assigns the meaning to the form; the form itself does not carry the label of "request" in all instances of use, an incorrect interpretation of this verb pattern in Japanese language textbooks.

Limitations of Speech Act Theory

Austin's work helped move language analysis away from an exclusive concern with formal features and truthfulness. Speech acts continue to constitute a main area of interest in pragmatics research, as will become apparent in later chapters. Nevertheless, SAT faces limitations in terms of accounting for pragmatic meanings. First of all, because there is no one-to-one relationship between form and function, the classification of speech acts is indeterminate. With regard to illocutionary force, "Could you shut the door?" can be a request, suggestion, or order. This indeterminacy is particularly problematic with nonconventional, indirect speech acts, where the illocutionary force may be difficult to assign. With "It must be time to go," only world knowledge or common ground between speaker and addressee works to assign the force as a request for information, a comment to escape from a boring or unpleasant situation, or a reminder of an important appointment.

Second, the analysis of speech acts does not facilitate greater understanding of how conversations proceed. The sociolinguistic context is largely ignored and it typically only looks at single utterances or an adjacency pair. Austin himself (1962: 138) expressed doubts about assigning special status to "statements," writing that "it is important to take the speech situation as a whole."

A third limitation derives from the fact that it is not possible in a nonarbitrary way to claim that an utterance is a single- or multifunctional act.

Hey, Miguel, you passed your thesis defense!!

This could be an assertion, a form of congratulation, and/or an apology for any previous doubts. The intonation and other prosodic or contextual features will hopefully enable Miguel to disambiguate the speaker's meaning. SAT itself cannot explain the multifunctionality of illocutionary acts.

Finally, speech act analysis does not address the question of the psycholinguistic reality of speech acts, that is, how a particular combination of linguistic forms comes to have a distinctive illocutionary force. The theory is based on observable linguistic forms and says nothing about the psycholinguistic reality of the theory.

Speech Events and Activities

Recognition of these four limitations led to an expansion of analysis of language use to include both the linguistic and nonlinguistic context of utterance. Included would be the listener's comprehension of pragmatic meaning and then subsequent production in response to previous utterances; in other words, the adjacency pairs that comprise sequences of talk. Researchers began to study longer texts, both spoken and written, to explore human use of language in a variety of situations. One expansion was to study speech events, both ritual events such as weddings or other ceremonies, and less conventional situations such as classroom discourse or courtroom trials. A conventional speech event such as a wedding ceremony would be a macro category with micro categories, such as giving compliments or teasing the groom, embedded within the frame of the wedding.

An underlying assumption is the expectation that the speech event will be coherent. A speech event is a discourse structure larger than a collection of speech acts or adjacency pairs. Examples include short, conventional interactions such as making introductions or complaints and giving advice or compliments. Here is an example to illustrate the structure of a compliment.

Compliment	→	A: hey, that's a beautiful tie
Acknowledgment	→	B: thanks, I kinda like it … got it in
Acceptance	→	Bangkok, you know, Thai silk …
		A: well, it's really lovely …
Bridge	→	B: so … where did you spend your year-end holiday?

This speech event example displays the function of the compliment to open a conversation with a colleague to develop more talk, introduced by the bridge. Note that not all participants accept compliments and may downgrade them, saying, "oh, it's just some old thing my mother gave me years ago." Direct denials are expressed with "oh, it's nothing" or "it's a silly present someone gave me." Another strategy is to shift the focus or change the topic entirely: "Oh, I got a whole bunch on sale at some market. I needed to bring some presents home."

The speech event analysis links individual speech acts in a larger textual unit. It is ethnographic in nature, as a complete speech event analysis would include descriptions of the setting, the participants, and their perceived goals. Hymes' (1972) SPEAKING mnemonic framework was developed specifically to facilitate speech event analysis.

A second form of expansion beyond the study of individual speech acts is activity type, an analytical perspective that comes from Levinson (1992). Levinson drew the basic concepts of embedding language use in human activities from Wittgenstein's (1958) "language games." The main claim is that the activity type, generally equivalent to a macro speech event, constitutes a culturally recognized activity within which language use is performed, although actions other than talk may occur during the activity as well. The focus in Levinson's elaboration is on allowable contributions by the participants, that is, who, what, and when co-participants contribute to the interaction, and on the constraints of the setting. He sought to describe the structure of the activity and the language use that was characteristic of a particular activity. Chapter 8 discusses this approach to analysis of speech events in more depth. Here is an example of classroom discourse as interactions between teachers and students can be viewed through the lens of the activity type framework. This excerpt comes from K. E. Johnson's (1995: 94) research on classroom learning.

1.	T:	What is this advertisement about?
2.	S1:	Radio ... sale
3.	S2:	Cheap sale
4.	T:	What is the word that is used there?
5.	S3:	Clearance sale
6.	T:	Clearance sale. OK, in the first place, do you know the meaning of *clearance sale*?
7.	S3:	Clearance sale
8.	T:	Clearance sale. Let's look at the word *clearance*. What word does it come from?
9.	S1:	Clear
10.	T:	Therefore, *clearance* sale will mean what?
11:	S3:	To clear up
12:	T:	To clear up, that's right. To clear up all the goods in the store. OK, let's look at the items which are for sale.

Source: Johnson 1995: 94

The activity type in this example involves a type of classroom event where the teacher reviews an assignment with her students. It could be called "reviewing vocabulary," a type of activity that teachers all over the world do to ascertain that the students had completed the assignment and understood the lexical items. Features of this activity include a predictable pattern of teacher (T) and student (S) interaction, a pattern of communication where the students respond to questions posed by the teacher. This framework is often referred to as the IRE pattern, where I refers to the teacher's initiation, R, student responses, and E, the feedback and elaboration by the teacher. This pattern is noticeable in the short excerpt above. Lines 6, 8, and 12 demonstrate instances of teacher elaboration; line 12 in particular includes the feedback from the teacher on how to use the two-word verb, *clear up*, with greater accuracy.

Thus, interactions illustrate the role of the context, both interactional and physical, on the participants. The students' contributions are influenced, for example, by the sociocultural practices from their L1 background, involving beliefs about respect, social class differences, and power. The constraints on contributions by the teacher and the students comprise the underlying inferential schemata for the interpretation of pragmatic meaning. In other words, by asking questions, the teacher not only wants to assess the students' understanding of the assignment, but also displays her more powerful role in the classroom.

As Clark (1996: 139) points out, speech acts can only be interpreted within the context of the social practices of a speech community. Some practices are formalized, such as those at graduation ceremonies or arrests by police; others are not codified and remain informal and indeterminate, such as directives at a dentist's office or requests for advice on radio talk shows. The main point remains: the joint activities of speaker and listener do not take place in a vacuum, but in the social world of which they are active, participating members.

Interactional Sociolinguistics

Interactional sociolinguistics is a theoretical and methodological approach to language use in interactions that does just what it says, i.e. it brings in features of the social world of participants. Among frameworks that guide data collection and analysis, IS is one of several that researchers adopt for their studies. Others also drawn from linguistics, sociology, and anthropology are introduced in the chapters of Part II.

Interactional sociolinguistics concentrates on verbal and nonverbal features of the context that are likely to have an effect on the participants' linguistic and communicative strategy choices for performing intended meanings. Gumperz (1982) centered his studies on appropriacy and the degrees of success of interactions in gate-keeping situations, such as job interviews and interethnic communication. Here is a short, illustrative example provided by students in a seminar on pragmatics (LoCastro 2005):

V: [pointing to the cigarettes] huh, did you smoke before, or you picked up this "bad" habit from Professor C?
P: [smiling nervously and stammering] um …
J: oh, before, we … um … before!
V: [smiling] OK, OK, I was just teasing you
P and J: goodbye
V: bye

Two international students, P and J, were smoking in a corner outside a classroom building when professor V walked towards them. P was from North India and J from Taiwan; both were in their early thirties and still not used to the American casual style of interaction between students and faculty. Thus, they were not used to V's questioning them in Line 1. There were cues in the discourse that enabled V to infer that P and J were uncomfortable with her question: the nervous smile, the stammering, and the curt goodbye by both of them. She tried to allay their nervousness with "*OK, OK, I was just* teasing you." The repetition of "OK" signals an effort to soften the effect of her earlier question and including "just" was a downgrader, a form of mitigation as well.

P and J introduced the example in a seminar session about daily instances when there seemed to be mismatches of pragmatic meaning. In the course of the discussion, it became clear that what V intended to be an ironic, joking comment was interpreted by P and J as an admonition not to smoke in front of faculty, even though Prof. C (another teacher of theirs and a colleague of V's) would smoke outside classroom buildings as well. They assumed the sociocultural belief of their Asian countries was in operation; i.e. while faculty, having more power in the campus hierarchy, could do as they pleased, students had to obey the rule against smoking within or near classroom buildings and especially not in front of faculty. They interpreted V's comment as an indirect criticism of their behavior. Her intentions to use indirectness to be ironic and, further, to display friendliness towards them, was misinterpreted. An interactional sociolinguistics analysis, coupled with sociocultural knowledge about expected behavior for students in Asian countries, facilitated understanding of this less-than-successful interaction.

Among scholars who have contributed to interactional sociolinguistics, the work of John Gumperz has figured significantly in developing awareness of the interaction of language, context, and sociocultural factors. In particular, Gumperz explores the role of values, beliefs, and norms that underlie interactional discourse and that can be examined at the micro level to bring out the dynamic relationship of social processes. Situated, local inferences arise in the course of face-to-face interactions that link to the larger sociocultural context and provide interpretations of pragmatic meaning that go beyond individual instances. Gumperz emphasized verbal features of interactions and the implied meanings that are formed during the talk-in-interaction.

Schiffrin (1996) summarizes Gumperz's contributions. His early work in India is collected in a 1971 set of essays where he showed that "meaning, structure, and use of language are socially and culturally relative" (Schiffrin 1996: 312). Gumperz studied Hindi-Punjabi code switching (Gumperz 1971), work that led to his introduction of three terms that describe features of interactions: contextualization cues, contextual presuppositions, and situated inferences. These three central concepts can be observed in this example (Gumperz 1982: 147):

Teacher: James, what does this word say?
James: I don't know
Teacher: Well, if you don't want to try, someone else will. Freddy?
Freddy: Is that a p or a b?
Teacher: (encouragingly) It's a p.
Freddy: Pen

This excerpt comes from classroom data with African-American students. In the African-American variety of spoken American English, the use of final rising intonation on James' response "I don't know" is a cue that he is seeking encouragement to provide an answer. It is functioning as a contextualization cue, based on this situated, contextual presupposition of seeking encouragement. The cue and its situated inference, however, were not accurately interpreted by the teacher, and she chose another student who was more willing to risk presumably making a mistake.

In addition to these three key concepts, Gumperz's work led to the use of two more terms: situated and local. Both, essentially synonyms, refer to dynamics of the language use and interpretation in the example above. The teacher cannot entirely be faulted for not interpreting James' response in line 2 as she may be from a different part of the United States, possibly of a different class background or ethnic group, from James. Thus, she does not share his background knowledge regarding use of a rising intonation contour. In the school environment, James was using the response and intonation contour that he assumed would be interpreted as he wanted them to be in the "local" situation. Physically both James and the teacher were in the same environment, yet they did not share the same background knowledge and practices for language use. In sum, inferences are always situated or local and to fully understand language use of any group of people, no matter how large or small, the situation of use is vital. Interactional sociolinguistics is thus interested in linguistic and social construction of meaning in situated, local interactions.

IS studies have tended to deal with native and nonnative speakers of one variety of English, or of a world English, such as subcontinent immigrants from India, Pakistan, or Bangladesh (see Gumperz 1982; Roberts, Davies, and Jupp 1992). The various speakers, although of the same language, do not share the same interpretations of Grice's CP and maxims. The data analysis is what is called "unmotivated looking," that is, the analyst does not approach the data with preconceived notions, but rather observes what is happening among the participants. The analyst studies the roles, relationships, and self-presentations to learn how those variables influence how social actions are carried out and how the situated inferences are created. In the example below (Gumperz 1982: 165), a waitress is talking with a friend at the counter who had come to the restaurant for lunch:

Friend: I called Joe last night.
Waitress: You did? Well what'd he say?
Friend: Well, hi!
Waitress: Oh yeah? What else did he say?
Friend: Well he asked me out of course.
Waitress: Far out!

Gumperz presents this excerpt as an example of contextualization cues that contributes to understanding the speakers' intended meanings. There is clearly sociocultural knowledge that contributes in this instance concerning dating situations and local knowledge about the friend's interest in a particular man, Joe. One of the contextualization cues is the very first line which is a lead-in to the story the friend wants to tell. The waitress cooperates by asking for details. She knows that "called" means a telephone call, who Joe is, and that a woman telephoning a man has some special meaning. By adding an exaggerated intonation contour on "you did?" she signals her understanding of the importance of the call. Prosody in fact plays a major role in this excerpt as the question and exclamation marks suggest in the transcribed data. Here even the word *well* uttered by the friend is pronounced in a way to dramatize the effect on the friend regarding Joe's asking her out. The contextualization cues and the situated inferences are part of interactional sociolinguistic analysis of data.

In another study, Gumperz, Roberts and other researchers used interactional sociolinguistics to look at gate-keeping environments where members of minority groups in courtroom trial discourse may be disadvantaged due to language issues. The following example demonstrates how difficulties with English constitute a contextualization cue of potential importance for legal decision-making (Lifesouth 2006).

Lawyer: would they take your temperature and your pulse and your blood pressure every time?
Witness: yeah
Lawyer: would they do that while you were waiting to give blood?
Witness: no, after
Lawyer: after you gave blood?
Witness: after, wasn't it? (speaks in Spanish to the interpreter)
Witness: before
Lawyer: OK, and once again, if you don't under ... understand anything just like you did ...

The witness was being questioned by the plaintiff's lawyer during a deposition; one issue in the case of contaminated blood having been collected from the witness, a donor, is the extent to which the donor was able to understand and speak in English. His native language was Spanish. The lawyer was trying to build a case that due to his low proficiency in English, the donor should not have been allowed to donate blood because the intake procedures were conducted in English. The case was against the blood donation agency that was being accused of negligence in their blood collection procedures. This excerpt suggests that the donor would have benefited from the services of a trained interpreter who provided constant language support. Whether his blood was checked before or after the blood donation was a detail of importance in building the inference that the agency was negligent.

In studies of code switching, Li Wei (1998) zeroed in on the underlying motivations of code switching and in particular code switching in the course of interactions among Cantonese bilingual speakers in England. The findings of his CA study displays, through the micro features of the exchanges of talk, how language change functioned as a contextualization cue concerning "higher-level social meanings such as the speakers' language attitudes, preferences, and community norms and values" (1998: 173).

Undercurrents in the local Chinese community in Tyneside regarding relationships among parents and children, which language should be used when speaking to parents, and authority over children led to uncomfortable communication.

A is an eight-year old girl, and C is A's fifteen-year-old brother. B is their mother who is in her forties (Li Wei 1998: 171–2).

A: Cut it out for me (.) please
C: (2.5)
A: Cut it out for me (.) mum
C: [Give us a look
B: [*mut-ye*? ('What?')
A: Cut this out
B: *Mut-ye*? ('What?")
C: Give us a look
   (2.0)
B: *Nay n ying wa lei*? ("YOU DON'T ANSWER ME?")
A: (To C) Get me a pen

In this example, the mother, B, signals her desire to assert her role as an authority figure in the family by using the contextualization cue of speaking in Cantonese, *mut-ye*? By using this particular phrase, she conveys the situated inference that her children's use of English is a mistake or minimally that she wants them to switch to Cantonese. In the following line, with the English translation in capital letters to convey her insistence, B appears to have become angry with her children due to the non-convergent language choice and their unwillingness to respect her authority (Li Wei 1998: 173). Language choice carries symbolic value, functioning as a contextualization cue and communicating situated inferences for the participants, about not just language choice.

Interactional dimensions can alter the participant framework, that is, who talks when, and the situated inferences that can be drawn. For example, Hispanic students may not code switch into Spanish during classroom work with other students and the teacher. However, on their way out of class at the end of the hour, they may switch into their variety of Spanish to comment about a topic of concern and to display solidarity with members of their in-group. This situated, local change of code communicates the pragmatic meaning of distancing other, non-Hispanic peers and the teacher, even if the teacher also speaks Spanish. The usual power ascribed to the teacher is diffused.

Displays of involvement (Schiffrin 1996: 318–19), such as hand raising, can function as a contextualization cue; however, it may be a culturally sensitive issue as practices vary. In the U.S., students raise their hands with an open palm facing the teacher. However, in several other parts of the world (Japan, Latin America), that same gesture is used to "call animals." Either no hand is raised (in Japan, students wait until class is over to approach the teacher) or a closed fist, pointed downwards, while opening and closing one's fist, is used. This difference can be troublesome until individuals become accustomed to local practices. Here is one international teaching assistant of a group of American undergraduates expressing his feelings.

R: has anything surprised you about teaching in the environment here?
P: there was something that caught my attention, they raised their hands like that (.) I was pissed off, it's like ...
R: disrespect?
P: yes, come on man, you have a question, don't raise your hand just like he's racing a new fly and ... yeah, it's like pushing the button for the flight attendant ... it's not like a big deal, but I remember that a couple of times, I intentionally ignored him

(LoCastro and Tapper 2006: 203)

The researcher had asked Pedro about students' behaviors that most surprised him from his perspective as an international student from Peru, doing doctoral studies at an American university. The display of involvement from the American students, the hand raising, to signal they had a question or wanted to contribute to the class presented a mismatch with the norms in his home country.

Conclusions

The goal of Chapter 3 has been to continue to build the reader's knowledge of pragmatics and, in particular, four areas of theory and research that have contributed greatly to understanding speaker meaning. The discussion moved from Grice's theory and model of communication to a perspective, interactional sociolinguistics, which emphasizes analysis of data to uncover the workings of cues to signal meanings beyond the linguistic forms, especially regarding questions of gender, inequality, and inter-ethnic communication.

Part II follows. Each chapter focuses on a particular topic area and reviews research studies and methodologies. Chapter 4 explores the ways people from different sociocultural backgrounds communicate despite mismatches from different norms and values expressed through language in use.

Suggested Readings

Austin, J. L. (1962). *How to do things with words.* Oxford: Clarendon Press.
Davis, S. (Ed.) (1991). *Pragmatics: A reader.* New York: Oxford University Press.
Goffman, E. (1963). *Behavior in public places: Notes on the social organization of gatherings.* New York: Free Press.

Grice, H. P. (1975). Logic and conversation. In P. Cole and J. L. Morgan (Eds.), *Speech acts*, Vol. 3 of *Syntax and semantics (pp. 41–58)*. New York: Academic Press.

Levinson, S. C. (1983). *Pragmatics*, Chapter 3. Cambridge: Cambridge University Press.

Pomerantz, A. (1984). Agreeing and disagreeing with assessments: Some features of preferred/dispreferred turn shapes. In J. M. Atkinson and J. Heritage (Eds.), *Structures in social action* (pp. 57–101). Cambridge: Cambridge University Press.

Tasks

1. What maxims are flouted in the following interaction?

    A: I'd like a coffee
    B: black? white? with or without?

2. Advertisements in magazines and newspapers, on television and billboards flout maxims regularly. First, collect several examples – three to five is a good number – and then analyze them to see what maxims are being flouted. Second, explain why advertising companies like such ads. For example, an English ad around Tokyo several summers ago proclaimed, "I feel Coke." The accompanying picture was of a young person in stylish summer clothing. An ad in Mexican Spanish reads "*Disfruta Coca-Cola!*" [Enjoy Coca-Cola!]

3. How do you indicate that you are not sure of the truthfulness, correctness, manner of presentation, or relevance of what you are saying? Give examples in at least one language you know well.

4. Do you agree with Grice that people follow the CP and the four maxims in their interactions with others? Why? Why not? Give evidence to support your opinion.

5. Provide an analysis of this bit of talk.

    A: where've you been?
    B: out
    A: where'd you go?
    B: somewhere

6. Construct at least one example for each of the following speech acts: request, disagreement, and warning in any languages you know. Compare and contrast your examples with those of others in the group or class.

7. What follows is Searle's description (Searle 1969: 66–7) of some of the felicity conditions for requests and warnings. Develop a similar list for the speech act of complaints, including the four conditions given in Searle's list. Discuss the difficulties you encounter.

Conditions	Requests	Warnings
Propositional content	Future act A of hearer	Future event E
Preparatory condition	1. Speaker believes hearer can do A. 2. It is not obvious hearer will do A without being asked.	1. Speaker thinks E will occur and is not in hearer's interest. 2. Speaker thinks it is not obvious to hearer that E will occur.
Sincerity condition	Speaker wants hearer to do A.	Speaker believes E is not in hearer's best interest.
Essential condition	Counts as an attempt to get hearer to do A.	Counts as an undertaking that E is not in hearer's best interest.

Compare your schema for the act of complaining with others in your group. Are there any differences? If another member of your group knows another language well, are there, for example, special verbs for complaints? Are there any noticeable differences in the act of complaint across cultures?

8. Conventional forms for requests in English are "Can you . . . ?" "Could you . . .?" or "I would be much obliged if you . . . " How does one make a request in other languages you or your group members know?
9. What is the form–function problem? Do the following task (from Astley and Hawkins, 1985: 4).

Here are the spoken messages exchanged by one family as they got up and came down for breakfast:

1. Do you know what time it is?
2. I *am* getting up!
3. I can't find my socks!
4. Cornflakes please!
5. Ta dad!
6. Thank goodness it's Friday!
7. Have you seen my trainers?
8. No, why should I?
9. What do you mean, I haven't combed my hair?
10. Try taking the top off first!
11. Well done!
12. Bye mum!
13. Be careful!
14. Okay. Don't worry!
15. What a lousy day!
16. Somebody's left the door, open!

Each of these speakers was trying to do something with words. Below is a list of things we do with language. Find an example of each in the family's spoken messages. Note which examples could have more than one function. Example: Asking for information: 1. Do you know what time it is?

a. Asking (i) for information (asking a question)
     (ii) for something or asking someone to do something (making a request)
b. Telling (giving information)
c. Refusing (to do or say something)
d. Advising (warning or threatening or persuading or suggesting? What is the difference between these uses of language?)
e. Ordering
f. Promising
g. Greeting
h. Thanking
i. Denying (saying something is not true or hasn't happened)
j. Showing friendship
k. Congratulating
l. Saying how you feel

FIGURE 3.1 'Get the message' (From Astley and Hawkins (1985), pp. 4–5. Copyright ©1985 Cambridge University Press. Reprinted with the permission of Cambridge University Press.)

Data Analysis

What is the speech event in the following interaction? What can you state about the speech acts that occur? Are there contextualization cues that play a role in the discourse that enable the intended speaker meanings to be interpreted? Note any other linguistic behaviors and sociocultural background knowledge that appear to be important in the successful completion of this interaction.

1. E: hi
2. C: hi what k'n I do for yuh?
3. E: I'm returning this "grolit." It doesn't work
4. C: yeh? What's wrong with it?
5. E: don't know. I plugged it in and it just doesn't work. Not your fault (.) but
6. C: you buy it here? You got your receipt?
7. E: yeh here
8. C: uhh OK. You wanna get a new one or you want your money back?
9. E: no, I want another one (.2) that works
10. C: yeh, OK, so go back and get another one and bring it up here and I'll write it up for you
11. E: okay, thanks
12. C: yeh

Source: Hatch 1992: 144

PART II
Core Areas of Pragmatics

4

CROSS-CULTURAL PRAGMATICS

Introduction

Cross-cultural pragmatics (CCP) is arguably the subfield of pragmatics that draws the most attention in the modern world where on a daily basis participants interact while not sharing the same native or primary language for communication. Both comprehension and production of pragmatic meaning become quite complicated. A neighborhood in Washington, D.C., for example, has supermarkets where the cashiers use English as a second language to communicate with customers, who themselves do not have English as their main language. English is the lingua franca. The same scenario plays out at the local automobile emissions check agency, where a young Asian mechanic can't quite explain in his rudimentary English the reason a car didn't pass the emissions check. He calls over a supervisor, an African, to explain to the car's owner. The final stage of explanation comes from an official in the office who uses English, also not his primary language. Moreover, "cultural" difference also includes sociocultural dimensions, a term that refers as well to ethnic, group, educational, and other features of people that may influence their language use and nonverbal behaviors. An illustrative example of sociocultural differences would be the great diversity in speakers of Spanish, from peninsular Spanish to different varieties of Latin American Spanish speakers. The diversity not only regards language dialects and accents, but also language use due to divergent socioeconomic, educational, and historical influences in the communities.

On a daily basis, instances arise that challenge interpretation of participants' verbal and nonverbal behaviors. It is precisely those occasions, when something expected occurs or a conversation goes awry, that draw the attention of researchers. CCP thus focuses on illustrating and explaining the reasons for miscommunication and the influences on participants' interactional strategies.

In this chapter, the influence of cross-cultural dimensions on the comprehension and production of pragmatic meaning is the center of concern. Here, definitions and issues related to cross-culture pragmatics are examined and research studies are considered for insights. The following sections of this chapter explore these key areas in CCP.

- definitions of CCP and related terms
- values and beliefs as constraining influences on social action
- pragmatic failure and alternative views
- speech acts: comparisons of Western and non-Western speech acts and issue of comparability of speech acts
- contrastive rhetoric in written, institutional texts

Defining Cross-cultural Pragmatics

Kasper and Blum-Kulka (1993) defined CCP as the study of linguistic acts by language users from different cultural backgrounds. Within this macro-category, contrastive pragmatics has been a useful descriptive term for research on specific speech acts (e.g. requests, refusals, compliments) across, typically, English and one other language and culture (e.g. Mexican Spanish). The goal of such contrastive studies tends to target one feature or groups of features of one speech act. Contrastive pragmatics has a fuzzy boundary with interlanguage pragmatics (see Chapter 5), the study of pragmatic competence development of second and foreign language learners, which focuses on nonnative English speakers' use of and acquisition of pragmatic competence in a second or foreign language.

In contrast with interlanguage pragmatics, CCP looks at issues outside classrooms and concentrates on environments where participants are not explicitly learners, but rather full members of the target language community. Women and men who work in the business world in Europe describe themselves as speaking "continental English," proudly so, with the various accents of their first or primary languages, from Swedish, German, Dutch, Hungarian, or Italian. CCP also includes studies of short- or long-term sojourners, in the U.S. to obtain advanced degrees in their areas of specialization. A CCP project might assess their everyday use of, for instance, the quotidian negotiation strategies of L1 Chinese speakers of English, not their developing competence as language learners per se.

Another term – intercultural communication (IC) – occurs with more and more frequency, even in the English language mass media. This change reflects the connections with sociolinguistics. In this book, "intercultural" is used in a broader sense than CCP. CCP researchers narrow their studies to comparing two groups of people, one of which comprises the native speaker language use of the target language. IC refers to research on the language use of groups of individuals resulting from the phenomenon of transnational movements of people from a variety of languages and backgrounds. They interact with each other in schools, health clinics, courtrooms, universities, and international forums on a regular basis. Thus, it is not possible to consider only a particular language feature of language A with a similar one in language B, or even to compare speakers of language A with those of language B. There is clearly a multiplicity of language features and culturally influenced social actions that raise issues such as comparability of a specific speech act or of displays of politeness across cultures, even regions or generations within one culture.

These definitions serve in this chapter as a base for discussing the terrain of CCP. The next section looks specifically at CCP and values and beliefs that underlie linguistic and nonlinguistic behaviors.

Values and Beliefs

In the sociolinguistic approach to pragmatics, "culture" is not Culture, with a capital C – that is, the literature, music, and art of one speech community or grouping of people. Rather, it is culture as a reflection of the values and beliefs about the world, held by the members of a community which form, in effect, the substratum of their everyday life. The largely unexamined values and beliefs constrain perceptions, expectations, and assumptions about the role of language and communication in general and the interpretations of language use.

What must be taken into consideration to account for cultural influences on language and related behavior?[1] CCP investigates how human behavior, influenced by participants' underlying values and beliefs, is translated into instances of language in use. Most researchers in pragmatics have adopted the view that culture does indeed have a role to play in language behavior. Specifically, research has shown that a speaker's intended meaning, mediated by linguistic symbols, may be interpreted or misinterpreted in cross-cultural contexts due to each interactant's own norms of interpretation. That is, social actions of speakers mirror the underlying worldview of their primary language. For instance, teachers' use of praising language in classrooms may be viewed very positively and even as a requirement to encourage and reward students for class participation and the quality of their written work. However, not all teachers and students share this value and belief; constant praising can be interpreted as patronizing, repetitious, and discriminatory behavior, especially if the teacher does not praise all students equally.

The values and beliefs from cultural models of thought are embedded in talk both at the micro and the macro level. The list of micro features includes prosodic cues, turn taking, indirectness, nonverbal cues, and speech act realizations. With regard to macro level aspects, researchers look at such pragmatic concerns as interpretation of illocutionary force, perception of politeness, and violations of the CP or maxims. As for production, form/function mismatches and topics that may be taboo in the second language culture may interest communication research experts. The influence of background knowledge may result in individuals' adhering to the cultural norms of their primary tongue to maintain ethnolinguistic identity. These lists are not exhaustive, but suggestive of the everyday features where culture influences production and interpretation of meaning.

CCP examines behaviors that are manifest or overt and others that are latent or covert. For example, an intonation contour that accompanies a phrase may be interpreted only by examining the latent meanings, such as how a particular society conceives male and female roles. The language use may signal that women are expected to use language differently than men. The 2008 presidential primary and election campaigns in the U.S. provided multiple examples; women such as Hillary Clinton were criticized for sounding too strong or severe, while the media did not comment on the language use of men in the same contexts.

Researchers (see Holland and Quinn 1987) have studied the language use of subcultural groups to understand the conceptual categories of their worldviews. Young women's and men's dating habits in the U.S. derive from their family backgrounds and mass media depictions of roles in gendered relationships. A well-known work that deals with cultural models of thought is that of George Lakoff (1987), entitled *Women, Fire, and Dangerous Things*. Lakoff found that the Australian aboriginal language Dyirbal has a conceptual category, *balan*, which includes the items mentioned in the title of his book. Thus in the Dyirbal model of the world, the items are grouped into the category of "dangerous." Arabic also includes a category of *haram*, that is, unclean or taboo things; that category or grouping contrasts with *halal*, that is, clean or appropriate.

It is useful to learn how cultural groups perform their values through speech events and language use at the event. They provide important baseline data for comparison studies. Cultures deal differently with values such as authority, individualism and interdependence, secular and sacred aspects of life, trust, spontaneity, and restraint.

Thai people, for example, value dependence, restraint, hierarchy, and separation of public and private life. Thailand is one of many countries where sacred dimensions play a role in daily life. For example, Thai Buddhist monks visit homes early in the morning, begging for food. Families fill their bowls with food. This practice earns the donors "merit" with Buddha. This nonverbal behavior is accompanied with verbal messages in the local language displaying respect for this sacred practice and the monks themselves. In the U.S., cooperation and competition are often cited as two values that characterize the differences between male and female interactional patterns. Holmes (2008: 307) includes this example in a discussion about the higher frequency of men interrupting women in conversations; interruptions are evidence of competition.

Woman: How's your paper coming?
Man: Alright I guess. I haven't done much in the past two weeks

Woman:	Yeah. Know how that [can]
Man:	[Hey] ya' got an extra cigarette?
Woman:	Oh uh sure (hands him the pack) like my [pa]
Man:	[How] 'bout a match?
Woman:	'Ere ya go uh like my [pa]
Man:	[Thanks]
Woman:	Sure. I was gonna tell you [my]
Man:	[Hey] I'd really like ta' talk but I gotta run – see ya
Woman:	Yeah

The words inside the brackets are uttered simultaneously and as the data shows, each time, the man interrupts the woman and steals the turn of talk, continuing with the topic he is interested in, rather than hers. Although Holmes herself is from New Zealand, her studies are representative of language behaviors in the U.S. also.

This type of information can be helpful for understanding language use and related behaviors in Thailand and the U.S. It must be kept in mind, nevertheless, that CCP is based on generalizations; no country of the world is homogeneous and this fact requires guarding against overgeneralizations, stereotyping, and discrimination. Further, societies and cultures change. Cameron (2000) delves into a recent phenomenon in the U.K., what she calls customer care philosophy. She found changes in the politeness strategies of the language use of sales clerks and others involved in providing customer services in the U.K. Urban areas all over the world exhibit examples of language use that may differ from that of the countryside in multiple ways, from lexical choice to phonological variables and evidence of social distance signaled by choice of address.

This overview of potential sources of discomfort or misunderstandings in cross-cultural contact situations illustrates the difficulties in interpretation of pragmatic meaning in general. What is left unsaid becomes considerably more complex in CCP, and the determination of what is meant from what was said a virtual quagmire. The next section examines one approach to the analysis of causes of communication glitches in cross-cultural contexts.

Pragmatic Failure

Pragmatic failure refers to mistakes in producing and understanding situationally appropriate language behavior. According to Thomas (1983), the inability to interpret intended meaning may be due to regional, ethnic, gender, and class differences within a community and across cultural boundaries. In other words, there are intracultural and intercultural differences. Culturally influenced patterns of behavior not only result in production difficulties, but also incomprehension problems, as listeners tend to interpret others' language use through the lens of their own worldviews. Even within one culture, pragmatic norms differ from region to region. Tannen's studies of New York conversational style (2005) indicate that the machine-gun style questions of some Jewish New Yorkers may communicate positive, solidarity friendliness, a pragmatic norm, whereas Midwesterners or Southerners may regard the speaker as overbearing, nosey, and aggressive. Here is an excerpt from Tannen's conversational style studies (2005):

Deborah: Did you two grow up with television?
Peter: Very little. We had a TV [in] the Quonset
Deborah: [How] old were you when your parents got [it]?
Steve: [We had a TV, but we didn't watch it all the time. We were very young. I was four when my parents got a [TV].
Deborah: [You] were four?

This excerpt demonstrates two features of the machine gun style: (1) the overlapping talk; and (2) the questions that Deborah asked, as if she were interviewing them. An additional feature that is not transparent in the printed excerpt is the rapid pace of Deborah's questions.

Another sociocultural feature that is not often recognized is class differences. A recent example in the U.S. media presented the case of a policeman who attempted to arrest a highly educated professor from a famous U.S. university who is also of a different racial background from the policeman. Policemen are stereotypically of middle-class backgrounds while a professor would be in a higher class, despite other characteristics of the individual. The discussion in the media about these dimensions of the two individuals went on for days.

Categories of Pragmatic Failure

According to Erickson (1984), there are three categories of pragmatic failure. First, at the level of explicit, referential meanings, there can be inappropriate transfer of speech act realization strategies or of expressions from the L1 to the L2 that can be interpreted differently. This is termed pragmalinguistic failure, which involves differences in the linguistic encoding of pragmatic meaning or force. This type is usually due to transfer or interference from the first language and can be observed in the linguistic forms used to, for example, apologize, to enact politeness, or to hedge a request. The differences may arise in the additional phrases that accompany, for example, an apology. Bergman and Kasper (1993) studied speech act by native speakers of Thai and of English as well as nonnative Thai speakers of English, where they considered such features as the role of contextual factors in choice of apology strategies by those three speaker groups. The apology strategies could vary along several scales: severity of the offense, obligation to apologize, degree of offense to the addressee's face, social distance between the participants, and the need to take responsibility. Bergman and Kasper found differences in the use of apology routines by the three groups in their data collection. In particular, 50 percent of the apology routine use by the Thai nonnative English speakers reflected transfer from Thai apology patterns.

Nonnative English speakers may express surprise when they hear Americans use the word "sorry" when giving condolences to someone whose family member has recently passed away. Another everyday context where pragmalinguistic mismatch arises is regarding the form of address for waiters and waitresses in restaurants throughout the world. In Mexico, *joven* (young person) is used even with older servers; in Japan, at noodle shops, *onisan* (little brother) or *onesan* (little sister) is common. In the United States, clicking one's fingers or whistling would result in no service at all as most American service personnel would be insulted by a signal they would consider "rude." In Peru, clapping to get the attention of a waiter, however, is the norm.

The second category of pragmatic failure – sociopragmatic failure – refers to mismatches in terms of the implied social meaning of a word, phrase, or speech act. The mismatches derive from divergent assessments of the social aspects of the context of utterance, such as the social distance between the speaker and addressee and the rights and obligations of speakers and listeners. One example involves the assumption that calling a senior faculty member by his first name entitles the graduate student to telephone that person at his home late in the evening or during the weekend.

Third, there can be misattribution or faulty assessment of other participants' intentions, competence, and background knowledge. In this category, the presuppositions underlying speaker meaning need to be unpacked. In the north of England, postal clerks, both male and female, may address their regular customers with "Morning, luv, what can I do for you?" Customers not used to the word "luv" may take offence, seeing the male clerk, in particular, as sexist or too familiar with the woman customer. The effect of misunderstandings of this sort in cross-cultural or regional cultural contact environments is to attribute them to personality flaws (someone may be regarded as rude as the result of her or his personal communication style). Or the discomfort may be due to ethnocultural origins, thereby stigmatizing or stereotyping all members of an ethnic group (see Tannen 1986).

Grammatical errors made by a nonnative English speaker may be forgiven, a mistake attributed to low proficiency in the target language. However, speakers are less willing to explain away pragmatic failures. Personal fault is given to even native speakers of English who do not know the local city customs for ordering coffee to go in a New York deli or using mutual complaining as a way to create solidarity with new colleagues in the South.

Pragmalinguistic Failure

In one example of pragmalinguistic failure (White 1993), the speech act realization strategies of Japanese and English requesting behavior were found to cause discomfort, particularly because of the word "please," when used by Japanese speakers of English to make requests. In the case of requests by native speakers of English, the speaker wants the addressee to do something that will benefit the speaker. This is a standard felicity condition for requesting in English.

> Could you please open the door for me? My hands are full.

A request can be a face threat for the addressee, that is, an imposition. That possibility typically causes the speaker to use a form of mitigation to do redressive action. Moreover, a request is not deemed to be successful if the addressee is the beneficiary. For instance, an office worker who received a box of chocolates as a gift may share the present with her colleagues by saying: "Have a chocolate" or "help yourself." She wouldn't add "please." If she did, her colleagues would assume she wanted them to help her eat the chocolates to avoid breaking her diet! So the word "please" correlates with a benefit to her.

However, it is common for Japanese speakers of English to use the word "please" in English when they would use *dozo* in Japanese. *Dozo* is normally translated as "please" even though the two words are not functionally equivalent. *Dozo* can be used with speech acts of requesting, inviting, giving permission, and offering. In the case of invitations and offers, the speaker wants the addressee to do something that benefits the addressee; in other words, the addressee obtains something she/he wants. Consequently, a Japanese speaker of English may use "please" inappropriately with invitations and offers, transferring from Japanese.

> Have a seat, please [*Dozo okake kudasai*]

Due to the transfer from the first-language strategies, the Japanese speaker causes a pragmalinguistic mismatch. One can argue that there is no serious misunderstanding in such a case, particularly in informal contexts with conversational partners of the same social status. Nonetheless, a level of discomfort may result in a Japanese employee being perceived as not being appropriately aware of role and status differences with the mismatch of "please" with a speech act of giving permission. The following example occurred; it is an imperative form, transferred from the V+*te kudasai* pattern in Japanese, used by a secretary to her non-Japanese boss. What may have been intended as a polite invitation to go back to his office while he waited for her help turned into a command, from his point of view.

> Please go back to your office now.

The implicature of the English speech act realization is that the superior is being treated as a subordinate, thus threatening his face needs to be acknowledged as the director of the program. Felicity conditions can be tricky across cultures and social roles.

Sociopragmatic Failure

Mismatches are more likely when interlocutors do not share the same sociocultural background. Social situations may be viewed differently across cultures. Also, some events may be culture-specific: a Buddhist ordination ceremony for a young man in Thailand has no counterpart in another part of the world. A corollary is that the linguistic and nonlinguistic behaviors vary and reflect the values and beliefs about the event as it is defined by the culture in which it is embedded.

Sociopragmatic failures come up in the context of job interviews in cross-cultural situations that are highly charged as such gate-keeping events require that an interviewee respond to questions according to the expectations of the interviewer. If the interviewee has difficulty with the language and, in addition, does not share the same expectations about job interviews, there are likely to be unpleasant consequences. Roberts, Davies, and Jupp (1992: 42–8) claim, specifically, that interviewees may not be able to "read between the lines" to correctly interpret the interviewer's covert meanings. Anglo-American interview style, for example, requires candidates to sell themselves, whereas interviewees from a different sociocultural background may shy away from such explicit self-presentation. Here is an example of part of a job interview in London, with N, the English interviewer, talking with B, a bilingual man probably from India or Pakistan, with near-native proficiency in English, but with different expectations about job interview discourse.

In line 9, N asks B to make some positive comments about his work at his current place of employment. However, B misinterprets the question and it

1. N: Yes, and you've been there for a long time?
2. B: Four years
3. N: Four years . . . why do you actually want to leave? It's a nice steady job
4. B: Well, the thing is um you know it's better to change the jobs and get other jobs I was very interested in working for L___ Transport you know right at the beginning so . . . because I couldn't get the job I had to take the R___
5. N: Uh huh so did you actually apply to us before for a job?
6. B: I applied once very I . . . once when I came here you know a long time ago
7. N: And what happened then . . . at that stage?
8. B: Well um I failed the test [chuckles]
9. N: For a guard and you failed the test at that stage OK and since then you've worked as a process operator what do you think L___ Buses is going to offer you that R___ don't offer you?
10. B: Well, quite a lot of things for example like um . . . Christmas bonus
11. N: Uh huh
12. B: So many things holidays and all that well we get holidays at R___, but you er . . . get more holidays than you get in R___ [laughs]

Source: Roberts et al. 1992

appears that he wants to get the job with N's company out of personal desires and not because he would find the new company better in ways that would make him a desirable employee. "The candidate's honesty combined with rather different assumptions about how personal to be or how to present one's commitment and worth, set the interview off on the wrong footing" (Roberts et al. 1992: 46). In essence, B could not interpret the pragmatic meaning of line 9 because he did not share the same view of the function of interviews in this different sociocultural context. Consequently, B did not produce the expected sociopragmatic meanings of emphasizing his positive qualifications that might have gotten him the bus driver job.

Misunderstood Intentions

The third type of cross-cultural pragmatic failure involves mismatches of expectations and intentions at a more macro level. Both pragmalinguistic and sociopragmatic glitches concern linguistic features and communication strategies, such as the performance of speech acts. A classic book in the field of pragmatics that focuses on this third type is Tannen's *That's Not What I Meant* (1986). The subtitle is "How conversational style makes or breaks relationships." In Part II, she elaborates on conversational strategy use in relationships that are based on divergent presuppositions. On the topic of indirectness, she states: "Many people, especially Americans, tend to associate indirectness with dishonesty and directness with honesty, a quality we see as self-evidently desirable" (p. 57). Yet, upon analysis of American spoken language, it becomes clear that Americans do practice indirectness, despite the belief. The presupposition that Americans value directness is not sustained.

There are several reasons participants do not always "mean what they say." Speakers use this strategy intentionally to soften messages to maintain rapport with others. It is a form of politeness to avoid conflict and to signal camaraderie and membership in the same group. Honesty can damage others' feelings, be insulting, and break boundaries between people who prefer less encroachment.

The motivations for use of directness or indirectness can differ cross-culturally and across ethnic groups. One cross-cultural example concerns a secretary in a university office in Japan who used English to greet a visiting professor from the United States.

Secretary: oh, you look like you're ready to go to the beach

Given that the university was not located close to a beach, the American professor was unable to interpret the pragmatic meaning. Some possibilities are:

- A compliment about the dress and sandals she was wearing
- A criticism for wearing casual clothing to the university

- An icebreaker, showing her desire to be friendly in a way she may have seen Americans do elsewhere.

What made this indirect comment particularly difficult to interpret was the social distance between the two: a secretary, especially one virtually unknown to the professor, would not be expected to make such a comment in the U.S. Moreover, the professor knew that the general practice in Japan is to deny or avoid compliments and thus she assumed that the secretary was criticizing her attire. Yet, in the professor's culture, secretaries don't criticize people with higher status. A "correct" interpretation is impossible to arrive at due to the mixture of cultural norms and assumptions about the appropriacy of this indirect use of language.

A more elaborated example of indirectness and underlying assumptions about its purpose comes from a study by Morgan (1996) of African-American talk, specifically among women. The text that follows is a segment of a conversation where four women are using indirectness in what is called "signifying" (Morgan 1996: 405). Signifying is described by Mitchell-Keenan (1972: 317–18) as "the recognition and attribution of some implicit content or function which is obscured by the surface content or function."

According to Morgan, two forms of indirectness are used in signifying in African-American communities. The first is pointed indirectness, where a speaker makes a statement to an addressee, whose message is actually intended to be recognized by an overhearer, who is the "real" addressee. The second form is called "baited" indirectness: the speaker claims that a co-participant has a particular feature, which is untrue or which the speaker knows the addressee does not consider to be true. Pointed indirectness has a "mock receiver," the presumed addressee, although hearers who share the same background knowledge understand the conversational strategy that masks the "real target." Neither the mock target nor the actual target responds, as to do so would indicate agreement with the speaker's comments. If the mock target does respond, the result is embarrassment, a signal that the individual is not a member of the group.

Baited indirectness involves a negative assessment about the real target. The pointed indirectness is about a target who is within hearing distance, but is not named or cued via eye contact. Any response from that person signals that the content of the signifying is true.

1.	MM:	What – what – I mean – what was teena – being a teenager like I mean what was
2	JM:	O::h I was (.) gor [geous
3	BR:	[OH well by that time HO:NEY? Her hea:d was SO: big
4.	R:	O:H my GO:D I:H my GO:D (.)
5.	MM:	This is the Coca-Cola pha: se?

(*Continued Overleaf*)

6.	BR:	O::H BABY the whole works (.) she was the only one (.) she ran in the Miss black WHAT (high pitch) EVER thing they was RUNNING in those [da:ys
7.	R:	[sure di:d

Source: Morgan 1996, 405–34
Notes: MM = Marcyliena, JM = Judy, BR = Baby Ruby, R = Ruby

All of the participants are relatives and all grew up together. Judy, sixty-three years old, and Ruby, seventy-eight years old, are sisters, and Baby Ruby, who is also sixty-three, is their niece. Marcyliena is one of Judy's daughters. The talk takes place in a dining room, and they are surrounded by their grandchildren and other family members. Marcyliena opens the topic of "teenage years" about their shared adolescence. Judy immediately gives a focus to the talk by making a comment about herself. Baby Ruby and Ruby then start signifying in line 3, using both pointed and baited indirectness. Judy is the mock receiver, while the baited indirectness occurs in the form of negative attributes about her. Marcyliena adds to the baiting by recalling that Judy used to describe her body as resembling the shape of a Coca-Cola bottle, which Marcyliena calls the "Coca-Cola phase." Judy's silence is noticeable behavior. She can only wait until the topic changes. The communication strategies of signifying behavior is accompanied by lexical items ("honey," "baby," "god") and prosodic cues such as the elongated vowels and the high pitch and loudness.

The indirectness is performed through the signifying act, with an audience and the baited person, Judy, present. This example of CCP concerns members of an African-American community in the United States. Nonmembers unfamiliar with this use of indirectness and the presuppositions about this performance of pragmatic meanings are likely to be unable to interpret the meanings.

Criticisms of Pragmatic Failure Perspective

The notion of pragmatic failure has met criticism. First, the original designation of pragmalinguistic and sociopragmatic types of failure, assumed to be a dichotomy where a researcher could distinguish one from the other with confidence, is not tenable as, in fact, both categories involve underlying perceptions of sociocultural norms. When ordering food in a restaurant, whether one can use a direct imperative, call the waitress your sister, or use politeness markers relates to dimensions of power, social distance, and how service personnel are viewed in different countries. Kasper has suggested that pragmalinguistic dimensions tend to be context or text-internal factors, whereas sociopragmatic concerns are more likely to be context-external in nature (1992: 209). The main point is that these two categories are not dichotomous, that is, two separate classes of pragmatic failure; rather, they represent two ends of a continuum or scale. Clearly, the linguistic enactment of politeness demands awareness of sociocultural norms. A response such as the following in an email message indicates that the writer has been socialized to address the professor with the formal address pronoun, *usted*, according to the social practices of Mexican society: "**su** *respuesta me ha ayudado mucho y* **le** *estoy muy agradecido*" [Your answer has helped me very much and I am very grateful to you.] The two bolded words, *su*, *le*, are all functioning as third person singular pronouns, despite the fact that the student is writing to the professor, where, in English, the second person plural forms would be used. Spanish is one language that requires the third person forms to address someone of higher social status.

Second, and perhaps a more difficult issue to resolve, is the criticism that labeling the linguistic and nonlinguistic behaviors of nonnative speakers of a language as instances of "failure" expresses a "deficit" view of the individuals and by extension negative attitudes towards nonnative speakers in general, their languages, and cultures. In the mid 1980s, in the U.K., the field of critical discourse analysis developed (Fairclough 2001) with the goal of examining the extent to which power was enacted in and through discourse in social actions. While the initial studies concentrated on power in written, media texts, the approach expanded to include the analysis of power, for example, in the use of tags to clarify earlier assumptions about differences in male and female talk (Cameron, McAlinden, and O'Leary 1988). What began as a call for a non-deficit perspective on nonnative speaker talk and interactional discourse has evolved into a much stronger stance against discrimination regarding nonnative speakers. It is beyond the scope of this book to provide a detailed overview of this body of research; the following discussion focuses on the premises of the non-deficit view *vis-à-vis* language users. The reader is referred to Chapter 9 on language, gender, and power and the suggested readings at the end of the chapter for sources on the topic.

Applying critical thinking to the issue of pragmatic "failure," it becomes obvious that this view unfairly targets nonnative speakers, often in an unexamined way. First, the underlying assumption is that the point of view of native speakers of language constitutes the norm for, say, the use of compliments in a conversational interaction. The simple, daily occurrence of this speech act is just the tip of a large iceberg of the reality of communication that is pervaded with the view of the de facto superiority of native speaker expectations in language use. Second, scholars in the field of World Englishes pointed out (Crystal 1997: 54) a couple of decades ago that English is no longer "owned" by native speakers. Crystal estimated that 670 million people at that time had native or native-like speaker command of the language. Moreover, he pointed out that this conservative estimate may be flawed if the criterion for inclusion is revised to consider all individuals who have "a reasonable competence" (Crystal 1997: 61). The revised number would be more like 1,800 million people.

Further, Kachru (1989) presented a now famous model of Inner, Outer, and Expanding Circle countries. The Inner Circle countries are the U.S., U.K.,

Australia, New Zealand, and Canada, while the Outer Circle includes such countries as India, the Philippines, and Singapore. The Expanding Circle is the largest group, with China, Germany, France, and Japan as examples. The countries in the Outer Circle were exposed to English typically during the periods of colonization by English-speaking countries and the language has become institutionalized in their government, educational, and business sectors. The Expanding nations have developed their use of English mostly through the instructed learning of English by their citizens. That development continues today as competence in English is seen as a ticket to a better and more prosperous life even within those countries.

This model clearly draws attention to the relatively small number of countries where native speakers of English dominate. As for the Outer Circle, this domain encompasses many countries where English is a language of daily communication and thus is developing into recognized varieties of World English. In addition to many countries in Africa and south Asia, former British colonies, where a variety of English is present, other areas of the world that were not British colonies have become sites of other varieties of English where it is used as a lingua franca. International trade and transnational movements of people for education, immigration, and even health care have fostered the increasing role of speakers of developing varieties of English.

Applied linguistics has taken on a critical perspective in research on language use in societies undergoing rapid change. Given that CCP is clearly involved in the study of language use and, in particular, interactional discourse with participants from varied language and social backgrounds, a non-deficit stance is warranted in studies and in everyday cross-cultural communication so as to avoid biased, discriminatory views and decision-making.

In effect, the term "pragmatic failure" may no longer be appropriate to describe language use that does not adhere to native speaker language norms for the communication of pragmatic meaning. A preferable term may be "infelicitous" or just "inappropriate." It is clear that a more inclusive perspective is required. New approaches have been evolving within pragmatics as more and more studies focus on situated linguistic and interactional practices to examine how sociocultural contextual features influence comprehension and production of pragmatic meaning. Micro-level analysis in interactional sociolinguistics seeks to avoid essentializing cultural factors and to see in social actions the diversity of language use within societies.

Background on Cross-cultural Speech Acts

One area of research that has contributed immensely to CCP is speech acts.

A: would you mind giving my lecture for me?
B: I have one of my own in an hour

After hearing some bad news that requires she go home immediately, A makes a speech act of requesting to B, a colleague. B has to refuse – another speech act – A's request and he does so by offering an explanation rather than giving a direct refusal.

Since the 1960s anecdotal evidence has been replaced by empirical studies on the transfer of speech act realizations from one cultural and linguistic background to another. The goal of the research has been to apply the findings to avoid stereotyping ("New Yorkers are unfriendly and complain all the time") and to contribute to the teaching of pragmatic competence of second/foreign language learners.

Important work on speech act realization strategies was done by Olshtain and Cohen (1983). They particularly targeted apologizing, a speech act which involves some violation of social norms that occurred and about which the speaker and hearer believe an expression of regret is necessary. The precondition – behavior that warrants an apology – leads the speaker to make amends, which is the goal or purpose of the apology. Olshtain and Cohen (1983) list five semantic formulas or strategies for the speech act set of apologizing.

1. I'm sorry; I apologize.
2. The bus broke down.
3. It was my fault. I didn't leave enough time to get back to my office.
4. Let me treat you to lunch.
5. I'll be more careful next time.

Olshtain and Cohen claim that apologies in English consist of one or more of the five strategies: (1) an expression of apology; (2) an explanation for the behavior; (3) acknowledgement of responsibility; (4) an offer of repair; and (5) a promise not to repeat the same action (Ellis 1994: 176). An important point regarding speech act sets is that apologies by a speaker of English may include one or more of these strategies depending on the severity of the act that required an apology. Another point to be kept in mind involves nonnative speaker realization of apologies, which may differ due to influence from primary language backgrounds, as discussed briefly above concerning apologies by native Thai speakers.

Another invaluable contribution to CCP is the comprehensive empirical study called the *Cross-Cultural Speech Act Research Project* (CCSARP) edited by Blum-Kulka, House, and Kasper (1989). A group of researchers in Europe developed a Discourse Completion Task (DCT) to study speech act realizations of apologies and requests in French, Danish, German, Hebrew, and three varieties of English in seven different countries. The researchers collected data through the DCT on these particularly face-threatening acts and the redressive language used, particularly to attend to the hearer's face needs. While the use of a DCT has been criticized due to the fact that it is based on self-report data, Blum-Kulka *et al.* chose it on the argument that it is the most appropriate instrument to gather large quantities of data while maintaining the same micro contexts provided in each item of the DCT. For example, this item was designed to elicit a request:

> At the university
> Ann missed a lecture yesterday and would like to borrow Judith's notes.
> Ann: _____
> Judith: Sure, but let me have them back before the lecture next week.

This item, along with the contextual information, was translated into the other languages in the CCSARP.

A particularly useful feature of the CCSARP is the coding manual in the appendix of the publication (pp. 273–94), still used today for analysis of data. The following is the basic frame for the data coding procedures (Blum-Kulka *et al.* 1989: 275).

> John, get me a beer, please. I'm terribly thirsty.

The actual request is called the head act: Get me a beer. Then there are alerters and supportive moves. In this example, "John" is an alerter. Alerters are opening moves such as an address term or an attention getter (Excuse me, *Oye, ano*). Supportive moves are external to the request and can mitigate or maximize the speech act. Giving a reason or explanation like "I'm really thirsty" can also function as a mitigator. However, if someone makes a request such as "Stop bothering me or I'll call the police," the second clause aggravates or maximizes the request. These phrases are external to the request and the information is not necessary for the request to be understood. The coding manual is used successfully for the analysis of speech acts and other forms of naturalistic data (see LoCastro 1997).

Since the 1980s, CCP speech act studies have concentrated on the following: apologies, refusals, rejections, compliments, complaints, requests, expressions of gratitude, disagreement, chastisement, giving embarrassing information, and corrections. This list is undoubtedly not exhaustive or definitive. Research in CCP has addressed a wide variety of issues related to speech act realization, such as variation in levels of directness, gender differences, L1 pragmatic transfer, communication strategies, comprehension and production differences, conversational routines, and formulaic language. In the next section, some representative studies by scholars of other languages, often underrepresented in CCP research until recently, are reviewed.

A Sample of Cross-cultural Studies

According to Blum-Kulka (1983), comprehension of a speech act depends on linguistic, sociocultural, and pragmatic knowledge. Even felicity conditions can differ depending on cross-cultural factors. Labov and Fanshel (1977) state that one precondition for requests, for example, is "the hearer must believe that the speaker believes there is a need for action and the request, that the hearer has the ability and the obligation to carry it out and that the speaker has the right to tell the hearer to do so." In other words, Labov and Fanshel contend that felicity conditions are likely to be universal and, further, that there may be neurological evidence of this social action. However, Blum-Kulka (1983) claims that, while these preconditions can only be possible at a very general level, the actual realization strategies of a request vary depending on contextual features, including the values and beliefs of the cultural background of the interactants. She found that a request in Hebrew always involves asking the addressee if they can perform the request:

Child: Can you fix the needle?
Adult: I'm busy.
Child: I just wanted to know if you can fix it.

Thus, a direct questioning of the addressee's capacity to carry out the request is normative in Hebrew, according to Blum-Kulka, while the pragmatic meaning of a commonplace request in American English – Could you pass me the salsa? – does not carry the meaning of inquiring about the addressee's capacity to pass the salsa. It is interpreted as a mitigated speech act of requesting.

Clearly, cultural norms are embedded in speech act realization strategies. At issue is the concern to avoid Anglo-American interpretations of cultural models of thought. One scholar who has attempted to address that problem is Wierzbicka (1991). She developed a form of semantic analysis to avoid culture- and language-specific labels based on a shorthand of universal meanings to capture the core features of speech acts. The goal is to illuminate cultural differences while avoiding interpretations that are loaded with a researcher's culturally influenced view. The following is an example of the verb *ask* in English and its semantic core meanings and the functionally equivalent Walmatjari verb. Walmatjari is a Western Australian language; the sentences are created by Wierzbicka (1991: 159).

ask	*japirlyung*
(a) I say: I want you to do something good for me (X)	(a) I say: I want you to do something good for me (X).
(b) I say this because I want you to do it.	(b) I say it because I want you to do it.
(c) I think: you don't have to do it.	(c) I think: you have to do good things for me.
	(c') I think you know: everyone has to do good things for some other people (because of the way we are related)
(d) I don't know if you will do it.	(d) I think: you will do it because of this.

It is clear from this listing of the semantic features of the two verbs that there are different pragmatic meanings. Specifically, the aboriginal language reflects values attached to kinship rights and obligations. The request speech act (see especially c′) indicates that due to the kinship system of Walmatjari people, the request will not be refused, as it might be in English.

In the next section, a sample of CCP studies illustrates the type of studies, the findings related to the nature of cross-cultural communication, and the development since the early studies. The focus here is on users of the language as a lingua franca for the purpose of everyday, authentic communication.

Listener Behavior

One aspect of interactional talk is the relative lack of attention given to the role of the listener in the co-construction of meaning in conversation. Yet it is important not only cross-culturally, but also within a pluricultural society. E. T. Hall (1969: 379) stated the following regarding his insights from doing ethnographic research with Navajo people: "I slowly learned that how one indicates that one is paying attention is different for each culture. . . . I ultimately learned that to look directly at a Navaho was to display anger." How one displays listenership is important in the everyday world of academic counseling contexts, particularly when the counselor is from a different ethnic background than that of the student advisee. Erickson and Schultz (1982) carried out a micro analysis of videotaped counseling sessions at a U.S. university to learn about what might be considered fine distinctions in listener display between a variety of pairs of students and counselors. For one thing, they learned that African-American students displayed attention and listenership in less overt ways than those expected by the white counselors, even when there were no gender differences. A more recent study of Japanese students and their Australian teachers in an English for academic purposes program and mainstream university classes (Ellwood and Nakane 2009) demonstrated how the Japanese students' use of silence as a form of listenership display led too often to the Australian teachers' perceptions of their lacking competence, being shy, or lacking a commitment to study. Thus, the display of listenership is a particularly sensitive feature in CCP whether one is concerned with communication across cultures within one speech community or across geopolitical boundaries.

The case of listener behavior across cultural boundaries was the focus of studies by both U.S. and Japanese researchers: LoCastro (1987, 1990), and Maynard (1986). Their research questions centered on (1) how frequently verbal and nonverbal listener cues were used in Japanese talk compared with American English talk; (2) the functions of the listener cues across the two cultures; and (3) the location of the occurrence of the cues in the stream of talk.

Listener cues are also called "back channel cues," or "*aizuchi*" in Japanese. The term "back channel cues" designates the fact that the cues are believed to be given by the listener while the speaker, often in the context of telling a story or narrating recent events, is talking in the "main" channel (Yngve 1970). While such cues are common in all world languages, there may be cultural values attached to them more explicitly in one culture than another. Japanese culture does transparently discuss the need for the listener to "chime in" in a patterned manner to show polite listenership (Mizutani and Mizutani 1987). Learners of Japanese may have a lesson on this behavior in their textbooks. This greater sensitivity to an overt demonstration of conversational harmony and the existence of a folk linguistic term for it, i.e. *aizuchi*, contrasts with Anglo-Americans' lesser awareness of this behavior. However, even in the U.S., lack of overt attention on the part of a listener while talking will cause the speaker to stop talking, seek eye contact with the listener's eyes, and then resume talking or not resume talking if there is no eye contact or gaze returned (Goodwin 1981).

The cross-cultural mismatches between Japanese interlocutors and American English speakers may arise regarding the location and frequency of listener responses. Research on the location of listener responses shows that they tend to occur at the ends of phonemic clauses and usually prosodic, grammatical, or semantic cues co-occur. Given that the listener responses help the speaker monitor whether or not the interlocutors are following the talk, lack of responses or asynchronic responses by the listener signal that the talk is not being understood or that something has gone awry in the interaction. In addition, the timing is important. They are expected to occur more frequently in Japanese talk than in American English, and thus, when a Japanese speaker of English is interacting with an American in English, transfer from the L1 practice may be noticeable. Needless to say, the less frequent cue pattern in English is also likely to be transferred to the talk of an American speaking in Japanese. Frequency and timing are both important cross-culturally.

In addition, the functions of listener responses can differ as well. Researchers have found listener behavior in general may signal (a) attentiveness, (b) understanding, (c) agreement, and (d) continuation of the talk (see Schegloff 1982). As noted above, expected listener displays let the speaker know the listener is being attentive to what the speaker is saying. In addition, beyond attentiveness, the listener may wish to demonstrate agreement with the content of the speaker's talk or at least understanding of the content of the talk. Understanding and agreement are not the same thing; there are instances when the listener wishes only to signal understanding while not wanting to display agreement for a variety of reasons. As a continuer, listener behavior cues tell the speaker to continue talking as the listener does not wish to take a turn at talking. However, the cues are indeed ambiguous and there are likely to be more than one cue and one function for any one instance. Then, the context serves to disambiguate the listener's pragmatic meanings.

Needless to say, there are cultural differences with regard to all of these functions. The greater attentiveness in Japanese culture expects the listener to give vocal verbal and nonverbal support in the form, typically, of head nods, and to encourage the speaker, often in tandem with the speaker's use of interactional particles (*ne*, *nee*, *na*) to elicit responses. Tannen (1986) suggests that Americans are more likely than Japanese to expect listeners to show agreement with the content of the speaker's talk. Further evidence of cultural variability in the role of listenership can be found in Philips (1976) and Clancy *et al.* (1996).

In addition to recognized cultural differences, it is not surprising to find ambiguity with regards to the listener cues. As suggested earlier, indeterminacy is a strong feature of languages and language use. The indeterminacy has a function to play in interactional discourse as back channel cues allow the listener to create a fuzzy meaning, enabling denial of responsibility concerning the content of the talk.

Indeterminacy does not just occur due to listener cues. It is a ubiquitous feature of language and plays a role in the use of vague language to signal politeness, obfuscate the veracity of, for example, a response to an interviewer's question on TV, and to avoid the need to get precise numbers of things, as in "*le film a duré environ trois heures*" [The film lasted about three hours] (Channell 1994). The use of indeterminacy can be intentional or due to lack of proficiency in the target language. Eslami-Rasekh (2005a) looked into invitations in Persian and English to learn how to distinguish genuine from non-serious invitations. International students from many countries complain that, when an American says "let's have coffee together," they cannot understand whether the invitation or suggestion is "real." The same complaint can be heard, however, in England from American exchange students!

Eslami-Rasekh (2005a) used a data set of unplanned Persian invitations and an interview data set to describe features of the two types of invitations in that language. Her comparison data of English invitations was from Isaacs and Clark (1990). She used their framework for data collection and analysis for her study. Eslami-Rasekh's results point out several features:

- The structure of non-genuine invitations in Persian is more complex than those in English.
- Features of non-genuine invitations are present in the English ones.
- Those same features, while present, in invitations in Persian are not adequate to allow a distinction to be made between non-genuine and genuine invitations.
- Invitations that could be categorized as genuine in English could be classified as non-genuine by Persian speakers.
- Persian speakers are likely to use a greater number of non-genuine invitations in their daily lives as a form of ritual politeness (*ta'arof*).

This list of descriptions of Persian vs. English non-genuine and genuine invitations paints a picture of the indeterminacy of enacting the speech act of inviting others to have coffee or to attend a special event together. One striking feature of the Persian acts is the higher frequency of non-genuine invitations. Ritual politeness or courtesy is found to be highly frequent in many cultures, ranging from Japanese to Persian to African languages in multiple circumstances. Here are some examples from Eslami-Rasekh (2005a: 457):

> *Maen ta'arof nistaem, jedi migoem, biya tu*: I am not *ta'arof*, I am serious, come in.
>
> *Ye ta'arofe xosko xaliyaem naekaerd*: S/he did not even make an empty *ta'arof*.

In the first example, the person speaking is trying to convince a guest outside her/his door to come in and that the invitation is genuine. It is not offered only out of politeness. The second example is a complaint about a person who did not make even an empty gesture to excuse some action. Clearly these examples demonstrate the extent to which ritual politeness is part of the sociopragmatic norms of Iranian discourse. It is not that American interactional norms have no means to engage in ritual politeness. Flattery and complimenting are often forms of ritual attention to face needs of the addressee in American culture.

Non-English Cross-cultural Studies

One major development within pragmatics is the considerable increase in the number of studies by researchers outside the Anglo-American/Western-centric world where the field has been dominated by (1) native English speaker researchers, (2) standard varieties of English, and (3) English data as the baseline, default norm for analyzing interactional data for theory building and/or descriptions of communication strategies and pragmatic failure. This state of affairs has changed markedly since the mid 1990s in particular, when an increase of data-based research by non-Western scholars providing perspectives on interactional talk in their own cultures, nations, and ethnic groups became noticeable in the literature. In addition, conferences on "Cross-Cultural Pragmatics at a Crossroads" are announced on The Linguist List. This section presents some recent studies carried out in Africa and France where English does not feature as one of the languages.

Regarding sociolinguistic variation in communicating pragmatic meanings within one country, Kasanga (2006) investigates the assumption that the pragmatics of South Africa's indigenized variety of English (Black South African English: BSAE) has been influenced by transfer from various L1s, i.e. the local indigenous languages of educated bilingual speakers of BSAE, and nonnative varieties of English. Specifically, Kasanga uses notebook data of BSAE, a DCT completion task, and acceptability judgments to assess the politeness of requests in BSAE and in Northern Sotho (SeL), an indigenous language of that part of the country. The findings support anecdotal evidence concerning the origins of the pragmatics of requesting in BSAE. Kasanga found pragmatic transfer from the indigenous language into the local variety of English, rather than the population adopting the pragmatic norms of any standard form of English. For the speech act of requesting, the following verbal structure is used (Kasanga 2006: 75):

> *Ke kgopel-a   ranta*
> I ask-Pr.TENSE   one rand.
> I am asking for one rand.

In this case, the person wants one rand, the currency of South Africa. This use of the performative verb form is "commonly used in African languages" to express politeness or deference (Kasanga 2006: 75). The point here is that this requesting strategy is found in the local variety of English, having been adopted from SeL.

These findings illustrate the role of African cultural norms in local language contact situations to produce an indigenized variety of English.

Mashiri (2003) collected data on polite request strategies and responses to requests on commuter minibuses in Harare, Zimbabwe. In the microcosm of that environment, the participants' language is Shona, one of the main languages of that country. Yet Zimbabwe is similar to many African nations: it is essentially a multilingual society that has evolved and continues to do so in a language contact situation that is a particularly marked example of the diversity and contradictions inherent in all societies. The complexity of the local society translates into pragmatic meanings such as co-membership in the same group and camaraderie or solidarity through code switching. The practice of code switching among the former colonial languages and those of people returning from the African diaspora, the local indigenous languages, and lingua francas entail not only daily language switching, but also a mixing of cultural practices.

Drawing on questionnaire data from informants of four different language families, field notes, and examples from African literature, Egner (2006) looks into the speech act of promising in West African cultural practices. On the basis of intercultural experiences while living in Ivory Coast, Egner studied the cultural premises underlying the act of promising for Africans and Westerners. She learned that in African cultures promising is a strategy that signals politeness, orienting to the hearer or addressee, typically occurring at the close of a period of talk. The ability to carry out the act may not be relevant in the African context, in contrast to the assumption of ability underlying the act of promising by Westerners. Egner was able to ascertain that, through negotiation during a conversational exchange, a binding promise could be reached between the African speakers, suggesting the existence of two speech acts, polite promises and binding promises (2006: 462). In fact, different speech act verbs are used for the two types, a finding that further supports her conclusion.

In a data-based study comparing conversational routines and verbal rituals in French and Syrian service encounters in France, Traverso (2006) explains the inherent connection between two interactional practices: (1) conversational routines and (2) ritual acts. Conversational routines can be used to carry out ritual acts and, while the core feature of ritual acts is their symbolic value, conversational routines possess functional or pragmatic value rather than symbolic value.

A possible pragmatic mismatch due to the overlap may not be transparent to interlocutors in the course of an intercultural interaction. Traverso investigated the conversational routines that are used in verbal ritual acts and the differences in Syrian and French data, collected in France and Syria. She audiotaped interactions in small shops in both countries. In Syrian commercial transactions, Traverso argues that there are cultural values of affectivity, communicated through expressions of "closeness and familiarity" and of deference, typically used to address a superior. Receipt or acceptance of a requested item in a shop becomes a ritual act in Syrian Arabic: "Thus, whereas in the French corpus acknowledging a request is not more than a practical matter, dealt with by a functional act, in the Syrian corpus it becomes the occasion for stating a certain type of relationship and for assuring the co-participants of one's good will" (Traverso 2006: 120). The example below evidences the acceptance of the product that had been requested.

C = customer; SC = shop clerk

<u>French shop</u>
C: *oui, oui, oui, oui j'vais prendre le (inaudible) j'sais pas si je prends la boîte*
SC: *ben d'toute façon j'vais la garder hein*

Translation
C: yes, yes, yes, yes I'll take the (inaudible) I don't know if I'll take the box
SC: well, anyway, I'll keep it

<u>Syrian shop</u>
C: *ʔe maːʃiː l-bajda lakaːn,*
SC: *ʔajj wahde*
C: *hajj*
SC: *maːʃi (.) mabruːk*
C: *ʔalla jbaːrik fiːk*

Translation
C: yes, it's all right with the white one then

SC: which one?
C: this one
SC: it's all right (.) may it be blessed
C: God bless you (silence)

The dialogue with the shop clerk in French includes talk about other topics while accepting the shoes the customer decided to buy. The acceptance itself is a routine formulaic phrase and then a practical matter about whether or not to take the box ends the transaction. In the Syrian example, the customer's acceptance is followed by the shopkeeper's blessing of the customer for buying the product. Her blessing reciprocates the customer's blessing, literally, of the shoes. Traverso explains that this *mabru:k*, an exchange of blessing, is repeated at the end of the transaction. It is a ritual exchange and after it no more talk about the item occurs.

These three studies are just a sample of the research that is taking place on differences in communicating pragmatic meanings in languages other than English. This growing body of research not only contributes to the recognition of the sociocultural diversity of the world, but also provides valuable information on baseline data needed for comparison studies of the enactment of pragmatic meaning.

Intercultural Rhetoric

The final section in this chapter reviews another area of CCP that involves cross-cultural differences in literacy skills. Academic literacy skills include oral production of such text types as class and conference presentations as well as writing skills for this particular discourse community. A result of geopolitical changes throughout the world and transnational migrations of populations in search of education and better economic conditions have led to large increases in the number of international students at all educational levels, from the influx of Mexican children into public school systems throughout the U.S. to Chinese and Latin American students in search of doctorates in engineering, computer science, and pharmacy at most tertiary level institutions. Many of the international students lack the educational training needed in the area of academic literacy skills. At times, despite relatively high proficiency levels in English on standardized tests, and good oral fluency in the language, such students are at a loss when it comes to producing reports and examination papers that reflect their academic potential.

Teachers, curriculum planners, and educational policy stakeholders become involved in developing ways to overcome the gap and prepare the learners to succeed in the educational system. One key aspect is promoting awareness of the cultural influences on the learners' literacy skills. This field shares the premises of CCP and is called "contrastive rhetoric" or "intercultural rhetoric."

An interest in academic writing has developed over the past two decades as a result of the increasing number of second language learners and users of English who have left their countries to pursue tertiary level education, in undergraduate and graduate educational programs, typically in North America, the United Kingdom, and Australia. What at first seemed an easy task, to provide study skills courses for this student population, soon led to the realization that empirical studies were needed to understand what academic writing is from a cross-cultural perspective.

Some early studies focused on politeness. At first glance, it may not be clear how an extended written text can present information in accord with cultural norms of politeness. Generalizing, there are two styles of information structuring or flow: inductive and deductive. With the inductive style, the supporting arguments or reasons for writing, for example, a business letter to someone, come first, followed by the main point: a request, complaint, or inquiry. In the deductive style, the main point is introduced at the beginning before stating the reasons or providing supporting evidence. A number of researchers claim that the deductive pattern is preferred by writers influenced by Western rhetorical practices, while the inductive or delayed introduction of the main topic is more likely to be used by Asians. A common stereotype claims that British rhetorical style prefers presentation of the facts first, while Asians find it insulting to provide a conclusion at all! Consider the following two letters (the first one is from Kirkpatrick 1991 and has been edited). Formal business letters provide short, illustrative evidence of the two styles of information structure.

Miss _____,

How are you? ... I heard Radio Australia's Cantonese programs. I really liked them! Because I, the lover of Cantonese and Cantonese songs.... Now I listen to your program every day and my Cantonese has greatly improved ... [I] feel great affection for Radio Australia ... I shall always remember that at 11800 kilohertz, I have a good friend.... Here, I want for my good friend ... a Li Keqin song.... Also heartfelt wishes for happiness to all listeners of Radio Australia! In addition, I would like to ask for a program schedule for Radio Australia's Cantonese programs ....

Wishing you happiness at work.

Loyal Listener _____

> Dear _____ School:
>
> I would like to congratulate you on your ninetieth anniversary of your fine school's existence. I know that you have been a great help to the many Americans in Japan.
>
> I would like to wish you many continued years of excellence in education. Please let me know if my staff or I can ever be of any assistance in your fine school.
>
> Sincerely

The first letter, written in the second language of a Chinese young adult, demonstrates the inductive style, in that the main point, a request for the program schedule, is delayed to the end. The writer of the second letter states in the first sentence the reason for the letter, exemplifying the deductive style. The text of the letter indicates the author was more likely an American or someone heavily influenced by the American style of business letter writing.

Scollon and Scollon (1995) did a study of factors that affect the style choices Chinese university students make in their academic work. They note that Chinese students tend to use the deductive pattern in two contexts: (a) when they interact with their peers and (b) in transactional contexts, such as when purchasing something or using a taxi, thus in service or "outside" encounters. These situations contrast with "inside" contact situations that require more sensitivity to interpersonal dimensions, such as with people at one's place of work that one expects to have an ongoing relationship with. Scollon and Scollon further claim that Confucian influences on teacher–student relations are still present in contemporary Hong Kong and China. Consequently, students, low in the university hierarchy, are not in a position to introduce a topic, entailing the inductive pattern in writing essays. In other words, students are expected to acknowledge social positions, humbling themselves and showing restraint through discursive mitigation in the form of introducing topics only after providing reasons and evidence.

Western use of the inductive pattern provides further support for the claim that the delayed introduction of a topic is a form of politeness. The inductive structure can be found in instances where a Westerner is hesitant to broach a difficult subject such as borrowing a large sum of money or giving embarrassing information in writing (Scollon and Scollon 1995). Topic introduction is delayed to buy time to feel out the mood or opinions of others and to avoid stating abruptly one's view.

Here is an example of an edited student-written essay from a class at a Japanese university. The students had been given the following essay prompt:

According to the theory about attitudes and motivation, the "best" kind of motivation is the desire to acculturate to the target language community, i.e. to want to be a member of that community and to become like a native speaker. How do you feel about this?

The theory about attitude and motivation is very interesting, because language is a culture. If we can speak the target language like a native speaker and we don't know the culture the culture of that language, it seems like one play baseball without knowing how to fun.

By the way, I heard that the easiest way to learn the foreign language is to go to the country spoken the target language. And I agree with it, because it is easy to learn the culture of there.

In Japan it is hard for us to learn it. But there are many foreigners in Japan. We have the chance to learn the culture and the language from them.

So we have to learn the culture of the target language. *I believe* it is the best way to study the foreign language.

Of this four-paragraph essay, only the final one contains the student's opinion, explicitly marked by the words *I believe*. The content of the other three paragraphs summarizes class discussions as well as common beliefs in Japan about language learning. Given the task the students had been given in the essay prompt, this student embedded the important point, that is, his opinion, only at the end of the essay.

From a functional perspective on language use, the motivation for one particular organization of information in a written text has to do with displaying attention to the likely audience or readers of the text in any culture. An Asian may describe the organization of the photos on a website as not being very "polite" for the readers while an American may be concerned about the degree of user-friendliness of the website. These may simply be different terms for the general, overriding issue of communication with the audience through linguistic and nonlinguistic means.

Other cultural influences on writing styles are apparent in Mexican multilingual writers. One characteristic of Mexican writing is "long sentences and floating commas," a comment made by a colleague with long experience teaching linguistics to graduate students at a Mexican university. The sentences tend to be elaborated by adding multiple clauses with a string of related ideas or topics, one following after another. Other related characteristics include different punctuation conventions, few cohesive markers to combine clauses or sentences, and repetition of lexical items. The following example from the M.A. thesis of an L1 Mexican Spanish graduate student was described by the student as being "polite" in his sociocultural context. This remark is insightful as it explains the value the student attached to his writing style.

> *Al comparar el método comunicativo y participativo de la enseñanza de la matemática con el método de enseñanza tradicional, se encontró que el primero fue mas eficiente sobre el segundo debido a que el método tradicional tiene una estructura rígida en su forma de enseñanza y en donde se hace énfasis en procedimientos rutinarios, formulas y demostraciones carentes de significado para los estudiantes, este tipo de procedimientos es para la mayoría de los estudiantes estériles, aburridos y carentes de sentido, fuera de contexto y del ámbito cultural de los estudiantes, además la impartición de la clase se realiza a través de monólogos par parte del maestro con lo que la parte interactiva de la enseñanza se pierde.*
>
> [Comparing the communicative and participative method of teaching mathematics with the traditional method, one finds that the first one is more effective than the second, due to the traditional method having a rigid structure in its form of teaching and where emphasis is put on routine procedures, formulas, and demonstrations devoid of meaningfulness for the students. This type of procedure is for the majority of the students sterile, boring, and devoid of meaning, without context, and outside the cultural context of the students, in addition to the fact that the class is realized through monologues by the teacher where the interactive dimension of teaching is lost.]
>
> (LoCastro 2008b: 204)

There are several features to notice here. First, the Spanish language original is one sentence or one paragraph. In Spanish, the word "*oración*" is translated as both "sentence" and "paragraph." Students in classes in the Mexican educational system are taught that an *oración* should include all ideas associated with the topic. This description is very similar to what U.S. students find in their writing textbooks regarding paragraphs. Second, the translation has two sentences in contrast to the one-sentence original Spanish version. It would be ungrammatical if it were rewritten verbatim in English. This syntactic difference between Mexican Spanish and standard U.S. English creates a cross-cultural stumbling block for literacy skill training.

The features of this one passage demonstrate quite clearly the linguistic differences between the writing style of Mexican Spanish writers and American writers. These syntactic structures are rendered following cultural practices. The additive clauses in the Mexican example above are mostly linked with commas or semicolons, resulting in what are called "run-on" or "fused" sentences in English. Building "paragraphs" to include all related sub-ideas is viewed as positive and very polite, demonstrating to the teacher, the main reader of the essays, the student's intelligence by writing long sentences.

Thus, what is appropriate language use in an academic text varies with the sociocultural context. The syntactic patterns of the Mexican student or information structure of the Chinese students convey information in the manner deemed appropriate for the particular sociocultural context. Writers have communicative purposes in mind in creating texts, in line with the norms of their sociocultural background. One of the communicative goals is to display pragmatic meanings, in this case politeness, in written texts.

Applications to Language Teaching

There have been undoubtedly more cross-cultural studies of pragmatic competence than any other area of pragmatics, particularly addressing the conversational contributions of nonnative speakers of English as a second or foreign language. Most of the research has been on perceptions of speech act force, levels of politeness, and the role of contextual variables in choosing realization strategies (see Kasper and Rose 1991). Questions regarding development of pragmatic competence have been less frequently addressed (see, however, LoCastro 2001; Salisbury and Bardovi-Harlig 2000). CCP studies have concentrated on users of a second/foreign language rather than learners per se. However, the nonnativeness of those users reflects many aspects of their earlier acquisition of a second/foreign language. The next chapter on interlanguage pragmatics delves into some of the work on second language pragmatics. In addition, Chapter 10 reviews classroom pragmatic development.

Adult speakers of second/foreign languages find efforts to move towards more native-like language use hampered by numerous factors: inadequate time available to study, formally or informally; lack of teachers trained to work with adults at advanced stages; and materials published solely for lower proficiency learners. The issue of exposure comes up, particularly with pragmatic competence development. Studies of immigrants find that if an individual lives and works in the first language community, for instance in Montreal, that likelihood of attaining high proficiency in Quebecois French is problematic. Thus, in the typical domains of people's lives – home, work, and outside activities – there needs to be an immersion degree of exposure to the new language and the community for pragmatic competence to develop. Classroom instruction in pragmatics for adult users of the new language needs to include, consequently, opportunities to learn about pragmatics, conversational routines, and other dimensions of communicative competence. Tailored instruction by teachers trained for working with adults can go a long way in helping them integrate the everyday learning "on the street" in their new communities with formal instruction where they get help to become the more competent speakers they may wish to be.

Conclusions

This chapter reviewed the important field of CCP, starting with the first phase where the focus was on pragmatic failure, typically when learners of

English miscommunicated in the target language due not only to their proficiency level, but also transfer of use from their first or primary language into English. That narrow view has broadened to focus on users of English and other languages in everyday interactions, where acquisition is not an issue. Further, CCP has moved beyond seeing misfires or communicative glitches as evidence of failure to a perspective that studies differences, for instance, in requesting speech acts that may arise due to divergent cultural beliefs and practices of the participants. Cross-cultural differences are not per se negative. Rather than a deficit view, that nonnative speakers produce defective language use, the modern stance of difference fosters an inclusive view, avoiding judgment and discrimination. Perhaps one way to sort out the tendency to judge is to focus on intelligibility (McKay 2002: 78). In McKay's view, there is a need to investigate how cultural patterns, transferred into English as a lingua franca, the most prominent international language, affect comprehension.

Chapter 5 takes up the topic of interlanguage pragmatics, where acquisition and pragmatic competence development by learners of English become the center of attention. Learning English continues to be an important goal of people, just as learning to be an expert in technology is in the modern world.

Suggested Readings

Fairclough, N. (2001). *Language and power.* 2nd edition. Harlow: Pearson Education.
Hall, E. T. (1977). *Beyond culture.* New York: Anchor Books.
Holliday, A., Hyde, M., and Kullman, J. (2004). *Intercultural communication: An advanced resource book.* London/New York: Routledge.
Kecskes, I. and L. R. Horn (Eds.) (2007). *Explorations in pragmatics: Linguistic, cognitive, and intercultural aspects.* Berlin: Mouton de Gruyter.
Spencer-Oatey, H. and Franklin, P. (2009). *Intercultural communication: A multidisciplinary approach to intercultural communication.* London: Palgrave.
Tannen, D. (1986). *That's not what I meant: How conversational style makes or breaks relationships.* New York: Ballantine.

Discussion Questions

1. Discuss with group members your experiences of communication problems that seem to be due to participants' cultural backgrounds. Use what you learned in this chapter to analyze these events. Categorize them in a table to present to class.
2. Name two or three values and beliefs you have about the contemporary world that differ from those of your parents' generation. How would you handle a heated discussion with participants of different generations?
3. Do you think pragmatic misunderstandings are a common problem in the daily world of intercultural communication? Explain.

4. Discuss situations you have experienced where the outcome was successful and others that were unsuccessful. Job interviews, for example. Can you explain the reasons and the differences for the successes and the failures?
5. Select a speech act and study it. Collect naturally occurring data and then compare and contrast your findings with classmates. Consider the variables connected with speech acts that have been discussed so far in this book.
6. Have you noticed that some people jump into a conversation as soon as the speaker has barely finished talking? And others don't and even seem to wait too long? Have you considered the reasons for the different conversational styles in the instances you have experienced?
7. What are intr_a_cultural differences? That is, subcultures within a country, community, or society. Discuss with other members of your group intracultural differences in countries that you know well.

Data Analysis

The duration of the speaker exchange point in talk, i.e. the brief silence or pause that occurs before the listener starts talking – varies by culture. Scollon and Scollon (1983) carried out a study in northern Alaska with Athabaskans, a local indigenous people, who, when they interacted in English with non-Athabaskans, could not get a word in edgewise. In the Scollons' study, the response latency or pause before responding exceeded 1.5 seconds in conversational talk between Athabaskans; a shorter pause, less than one second, is the norm between English speakers. Both groups transferred their practices when conversing in English with each other. Consequently, the Athabaskans felt that they were never given an opportunity to speak by the English speakers as the English speakers failed to wait long enough for them to speak.

The question now is whether this pattern of pause length can be found in other cultures. The accompanying table presents statistics from a study of Japanese and American television interviews. There were three types of interviews: the first with all the participants speaking in American English; the second with the participants speaking in Japanese; and the third conducted in English, with one participant speaking his first language, Japanese, and the second speaking his second language, English.

In the table, for the first two rows, the speakers were using their first language, English and Japanese, respectively. The data in the first row came from American TV interview programs, whereas the data of the second row was obtained by counting pause lengths from a Japanese TV interview program. The third and fourth rows include pause lengths from one interview program on Japanese TV, where the interviewer was a Japanese speaking in English and the American was using his first language, English, to respond to the questions. In the third row, the American speaker's response was followed by the Japanese who introduced the next question, and the fourth row is the reverse order. In the interview between two Americans, for example, twenty-nine pauses were measured, lasting from a minimum of 38 milliseconds in length to a maximum of 1,550 milliseconds in length. The mean was 635 milliseconds.

Type	Minimum (ms.)	Maximum (ms.)	N size	Mean (ms.)	SD
American–American	38	1,550	29	635	496
Japanese–Japanese	32	582	28	280	158
American–Japanese	83	2,930	20	869	783
Japanese–American	62	1,036	18	373	314

Source: LoCastro 1990: 232.

Discuss the data and come to some conclusions about the pattern of pauses and cross-cultural influences on pause length. Generate a list of explanations related to CCP for the data in the table.

5
INTERLANGUAGE PRAGMATICS

Introduction

Chapter 4 dealt with cross-cultural pragmatics, where the main concern is the influence of sociocultural background on the comprehension and production of pragmatic meaning. While the effect of a speaker's primary language and its underlying values and beliefs on the performance of pragmatic meaning may result in misunderstandings and communication breakdowns, positive transfer from the L1 into L2 language use does occur and paves the way for successful communication across languages and cultures. In Chapter 4, the emphasis was on multilingual participants who are not primarily learning or studying a language, but rather use it for purposes of communication in a variety of environments.

This chapter, as the title suggests, focuses attention on learners of second/foreign languages and their pragmatic development as they seek to become proficient, successful users of the target language. Learners and teachers of languages need to understand the domain of interlanguage pragmatics (ILP) to facilitate our understanding of how people comprehend and communicate meaning beyond what is said. ILP may be considered a sub-area of second language acquisition (SLA) and thus is inherently anchored in acquisition contexts. This chapter looks into a range of relevant topics, including learner language characteristics, developmental stages, ILP research in discourse contexts, and methodologies for studying ILP.

Since the 1960s, the field of second language acquisition (SLA) has reflected the dominance of the mentalist paradigm in formal linguistics, strongly influenced by the seminal work of Chomsky and his colleagues. This background has translated into an almost exclusive interest in studying language learners' ability to employ linguistic resources – phonological, lexical, and grammatical systems – according to the norms of the target language (Ellis 1994). Further, the mentalist agenda of the Chomskian perspective has placed high priority on the extent to which language learners have access to the Universal Grammar, theorized to be the cognitive apparatus, the Language Acquisition Device (LAD), that supports and structures acquisition of all languages, from one's first language to any and all subsequent languages. However, since the 1990s, SLA has shifted to include a greater interest in language use; in other words, how learners understand and communicate pragmatic meanings and achieve successful communication in their second language. Further, rather than concern for sentence-level production in the target language, attention has prioritized language as discourse, or extended text, from utterances in conversational talk to texts in academic writing. Along with these changes, in the early 1990s, the acquisition of pragmatic competence has found a place in SLA research. In this context of acquisition, cognitive approaches, based on current advances in brain research, have drawn attention to what is called the cognitive–pragmatic interface.

Chapter 5 explores learner language and issues related to acquiring L2 pragmatic competence to function at advanced levels of communication. After providing definitions for terms in ILP in the next section, the following ones address the value of studying learner language, two important influences on learner language, i.e. transfer and developmental stages, and evidence from speech act and speech event data of pragmatic competence of interlanguage pragmatics.

Definitions

ILP takes the first word of the term from SLA, specifically from the efforts of Selinker (1972) and Tarone (1980) to account for the developing linguistic system of learners that is neither that of their L1, nor that of the L2. Interlanguage refers to intermediate, dynamic, and transient linguistic systems that, according to the theory, continue to develop over time as learners move closer and closer to attaining native-like proficiency. The interlanguage is a reduced system at the early stages of development. There are fewer grammatical markers (omission of the third person singular marker, "s" as in "She make good cookies") and, at the very beginning stages of learning a language, learners may use one word, say, "please," to perform a variety of functions. Learners progress along a trajectory towards their desired goal in fits and starts, sometimes regressing and sometimes making rapid progress with particular skills, for instance in academic speaking skills, while still struggling with conversational chat unless they live with a native speaker of the target language. Although, in theory, all learners can progress to native-like proficiency, this desideratum may not be attainable for most learners unless they study the target language before puberty, before the age of 11 to 13. Beyond the critical period of language acquisition (birth to puberty), learning second or third languages becomes more difficult for a variety of reasons, including physiological and cognitive factors and individual differences. Many, if not most, experience fossilization where development of their L2 skills ceases or lessens so that native-like competence becomes more and more unattainable.

The main point with the interlanguage concept is that learner language use is informed by an underlying system, or rather systems, that overlap and are constantly being revised by learners, usually out of awareness, as long as there is regular exposure and tutored learning. Their talk is not random and can inform researchers and teachers about SLA developmental stages for curriculum and materials planning.

ILP is essentially interested in how L2 learners use their developing abilities in the target language to communicate successfully despite gaps in knowledge about the linguistic systems and about the sociopragmatics of the L2. In other words, to interact in the L2, learners need not only to have a yet to be defined level of proficiency regarding the phonology, lexis, and syntax, but also the norms of communicating pragmatic meanings in the L2. One way to learn about their abilities is to study their production, their performance in the L2 in classrooms and outside of classrooms. This interest in learner language spans analysis of their pronunciation mistakes, such as using a sound or phone that is neither an /r/ or /l/ phoneme in English; to interactional strategies when there is a lack of understanding of the speaker's intended meaning (Tarone and Swierzbin 2009). Studying learner language has several purposes. One is a concern of researchers to build a knowledge base of learners' interlanguages and to advance a more comprehensive theory of that phenomenon. A second goal involves enabling teachers to diagnose weak areas that can then be attended to in actual classroom lessons. A third objective is to help learners evaluate their own interlanguage production and work on self-study activities to improve their L2 skills in resources online, in media centers on campuses, and in libraries.

Pragmatic Transfer from L1 to L2

One feature of learner language that researchers and teachers are particularly interested in is the transfer from the L1 into comprehension and production of the L2. As with CCP, interference or the more neutral term "transfer" is again an issue. In this case, for ILP, the focus is on learners of the L2, that is, the types of errors and mistakes, possible causes, and the effect on pragmatic development. Although research has shown consistently evidence of transfer in cross-cultural and interlanguage pragmatics, it is not yet clearly understood. Further, the psycholinguistic basis of transfer in pragmatics has not been fully established, despite the recognition of researchers, teachers, and learners of second/foreign languages that this phenomenon is a part of language learning and use.

The cognitive ability to infer implied or pragmatic meaning is not an issue, as it comprises basic processing skills that are universal. Brain research in the future may provide explanations of the cognitive processes involved in transfer of language use strategies from the L1 to the L2. For right now, by means of microanalysis of local instances of transfer in learner language, the goal is to zero in on factors that contribute to less than successful communication of pragmatic meaning by learners, and evidence of reliance on the L1 during the acquisition stages.

Conventional and conversational implicatures are particularly difficult types of pragmatic meaning for learning, involving such topics as attribution of illocutionary force and perceptions of politeness. For example, a learner of Japanese who needs to make requests for information and help at one of the ward offices of a city government in Japan achieves that goal more successfully and appropriately by having the knowledge that a negatively worded request is preferred to other forms of requests in Japanese:

Pamfuletto o itadakemasen ka? [Don't you have a brochure I could have?]

And in Mexican Spanish, use of the imperfect of *querer* with requests is preferred:

Hola, quería unos billetes para ir a la Canarías. [Hello, I'd like some tickets to go to the Canaries.]

(Chodorowska-Pilch 2008: 34)

Such request realization strategies communicate pragmatically greater politeness and attention to the addressees at the city office and a travel agency. What are conventional routines in the L1 may leave a learner feeling perplexed; grammar lessons in classrooms tend not to teach learners the uses of negation in Japanese or the imperfect in Spanish to make requests. The next example of complaints with Russian immigrants in Israel concentrates on misunderstandings that developed due to the unexpected language use.

Gershenson (2003) took a pragmatic perspective to look into misunderstandings between Israelis and Soviet immigrants. During the 1990s, over 900,000 Soviet Jewish immigrants, about 15 percent of the total population, arrived in Israel where, in addition to economic, political, and social problems, negative stereotypes developed among both groups about each other. Gershenson states: "I argue that linguistic and cultural factors, stemming from pragmatic differences between the Russian and Hebrew languages, also play a role in explaining differences between some Soviet immigrants and veteran Israelis" (2003: 275). She studied both the interlanguage of Hebrew spoken by the Russian immigrants and the different communication styles of the Russian and Israeli populations. Specifically, Gershenson looked at the speech act of complaint, where one interlocutor breaks a social norm and the other seeks retribution for the act deemed unacceptable. The research methodology involved two groups of university students, one in Russia and the other in Israel, who completed two tests to identity problematic situations. This mixed-methods empirical study used retrospective interviews and statistical analysis of the two tests. Both the quantitative and qualitative results illustrated problematic behaviors. For example, the Israelis tended to complain more readily and directly, whereas the immigrants were more likely to opt out and not complain.

Here is an example of complaints regarding music, translated into English:

> Russian immigrant: This music rocks, but it would sound even better if it were softer.
>
> Israeli: Come on, really, I already asked you to lower it [the music], it's really not nice what you are doing to me.

The immigrant uses slang (*rocks*), a strategy to lessen social distance and create informality, with an indirect request for the other person to lower the volume of the music. With the Israeli informant, there is direct expression of complaining along with politeness in the use of "come on, really," signaling group identity. Thus, although both groups used positive politeness and in-group markers, the Russian speakers of Hebrew were more likely to use indirectness, a negative politeness strategy, signaling more concern for the addressee's wants. Another pragmatic strategy where there were noticeable differences involves the use of questions for complaints. While the Israelis used them frequently, the Russians did so less frequently.

Gershenson's conclusions concern the use of indirectness by the Russian informants in their interlanguage of Hebrew, which leads to a cultural clash between them and Israelis, particularly in situations that are apt to be conflict-ridden. She explains that while the Russian immigrants transferred pragmatic strategies from their L1 into their interlanguage to avoid conflict, the Israelis, who tend to see conflict as a "normal part of human relationships" (p. 286), prefer to address the conflict directly, resolve it, and move on. Gershenson also found that the Russian immigrants did incorporate Hebrew pragmatic strategies, thus creating a hybrid interlanguage, which presumably will change towards the native Israeli use of Hebrew as the immigrants become more integrated into the local speech community.

ILP, then, seeks to identify instances of gaps in the knowledge of the L2 in learner language. According to Kasper and Blum-Kulka (1993), the main reasons for difficulty in enacting pragmatic knowledge derive from either insufficient knowledge of the target language and its communicative practices, or problems in accessing it with automaticity in a real-time, interactional context.

Learner Language

Clearly, a very important source of information on pragmatic development is learner language, that is, the production of learners that has evidence of errors, mistakes, slips of the tongue, hesitations, rephrasings, silences, and so forth. It is the performance data of their efforts to use the target language. By analyzing learner production, teachers can diagnose the progress learners in their classes are making as well as derive ideas for future lesson plans, even a whole semester worth of lesson plans.

History

The idea that learner production plays an important role in learning about language development, including pragmatic competence, began with Contrastive Analysis. During the period of behaviorism and the audiolingual method of language teaching in the 1960s in the U.S., teachers regularly made decisions about lessons based on predictions of what linguistic features would be most difficult for their learners, given their L1. Comparing systems of the L1 with those of the L2 and developing teaching materials was a salient feature of language education during that period. In the 1970s, error analysis was the next stage in developing L2 proficiency as research had shown that contrastive analysis did not produce the hoped for results in classrooms. So, rather than carry out comparison studies of two languages, to find areas of difficulty, error analysis began to play a major role. It entailed looking at what learners produced in the L2 in classroom contexts. It was assumed that, if a learner did not use the third person singular marker on verbs in English ("He don't want to go to the library.") the student had not learned that rule of English grammar. Again, teachers and materials writers made pedagogical decisions, targeting the areas of a language's grammar, phonology, and vocabulary that seemed to present learning problems for learners.

The current state of affairs has evolved from that start and learner language has become a much more sophisticated tool for teachers. We now know that, given the situational context, a student may continue to delete the "s" on the third person singular to signal their identity by speaking a non-standard variety of American English. Another possible explanation derives from the distinction that is made between "errors" and "mistakes." If indeed the student has not been taught at all or inadequately about the third person singular form, then the learner is likely to be making an error. However, it is only a mistake if, in the context of focusing on meaning to get a point across, learners are not monitoring their talk and so slips of the tongue do not necessarily indicate lack of knowledge of the standard form.

While studying learner language may most often be a tool to assess grammatical, lexical, and phonological progress and accuracy of students in instructed

SLA environments, studies now deemphasize learners' errors or mistakes and focus on how researchers can not only learn about interlanguage development, but also better understand the stages of language learning and the exploratory nature of the learner language (Allwright and Hanks 2009), to ultimately inform more comprehensive theories about second language learning. A major step in SLA and thus ILP research transpired in the 1980s when interactional studies took on greater importance with Long's (1983) Interaction Hypothesis. He argued that conversational interaction was a necessary condition for SLA. Then, in 1996, Long's revised view of the Interaction Hypothesis (Long 1996) emphasized the need for modified forms of interaction. Clearly, any discussion of interaction overlaps with pragmatics; interactional discourse is the primary context where pragmatic meanings form.

Learner Language Study

An example of ILP talk in an academic context includes two language learners using L2 English to enact targeted speech acts during a comparison task with two pictures of American houses. This study of learner language by Tarone and Swierzbin concentrated on the academic language the learners used to express inference and justification, two common academic language functions (2009: 80, 86). The learners are Antonio and Rodrigo, brothers, both native speakers of Spanish from Mexico who were studying in the same intensive English program at a university in the U.S.

A: eh this house, eh eh show me, that that eh, the the the people, the property, are, maybe eh they, eh, they had a a a good job, eh, because, eh the house, eh show it. It's it's it's big, it's it's clean, eh, there is a car, and and, this eh house it's it's small, it's no clean, em I I I think I think so.

R: Yes, is correct, I think so too. Eh, this house eh eh eh, show, eh, the the the, poor, poorer money, I don't know, I I, this house, show, there are very money and this house no. This house is, is, it's a good house but, eh, is better this house and and and, and the and are worth in Mexico, in United States, in other countries, yes, I I I eh, um, I am, m, is is, em, show, eh, different . . .

(Tarone and Swierzbin 2009: 138)

Jointly, the two learners discuss the evidence from the two pictures to make inferences about the residences. They argue that one of the houses must belong to people with money: it's big, clean. There is a car. On the other hand, those living in the other house are viewed as being less financially well off: it's not clean and is small. Note that Rodrigo draws on his world knowledge to make the inferences. When he says "is the same in in other countries," he is comparing the American houses with those in his home country in terms of how one can infer that the owners are either wealthy or not. It is clear that Antonio and Rodrigo can explain their inferences and justify them. Thus, despite many repetitions, hesitation markers, and grammatical mistakes, their ability to communicate pragmatic meaning is successful.

The next section turns to another area of ILP that seeks to contribute to understanding the complexities of acquiring and learning another language. Early researchers on child L1 language acquisition learned that there were developmental stages that all children went through to acquire their first language. Irrespective of the L1, the stages were similar and without much variation. L2 scholars shifted their interests and proposed theories and carried out numerous studies to develop the concept of interlanguage.

Developmental Stages of Pragmatic Development

Interlanguage pragmatic development derives from the notion that learners move through developmental stages as they make progress towards L2 pragmatic norms. The interlanguage concept is based on a developmental model. Specifically, morpheme acquisition studies, according to Clark and Clark (1977: 345) demonstrated the existence of stages of increasing syntactic complexity that learners pass through to reach a higher level of proficiency in the L2. On the basis of their work with second language learners, researchers such as Pienemann, Johnston, and Brindley (1988) and Doughty (1991) claim that the developmental sequences found in learner language are very similar to those of children acquiring the target language as their L1. Further, Lightbown and Spada (1999) found that the stages are similar across learners from different L1 backgrounds, results that lead to a questioning of the role of transfer alone in explaining early interlanguage development.

This claim for a strong role of the effects of developmental sequences in learner progress tends to be based on interlanguage syntactic evidence. Here is an example of developmental stages involving relative clauses (Lightbown and Spada 2006: 90).

Part of speech	Relative clause
Subject	The girl who was sick went home.
Direct object	The story that I read was long.
Indirect object	The man who(m) Susan gave the present to was happy.
Object of the preposition	I found the book that John was talking about.
Possessive	I know the woman whose father is visiting.
Object of comparison	The person that Susan is taller than is Mary.

In the case of acquiring the ability to use relative clauses in English, learners go through all of these stages in order. This table provides an accessibility hierarchy for relative clauses. Learners who can form relative clauses correctly for the possessive structure, for example, can already produce relative clauses for the four stages higher in the hierarchy. This generalization holds for other languages that have been studied. In other words, a similar hierarchy exists for French, for example. Studies have shown other hierarchies for grammatical morphemes, questions, negation, possessive determiners, and reference to the past (see Lightbown and Spada 2006: 83–92).

However, the existence of stages for pragmatic development is underresearched. Although Kasper and Schmidt (1996) state that so far no overall order of acquisition for ILP has been described, such as the developmental sequences for morphosyntax, Tanaka (1997a, 1997b) has found evidence for an acquisition order in the acquisition of point of view and passive voice in Japanese as a second/foreign language. Kasper and Rose (2002) review more recent studies of developmental sequences for pragmatic features with learners of Japanese as a foreign language (Ohta 2001) and Indonesian also as a foreign language (Dufon 2000). A related issue is the extent to which high levels of grammatical competency in the L2 are required for pragmatic competence development. Kasper and Rose (2002: 133) state:

> What we see across the studies is a tendency for learners to rely on routine formulas and repetition at first, which gradually gives way to an expansion of their pragmatic repertoire.

It is possible to argue that learners must reach a minimum or threshold level of L2 proficiency and knowledge to comprehend and produce appropriate pragmatic meaning in a language. However, pragmatic competence entails more than knowledge of the language and even at high levels of proficiency, especially if it is measured on a discrete-point, multiple-choice test, it requires complex interpersonal skills. Bialystok (1993: 47) attempts a theoretical account, comparing child and adult acquisition of "the social uses of language." Kasper and Schmidt (1996: 258) state that pragmatic competence is "an area of communicative competence which is closely tied to cognitive ability and social experience" in any language, L1 or others. Blum-Kulka (1991) describes three phases of pragmatic competence development in learner language that address competencies beyond syntactic knowledge. She found evidence in the learner language she studied of:

1. reliance on situational cues to infer illocutionary force;
2. differentiation of alternative realizations and evidence of transfer from the L1; and
3. approximation of native speaker norms, but continued display of transfer of "deep" cultural elements.

At the first stage, learners can use the situation to acquire pragmatic routines and accompanying vocabulary. At a fruit stand in a Mexican market town, in a speech event of buying and selling, making requests is, needlessly to say, ubiquitous, and with lots of cues that facilitate learning the routine, formulaic language. Even requesting a ripe papaya, for use that day, transpires easily, aided by the seller, who demonstrates with her hands how a papaya feels when it is ripe, as she says "*Sí, está bien cocida*". It is not too much of a stretch to figure out that that phrase, which means "well cooked," can also be used to refer to a ripe papaya. The second stage may entail learning to differentiate closings in the late afternoon. In Mexican Spanish, it is common to hear *buenas noches*, literally "good night," in a context where French speakers prefer *bonsoir*, good evening.

For the third stage, LoCastro (1998) and Siegal (1994) provide an illustrative example of the role of deep cultural features. They claim in their work that Anglo-American women find it difficult to learn the social appropriateness rules for what is called "female" language in Japanese. The movement toward non-sexist language has influenced the United States and Britain to the extent that language overtly cueing male–female roles is not tolerated. Siegal (1994) cites phrases used by women, typically in their early twenties, to reference an enthusiastic speech style by uttering *sugoiwa* (that's great), *kirei ne* (that's beautiful), or *tsugoi* (wow!). The American women in her study, though young themselves, found such phrases to be "silly and shallow" (Siegal 1994: 334). Thus, both researchers found that use of "female" language according to the current norms of Japanese society was unpleasant for them and their informants as doing so violated a deep cultural norm of their subculture in the U.S. regarding such overt and stereotyped cues of gendered language use.

Another example of the complex requirements of enacting pragmatic competence and the likelihood of developmental stages is observed in the use of modality, a subsystem of English frequently employed to signal pragmatic meaning. Correct use seems to require a high level of proficiency as it is a more cognitively demanding subsystem. Kasper (1984) shows that, in early stages of learning, modality reduction occurs in situations where learners appear to be focusing on the propositional content of their utterances and not as much on linguistic forms such as modal verbs and adverbs, commonly used to show hesitation and possibility in English. One developmental sequence could involve distinguishing between *must*, *have to*, and *should* to discuss what a person needs to do to, for instance, avoid a parking ticket. The distinctions in English have fuzzy, overlapping boundaries with those in other languages and, consequently, the area of modality tends to provide evidence of cross-pragmatic transfer as well. This evidence suggests a developmental sequence, where appropriate use of modality comes only after learners have consolidated other skills regarding communicating propositional and pragmatic meanings.

Interlanguage Realization Strategies

The main focus of ILP until the 1990s was on linguistic actions, specifically individual realization strategies to communicate pragmatic meaning of learners.

Kasper and Blum-Kulka's edited book on ILP (1993) includes speech act studies of expressing gratitude in American English, native and nonnative apologies of Thai and American English speakers, complaining, requestive hints, and correction. The example below provides one of the studies that exemplify the historical basis of the more recent work in ILP.

Bergman and Kasper (1993) looked at apologies as speech acts to compensate for offenses the hearer had experienced as a result of some behavior by the speaker. The apologies might have been actual or virtual. Following Goffman's conceptualization of apologies (1971), Bergman and Kasper include both types to account for ritualized apologies for virtual offenses and redressive actions for real or actual damage to the hearer. In other words, apologies may be offered for real offending behavior, such as stepping on someone's feet while attempting to find a seat at a movie theatre, or be only virtual, a behavior that the hearer might only regard as offensive, such as passing in front of someone at a crowded party. A typical virtual or ritual apology in American English is the use of "excuse me," where the purpose is more to maintain interactional or social harmony and to display one's efforts to abide by the local social norms. It contrasts with "I'm really sorry," that may be used, again in American English, for a more serious offense to the hearer such as when the speaker has been very late for an appointment or forgot to telephone about an important matter. All societies perform both forms of apology. However, there is cross-cultural variation. Many native speakers of English who interact regularly with Japanese speakers of English in Japan notice that Japanese interlocutors use such word as *sumimasen*, *gomen nasi*, or *shitsure shimasu*, all words of apology in Japanese frequently used for many functions. Bergman and Kasper studied the use of apologies by Thai nonnative speakers of English and American informants to answer these three research questions (1993: 87).

1. How are contextual factors in a variety of offense contexts perceived by Thai and American informants?
2. How is the selection of apology strategies determined by contextual factors?
3. What patterns of intracultural and intercultural variability are observable in the selection of apology strategies by Thai nonnative speakers of English as compared to native speakers of Thai and American English?

The informants for the study were 423 Thai graduate students at Chulalongkorn University in Bangkok with intermediate proficiency levels of English and 30 native speakers of American English, all students at the University of Hawaii, Honolulu, U. S. The researchers collected data by means of two questionnaires: (1) an assessment instrument where the informants were asked to rate on a five-point scale the severity of the offense; and (2) a discourse completion questionnaire that asked the informants to provide themselves the apologies they would use for the same offenses used in the first questionnaire. Twenty items were used. The analysis focused on the sociopragmatic knowledge of apology of the Thai learners of English, not on the linguistic items of their apology strategies in the second questionnaire.

The results from the data analysis of the two questionnaires indicated that the Thai informants overused apology strategies in English, a phenomenon labeled "waffling" by Edmonson and House (1991). This behavior, of using too much language to apologize, has been observed in the L2 pragmatics of other learners of English. Bergman and Kasper suggest that this overuse may be due to the nature of the instruments used to collect data and that, in studies using role plays to elicit speech act realization strategies, there were fewer examples of waffling under the pressure of face-to-face interactional discourse.

Clearly further study is needed regarding the use of apology strategies cross-culturally and cross-linguistically to sort out the likely motives for the greater use of apologies by speakers of different languages in the L1 and L2. The early stages of ILP focused on a narrow range of language features, specifically the performance of speech acts by second language learners. Due to developments within pragmatics and other areas of linguistics and applied linguistics, a more inclusive stance has taken over. Increasingly, researchers and educators are interested in taking a discourse perspective, which engages researchers in analysis of natural language data, composed of extended text, to learn about such features as conversational topics, nonnative speaker responses in tutorials, and the achievement of successful communication despite relatively low proficiency levels in the L2. Discourse data, primarily naturally occurring talk, offers the context needed to assess more fully learners' L2 language competency. The next section looks at an area of language use, regarding a variety of the forms to show how reference is created in a discourse context.

Referential Communication

Tarone and Swierzbin (2009) chose to study how learners used language resources to signal given and new information to achieve effective referential communication. They state (2009: 68):

> Effective referential communication is inherently interactive .... Speakers must take into account any information the listener already has, and any information the listener needs to know in order to identify the entity being referred to.

As an interactive feature of talk, discussed in Chapter 2, reference entails pragmatic meanings. It is also an aspect of language use that depends on careful decisions by speakers regarding linguistic forms. So, for example, if a speaker asks a listener to pass "the" book, when there are several books on the desktop, it is unclear which of the several books the speaker is referring to. The speaker assumes that the listener has enough old or given information in the context to know which book the speaker wants to examine. However, in the case of L2 learners of English, particularly if their primary language does not include a subsystem of indefinite and definite articles, i.e. "a," "an," "the," and sometimes "that" or "this," as English does, they may not have enough pragmatic knowledge of English to understand which linguistic form is needed in this case. Further, the use of modifiers takes on a new light of importance once the functions of adjectives, prepositional phrases, and relative clauses in referential communication are studied. Which book is it? The one with the black cover, the black book, or the one at the bottom of the pile next to the coffee cup?

Here are two examples that illustrate the referential function in talk among native English speakers:

B2: so **this other** lady who was on the phone wouldn't know
A1: what colour hair did **the girl** – **the** lady **with the telephone** + did she have
B1: long brown hair
A1: brownish **sort of**

(Brown 1995: 136)

In this excerpt of talk, the bolded words indicate the efforts on the part of the interlocutors to settle on a description of a third person being talked about, who all of them know. Thus, they are referring to given information so that A1 can infer just who B1 and B2 are referring to. Here is another example.

A: go – up towards between the mountains and across **the bridge** on the big river
B: what **bridge** on the big river?
A: the river on the –
B: och aye
A: and you go + round towards **the wood** + but you cut off between + the top of the – river and **the woods** + + and then up towards the castle

(Brown 1995: 79)

This instance of talk comes from a paired task given to native English speaker teenagers at school to study how they carry out referential language use when one of the students has a map with a trail on it and the other's map lacks the trail. The first student must explain to the partner how to get from the start of the trail to the end. Here the speaker and listener struggle to figure out which bridge and which woods (small forest) on the map without the trail needs to be considered. Note that the speaker assumes that the listener has all of the given information by virtue of the fact that they both have the same map. However, the "new" information resides in the evidence on the maps of more than one bridge and more than one wood. This referential task (see Yule 1997) demonstrates the difficulties of communicating details on a map to fellow native speakers.

Academic Speech Event

A particular speech event that university students experience that may affect their academic development is the advisement sessions with a faculty member in their major field. Bardovi-Harlig and Hartford (1990, 1993) focused their analysis on what are called status-preserving strategies in the interactions between the advisors and advisees who were international students. This speech event is an educational setting where native and nonnative speakers of the L2 have their pragmatic competence tested. Highly proficient nonnative speakers may lack the ability to negotiate an advisement interview that is dependent on appropriate speech acts and communication strategies. At issue in the study is impression management, important to graduate students who seek to be well regarded by their advisors. Appearing to be too assertive with faculty members may lead to negative repercussions.

Bardovi-Harlig and Hartford's study concentrated on advisement sessions with faculty members and both native and nonnative graduate students at a Midwestern university in the U.S. to learn, first of all, which speech acts and strategies were used by professors and students and, second, the extent to which the nonnative speakers' pragmatic ability improved over the course of a semester. Their findings bring to light some important dimensions of this type of institutional discourse.

Faculty advisors have a higher status within the university than students do. At the same time, graduate students in U.S. institutions are expected to demonstrate independent thinking (Kress and Fowler 1979) by arriving for the advisement session with knowledge about the schedule of classes, and a plan of action for the courses they want to take for the next semester. Thus, the dilemma for the students is to acknowledge the advisor's status, while, at the same time, taking the initiative. This use of language requires careful use of "congruent" speech. Both participants should perform the expected roles for students and advisors, using status-preserving linguistic forms and appropriate timing of their turns at talk. In the following example, a native speaker student talks with an advisor (Bardovi-Harlig and Hartford 1990: 488):

S: Now, for the uh, I think when I talked to you oh a year ago or so, un, I had, I was asking about electives.
A: mhm
S: and, if I understood it correctly, they have to be electives that are not used for, in another degree

A: right
S: now, my first year when Mongol language courses cannot be used for the Master's degree in Mongol
A: mhm
S: it can apply for the Ph.D.
A: I don't think that's a problem
S: oh, it's not a problem? Otherwise, I's thinking I, you know, could I just use it that, uh, here, and then, you know, not plan on using it over there

As they look at a document with information and maybe a blank schedule that needs to be completed, the student uses downgraders to mitigate the suggestion made in the last turn of the example: past tense, showing tentativeness (I was thinking), a downtoner (I think), and a cajoler (you know). The teacher appears to agree with the student-initiated suggestion. The student's status-preserving strategies were successful.

In another example from the study, an international student whose L1 was Spanish illustrates a less-than-successful enactment of pragmatic meaning for an advisement session (Bardovi-Harlig and Hartford 1990: 484):

A: do you know what you want to do?
S: more or less
A: let's hear it [pause] you've done 530, 31, 34, so you probably want to do 542, I bet you
S: yes, that's phonological
A: yes, phonology

In this case, the international student does not initiate discussion of a plan for the next semester's courses. The student waits to be asked questions and only agrees with the advisor in the second turn of talk, thus not demonstrating independence, knowledge, or careful preparation for the advisement session. Rather than lacking knowledge, it is likely the student was transferring language behavior acknowledging the advisor's higher status that would be pragmatically congruent in their L1 environment.

Bardovi-Harlig and Hartford (1993) continued their study of academic pragmatic competence development over a semester to learn whether the international students improved in their ability to employ appropriate strategies for the American educational context. The findings evidence some improvement in the ability to use speech acts in advisement sessions; their advisors were able to understand their indirect requests, although the form might not be standard for the U.S. However, the international students were still having difficulties using appropriate levels of mitigation to soften speech acts in the discourse context. The academic context is a gate-keeping environment where international students' linguistic competence and pragmatic competence influence success on many levels. The next section looks into another topic of interest in ILP.

Pragmatic Markers

It is not unusual to hear one American speaker of English make a comment to a conversational partner as in the following example:

A: I'm having a really hard time getting my daughter to do her homework
B: Well, you know, maybe if you sit down with her, help her a little, she might get motivated

A friend who overhears B's suggestion may ask: "why do you use *you know?*" The friend is clearly not a student of pragmatics as he does not realize that *you know* functions as (1) mitigation device and (2) a signal that B is inviting A's reaction to the suggestion. *You know*, as well as many other words, phrases, paralinguistic markers, and noises are what are called discourse or pragmatic markers that frequently occur in spontaneous conversation, mostly out of awareness of the speaker. The mitigation function of *you know* aims to achieve a softening of any perceived threat A may feel regarding B's suggestion about how A might entice her daughter into doing homework. It is a politeness strategy, in sum, recognized in taxonomies of politeness strategies. Further, it communicates B's positive attitude toward A, lessening social distance, and can be labeled an "interpersonal marker." B is expecting A to respond with agreement or disagreement, such as "I've already tried that, but it didn't work very well."

Note that the label for this category of linguistic items varies; studies discuss "discourse markers," "pragmatic markers," and "interpersonal markers" sometimes interchangeably. In this brief overview, fine distinctions are not made. The important point here is that these often unexamined, yet pragmatically important linguistic cues signal interpersonal pragmatic meanings that may help keep a conversation going or do the exact opposite and lead to hurt feelings among the participants. They are also particularly problematic for language learners.

Schiffrin (1988) in *Discourse Markers* provides a list of discourse or pragmatic markers in American English, with commentary and textual examples, as well as a definition often cited in research work on this topic of pragmatics. The basic definition states that pragmatic markers have three features. They are grammatically optional and independent of the utterance; if they are removed from an utterance, the meaning remains the same. They are also "semantically bleached," that is, they have little or no propositional meaning. Finally, they carry out textual and interpersonal functions. Going back to the example above, B could say: "maybe if you sit down with her, help her a little, she might get motivated." Both of the pragmatic markers, *well* and *you know*, contribute nothing to the propositional meaning and do not cause an ungrammatical sentence to be formed if they were deleted. Specifically, they enact interpersonal functions, the two outlined in the example above. *Well* also has the function of signaling hesitation, used in the context of B's suggestion possibly being perceived in a negative light by A. B's comment is a non-preferred response.

No one list of pragmatic markers is complete. Very common ones in American English are, in addition to *you know*, *you see*, *I mean*, *like*, and they can be combined as in *like, you know, like*. Aijmer and Simon-Vanderberger (2006) discuss a cross-linguistic approach to discourse markers in *Pragmatic Markers in Contrast*. The volume includes contributions that are based on corpora to investigate the functions of several pragmatic markers in natural discourse across European languages.

It goes without saying that pragmatic markers are likely to be universal and present in all languages. Studying Chinese discourse markers in oral speech, Liu (2009) collected data on fourteen such markers in the speech of ten native Mandarin speakers who were doing graduate work at an American university. She described each marker's textual and/or interpersonal functions in the data from individual, sociolinguistic interviews with the international students. Here is one example from her study (Liu 2009: 370):

> Peng: (. . .) *you yi ge laoshi,* wo juede *ta bushi na zhong tebie fu zeren de. Yinwei si zhou xialai, ta zhi chuxian guo yici* (. . .)
>
> One of the teachers, I think, he is not the kind of very responsible teacher, because he only appeared once during four week.

As Liu explains, *wo juede* is translated as "I think", and can occur at the start of an utterance, in the middle, and at the end. It functions as an interpersonal marker to communicate to the listener that it is only his opinion and he does not presume that the listener will or should share his view of the teacher. Another way of interpreting the function of *wo juede* is to see it as a politeness marker. The directness of Peng's view is softened through his claim that it is his opinion only. Liu's study compared the use of *wo juede* in Chinese with the use of *I think* in English in naturally occurring talk of her informants and the findings suggest L1 transfer into their interlanguage production.

Netsu and LoCastro (1997) earlier studied instances of use of the Japanese verb *~to omou*, translated as "I think." It appears with high frequency in both spoken and written texts in Japanese. In response to a question about how students have to change in many ways when they enter university, a student stated during the group discussion:

> F: *soo da to omoimasu, de, koko oseino ishiki no mama datta kara, ishiki no kaikaku to iu no ga hitsuyoo da to omoimasu.*

> F: I think so, I think it is necessary for us to change our thinking since we are as we were in high school
>
> *(Netsu and LoCastro 1997: 144)*

The student's response includes the form twice, at the beginning and end of the utterance. It is important to note that, while conversational data of American speakers of English may include an utterance similar to this one, there has been grammaticalization of a pragmatic marker in Japanese. The use of ~*to omou* in Japanese is not a matter of speaker choice; ~*to omou* appears in these positions in the students' writing as a required form. Here is one such example that is in the last paragraph of three pages of the student's written essay.

> When I had to memorize English words, I often used *gorowase* which is a similar strategy to KM. People can memorize few items unless they understand the meaning of the items . . . . It is useful to associate meaning with target items whenever we have to memorize something. *I think.*
>
> *(Netsu and LoCastro 1997: 136)*

It is evident that despite the essay having been written in English, the student included the English equivalent of ~*to omou*. In Japanese language essays by students, some appended the form to the end of each paragraph. The interlanguage in their essays, consequently, evidenced transfer from the pragmatic norms of their L1.

For second language learners and teachers of second/foreign languages, L2 pragmatic competence development requires attention to these small words. The two studies cited above clearly point to evidence of L1 transfer of pragmatic markers, resulting in interlanguages that mismatch the expectations for English language discourse. They are important features of everyday talk as they occur frequently and tend to appear with noticeable prosodic features, and in predictable locations in utterances. They signal a variety of pragmatic meanings, such as friendliness and camaraderie, respect for an addressee's potentially contrary point of view, and mitigation of bad news and uncomfortable moments. Yet, nonnative speakers find learning about pragmatic markers difficult, particularly in a foreign learning environment. Moreover, signaling status differences through language use varies cross-culturally; not all societies value overt expression of such differences.

Thus when to use pragmatic markers and how to use them are learning tasks problematized outside of constant and appropriate exposure to their use in the stream of L2 speech. The wrong intonation contour can have a different meaning from the one intended, resulting in misunderstandings.

Influence of Third Languages

Pragmatic competence development is dependent on the complex ability to use (1) phonological cues, including prosodic features such as stress and intonation; (2) rules of the grammatical system; and (3) knowledge of social appropriateness norms. However, this ILP description is deceptive: it presents a simplistic view of the SL learner. Researchers have challenged the view that such aspects of ILP as transfer from the L1 to the L2 are always unidirectional. Cook (1992, 2002) concentrated on a perspective that sees the learner not through the eyes of native speaker pragmatic norms, but rather as a multidimensional individual with multicompetences. Cook argues, for instance, that the L2 can influence the L1. Residence in Japan may change how a native speaker of English gives listener responses; the frequency and forms of listener cues, even when speaking in English, display influence from Japanese.

Further, pragmatic realization strategies are not only influenced by the social norms of the first language (Blum-Kulka 1983). Other languages a speaker may know can create an unexpected use of language that reflects more than L1 influence. A plurilingual speaker may modify, for example, the degree of directness and indirectness in making requests according to the norms of another culture and language (an L3), rather than their L1. Their communicative resources may have become influenced due to residence abroad over a number of years, particularly if they have proficiency in several languages.

Again, residence in Japan created awareness of the role of politeness in everyday talk in ways that, to an American, were not transparent. Just as native speakers may not know the grammar of their L1, it is not unusual to find the same pattern with regards to pragmatic awareness and strategies. Then, while living in Mexico, the same person recognized similarities in politeness use in local contexts. Women selling goods at the local covered market, from noticeably indigenous backgrounds, used politeness routines much more frequently than clerks in shops on the *zocalo*. The differences are likely to be due to the lower social status of the market women as well as their L1, an indigenous language that has a system of honorifics as the Japanese language does.

Kasanga (2006 – see Chapter 4) documents the influence of local indigenous languages in Africa on the development of varieties of English in that part of the world. There is a complex dynamic of influences on languages, including pragmatic development, creating interlanguages with nonstandard forms that eventually become grammaticalized into the local languages. Unfortunately, this area of ILP lacks research by scholars.

Limiting Factors on ILP Development

It may seem obvious that the greater the exposure of learners to the pragmatic norms of the target language, the more easily and quickly the learners improve their pragmatic competence. And indeed, there are certainly arguments in favor of leaving behind the classroom environment to find ways to increase exposure with conversational partners and swapping lessons, watching films and other media in the target language. Needless to say, study abroad programs can play a role, although there are issues such as willingness to communicate on the part of both the study abroad students and the local host families and communities.

An instructional environment may be limited for many reasons. In considering the effect of explicit teaching of pragmatic competence, that development is likely to be facilitated if the classroom practices focus on communicative activities in a learner-centered environment. Pragmatic competence develops where learners can enact a variety of social roles; rather than restricting participation to answering teachers' questions or responding to set prompts by peers, students need to practice asking questions, eliciting information, and engaging in a variety of speech acts in such activities as role plays, simulations, debates, and other tasks. Classroom environments worldwide are commonly teacher-centered, structured to complete the syllabus with little time during lessons to facilitate practice of language where learners are involved in comprehension and production of pragmatic meaning. The opportunities to use the target language in situations that approach real world conversation are limited.

In addition, teachers of the second or foreign language may lack the metapragmatic awareness and knowledge of the target language to help learners develop their L2 pragmatic competence. Many teachers of a foreign language may themselves feel at a loss, as they may not be native speakers of the language or may not have the proficiency level or have experienced sufficient periods of exposure to the L2 pragmatics to be able to develop lessons to help their learners. Further, inadequate or uninformed teaching may be a major drawback in socializing the learners regarding interactional practices and formulaic language use to create pragmatic meaning. As Rampton (1990) notes, the main qualification of the teachers need not be that they are native speakers of the target language, but rather that they have knowledge and experience of the sociocultural background and linguistic behaviors of the L2 to engage in awareness raising and explicit teaching of the L2 norms. These requirements of teachers are particularly important in foreign language teaching environments where the community language practices are not available to the learners on a daily basis. Ideally, teachers can serve as role models; minimally, they can serve as rich sources of information on how to be pragmatically appropriate in the L2.

Another source of exposure to L2 pragmatic norms can be the instructional materials. However, they are often inadequate, simplistic, and sometimes incorrect regarding presenting learning content and opportunities in the published resources. Despite efforts since the early 1970s in the teaching of language functions, notions, and gambits (see, for example, Wilkins 1976 and van Ek 1975), textbooks and other teaching materials still tend to be based on the author's or editor's intuitions and the personal experiences of native speakers, and not on empirical studies of pragmatic norms and strategies for the signaling of pragmatic meaning. A couple of examples illustrate the type of textbook input provided to classroom learners.

Abdullah: gosh, you look great, Beverly! Have you lost weight?
Beverly: That's nice of you to notice – I've lost about 10 pounds, but I still need to lose another 5 or 6.

(Wall 1987: 191)

This is not the way people talk! Even in the United States, men do not compliment women unless they are close friends: in particular, comments on weight are inappropriate. Further, the name of the male student indicates that the man is likely to be a Muslim, and it is highly unlikely that a Muslim male would compliment a foreign woman in that way. Such contrived examples, perhaps reflecting efforts to promote the image of diversity in language learning materials, communicate an incorrect view of pragmatic appropriacy.

Another example comes from a reading and translation practice passage in a senior high school textbook for English as a foreign language in Japan.

He hurried to San Francisco and went to a tailor. He showed the tailor his roll of canvas. "**I want you** to make a pair of pants out of this material," he said. "**Can you do that**?" "Yes, of course," said the tailor. "And your name? "Strauss, Levi Strauss."

(LoCastro 1997)

Notes in the teachers' manual for the book provide translations of may/can/could/might, with no comment about the use of modals to make requests. This lost opportunity to prepare learners for the variety of pragmatic meanings of the modals in English is not uncommon in such materials. Further, the phrase "I want you to . . ." is frequently found in learner language as modal reduction is a characteristic of the early stages, rather than the more polite forms such as "I'd like to ask you to. . . ." This example reinforces the tendency of learners to depend on translation rather than functional equivalents and thus the acquisition of what are pragmatically inappropriate forms of language use.

A worldwide survey of textbooks and other materials for language learning would no doubt generate numerous examples of inadequate materials which put teachers and learners at a disadvantage in fostering pragmatic development, particularly in foreign language learning settings.

In addition to factors that may, to a certain extent, be controlled by teachers and language educators in general, there are individual differences among learners of second or foreign languages that are much less open to influence. One such individual factor is learners' L2 identity concerns. A learner's attempt to acquire and use L2 pragmatic norms may not indicate inadequate knowledge or fossilization of L2 development. Rather, learners may wish to maintain their L1 cultural identity. Just as human beings on a daily basis select the clothes they wear, the car they drive, and the friends they hang out with, so do they speak in ways to construct their identity as members of a particular group and show disinterest in belonging to another group.

Teacher: So you went to Australia for the New Year's break to play women's basketball with an Australian team?
Female student: Yes, I did. I had a good time.
Male student: Oh, so now you're speaking English . . . so you're showing off your English

This example is reconstructed from an actual classroom incident in a Japanese university freshman class of English as a foreign language. It took place in January, just after the end-of-year holidays, and the teacher, an American native speaker of English, was attempting an icebreaker activity to bring the class together before starting the lesson. The female student, a local basketball star on the women's team, had won a prize that enabled her to go to Australia to play there. Her response to the teacher was unusual as normally she did not participate in class spontaneously. She spoke hesitantly, but seemed happy to be able to speak in English with the teacher. The male student's comment, loudly from the back of the class, suggested she was breaking co-membership with the other students in the class by using English to converse with the teacher. The presentation of self is part and parcel of pragmatic competence and may hinder or foster development and the studies of language learners too often impose a learner identity that is narrow and unrelated to the wider community outside classroom learning contexts.

Connected with identity issues are attitudes towards the L2 and its pragmatic norms. One important variable in this context is that learners have to be motivated with positive attitudes to take advantage of opportunities to become more proficient regarding appropriate L2 language use. A particularly telling instance of the role of attitudes and motivation comes from a study by Bouton (1994: 157); he looked into the extent to which nonnative speakers can communicate implicatures in the L2 with "little or no instruction." Although the ability to infer conversational implicature seems to be a universal feature of human communication, Bouton found that approximately one-fifth (21 percent) of the time, reasonably proficient nonnative speakers of English could not interpret implicatures in the same way as the native speakers of American English in his study. He carried out a longitudinal study of two groups of international students at an American university, testing their ability to interpret implicatures three times: (1) on arrival in the U.S.; (2) after eighteen months; and (3) after fifty-four months of residence. At the time of the second test, the international students still had problems understanding implicatures involved in such instances as flouts of the relevance maxim. Here is an example from Bouton's questionnaire (1994: 163):

> Relevance Maxim: Bill and Peter have been good friends since they were children. They roomed together in college and traveled Europe together after graduation. Now friends have told Bill that they saw Peter dancing with Bill's wife while Bill was away.
> Bill: Peter knows how to be a really good friend.
>
> Which of the following best says what Bill means?
>
> (a) Peter is not acting the way a good friend should.
> (b) Peter and Bill's wife are becoming really good friends while Bill is away.
> (c) Peter is a good friend and so Bill can trust him.
> (d) Nothing should be allowed to interfere with their friendship.

Only half of the nonnative speakers indicated (a) was the best choice, in comparison with 84 percent of the native speakers. When the same task was given earlier, that is, on arrival, only 33 percent of the nonnative speakers chose (a). Most of the nonnative speakers chose (c) on both occasions, a response that indicates transfer from their different L1 sociocultural norms about marriage and friendship. In general, after fifty-four months of residence in the U.S., the nonnative speakers were more proficient in interpreting the implicatures, suggesting that a long period of residence in the L2 community is necessary. Note that understanding the implicatures does not necessarily correlate with the ability to produce them in relevant contexts (Hinkel 1996).

Conclusions

ILP is an area of pragmatics that includes many dimensions. In this chapter, major areas have been touched upon: transfer, learner language, developmental stages, limitations of pragmatic development, and relevant studies for each area. All of the sections illustrated the diversity of research on learner development towards higher levels of use of interlanguage pragmatic competence. Further discussion of the teaching and learning of pragmatic competence in instructional contexts is found in Chapter 11.

Chapter 6 turns to a popular topic in pragmatics: politeness. It is a topic that touches directly on the complexity of attitudes and values of human beings in everyday contexts regarding language use. Indeed, one task of researchers is sorting out the folk linguistics aspects of politeness from the task of developing a theory of this very value- and culture-loaded dimension of interaction.

Suggested Readings

Alcón Soler, A. and Martínez-Flor, A. (Eds.) (2008). *Investigating pragmatics in foreign language learning, teaching, and testing*. Clevedon: Multilingual Matters.
Cook, V. (Ed.) (2002) *Portrait of the L2 user*. Clevedon: Multilingual Matters.
Lightbown, P.M. and Spada, N. (2006). *How languages are learned*. 3rd edition. Oxford: Oxford University Press.
LoCastro, V. (2011). Second language pragmatics. In E. Hinkel (Ed.), *Handbook of research in second language teaching and learning* (pp. 319–344). New York: Routledge.
Saville-Troike, M. (2006). *Introducing second language acquisition*. Cambridge: Cambridge University Press.
Tarone, E. and Swierzbin, B. (2009). *Exploring learner language*. Oxford: Oxford University Press.

Discussion Questions

1. What is interlanguage pragmatics? What is included in analysis of language use from this perspective?
2. What is pragmatic transfer? Is it always negative? Give examples for discussion in your group.
3. What is learner language? Why is this an important concept in ILP?
4. What are developmental stages? Are there any documented examples regarding such stages in pragmatics? Can you come up with an example that might be researched?
5. Discuss differences between cross-cultural and interlanguage instances of communication. What type is more likely to cause problems of communication? Which one is more difficult to overcome for learners? Explain and give an example.
6. Generate examples of miscommunication between speakers of English, native and nonnative. Draw on your own experiences. Be nonjudgmental. If you were teaching, how would you help your students to handle such instances?
7. Discuss the reasons learners may not want to become pragmatically competent in the L2. Add any you can think of with your group members.
8. Discuss what you learned from the studies reported on in this chapter. If you could do a study of ILP, what would you focus on?

Data Analysis

1. Here are two examples of talk between a British tutor and British students. Compare and contrast them. Which one do you think the tutor is likely to give a high mark to? What are the reasons for your opinion? (Hiraga and Turner 1996)

Tutor: have you visited any art galleries recently?

Student A: Yes, I went to see the X exhibition at the Y gallery. I'd seen a previous exhibition of her work about three years ago. . . . It seems to have become more architectural. . . . The objects are much larger in scale, . . . and more to do with architectural space . . . . It's quite an unexpected turn in her work to take . . ., much richer than the previous formula.

Student B: Yes, I went to see the X exhibition at the Y gallery. It was very impressive . . . . The gallery also featured the Z as a special display of the month. . . . I just saw the X because it was what Prof. A recommended in class . . . . I would certainly like to go back there . . . .

2. Now, provide an interlanguage pragmatic analysis of this fine arts tutorial with a British tutor and a Japanese art student. Justify every point of your analysis by citing examples from the data (Hiraga and Turner 1996: 102–3)

BT: Which is the best one?
JS: Mm, I can't say that because –
BT: Which is the worst one? . . .
JS: Just . . . these . . .
BT: They're not all of the same value . . . understand? . . . mm . . . I'm going to ask you to choose four –
JS: Mm-m
BT: . . . I'm going to put eight of them on the fire . . . save four . . . which four would we keep?
JS: I cannot choose
BT: Yes, you can. You must.
JS: Why do you know, why do you want to know that?
BT: Because it will tell me something.
JS: Mm. It's a universe, they're part of the universe . . .
BT: . . . But, but if you say, "because I made it, it therefore is OK – you will never develop any . . . critique.

6
POLITENESS

Introduction

Perhaps of all the forms of human behavior the one that is most likely to be noticed in interactions is how polite or impolite a person's language or nonverbal actions are. If an individual cuts into a line at the airport ahead of others or doesn't make a request for help getting through a door with heavy luggage with "please," these are noticeable behaviors that are typically regarded as "rude," at least by members of the local community. Labels such as "low class" or "uneducated" may also be uttered to describe the individual who has not followed the rules of interaction. Human beings cannot avoid communicating meanings about themselves and how they want to be perceived as they engage in displaying politeness, converging with or diverging from the norms of the local community. Clearly, second language learners must be not only competent in the target language, but also in the cultural practices of a community to avoid negative stereotyping, despite what might be sincere efforts to behave "politely." Learning how to be polite in another language is, however, not an easy task: doing so takes time, exposure to authentic, local practices, and mindfulness in communicative contexts. Anecdotal evidence indicates that learning how to be polite in the target language is a frequently cited goal for learners, and thus it is an important area for language educators as they seek to help learners develop their pragmatic competence.

First, this chapter provides a review of politeness theory to introduce key terms and concepts and it then summarizes important criticisms of earlier approaches. Due to the ubiquitous nature of politeness, which has even mistakenly been viewed as the core domain of pragmatics, researchers have been building theories of this category of behavior for several decades. Here, the review focuses on one of the main approaches only, the traditional or classic theory of Brown and Levinson (1987). In the second section, one of the alternative approaches is elaborated on with key concepts explained and criticisms of the approach discussed. It is followed by a case study of politeness in a multicultural classroom to illustrate this perspective and consider the value of this alternative approach, specifically the extent it can provide greater insights in language use in everyday talk.

Politeness Theory

The most influential work in politeness theory is Brown and Levinson's (1987) model, which provides a framework to describe and explain different linguistic resources that can be used to signal politeness in face-to-face interactions. Brown and Levinson claim that their theory is universal. However, the assumptions of their framework, while cited internationally by researchers, highlight the fact that it was developed in a Western-centric, academic context.

Their model does not consider non-linguistic behaviors, such as shaking hands or bowing upon greeting another person, as resources to enact politeness. To account for linguistic means to show politeness, they base their theory on several important premises. First, they view human beings as rational, i.e. motivated to achieve mutual benefit to both speaker and addressee in interactions. Specifically, the benefit involves the concept of "face," a technical or scientific term to denote the public self-image all human beings wish to maintain. Face comprises affective and social aspects, such as that one is honest, well behaved, and a member of valued social groups and institutions in the community. Consequently, an individual expects others to recognize and acknowledge their face needs through verbal behaviors of a great variety. In the South in the U.S., greetings from store clerks are common and expected, and holding a door open for another person is as well. Thus, in everyday social interactions, participants act in such a way as to show attention to the face needs and wants of their conversational partners and, reciprocally, have their face needs and wants acknowledged in return. This rational, reciprocal dance, so to speak, of politeness is displayed even with a simple exchange of greetings: "Hi, how are you" "Fine, thank you and you?" If a greeting in American English is not returned or reciprocated, the first person speaker in this adjacency pair will most likely view the second person as unfriendly, rude, an outsider.

Positive and Negative Face

The concept of face is broken down by Brown and Levinson into "positive" and "negative" face. Positive face needs concern the desire to be liked, involved, and included in the category of being the "right" kind of person. Negative face wants involve the wish to remain undisturbed, not imposed upon, in one's actions. Human beings, it is argued, essentially seek to be involved with others while simultaneously independent (see Tannen 1986). Further, Brown and Levinson theorize that there are both positive and negative politeness strategies. Strategies that show solidarity and make the addressee feel their wants are important and desirable to the other are categorized as positive, while those that seek to apologize for an action or to soften or mitigate any imposition on an addressee's time are labeled negative strategies. Negative politeness or avoidance-based strategies and positive politeness or solidarity-based ones make up the resources for engaging in polite behavior, according to Brown and Levinson. The speaker's choice of which type of strategy to utilize takes into consideration the face needs of the speaker and addressee.

Face-threatening Acts

Another dimension the Brown and Levinson approach must account for is the fact that speech acts may threaten the face needs of the speaker, the addressee or both. An act – an apology, request, or compliment – may cause the conversational partners to feel uncomfortable during an interaction. Japanese speakers of English may be aware that their cultural norm requires them to express gratitude more frequently than would be expected in the U.S., for instance. They then find themselves apologizing for thanking in English too frequently, where the American conversational partner may even blush due to the profuse repetitions of "thank you, thank you."

A salient example would be a nurse having to ask the medical doctor she works for to sign an insurance claim, something he forgot to do. Her perceived lower status, gender, and possibly age are social factors that may result in the doctor's feeling imposed on as he may consider his public self-image or face to be threatened by being reminded of something he had not done by a subordinate. The act the nurse needs to carry out – a request – is called a face-threatening act (FTA). In order for the nurse to carry out this FTA and to avoid showing disrespect for the doctor's face needs, she uses language in a way to soften or mitigate the threat. She might say the following:

> I know you are very busy, and I'm sorry to have to bother you, but could I get your signature . . . right here?

The nurse is using linguistic resources to mitigate the face threat. With "I know you are very busy," she takes responsibility, and she uses a conventional excuse for the doctor's not doing something. The nurse makes it clear the doctor did not offer any excuse. Then she apologizes, "I'm sorry," implying that it is not her own will, but some external force that is causing her to interrupt him ("sorry to have to bother you"). By uttering "could I get your signature," she is asking permission, indicating that the doctor has an option; that is, that he could refuse her request. The final phrase, "right here," suggests she is standing, pen in one hand, ready to give it to the doctor, and pointing with the other hand to the exact line on which he needs to write his signature. He does not have to do any extra work to comply with her request. Finally, an interrogative form also signals that the doctor may respond to the question negatively, should he wish to do so. Politeness theory attempts to explain the linguistic resources to soften or mitigate face threats, from asking for the time at the bus stop to geopolitics where apologies draw international attention.

The nurse–doctor example above illustrates some of the strategies that are used to soften or mitigate a request. Mitigation or redressive action is a salient feature of talk and Brown and Levinson's model attempts to account for this aspect. They theorize that conversational partners are likely to enact FTAs according to the following set of choices:

1. Do the act on record, baldly
2. Do the act with redressive action
3. Do the act off record
4. Don't do the act

The first choice, of doing the act "on record, baldly," means that there is no effort to soften the act to save the face of the addressee. If the speaker estimates that redressive action is called for, then there are two possible choices: (1) use redressive action, i.e. mitigation; (2) do the act "off record." The final strategy is to remain silent and not do the act at all. The following examples give possibilities for these choices in a situation concerning smoking.

1. A says to C, the smoker: "You can't smoke here!"
2. A says to C, the smoker: "Would you mind not smoking here?"
3. A says to B, a companion, about C, the smoker: "I wonder if there is a smoking section" (said aloud to B so that C can overhear).
4. No linguistic action; A and B move away outside the range of the smoke.

Within the strategy of redressive action, involving some form of linguistic modification, there are two subcategories: (1) do the act on record with positive politeness redress and (2) do the act with negative politeness redress. "On record" denotes that the speaker does do the act. The redressive action is a means to "give face" to the addressee to counteract the potential face threat or damage of the FTA. With positive politeness, the speaker appears to be friendly and helpful. In the smoker example above, to signal positive politeness, A could say to C, "You know, they do have a section for smokers over there," pointing to the other section or room. Or for negative politeness, A could say, "Would you mind our asking you not to smoke in the nonsmoking section?" Negative politeness does not mean that the speaker is impolite. Rather it reflects a greater degree of social distance between speaker and addressee, signaling the intended meaning that the speaker wishes to disturb the addressee as little as possible.

Here is another example that illustrates the strategies. If your neighbor in the apartment above yours has, for the third time, let the water from her washing machine run onto the floor rather than into the sink and, consequently, the water has come through the ceiling into your apartment in Tokyo, you have several choices as to what you can say and do:

Baldly, on record:	Do not let the water from your washing machine run onto the floor ever again.
On-record, negative politeness	I'm sorry to have to ask you, but I wonder if you could be more careful with the hose of your washing machine? It must need repair as it apparently comes unhooked and then the water seeps down into my apartment.
On record, positive Politeness:	Well, I guess you must have been busy with something else, because I got some water in my place again from your washing machine. How about my helping you fix it, or finding a repair person who can do it for us?
Off record:	Do you need a hand with your washing machine? Perhaps you aren't used to the kind of machine we have here in Japan.

If you select "Don't do it at all," the landlord or manager of the apartment building might be asked to act as a go-between to settle the problem. This is a strategy that would be less threatening to your upstairs neighbor's face than your speaking directly with the neighbor. The important point here is that the speaker's choice of which face-saving strategy to use is constrained by contextual factors, involving perceptions of degrees of social distance or intimacy, power, or weight of the problematic behavior. The repeated water resulted in mushrooms growing on the tatami mats! The speaker's assessment of how threatening the act may be, cultural practices, and even personality characteristics enter into the decision-making.

Face-saving Strategies

Brown and Levinson (1987) provided taxonomies of both positive and negative politeness strategies for a variety of communicative goals. The following two lists illustrate the core features of their theory.

Negative Politeness Strategies

1. Be conventionally indirect. Could you please pass the salt?
2. Question, hedge. I don't suppose you could loan me some money.
3. Be pessimistic. You don't have any envelopes, do you?
4. Minimize the imposition. I just dropped by for a second to ask . . .
5. Give deference. We very much look forward to your dining with us.
6. Apologize. I am sorry to bother you, but could I borrow a pen?
7. Impersonalize S* and H*. It appears that we may have to refuse.
8. State the FTA as a general. Passengers will refrain from smoking.
9. Nominalize. I am surprised at your failure to reply.
10. Go on record as incurring debt or as not indebting H*. I'd be eternally grateful if you could . . .

Positive Politeness Strategies

1. Notice, attend to H*. You must be hungry . . .
2. Use in-group identity markers. *Tu t'es bien amusé à la plage?* [Did you have a good time at the beach?]
3. Seek agreement and avoid disagreement. Yes, the weather is wonderful today, isn't it?
4. Presuppose or assert common ground. Help me with this bag, luv?
5. Joke. How about lending me a few fivers?
6. Offer, promise. I'll drop by sometime next week.
7. Be optimistic. I'm sure you won't mind if I . . .
8. Include S* and H* in the activity. Let's have a drink together next week.
9. Give or ask for reasons. Why not go to the beach?
10. Give gifts (sympathy) to H*. I'm really sorry to hear about your cat.

Note: *S=speaker *H=hearer

Politeness strategies have been shown to be ubiquitous in everyday talk in the languages that have been studied. Some acts are "inherently" face-threatening, according to Brown and Levinson. They argue that speakers make decisions on how to enact a FTA by considering three variables: (1) the social distance between the speaker and addressee; (2) the power difference between the speaker and addressee; and (3) the weight of the imposition. Their model proposes one way to account for the relationship among the three features of an interaction. Social distance and power differences arguably work together: an addressee who has high social status and a high degree of social distance from the speaker is likely to be perceived as having greater power. The weight of imposition concerns how "costly" the FTA is perceived to be: borrowing someone's cell phone briefly to make a local call may be less costly in terms of politeness than asking for money to get a taxi home from the train station in a rainstorm.

However, there is some discussion about the extent to which speech acts are generally threatening to interactants' positive or negative face needs. In recent studies on FTAs, researchers have shown that speech acts may in fact also be used to "enhance" the face needs of conversational partners rather than threaten them. Kerbrat-Orecchioni (1997, 2006) has suggested an expansion from Brown and Levinson's FTA concept to include "face-enhancing" acts (FEAs) or "face-flattering" acts (FFAs) to provide a more accurate interpretation of observable human behavior. In her view, politeness is a matter of managing the face work expected in local contexts. Her stance is supported by a data-based study of politeness in small, neighborhood shops in France where multiple examples motivate a four-part system of politeness, hyperpoliteness, apoliteness, and impoliteness to account for verbal behavior in the cultural context of this particular environment, where clerks and customers may flirt with each other to promote sales or get special deals. Here is an example where at least two forms of politeness interact. A professor at a university received this email from a student.

> Student: Hello, Steve. I'll email you to make an appointment to see you next week.

A distinguished professor may prefer to be addressed by his first name by graduate students, wanting to be regarded as a member of the departmental group, while, at the same time, he does not want to spend too much of his time interacting with colleagues and students, keeping him away from his research projects. By using the professor's first name, the students and colleagues are addressing his desire to have his positive face needs met – in effect, doing an FAE – while at the same time carrying out an FTA that attends to his negative face needs to not be imposed upon. That is implied at least in the second part of the email message from the student about getting in touch to make an appointment, rather than just dropping by the professor's office.

Cross-cultural Differences in Politeness

Cross-cultural differences have a role to play with regards to selecting politeness strategies. The three variables of social distance, power, and weight of the imposition are not interpreted equally across cultural and ethnic boundaries. Within the U.S., for example, borrowing money from a close friend or family member may weigh more heavily than the same speech event in Mexico. Thanking may be performed in everyday transactions such as supermarkets and post offices without much thought in the U.S. Yet, considered cross-culturally, thanking may threaten the face wants of a person who has higher social status, relative to the person being thanked (Hinkel 1994: 73). Faculty at American universities may feel uncomfortable *vis-à-vis* what seem to be verbose shows of gratitude by international graduate students.

Apologizing can also be problematic in some cultures where high-status individuals do not normally apologize to others of lower status; this speech act entails humbling oneself. Compliments tend to be avoided in Asian cultures where an addressee will be silent or refuse the compliment from a friendly North American who uses compliments as conversational openers. Requests and refusals are speech acts often found together where both speaker and addressee may experience face threats.

1. A   There's a new movie playing downtown
2. B   Oh really? What is it?
3. A   It's the new Pixar animated film, *Up*. I was wondering if you are free Friday evening to go see it.
4. B   Oh . . . well . . . I'm not so keen on animated movies.

In this example, A takes a risk in line 3 by asking B to go to this particular movie on Friday evening. B is also engaging in a risk by not only refusing the invitation, but also by explaining a dislike for this type of film. The refusal implies criticism of A's taste in movies, although not necessarily the person. A simple act of inviting an international friend to a movie may lead to discomfort for both A and B and can discourage further invitations.

Brown and Levinson's theory of politeness has sought to account for many features of this common human behavior. The fact that criticisms arose to challenge the premises and point out limitations does not negate the value of their framework. Rather, it promoted thinking and research about politeness and a concentration on developing a more inclusive, comprehensive theory. The next section outlines the work of researchers who recognized weak aspects of Brown and Levinson's theory.

Criticism of Brown and Levinson

While Brown and Levinson's model of politeness has been and continues to be arguably the most influential approach to this form of human behavior, criticisms, particularly by researchers from Asia, began to come to light as they challenged the universality of the model on the basis of observable cultural differences. Researchers such as Ide (1989, 2005), Matsumoto (1988) and Gu (1990) claimed that, on the basis of their studies regarding politeness in Japanese and Chinese respectively, Brown and Levinson's approach to politeness cannot explain all aspects due to different cultural beliefs and practices.

One of the main issues taken up by Matsumoto, Gu, and others concerns the Western-centric perspective of Brown and Levinson's framework. The rational actor model incorporates human beings as individuals with agency in their social worlds, free to interact with others on the basis of their own independently arrived at assessment of the particular interactional contexts. They can adjust the extent of involvement and independence to meet their own face wants and needs and those of their conversational partners. However, not all parts of the world adopt this view of human actors as individuals; other cultural groups have been influenced by other beliefs and values that view the individual as part of society, a community, that is, in terms of membership in one or more groups, from the basic family unit to institutions and nations. These societies and cultures may be labeled "communal" or "collectivist," where individuals primarily derive their identities and behaviors from norms of groups. Thus, one noticeable feature of a collectivist culture is subordination of the individual to the group.

For example, one very salient group that affects even a Westerner's life in Japan is the company or institution she works for. During social occasions, employees represent their place of employment. At a restaurant in Tokyo, a guest paged over the intercom system was identified not by her family name, but by the expression in Japanese signaling her membership in the company where she was working at the time: "*Simul no LoCastro irrashaimasu-ka?*" This utterance is the local phrase to say "There is a phone call for Simul's LoCastro." It is a simple example that communicates this notion of the individual as group member and the Asian view of politeness. Sociocultural decisions about levels of politeness in Asian languages and cultures are made on the basis of expectations of group membership; Ms. LoCastro is expected to use language to signal her membership in the Simul group in the interest of maintaining the face of the organization.

The Western rational social actor of Brown and Levinson's theory lacks explanatory strength for cultures that do not prioritize the needs of individuals. Asian cultures have different perspectives on the notion of the individual (Hofstede, 2001). Further, collectivist cultures are not only found in Asia. Eslami-Rasekh (2004, 2005b) links differences in the realizations of some speech acts in Persian to culturally distinct communication strategies. She claims, "Iranian society, being a more group-oriented society, . . . puts more emphasis on the importance of society, family, solidarity, and common ground as opposed to individual privacy . . . and autonomy of individuals" (2004: 189). These differences in cultural values translate into different "face-keeping" strategies (2004: 192) regarding reactions to complaints in her cross-cultural pragmatics study.

The important point to be remembered from this criticism of Brown and Levinson's theory is that a universal perspective on politeness may be beyond reach until empirical studies of many societies in different parts of the world can confirm patterns of behavior regarding politeness across a large variety of contexts and cultures.

A second criticism of Brown and Levinson, related to the first, is the depiction of politeness as if it were static, predictable human behavior, always carried out or enacted to fit a situation in a deterministic manner, as if social actors lacked agency to use language proactively or creatively. The collectivist conception of society also suffers from the same criticism. Ide (1989), in her critique of Brown and Levinson's universal model, argues that politeness in Japan is based on discernment instead of volition. Discernment is defined by Ide as the tendency of Japanese to follow the generally socially-agreed-upon rules rather than to use language creatively, dependent on situated features. In other words, the default for Japanese speakers' enactments of politeness is to follow societal norms. Ide contrasts the value of discernment with volition, where speaker agency is more likely to be implemented, resulting in politeness strategies chosen on the basis of individual speakers' views, rather than macro sociocultural factors. Ide views Western societies as emphasizing volition due to the cultural bias towards individualism.

However, Ide's point of view is not shared by other Japanese researchers. Okamoto (1999) points out that any claim that Japanese politeness is always enacted according to social norms is an empirical question, rather than an assumption based on static, stereotyped views of Japanese culture. As a result of Okamoto's study of "situated politeness" in Japanese interactions and his surveying of the attitudes of native speakers of Japanese to the use of honorifics in talk, Okamoto states that "it is highly questionable whether the use of such linguistic forms as honorifics is an automatic, or passive, response to the contextual features . . ." (1999: 52). H. M. Cook (2006) found evidence in her research of academic sessions with professors and students that students in Japan do not always limit their language use when interacting with their professor to honorifics to humble themselves. She explains that, in the collected data, the professors used the plain form of the verb, whereas the students would use either the formal verb morpheme, *masu*, or the plain form. The students could choose between two speech styles, depending on what kind of relationship they wanted to establish with their professor. The formal *masu* form correlated with a hierarchical relationship and the plain form was a strategy to avoid a hierarchical one. This example demonstrates the discourse of the collected data.

P: *kurisuchan no kazu to hontoni kurabemono ni naranai kurai kirisutokyoo ga*
   Compared with Japan, (in Korea) the number of Christians is
S: *[ooi]* large
P: *shinja ga ooi*
   The number is large.

(Cook 2006: 279)

The professor's utterance is completed by the student's word, *ooi*, which is in the plain form; in formal Japanese it would be *ooi desu*. Then, not only did the student complete the professor's turn at talk, but he also used the plain form. Both linguistic cues signal that the student wishes to develop a friendly, informal type of relationship with his professor. Cook's data provides evidence that the static, predictable enactments of politeness required, according to Ide, to reproduce the societal structures of Japan is not a valid picture, certainly, of modern Japan. It also opens the door to viewing politeness as a form of relational work to achieve comity in human relationships. The next section below develops this perspective in a new, current approach to politeness theory.

Another criticism that has developed in the past decade concerns the lack of attention in theoretical perspectives as well as research into impoliteness, a feature of everyday behavior, almost as if it were an aberration rather than a ubiquitous occurrence. Folk linguistic terms abound for labeling acts of impoliteness: rude, disrespectful, out of line, inappropriate, low class, and so forth. From the point of view of learners of second/foreign languages, having attempts to use their L2 or L3 be viewed as "rude" by native speakers may be a major demotivating factor in their communicative competence development.

Currently there is no agreement on how to define impoliteness nor on a methodology to study this form of social practice. Bousfield and Locher (2008: 3) suggest a summary definition: "impoliteness is behavior that is face-aggravating in a particular context." Some non-controversial examples in the U.S. of face-aggravating behavior would include spilling coffee on another customer at a café and not apologizing; inviting one colleague for lunch in front of another who is not invited; code switching with one conversational partner and excluding others who cannot speak the language; or not holding a door open for someone who is following right behind with her hands full. Locher and Watts (2008: 96) describe politeness/impoliteness as "the work invested by individuals in the construction, maintenance, reproduction, and transformation of interpersonal relationships." On their view, Locher and Watts propose an agenda of research where politeness and impoliteness are incorporated together, using the term (im)politeness. Studies are needed to learn what behaviors are polite or impolite and how the participants make those decisions. Clearly, situated expectations have to be clarified as well as other unexamined dimensions that may influence labeling of behavior as polite or impolite.

Lambert Graham (2008) has studied how members of e-communities evaluated utterances of others in email messages in terms of (im)politeness. Specifically, she looked at the FAQs (frequently asked questions), a manual that includes technical guidelines as well as advice on appropriate interactions for an online community. As Lambert Graham argues, it provides a baseline on polite behavior for this community. One part of her study focused on the FAQs' norms and expectations for polite behavior. For example, one item on the list of guidelines in the FAQ is the following: Don't send posts just saying "I agree," "Me too," or "Amen, Rev" (2008: 289). It includes an explanation for this item: "Nobody will know what you're responding to, you'll be wasting some subscribers' money, and you will be adding nothing to the discussion. Explain yourself, think new thoughts, explore possibilities, challenge wrong beliefs, make lists of good books, go into detail" (2008: 289). This example gives only a small look into the

FAQs, which seek to provide guidelines for computer behavior on chat sites. It reflects the emerging nature of this particular online community as it is changed and updated as issues arise concerning appropriate behavior. It is an interesting microcosm of other communities regarding everyday talk behavior.

New Perspective on Politeness

The criticisms cited above, as well as anecdotal evidence, have motivated researchers to explore other perspectives on politeness. In particular the view that politeness emerges within the interactional contexts of everyday talk has drawn the attention of scholars on politeness. The recognition that social actors communicate pragmatic meanings in the course of conversational discourse primarily for the purpose of establishing and maintaining relationships has evolved in the past decade. This alternative perspective challenges the classic view of Brown and Levinson (1987) and conceptualizes politeness as a discursive phenomenon, whereby the interactional participants co-construct (im) politeness in local, situated instances by means of linguistic and prosodic resources to achieve their communicative goals.

Watts and Locher

Two researchers, Watts (2003) and Locher (2004), have been particularly instrumental in developing this alternative model that addresses many of the criticisms of Brown and Levinson's theory. They argue that there are two ways to conceptualize politeness. The first, labeled politeness1 or first-order politeness, is the lay or folk linguistic notion that includes etiquette. In other words, politeness1 incorporates a prescriptive view of language use, where value judgments inform reactions to polite or impolite behaviors. Linguistics regards itself as a descriptive field of research. Cameron (1995), in *Verbal Hygiene*, discusses the fact that the folk linguistic view of language use is anchored in an inherently prescriptive view of language. On her view, however, ignoring the views of the average citizen regarding such features of language as politeness is mistaken. After all, sociolinguistic theories seek to account for everyday talk and perceptions of participants.

The second, politeness2 or second-order politeness, involves the theoretical concepts such as are found in Brown and Levinson's model. Much of the previous research focuses on theory building and virtually ignores folk linguistic accounts, viewed as judgmental and not descriptive. The tension between theory and everyday practice prevailed in politeness studies. In Watts' view, in order to build a solid, comprehensive theory of politeness, researchers need, first of all, to study what happens in everyday interactions to learn not only how politeness is done, but also how the participants react to and interpret it.

One change in politeness studies involves the introduction of new terms to avoid the use of "polite" or "impolite" as they carry too much baggage from earlier studies. There are no agreed-upon definitions for words like "polite," "love," or "democracy." Researchers have adopted what Watts designates as "politic" behavior. A dictionary definition of "politic" includes synonyms such as "prudent," "artful," "expedient," and "judicious". The following sentence provides an example: It would not be politic for you to leave the meeting early. All of the synonyms for "politic" capture Watts' intended meaning. His definition of "politic" is (Watts 2003: 144): "behavior, linguistic or non-linguistic, which the participants construct as being appropriate to the on-going social interaction." Watts focuses on what would be the expedient and judicious use of linguistic and non-linguistic cues. The way to assess what behaviors are "expedient and judicious" uses entails microanalysis of conversational discourse and of evidence in the data that the social actors meet the situated norms or expectations for language use in the context. For example, language use in an informal group of college friends may entail different language use strategies from those expected at a family dinner gathering with guests. Researchers pay attention to the situated norms or expectations as the social actors carry out talk. Rather than focusing on sociocultural differences and hierarchy, this view of politeness emphasizes communication, despite sociocultural differences, that maintains mutual respect and comity.

The following example evidences interactional discourse from a classroom task where two students negotiate help on a laboratory experiment with an international teaching assistant (ITA)(LoCastro 2008a).

1.	S1:	also I noticed that . . . with the pulley off
2.	P:	yeah . . .
3.	S1:	the track . . . some places it wasn't even
4.	P:	you say it wasn't even . . . may be
5.	S1:	(demonstrates the problem on the lab equipment)
6.	P:	ahha, now I think, yeah, OK, let's see
7.	S1:	but that's only if it's past 160 and we're stopping at 160, that doesn't really
8.	P:	yeah, you know what
9.	S1:	it doesn't really play too much of an effect
10.	P:	OK, look at this, here it seems to be OK . . . here it seems to be OK . . . here it seems to be OK . . . here it seems to be OK . . . here, well . . .
11.	S1:	once you get past 160 then it starts to
12.	P:	and here it doesn't seem to be OK
13.	S2:	(soft voice) because of the string
14.	P:	what?
15.	S2:	because of the magnets?
16.	P:	because of the magnets, you see?
17.	S1:	(smiles, realizing he misunderstood) because 160 . . .

Source: LoCastro 2008a

Student 1 engages the ITA in talk to try to figure out some irregularity he noted in the equipment for a physics laboratory experiment. Pedro, the ITA, rather than providing the correction, talks the students, S1 and S2, through some steps to help them reach the answer themselves. When asked to explain his teaching strategy in this instance, Pedro stated that it is his way of persuading the students that he respects their abilities, both as individuals and as group members to work collaboratively and solve the physics problems. Line 14, where he says "what?" could be viewed as being too direct, even rude, for a faculty member. However, all of his behaviors were politic for this classroom context. All the social actors, the students and the instructor, were concerned primarily about learning and then in maintaining cordial relations.

Further, Watts makes the claim that words are not inherently "polite." In the example, "I'd like a latte, please," the word *please* does not always make the speaker's utterance "polite." Indeed, *please* can signal displeasure if one person yells loudly "Would you *please* turn down that music?" In sum, politic behavior – language and non-language – is what is regarded as appropriate and expected for the context of use.

The next change of terminology concentrates on "politeness/impoliteness." Locher and Watts (2005) maintain that "politeness" and "impoliteness" can be used to characterize the "surplus" behavior of social actors. Conversational partners may engage in marked behavior in interactional contexts whereby they do more than what is necessary, producing "polite" language use, or do less than expected, resulting in the attitudinal label of their being "impolite." The assessment of what, then, is polite and impolite is tricky. Many examples can be cited. Thanking someone for bringing a cup of coffee, for instance, in some families is expected, i.e. is politic. In others, it could be regarded as excessive behavior and the person who brings the coffee would be viewed as "polite." The only way to begin to know what the norm is for the family is to observe the reactions to the thanking. Does the person who was thanked say "You're welcome?" Or "no problem?" Or "next time, get your own?" Or nothing?

In sum, there is a continuum of behaviors with labels from "impolite" to politic to "polite." Here is a modified continuum from Locher (2004: 90):

Impolite ←--------------- **Politic** ---------------→ **Polite**

The purpose of politic behavior, according to Watts and Locher, is to do relational work to support the struggle to maintain social interaction. While impolite behaviors may endanger the equilibrium of the interactional context, politeness seeks to insure social harmony and comity.

Relational Work

Naturally occurring everyday talk data enable the researcher to observe the flow of the "relational work" of the social actors, as they discursively co-construct meaningful talk. In Watts and Locher's framework of politic language use, they chose the term "relational work" to describe the conversational efforts of the participants. "Relational" emphasizes the purpose of much of human communication in seeking involvement or relationships with others. In the course of a conversation, two or more people may discuss children, car-pooling, cooking, animals, sports, and so forth, not so much to share information as to build and maintain their relationships where *how* they interact with each other is as important as *what* they say. The *how* of their talk comprises the features that are of interest to researchers regarding the extent to which their talk is described as politic or (im)polite.

Given that conversational norms or expected behaviors vary across cultures, gender groupings and occupational environments, for example, it may be difficult to describe with confidence not only what the social norms are, but also where they come from. A baseline knowledge of how participants know what the norms are is lacking. Watts addresses the need to have an explanatory framework for politic behavior by including Bourdieu's notion of *habitus* (1990). A famous French sociologist and linguist, Bourdieu claimed that human beings develop the ability to interact in the society where they are socialized, acquiring over time, in an unexamined, subconscious manner, the expectations of their particular community, both as individuals and as members of societal groupings, such as university lecturers of elite institutions in France. Bourdieu uses *habitus* as a term to signal "a set of dispositions to behave appropriately" (Watts 2003: 145). Watts' concept of politic behavior is thus related to Bourdieu's *habitus*; politic or normative behavior is acquired from one's primary language community and is slowly built from childhood. That socialization process includes linguistic and non-linguistic dimensions recognized by participants in situated interactions.

Note that, for Bourdieu, the socialization process does not stop with the end of childhood. Adults may learn different norms as they change jobs, move to a new part of the world, or spend summers in a second language community. For the outsider or newcomer, there is a lack of objective criteria to interpret and carry out politic and (im)polite behaviors in a new environment. The need to acquire new *habitus* knowledge arises as participants in interactions use this knowledge to interpret the behavior of others and to enact politic behavior themselves.

Laphasradakul (2006), for example, studied how a Thai-speaking international student, Panoat, at a U.S. university, accommodated to the American *habitus* when he was a teaching assistant of a course for undergraduate students. Laphasradakul's goal was to investigate whether the Thai TA made an effort to be politic or even polite to his students by following what he perceived as American culture or Thai norms for politeness with his students. On the basis of classroom observations and interview data, Laphasradakul found that he adjusted his behaviors in several ways to converge towards the American expectations. Panoat paid more attention to the stricter use of time and deadlines in the U.S., such as arriving for class on time and responding to students' emails in a timely fashion; he dressed more casually rather than use the formal style of teachers in Thailand; and he refrained from touching students despite the commonality of teachers touching students in his home country. Further, he ignored the Thai practice of not having students sit so that they were in a higher position than their teachers. He also lessened the social distance between himself and his students, particularly due to his being not that much older than the students. Regarding his classroom practices to facilitate learning, he engaged in scaffolding in the interactional classroom discourse, asking leading or open questions, rather than lecture exclusively, as is the case in Thai academic environments. Panoat made an effort to mitigate his talk when giving feedback to students so as to "avoid hurting them and teaching by suggestion not domination" (Laphasradakul 2006). Laphasradakul claimed that, when asking questions of his students in class, he paid respect to them by treating them as smart persons who have knowledge and their own opinions on the topic. He had become a bicultural individual himself by adopting American norms for his stay in the U.S. His Thai-style politenesss, based on his *habitus* knowledge from his upbringing in Thailand, expanded to include situationally appropriate American practices.

This alternative view anchors politeness in the notion that it is part and parcel of human efforts to create and maintain amicable relations with others. The enactment or performance of politic, polite, and impolite behaviors is inherently related to expected norms or assessments within particular groupings or communities, norms that develop over time through socialization. The goal of researchers is to search for commonalities across groups to inform the efforts to build theories of politeness and the teaching of pragmatic competence.

Doing Relational Work: Showing Respect

This section comprises an example of research informed by Watts' and Locher's perspective on politeness. The study focuses on one strategy of interactive behavior, specifically "respect," and demonstrates how respect is performed following the norms of a particular setting. It is an illustration of linguistic, non-linguistic, and attitudinal aspects of interactions that evolved into the communication of respect.

Respect

Respect is not equivalent to politic behavior, but rather one form or manifestation of the norms or expected behavior for a particular setting. The rationale for focusing on respect derives from several sources. In the politeness literature, respect comprises one strategy to signal negative politeness; Brown and Levinson (1987: 72) state that a speaker in an interaction can display respect or show deference to an addressee. However, Brown and Levinson use "respect" without defining it. Further, it is a lay term, used in daily life in the U.S. with some frequency. Respecting or disrespecting is a notion of U.S. popular culture, found in TV programs, movies, and popular magazines. Wikipedia (2006) provides an informative look at the current lay interpretation of the term.

> Respect is sometimes loosely used as a synonym for politeness or manners, though these are behaviors, whereas respect is an attitude. Intercultural differences in behaviors, self-perception, and outward appearance may result in the unintentional appearance of disrespect.

For example, attending a ceremonial event, such as a graduation ceremony, wearing flip-flops and informal attire would constitute showing lack of respect for oneself as well as other attendees. Wikipedia's definition further emphasizes that it is "an attitude of acknowledging the feelings and interests of another party in a relationship," where the other party can be animals or groups including countries. Respect is considered to be the opposite, in effect, of "selfish behavior." These quotations from Wikipedia illustrate, at least in contemporary U.S. culture, a change or shift in meaning of the concept of respect from a negative politeness strategy to one which has taken on shades of positive politeness in attending to addressees' feelings and needs.

The case study draws, first, on videotaped data of a multilingual teacher's classroom practices during two semesters in the physics department at a U.S. university. Required videotaping of the ITA's teaching practices was carried out three times during the spring 2006 semester as part of the training course for ITAs at the university. In addition, a second data set comprises two interviews, one with the researcher and the second, a fellow international graduate student in linguistics. These two data sets of a natural setting – a classroom – and semi-structured interviews are two methods of data collection that provide a rich picture of this institutional context.

The study concentrates on the extent to which the instructor communicates respect for his students. There is a strong motivation to do so to avoid damaging the interactional context (which has real-world consequences such as low student evaluations that can subsequently damage job prospects). The analysis for the study draws on the assumption that the instructor's efforts to be respectful are observable in the interactions with the students. The students would signal understanding of his intended behaviors in their responses in the data set of classroom discourse. The goal of the data analysis, therefore, is to assess the enactment of respect as a form of politic behavior in the ITA's classroom interactions with his students, triangulated with his own interpretation of his actions as evidenced in the interview data sets.

Participants

The multilingual teacher in the case study is Pedro, a 31-year-old male Ph.D. student in physics from Argentina. Given that he had been teaching in his home country before matriculating at the U.S. institution, he was assigned to teach an introductory laboratory course for lower division students, all non-physics majors, in his first year as a graduate student. At the end of two semesters, Pedro received high student evaluations in general (top one-third of the 18 physics teaching assistants for the spring semester) and in particular on the focal variable for this study on the student–teacher assessment instrument. The university instrument asked specifically if the teacher communicated respect and concern for the students in classroom interactions.

Data Analysis and Findings

The researcher carried out a data analysis of the videotaped sessions and Pedro's explanations about his classroom practices in the two interviews. The data evidenced seven strategies Pedro used to communicate respect in the relational work he did with his students. The following list of the categories includes excerpts from Pedro's talk for each category.

> #1. *He treats the students "all the same."*
> P: "you really try to treat each question as a potential, new instance . . . because it's not fair . . . for the last three tables to receive a worse explanation"

Pedro explains how he helped the groups of students equally as they were setting up equipment for experiments in the laboratory.

> #2. *He uses non-academic talk.*
> P: "if you speak very far away from, from the way the students speaking, the very academic way, it's not very good, I mean"

Pedro did not use elaborated academic language when he helped the students, to avoid communicating distance from them.

> #3. *He displays humor.*
> P: "humor hey, there's no one that doesn't like you . . . it's a way of making things a little . . . bit at least more fun, for them and for me"

Despite his sensitivity about using humor with his L2 speaker English, Pedro, nevertheless, tried to inject humor when talking with the students in his constant emphasis on prioritizing ways to communicate with them.

> #4. *He does not pull rank with students.*
> Q: you use the expression "sorry"
> P: I was treating him as a person . . . the fact that I'm a teacher doesn't mean that I can, OK, move away, you are in my way . . . they feel that, the thing is that if you respect them, they respect you"

When the researcher questioned Pedro on his use of "sorry" with a student, he explained his view regarding how he treats students in general.

> #5. *He focuses on what he can do to help them despite his nonnative speaker of English skills.*
> P: "there is some breaking point, I have to, go on . . . and then you start, you lose yourself, . . . you relax and people understand you . . ."

Here, Pedro described the need to transcend his feelings of inadequacy regarding his language skills to do his job as a teacher.

> #6. *He avoids using praising language.*
> P: "I know all the names, . . . but I don't think it's necessary [to use them]. If you're all the time using a positive reinforcement, it loses its value, you know, because they give it for granted"

Teacher training courses in the U.S. commonly emphasize the need to praise students. For Pedro, he did not see praising students as necessary; rather he viewed it as a form of false or dishonest behavior on the teacher's part.

> #7. *He discusses the need to respect students.*
> P: "be respectful, never mock students or humiliate students"

Here, Pedro talks explicitly of the students about his belief in interacting with them.

Pedro emphasized the need to respect his students, despite the fact that the researcher did not state the purpose of the research project. Respect is one dimension of relationships, a strategy to do relational work to achieve balance and harmony. Moreover, Pedro believed that a respectful attitude on his part would not only build positive relationships, but also help the students to learn.

Applications to the Classroom

The introduction to this chapter commented on the voiced concerns of second/foreign language learners about their desire to be perceived as polite when using their target language. Those concerns provide the starting point for language educators when they select textbooks and other learning materials for courses they teach and programs they supervise. While more and more publishers address the need to include the teaching of pragmatics in their materials, it still remains an area of language development that requires creativity and motivation to prepare appropriate tasks.

The first stage of teaching pragmatics, including how to be polite in the L2, concentrates on formulaic expressions or routines. These bits of talk do not change their grammatical form and can be used frequently in appropriate places in conversational talk. They are prefabricated and stored in memory for ready, automatic use. They can serve as communication strategies, to buy the speaker some time to think about what to say, and fill up silences when at a loss. Here are some examples:

> Shall we go?
> Do you have the time?
> Excuse me, I'm sorry to bother you. . . .
> Well, yes, I agree.
> Could I make an appointment to see you in your office?

Beginner students, in particular, can benefit from acquiring a repertoire of these expressions and practice using them where they fit into the flow of talk. However, learning formulaic language continues even to the advanced level when more complex and longer routines can be helpful for job interviews and formal, year-end parties. Learners of Japanese find it a challenge to learn and use appropriately greetings that seem ubiquitous, especially at the end of the year and for the New Year's celebrations. At first, a simple *"omedeto gozaimasu"* seems to suffice for "Happy New Year." However, the full expression that is required especially for more formal contexts is: *"Akemashite omedeto gozaimasu. Kotoshi mo yoroshiku onegaishimasu."* This greeting has two parts, the "Happy New Year" wish and then a second wish, where the speaker asks the person she is greeting to continue to extend friendship and support for the coming year.

In tandem with teaching the linguistic formulaic routines of the L2, teachers can raise awareness at the same time regarding when, which expressions, and why politeness cues are necessary. Just as parents intervene with their children, by requiring them to say "please" with each request, so teachers and materials writers can introduce and provide lessons on politeness even at the beginning levels. The strategies listed in Brown and Levinson (1987; see above) on how to mitigate a request, for instance, in the L2 comprise information for classroom lessons.

A second stage at an intermediate or advanced level would work on the concept of relational work as an underlying motivation of politeness. Teachers can raise awareness by using short excepts of talk in the L1 or, in a mixed student group, the L2 to observe and discuss what speakers and hearers do to display politic (what's normal for the situation) and (im)polite behavior. Once the students understand the concept of establishing and maintaining relationships through language in use, lessons could focus on how the L2 weaves through the discourse of conversation to accomplish communicative goals. One possibility for the collection of lessons is (in)directness, an area of pragmatics that commonly comes up in folk linguistics commentary on individuals' speaking styles. The cultural differences in speaking styles abound even among subcultures in one country. New Yorkers are said to be loud and direct, "too assertive." Southerners are "soft," "polite," and friendly.

Again, raising awareness is a useful starting point. Learners and teachers can generate a list of reasons why indirectness is preferred, based on their own experiences and perhaps through analysis of some talk excerpts. Here are some rationales for indirectness in interactions:

1. Hint, lead interlocutor to discover the intended meaning
2. Avoid responsibility and conflict
3. Joke, have fun
4. Show membership in group
5. Avoid saying the obvious and be insulting

Clips for TV programs – especially sitcoms – and movies can illustrate the variety of underlying reasons people use language indirectly. Chapter 10 discusses teaching pragmatic competence in classrooms more at length. Here, it is fair to say that students do express the need to learn how to be polite in the L2 and programs and classes are inadequate if they do not tackle those students' needs in an explicit manner.

Conclusions

This chapter has reviewed the classic theory on politeness of Brown and Levinson (1987) as well as some of the criticisms of their work, focusing particularly on cultural differences that point to the need for a more inclusive approach to this linguistic and non-linguistic phenomenon. The chapter continued with an introduction to a current approach that sees politeness behavior as part and parcel of human efforts to establish and maintain relationships with others. One of the basic premises is that conversational participants do a lot of relational work to achieve respectful, balanced human relations. One dimension of that relational work is the use of language to communicate that goal, what have been called displays of politeness. Politeness is just one type of social action that people seek to enact in interactions to reach comity. Chapter 7 looks into another goal of the interactive work people do: the construction of identity in everyday talk.

Suggested Readings

Bourdieu, P. (1990). *The logic of practice*. Stanford: Stanford University Press.
Brown, P. and Levinson, S. C. (1987). *Politeness: Some universals in language usage*. Cambridge: Cambridge University Press.
Hickey, L. and Stewart, M. (Eds.) (2005). *Politeness in Europe*. Clevedon: Multilingual Matters.

LoCastro, V. (2003). *An introduction to pragmatics: Social action for language teachers.* Ann Arbor: University of Michigan Press. Chapters 6 and 13.

Locher, M. A. (2004). *Power and politeness in action: Disagreements in oral communication.* Berlin/New York: Mouton de Gruyter.

Watts, R. J. (2003). *Politeness.* Cambridge: Cambridge University Press.

Watts, R. J., Ide, S., and Ehlich, K. (Eds.) (2005). *Politeness in language: Studies in its history, theory and practice.* 2nd edition. Berlin/New York: Mouton de Gruyter.

Tasks

1. Chapter 6 touched on the inclusion of nonverbal behavior to signal politeness. A well-known example from Japan is the bowing that accompanies the exchange of business cards. Working in groups, generate a list of other nonverbal forms of politeness from cultures, subcultures, or groups you know.

2. Collect copies of phrase books, for example from Berlitz, and study the books to assess the extent they teach politeness in phrases as well as language to engage in relational work. Be prepared with examples and a short oral report on what you have learned.

3. Find examples in letters to the editor in a local newspaper or an online source, and discuss to what extent the writers use politeness in their writing.

4. Rearrange the following phrases in order from the most to the least polite. Give reasons for your choices.

    Pass me the salsa.
    Could you please pass me the salsa?
    Can you pass the salsa? I'd like some.
    Please pass me the salsa.
    Salsa!
    Are you finished with the salsa?

5. Impoliteness draws the attention of researchers and members of speech communities. There are differences across gender, age, and ethnic or sociocultural groupings. Here is a list of types of impoliteness that occur. Work with group members to suggest examples for each case. Note that some of the items below refer to primarily linguistic forms while others are nonverbal or both.

    Address forms
    Lessening the social distance suddenly, shifting role relationships
    Inappropriate dress
    Time of arrival at an event
    Topics of conversation
    Refusals
    Greetings
    Starting and ending a meal

Data Analysis

Here is an example of a transaction in a bakery in France. In addition to the formulaic phrases, there are multiple examples of how B, the owner of the shop, and C, the customer, do politeness and relational work.

1.	B:	Madame bonjour?
2.	C:	Je voudrais un pain aux céréales [s'il vous plaît
3.	B:	[oui
4.	C:	Et une baguette à l'ancienne
5.	B:	Et une baguette (bruit de sac en papier) treize soixante-dix s'il vous plaît (C pose un billet de 200F) merci (C farfouille dans son porte-monnaie) vous voulez me donner de la monnaie?
6.	C:	Heu, vingt centimes c'est tout ce que j'ai
7.	B:	Heu non ça va pas m'arranger merci (sourire)
8.	C:	Excusez-moi
9.	B:	Oh, mais c'est rien je vais me débrouiller alors sur deux cents francs ça fait cent quatre-vingt-six-trente (. . .) cent cinquante-soixante soixante-dix hum quatre-vintgt-cinq quatre-vingt six (.) vingt et trente voilà on y arrive
10.	C:	Je vous remercie
11.	B:	C'est moi (.) merci madame bon week-end au revoir
12.	C:	Merci au revoir

Source: Kerbrat-Orecchioni 2005: 33

Provide an analysis of this data sample. Explain how the formulaic phrases and other linguistic features are used to do politeness and relational work by B and C.

English translation

B: good morning, madam
C: I would like a multigrain loaf, [please
B: [yes
C: and a regular baguette
B: and a baguette (sound of a paper bag) thirteen seventy please (C puts down a 200 F note) thank you (C searches in her purse) are you looking for small change?
C: er: twenty centimes is all I've got
B: er no that won't quite do it thanks (smile)
C: sorry about that
B: oh never mind I'll manage so with 200 francs that's one eighty-six thirty (.) a hundred and fifty sixty seventy hum eighty five and six (.) twenty and thirty see we made it.
C: thanks a lot
B: no my pleasure (.) thank you madam have a good weekend good-bye
C: thank you good-bye

7
INTERACTIONAL CONSTRUCTION OF IDENTITY

Introduction

Sociopragmatics focuses primarily on the social rules of speaking, those expectations about interactional discourse held by members of a speech community as appropriate and "normal" behavior. A major thread through the study of sociopragmatics is how communication of pragmatic meaning involves speakers' presentation of their identities. The choice of a cell phone or an intonation contour is as important as a greeting or lack of one in signaling to other community members who the speaker sees her/himself to be. Displays of convergence to the social norms occur where the speaker indicates a desire to be a member of a community. The speaker conveys that desire or need through language, such as adopting the local variety of a language, as Japanese from Kyushu do when they settle in Tokyo. Or the speaker may diverge from the local norms, consciously or in an out-of-awareness manner displaying unwillingness to join the local speech community by choosing to continue to speak a nonstandard form. Welsh and Irish speakers of English in the U.K. may retain features of their variety of that language. A social psychological theory, accommodation theory, explains speakers' choices of (in)directness in making requests, thereby enacting identity and group membership.

All of the categories that are often used to describe features of human beings, such as ethnicity, race, gender, socioeconomic background/class, are abstractions. Those abstractions become real or transparent as they are enacted through our choices of clothing, hairstyles, posture, lifestyles, and most assuredly how we use language. Word choice, prosody, tone of voice, degree of grammatical complexity, and interactional routines are components of sociopragmatics. Linguistic strategies and cues convey and build identities of speakers/listeners as they "perform identity." While individuals are likely to use more than one cue to display their identities in doing relational work in a group setting, one may suffice to signal one aspect of a person. For instance, using British English vocabulary (*lift* instead of *elevator*) or pronouncing French or Spanish phrases or names with a native speaker accent suggests involvement in one or more of those cultures.

This chapter considers the enactment of identity in the construction of interactional meaning. It is impossible to provide more than a sampling of the explanatory definitions and research studies concerning the concept of identity. The first section introduces definitions of identity as well as issues that revolve around this concept so important in second language acquisition (SLA) and pragmatics.

Explanatory Definitions of Identity

The traditional approach to identity claims that there are two aspects: (1) one's self-definition as an individual; and (2) a collective or social identity, which involves one's self-definition as a member of a social group. It is also possible to study, first, aspects of identity as macro features – those that relate to societal, ethnic, even religious groups – and micro features, which would encompass individual characteristics. However, both are always present in presentations of self, with some features being emphasized more than others depending on the sociocultural context. For example, Asian cultures place more salience on collectivism than individual needs in social interactions. Examples are found in popular culture, such as in the film *Shall We Dance?* which contrasts Japanese businessmen's public personas connected with their work at Japanese companies in Tokyo and then their personas as individuals in their dance classes and competitions. The American version of the film is not able to develop that theme as well because collective group behavior prioritized in Japan is not a strong feature of American culture.

A more recent approach to conceptualizing identity can be found in Simon (2004) and Spencer-Oatey (2007). Drawing from Simon, Spencer-Oatey argues identity is "an analytic fiction" that may be more correctly "taken as a shorthand expression or placeholder for social psychological processes" (2007: 640). Further, although identity entails cognitive dimensions, it is primarily relationally and socially enacted through interaction (Spencer-Oatey 2007). Pragmatic choices in interactions engage speakers in identity claims, about how they construct themselves in the dynamics of dialogue/talk. Simon's (2004) "Self-Aspect Model of Identity" describes characteristics of self-presentations, composed of beliefs about self-attributes. This list presents a sample of the features (Spencer-Oatey 2007: 640):

- Personality traits (e.g. shy)
- Abilities (e.g. poor dancer)

- Physical features (e.g. curly hair, slim)
- Behavioral characteristics (e.g. usually gets up early)
- Ideologies (e.g. Christian, democrat)
- Social roles (e.g. project manager)
- Language affiliation(s) (e.g. English, Chinese)
- Group memberships (e.g. female, academic, Christian)

Individuals and groups may vary in the extent to which they highlight some features over others. In a modern, urban work environment, for instance, physical features and ideologies will be of less importance than abilities, social roles, and personality. Self-definition or presentation may operate without any attention drawn to identity characteristics, until a problem arises. Generally, identity remains unexamined, off the radar screen, yet becomes transparent, even salient in interaction; for example, where an elderly person, sensitive to being viewed as an older person, may bristle about being perceived as needing help to get down from the bus. Such situations demonstrate that identity is an important feature of human beings and that it is a concept that serves several functions. Spencer-Oatey (2007: 642) cites this partial list from Simon (2004: 66–7).

- Identity helps to provide people with a sense of belonging . . . and a sense of distinctiveness.
- Identity helps people "locate" themselves in their social worlds . . . giving them a sense of "place."
- People's positive evaluations of their own self aspects help them build their self-esteem. . . . the respectful recognition of relevant others also plays a crucial role.

Identity is an important subject of study at the individual, group, and even national level, as seen in a recent summary (Dacey 2009) of sociolinguistic research on the topic in Switzerland. Switzerland's multilingualism has been a salient feature of its identity: it has four national languages – French, German, Italian, and Romansch. At issue currently is where English as a major international language fits into the nation's self-presentation. Over the past two decades, English has joined the mix in Switzerland due to (1) the influx of international firms, (2) the increasing use of English in academia, and (3) the worldwide recognition and use of English as a lingua franca, or language of wider communication. Specific evidence of the inroads of English includes its use for communication within Switzerland specifically among its citizens who do not share the same first language – for example, Italian and French speakers may use English rather than struggle in one of those two languages to communicate. Another example of the increased use of English is the translation of parts of the laws of the Swiss system into English. Further, English is being taught in all primary schools, where pupils study it along with a second national language. Given that multilingualism is a deeply rooted cultural view, Swiss identity is not being threatened by this addition of another language, a foreign one, viewed as very useful internationally especially for young people's futures.

Identity? Identities?

Traditional sociolinguistics conceived of social structure as being static and fixed, where an individual could be categorized as male, working class, Italian American, resident of Flushing, Queens, on Long Island, with a typical variety of New York City English, for his entire life. Psychology and related fields in academia also viewed identity as unchanging and singular. An individual had one identity and individuals with one, integrated view of themselves were accepted as healthy, stable community members. However, the Western view of identity has changed to reflect the interpretation of human beings as having multiple, situational identities, where features of the context would favor the enactment of some aspects of individuals. Researchers came to accept the possibility of agency and they recognized that all human beings can potentially change their language and nonlanguage behavior to reflect underlying motivations and new circumstances in their lives. There is ample evidence that individuals go about their daily lives, shifting from one social role to another, performing facets of their persona through language. Clearly, extremes, such as Dr. Jekyll and Mr. Hyde would not be tolerated in any cultural setting; that stereotype is outside the bounds of normalcy.

Block (2009) surveys the notion of identity in SLA, an area of noticeable interest only since the 1990s when the field of SLA started to catch up with research in other social sciences about identity. The poststructuralist perspective had introduced a number of terms to account for aspects of identity, such as subjectivity, positioning of self, and discursive construction, all appropriated by researchers in SLA. As Block explains, early SLA studies involving issues related to identity did not explicitly label the research as having a focus on that notion. Those studies rather couched the main concerns as motivation and attitudes to bilingualism (see Gardner and Lambert 1972), the language ego, acculturation, fossilization, and diary accounts of foreign language learning experiences. Block focuses his study of identity on specific contexts: (1) adult migrants and gate-keeping encounters in Western Europe; (2) foreign language learning contexts and the likelihood of foreign language identities developing in classrooms; and (3) identity in study abroad contexts where residence in the target language community does not guarantee increased acquisition of the L2 pragmatic norms.

This expanded view of identity has evolved following the modern developments in psychology, in particular psychoanalysis. Yet the Western view of integrated presentations of self still continues in theoretical and methodological frameworks to prioritize the importance of the individual rather than membership in groups. It is probably wise to place societies and cultures along a continuum regarding how much a person in a particular society or culture uses interactional discourse to signal group membership rather than features of her/his individual identity.

A recent addition to the study of identity is the use of "third" or "hybrid" spaces to account for the anomie that individuals experience while learning another language and culture, in particular in the target language environment. Kramsch (1993) states that individuals may experience "feelings of being on the fence" and "of being forever 'betwixt and between,' no longer at home in their original culture, nor really belonging to the host culture" (p. 234). Jackson (2008) documents in her study what she calls "the creation of an intermediary zone or third space," the result of the intercultural contact by student sojourners in a study-abroad program at a Hong Kong university. The three-year B.A. program incorporated activities in Hong Kong and a five-week sojourn in England. Jackson collected narratives from 15 L1 Chinese participants in her study where she focused on identity, language use, and intercultural transformation and a resulting personal expansion of their abilities to view and experience the world. One of her informants, Mira, wrote:

> Culture influences my use of expression when speaking different languages. For example, I feel most comfortable to use English when I am praising or encouraging other people, or expressing my enthusiasm towards something. I have tried applying Chinese in these situations, but no matter how sincere I was, it just did not sound natural to me. Also, when I am telling my close friends my opinions which do not fit traditional Chinese culture, I tend to switch to English, too, as if these thoughts belong to the culture it represents.

Mira is attempting to account for the changes she is experiencing regarding her evolving identity in the two languages she regularly uses. Here she is aware of how her home culture and that of the English world of Hong Kong seem to dictate the language she feels comfortable using for specific speech acts or routines. Eventually, she may accept her own evolving, dynamic identities as she interacts comfortably as a third culture person, functioning in an intercultural environment.

Role of Sociocultural Factors in Identity

Language learners may experience difficulties in relation to their L1 identities in acquiring a second language. Siegal (1994) and LoCastro (1998) found that L1 gender identities impeded acquisition of Japanese as a foreign language for themselves and informants in their studies in Japan. American women studying and working in Japan realized that their cultural values concerning gender roles were challenged while they were learning and interacting in Japanese. The many changes that American society had undergone with regards to women's roles and non-sexist language problematized not only their motivational levels, but also decisions about what variety of Japanese to study in the Japanese as a second language environment. Exposure to native speaker Japanese as well as opportunities to use the language were compromised by gender and status dimensions (a woman who was a faculty member was treated very differently from others who were students from U.S. universities (Siegal, 1994)). Siegal and LoCastro found that they had to face unexamined, external expectations, both at the individual and group level, that Japanese speakers would bring into interactions, even with Japanese language instructors. Instructors as well as textbooks and other teaching materials reproduced the gender assumptions of the local, Japanese cultural values.

Nonnative speakers of an L2 may seek to maintain their ethnolinguistic identity owing to pressures from their L1 community, fearing discrimination and disintegration of their community in the face of hegemonic moves on the part of a dominant culture, such as that of English as the international language of communication or lingua franca in many parts of the world. In addition, there is anecdotal evidence that maintaining a "foreign" accent, whether phonological or pragmatic, allows the speakers to avoid heavy sanctions for inappropriately signaling pragmatic meaning as a nonnative speaker. Although complete convergence or movement towards the L2 norms is virtually unattainable if the acquisition or learning of the target language began after the critical period at puberty, nonnative speakers may in any case seek consciously or out of awareness to converge or diverge from the second/foreign language community for ideological and personal reasons.

Some examples of ethnolinguistic identity maintenance are (1) code switching between languages, (2) maintenance of sociolinguistic markers in speech, such as "He don't know what he's talking about" in the talk of Spanish speakers of English in the U.S., and (3) unwillingness to use humbling, honorific forms of Japanese by nonnative speakers whose L1 culture values more egalitarian language use.

Al-Issa (2003) looked for evidence of sociocultural transfer from Jordanian EFL learners into their L2, English, in their enactment of refusals. He collected data of their sociopragmatic responses by means of a discourse completion task (DCT) based on observations carried out in the field, using notebook data. The DCT administration was followed by semi-structured interviews. He compared those results with baseline data of Arabic speakers using Arabic and native speakers of English data responding in English in the same situations. The comparison of the collected data demonstrated three areas of transfer: choice of semantic formulas, length of responses, and content of the semantic formulas, all of which connect with the local cultural values of the two groups. Here is a table of semantic formulas and examples from Al-Issa's data that demonstrate the values of the informants, reflecting the sociocultural influence on their choice of routines (p. 585):

TABLE 7.1 Semantic formulas used by both Jordanian groups not found in the American data

Semantic formula	Example
Define relationship	OK, my dear professor but . . .
Return favor	I'll pay for me and you
Removal of negativity	You know we've been very good friends
Request for understanding	Please believe me, professor

What is particularly of interest regarding identity is that Al-Issa found in the interview data that the informants indicated with their responses in the DCT that they were influenced by their pride in their L1 and their religion as well as their perceptions of the L2. Three interviewees used "God willing" (*insha'allah*) in their English refusal responses. When asked about the use of the expression, all seemed to emphasize the role of Islam in their lives and how Muslims should obey its rules. The following conversation took place during an interview (Al-Issa 2003: 594):

1. Interviewer: When refusing a faculty advisor's suggestion to take another course in writing, you said "I'm sorry sir I can't take it now, but God willing I'll take it next semester." What made you use the expression "God willing" in this response?
2. Student: You are a Muslim. I can tell from your name and you know that only God knows what will happen in the future.
3. Interviewer: Yes, but do you think Americans will understand what you meant?
4. Student: I don't know – only God knows.

In line 2, the student speaks directly to the interviewer, a fellow Muslim, a feature of the interview context that may have influenced the topics in the collected data.

Moreover, the informants indicated that they would use "I swear to God" (Arabic, *w'allahiy*) in their EFL utterances as in the following example: "I'm very sorry. I swear I have pain in my hands and I can't carry anything but my friend can help you" (in response to a professor's request for assistance). This swearing to God is considered a cue to signal their religiosity, as one student explained: "When someone swears by God, I believe him and I know he is sincere . . . because if he is not sincere God will punish him . . . ." (p. 594).

Some of the informants also explained that when they spoke English as their L2, they felt more comfortable not trying to use the sociopragmatics of American English. They felt they were imitating native speakers, something that is regarded negatively by other Arabs. One student explained that when he used the American expression "what's up?" a friend made fun of him and accused him of trying to be "too American" (p. 595). Al-Issa explains: "Arabs may find it difficult to justify the effort needed to speak English more fluently and more appropriately" (p. 595).

Studying the Enactment of Identity

The interest in the enactment of identity has sparked the search for a methodology to study the details of this commonplace, but often unexamined or unnoticed feature of everyday life. Postmodern theories have provided the framework of the co-construction of identity, such that participants in interaction discursively signal who they are in the context of the occasions for doing so provided by the other participants. Just as adjacency pairs (see Chapter 3) influence and constrain participants' talk, the second pair part especially, so too does the talk of participants provide the occasion or opportunity for others to enact their identities.

Action Theory

The performance of identity, like all human communication, entails the dynamic, interactive sending of signals, verbal and nonverbal, to receivers of the intended message. However, it is not one way! Speakers become listeners, and listeners become speakers. As such, the coordination of speakers and addressees involves both cognitive and social aspects. Clark (1996) developed a social action theory to attempt to account for the complexity of comprehending and producing meaning, including the enactment of identity. Beyond Grice's Cooperative Principle (CP) and maxims, essentially rules of thumb (Clark 1996: 146), and the exclusive focus on the listener's comprehension of the speaker's meaning as in Relevance Theory, Clark's theory represents his thinking and research about integrating both the individual or cognitive and the social dimensions in explaining interactive language use, particularly of interest in understanding how identity is created in the flow of talk.

Basic Notions

In Clark's view, language use is a form of purposeful "joint action." This action is more than the sum of two individuals using language to do things; rather, the interactants coordinate their actions, merging their cognitive processes in what is called "discursive production of intersubjectivity." That is, individuals construct, attend to, and understand the meanings each of them contributes to an interaction. It is a "discursive" creation in that their contributions occur during the flow of talk, without any planning or expectations. Further, the creation is "intersubjective" as the participants, two or more, share the "same" mental space during the milliseconds of the cognitive processing of attending to and understanding the intended meaning of one of the participants. Thus, these joint actions combine individual cognitive processes in a joint social action.

Conversation is the basic, prototypical setting to view Clark's theory. Clark attempts to account for the intersubjectivity of the joint action (1996: 9):

Co-presence	Speaker and hearer are physically present.
Visibility	Speaker and hearer can see each other.
Audibility	Speaker and hearer are within channel linkage.
Instantaneity	Speaker and hearer receive each other's talk immediately.
Evanescence	The talk fades as soon as spoken.
Recordlessness	No record of the talk remains.
Simultaneity	Speaker and hearer simultaneously receive and produce talk.

Given these prototypical features, how do the participants coordinate their joint actions? Not only do they "take actions *with respect to each other*, but they *coordinate* these actions with each other" (p. 11). This intersubjectivity happens when the "two essential parts" of a joint action are present: (1) a signal by the speaker and (2) a recognition of receiving the signal by the listener. "Signals are deliberate actions" that can consist of an "utterance, gestures, facial expressions, eye gaze, and perhaps other actions" (Clark 1996: 13). The important part is that the signals have to be recognized as deliberate, ostensible and marked as having meaning to be attended to.

Signals that can be identified by the listener require a common ground. All theories of pragmatic meaning include this basic notion, labeled shared background knowledge, world knowledge, or, as here, common ground. Interpreting the utterance "New York has gotten better over the last decade" is not possible unless the speaker and hearer share some knowledge about New York in recent years. Just that one phrase serves to provide information about the speaker's identity and how s/he wants to be perceived as well as to test the hearer regarding whether or not her/his background and identity includes familiarity with New York.

Action and Activity

Joint actions can consist of speech events, in which conversants "negotiate deals, gossip, get to know each other" (Clark 1996: 17). Clark also includes speech acts: requests, disagreements, or compliments. The frame of the joint actions is a joint activity, a construct Clark adopts from Levinson's (1992) notion of activity type. An example is a sales transaction in a retail store, carried out by participants in recognizable roles with specific goals. The participants achieve their goals by coordinating their joint actions. Conventional procedures, such as selecting an item and then proceeding to the cashier, can be incorporated in joint actions following the frame or script for purchasing items in a shop; common ground is shared by the participants.

Coordination Problem

In the developed world, the stereotypical sales transaction, of purchasing groceries at a supermarket, may be achieved without using spoken language. What Clark calls the coordination problem does not arise. However, when the frame for a joint activity is not shared, then the participants even at a supermarket may not be able to achieve their goals.

The first point concerns the reasons interactants coordinate their actions. Clark assumes that they do so to achieve their goals, which they realize are impossible unless they work together. Participants engage in joint actions, by conversing with each other, coordinating to plan, for instance, for a party. Coordination problems at the level of local joint actions are multiple, the primary one being "what the speakers mean and what their addressees understand them to mean" (Clark 1996: 73). Miscoordination can be worked out through language, the conventional signaling system par excellence, or through coordination devices such as gestures. The minimum criterion is joint salience: all participants must recognize the meaning of a signal, usually on the basis of common background knowledge. The following example (Clark 1996: 31–2) illustrates coordination.

> Clark walks up to a counter and places two items next to the cash register. Stone is behind the counter marking off items on an inventory. Clark, looking at Stone, catches her eye.
> Stone: (meeting Clark's eyes) I'll be right there.
> Clark: Okay . . . These two things over here. (Stone nods, takes the two items, examines the prices on them, and rings them up on the cash register.)
> Stone: Twelve seventy-seven.
> Clark: Twelve seventy-seven. (Clark takes out his wallet, extracts a twenty-dollar bill, hands it to Stone, then rummages in his coin purse for coins.) Let's see that two pennies I've got two pennies. (Clark hands Stone two pennies.)
> Stone: Yeah. (Stone enters $20.02 in the register, which computes the change.)
> Stone: (handing change to Clark) Seven twenty-five is your change.
> Clark: Right. (Clark puts the money in his wallet while Stone puts the items and receipt in a bag. She hands the bag to Clark, they break eye contact, and he turns and walks away.)

In providing this real-life example, Clark demonstrates the kind of joint activity he carries out with Stone through a series of joint actions, some of which are linguistic, some nonlinguistic, yet all important to the activity. Clark claims that there are levels of psycholinguistic processing which accompany these actions, which he calls "action ladders" (1996: 389).

Speaker A's actions	Speaker B's actions
A is proposing joint project w to B	B is considering A's proposal of w
A is assigning that p to B	B is recognizing that p from A
A is presenting signal s to B	B is identifying signal s from A
A is executing behavior t to B	B is attending to behavior t from A

These action ladders are part of a schema of the cognitive processing involved in coordinating joint actions. The ladders are not as distinct as they are presented here, however. At each level, they overlap and are linked in complex ways, mutually dependent to complete the joint action.

However, in Clark's theory of social action, "language is rarely used as a means in itself (1996: 387). Participants carry out activities in roles defined by the social context. Clark's sociocognitive model claims that many features of language use are more correctly viewed as features of the joint activities that facilitate communication, such as turn taking, repairs, and sharing the conversational floor. Turn taking is essential to cooperative talk: participants who dominate a meeting, for example, are accused of not allowing others to "take a turn." Opening and closing telephone conversations are noticeable phenomena of talk; when they are violated or ignored, speakers are uncomfortable, and misunderstandings arise.

Consequently, language adjusts to meet the functional needs of the participants to carry out joint activities (see LoCastro 1999). Features of language in use – length of clauses, the rhythmic placement of turn-taking cues, and tag questions – develop out of the need to achieve joint activities. Pragmatic meaning, that "extra" meaning that goes beyond the linguistic signals, is created in the course of a joint action. For example, if conversants on a neighborhood sidewalk talk in the U.S. do not share the same turn-taking schema, not allowing everyone to participate in the chat, a less positive view of those violating the expectations may construct them as unfriendly neighbors.

Clark's theory provides a framework for studying how speakers and listeners embed signals regarding their identities in their talk. However, as a sociocognitive approach, it is not possible to prove or disprove his theory. The only evidence to support action theory involves the social, language dimensions of interactional discourse. The next section takes up a methodology for data analysis that can join Clark's theoretical contribution: conversation analysis (CA).

Conversation Analysis

CA is both a theory and a methodology to study face-to-face interaction. Schegloff (1992), regarded as the originator of CA, argues that social structure can only be studied in "previously unnoticed particular details in talk-in-interaction" (p. 106). In other words, social structure, a concept of sociolinguistics, is not something external to talk, but rather created within talk and is discovered in "empirically based analysis" (p. 102). Schegloff addresses what he sees as two themes central to CA: (1) relevance and (2) sequentiality. Regarding the first theme, he claims that relevance of a contribution to the talk-in-interaction is established by the participants, who orient to a particular point in the talk. What is relevant, in other words, is what the participants indicate they are paying attention to. For example, if one participant in talk speaks with a heavy accent from a region of the U.K., the other conversation partners may comment on his accent. They make the speaker's accent relevant to the talk-in-interaction.

The second theme, sequentiality, refers to the fact that the context of talk is composed of sequences, a general characteristic of talk-in-interaction. That point may appear to be obvious. However, a premise of CA states that CA depends on microanalysis of the sequences in naturally occurring data. For example, speech exchange systems (Sacks, Schegloff, and Jefferson 1978) concern rights and obligations with regards to such features as turn taking, holding the floor, and repairs. The external social structure of a particular society, according to CA, may become transparent by observing the way turn taking occurs in talk among a doctor, a nurse assistant, and a patient. Schegloff (1992: 113) states that "by the very form of their conduct they show themselves to be oriented to the particular identities . . . provided by that setting and show themselves to be oriented to . . ." the doctor–patient context. One very transparent example of how language behavior in this setting displays the doctor's identity is the use of questions almost exclusively, whereas the patient is expected to respond. To go more deeply, if the doctor wishes to construct an identity as a caring physician, attentive to patients' needs, that identity is co-constructed with the patient in the face-to-face interaction by making open-ended comments and indirect questions, so that the patient may feel free to elicit information from the doctor. This linguistic evidence communicates the desire on the part of the doctor to assume a more modern identity as a health practitioner.

In addition to the requirements of studying how relevance is made apparent in the sequences of an interaction, CA has also claimed that a focus entirely on the actual talk is necessary. In other words, the researcher in this classic view should know nothing about the participants – their age, ethnicity, gender, and so forth. CA depends entirely on what is discerned in the interactional discourse. One motivation for this requirement is to avoid the researchers introducing any a priori or preconceived views on the data and the participants.

This arguably narrow approach does not serve the research goals of sociopragmatics, which prioritizes knowledge of the sociocultural context, participants' social status, and the norms and expectations about situated language use. Consequently, a more inclusive interpretation of CA has developed. Moerman (1988: 123) advocates for "a culturally contextualized conversation analysis" (CCCA) that includes a microanalysis of conversational data and information about the participants and the speech community to arrive at a richer, culturally informed view of meaning-making actions of the participants.

The studies in the next section of this chapter and in the next several chapters put into practice the combination of CA and other methodologies. The goal (Waugh *et al.* 2007) is to have the findings come out of the data, not to impose a view or theory on the data.

Studies of Identity

This section discusses several studies that exemplify how concerns about enacting identity get carried out in interactional discourse. The studies are all situated in different sociocultural contexts with native and nonnative speakers where attitudes, in particular, towards enacting identities are made transparent in the data analysis.

La Lotería

One study that clearly demonstrates the ways in which participants in local talk-in-interaction enact their identities in the flow of playing a game at a senior citizens' program was carried out by Cashman (2005). Rather than follow the more traditional or classic view of code switching, based on language code change as a reflection of the social structure of the urban Latino community, Cashman observed members of the community as they did "identity-work," embedded in the social activity of playing *lotería*, a Mexican version of bingo that uses pictures rather than numbers or letters. The participants employed code switching to claim or reject group affiliation and ethnic identities. The players of the *lotería* had varying degrees of Spanish–English bilingual proficiency and they used language preference and alternation as a resource to do identity work, such as signaling if they were English dominant, English monolingual, Spanish dominant, or Spanish monolingual – or members of both groups, as bilingual users of both languages. Their language preferences, inferred from the pragmatic meanings of the talk-in-interaction, served as a membership categorization device at this local, situated level. Language alternation is not solely enacted on the basis of the macro, social structure of the larger urban speech community. Here is an example from Cashman's study (2005: 305):

El Mundo: Yesenia (Y) and Ednita (E)

1. E: *el mundo*
2. Y: the world
3.   (1.0)
4. Y: the man with the world
5.   (3.0)
6. Y: *el mundo es el mundo con un hombre abajo (.) deteniéndolo*
7. E: *la bola*
8. Y: the ball

---

1. E: the world
2. Y: the world
3.   (1.0)
4. Y: the man with the world
5.   (3.0)
6. Y: the world is the world with a man below (.) holding it
7. E: the ball
8. Y: the ball

Ednita is calling a game of *lotería*, which entails, first, shaking a jar full of bottle caps, and then taking a cap out of the jar, saying aloud to everyone what the picture is on the cap she is holding. Although Ednita is bilingual, she tells the participants in Spanish that the bottle cap has a picture of the world with a man below holding the globe up. In this instance, Ednita signals she is Spanish-dominant. Yesenia, who is the program coordinator at the center, translates Ednita's talk and then elaborates in Spanish. Cashman claims that she does so, i.e. uses both languages, because, in her role as coordinator, she needs to attend to the needs of both groups, the Spanish- and English-speaking senior citizens. One could also interpret her behavior as a means to make it clear she is responsible to the entire group, where the members are likely to know enough of both languages to understand the descriptions on the caps. Indeed, the English speakers were busily covering the pictures of the world with the man holding it on their bingo cards as soon as Ednita called out what was on the cap in Spanish. In other words, Yesenia did not need to translate into English Ednita's words due to any fear of lack of understanding; she did so to communicate one aspect of her identity, relevant in that context, of being the coordinator of the program; she wanted to make all of the members feel included. This "preference-related codeswitching" is not necessarily related to the speakers' communicative ability in the language varieties in the community's linguistic repertoire (Cashman 2005: 306).

Occasioning Identity Work

Identity becomes transparent in the course of conversations, where an unexpected intonation contour provides a cue that the speaker is, despite fluency in English, originally from Italy, and this background information is a feature of that person's identity. Identity also becomes noticeable in the course of discussion of content where an individual contributes information about Middle Eastern food preparation, thus opening up the conversation to further comments and narratives about food preparation in other parts of the world. In other words, it is the occasion of the talk that opens up opportunities for identity display. One participant's talk occasions that of others, i.e. for them to do identity work. LoCastro (2009) assessed the value of retrospective interviews as a research tool to learn how an international instructor at an American university viewed his teaching practices. It becomes clear that he has used the interviewer's questions to occasion a display of his teaching identity.

Charley, a pseudonym for an international graduate student in electrical engineering, was originally from Taiwan, and was 30 years old at the time of the study in 2008. He was teaching a laboratory class for upper division students majoring in his field. He participated in a study to assess his teaching practices that had enabled him to receive high evaluations from his students on the required faculty evaluation instrument. Videotapes of several laboratory sessions and then a retrospective interview with him to go over the videotapes provide two data sets. In this summary, the focus is on the identity work he did while talking about his teaching practices during the interview. The researcher posed open-ended questions so that he could communicate his own thinking about his membership in the category of a professional, responsible teacher in the cultural context of teaching U.S. undergraduates. Reformulated questions and responses elicited expansions of his narrative, just as his comments led to the researcher's reformulations or further questions. The following is an excerpt from the recorded interview talk. LoCastro (V) had asked Charley (C) to explain his friendliness with his students:

1. V: . . . in your efforts to create rapport with the students it's the friendliness, the joking, using their names and using nicknames for the students etc . . . that when one wants to create rapport and have that friendly, humorous, joking atmosphere it's using more a conversational style and one of the things too that comes up – with the . . . transcription for your talk it's very . . . it's very interactive, teacher/student, teacher/student . . . constantly . . .
2. C: am only I speaking
3. V: yeah . . . very rarely do you go into
4. C: actually for other TA as far as I know only TA speaking
5. V: yeah

6. C: as far as I know . . . I ask other TA, other students
7. V: uh-huh
8. C: yeah, but um of course not every student come in that's the best way . . . they also say some TA cold, some TA nice but that's because that TA only speak when they need to speak, but I speak, no I don't speak when I don't need to speak – do you know the difference?
9. V: yeah, yeah
10. C: that's totally two different matters
11. V: right
12. C: so I speak as much as I can unless I should not speak
13. V: uh-huh
14. C: . . . and other TA basically speak as less as they can unless they need to speak
15. V: right right
16. C: but why some of the TA belong to that category uh as well as come to students . . . because when they speak they didn't speak I'm a teacher you're a student because most of TA I know who are cool are Caucasian or at least Americans
17. V: uh-huh
18. C: . . . but if they are Chinese, English, or Korean or other kind of European they just act like a teacher
19. V: lecture?
20. C: they just do their duty, finish that and go that's it, so student will say oh, they are good but they won't say oh, he's very cool, something like that, but this the reason why I'm very confident about my TA style
21. V: uh-huh
22. C: and uh . . . and I really want to know what students feedback and I confident that besides speaking, I think I should be the best one at UF.
23. V: OK . . . last comment . . . when you say "Go Gators" . . . it's because you were . . . why did you say "Go Gators"?
24. C: why do I say something about "Go Gators"? Because I was speaking something about baseball, no basketball, so I was asking them uh, are there some other activities for basketball yesterday – did you go there? and we just talk about that stuff . . . and later on I just go back to their desk and I say "Go Gators" uh, yeah, basically people don't know what's going on but for me uh . . . OK because I think, oh I know what's going on . . . "Go Gators" is a sentence you use when you try to group people together at UF

The noticeable topic of the talk that evidences his doing identity work is the comparisons he makes between "other" graduate teaching assistants and himself. He focuses on how much other teachers talk or dominate in the classrooms (lines 4, 8, 14), whether or not they help students (8, 20), and whether or not they know "what's going on" (24). Seemingly out of awareness, he distances himself from the others and tries to demonstrate how he is better than they are. He puts himself into the category of being a "good" teacher by modeling his behavior on the "cool" Caucasian or American teaching assistants (16, 18). He also wants to be viewed by the students as one of the "guys" in his use of a common phrase on campus to refer to the sports teams (24). Within the discourse of discussing his teaching practices with the researcher, he is expressing his resistance to being positioned as a typical teaching assistant, often denigrated at the university by regular faculty, students, and administrators. Charley wants very much to be perceived as a "cool" teacher who is not the same as the others.

Don't Want to Sound Like an American

In classroom language tasks or discussions, teachers may come across students expressing what seem to be positive attitudes towards learning English. Many claim an "interest" in that language and, when pushed to explain, state that "it's necessary" to study English to travel or study abroad or for their professional aspirations. Yet anecdotal evidence suggests that few desire, in fact, to acculturate to the Western values associated with English or to become "native speakers" of the language. LoCastro (2001) decided to conduct a study in the late 1990s at a major private university in Tokyo to assess the extent the Japanese EFL learners were motivated to adopt L2 communicative norms and include competence in English as part of their identity.

Both theories and research on individual differences in SLA prioritize the need for positive attitudes towards the target language, its speakers, and its culture. Schumann (1978) proposed a theory of acculturation to account for the lack of progress his informant, Alberto, made in acquiring English at a level that would have enabled more successful interactions in his adopted country, the U.S. Sociopsychological perspectives, such as Gardner's (1985) work on attitudes and motivation, and social constructionist approaches linking motivation or investment and L2 identity formation (Peirce 1995; Wertsch 1991) all focused on target language proficiency in terms of grammatical accuracy, native-like pronunciation, and accommodation to target language cultural norms. More recently, a strong interest in the acquisition of pragmatic norms has developed within the SLA/sociolinguistic frameworks. In conjunction with this revision of what it means to "know" a language, research has focused on individual differences and the impact of attitudes, motivation, and willingness to adopt L2 pragmatic norms for linguistic action. Kasper and Schmidt (1996) acknowledge that learners' willingness to enact L2 norms would be sensitive to affect factors. However, in a study of ESL learners' knowledge, attitudes, and self-reported behaviors of L2 pragmatic norms, Hinkel (1996) found awareness of the norms did not match willingness to enact the norms. Undoubtedly, attitudes and willingness to communicate in the L2 involve issues of identity, for individuals and members of migrant ethnic groups, as well as at the community and national level.

The upper division juniors and seniors in LoCastro's (2001) study in Japan were enrolled in content courses for majors in Languages, taught in English, such as "Pragmatics" and "Attitudes and motivation," and the first and second year students in "Pronunciation" or "Sophomore English" classes within the intensive English Language Program. This quasi-bilingual university made efforts to provide Japanese students with multiple opportunities on campus to improve their English language skills. A variety of data collection procedures was used: focus groups, reaction papers, and exam essays as well as role plays, tasks to raise awareness of pragmatic norms, and class discussions. In sum, four different classes and collaborating teachers provided opportunities to elicit learners' views and attitudes to the target language, their identities as English language learners and speakers, and their reactions to expectations that they would converge to the L2 pragmatic norms. The aim of the two teachers, one native English speaker and one nonnative English speaker, was to develop awareness of appropriacy regarding pragmatic use of language at a general level and then specifically the target language, American English.

This mixed-method, descriptive study posed two research questions (LoCastro 2001: 76, 79):

1. What is the evidence that learners seek to integrate into the TL community, thereby signaling a readiness to adopt L2 communicative norms?
2. What is the evidence that learners resist and contest the construction of a self-identity which acceptance of the L2 pragmatic norms would entail?

The data sources provided findings that the informants had an overall positive orientation towards developing their English language proficiency. Here is what two of the learners wrote in their essays:

> Wanting to become like a native speaker can't possibly have negative effects.

> I also think that the fact that I am eager to speak like a native speaker, which has not achieved yet, helps me to improve my English

Nevertheless, other essays suggest their motivations could be characterized as "instrumental," according to the Gardner model (1985). The following is one example.

> If one learns for business, it is not necessary to speak like a native speaker. For one, the target language is only a tool for one's business.

Another student felt that communicating in English with foreigners with a Japanese accent would be sufficient.

The students demonstrated an awareness of the effect of motivation, identity, and the L2 culture on SLA. One wrote: "I myself have motivation in learning a language. It's to express 'myself,' not to become like a someone in other culture." Another commented that motivation was not enough: "Desire is important." These two students demonstrated awareness of the complexity entailed in combining desire, effort, time, and motivation, as well as future goals and identity needs, to move towards proficiency in the L2 pragmatic norms.

That awareness represents a positive feature from the point of view of teachers who can then work with the more instrumental attitudes in class activities. Although the evidence was not strong, resistance to convergence to TL behaviors and L2 pragmatic norms was apparent with some of the learners, who expressed their desire to retain their Japanese identities, even stating it would be inappropriate to seek to become "native speakers" of English and that it would be "unnatural" to do so. Their voices are transparent in these excerpts from their essays and talk:

> I'm proud that I'm Japanese and that would never be changed. Even if I could speak English fluently as a native speaker, my personality and characteristics of Japanese won't change.
>
> What would you do with your first language and identity? Should you throw it away and head for a new one? I don't think it is possible to erase your first identity even how hard you try.

One thread through their discourse in class discussions was that there are different pragmatic norms for different native English speakers: "There are more than one set of pragmatic norms for English speakers, because those who use English as a mother tongue have different backgrounds." The realistic attitude expressed by this student enabled her to function comfortably in the modern world of Tokyo and elsewhere. Indeed, the majority of these students preferred to portray themselves as having an identity that included being a competent speaker of English as a foreign language, while fully retaining their first language culture and pragmatic norms.

Are You Hindu?

Cues of identify work in an interaction are also used to index membership in a group. An earlier perspective about identity adhered to a more static view of how conversational participants could include or exclude themselves or others by, for instance, their choice of a particular dialect of the local language of a community.

More recently, an approach within CA, labeled membership categorization analysis (MCA), seeks to describe how speakers use varieties or codes of languages they know as resources to enact their identities in the course of social actions. Higgins (2009) studied the resistance of one speaker to being classified as a member of an ethnic group, specifically the religious affiliation usually associated with that ethnic group, Hinduism. One of the two informants in her study, Irene, tried to establish "mutual identity" with Braj, the other speaker, by asking him if he were Hindu. Higgins explains that this type of question is similar to asking about the weather in other cultures; asking about one's ethnic or religious identity is more likely in the multicultural environment of Dar es Salaam, Tanzania. Braj resists Irene's categorization and distances himself through conversational strategies; both of the participants use alternation of Swahili and English to produce and resist identity construction concerning religious beliefs. Higgins (2009: 132) states: "Codeswitching appears to be a resource available to bilinguals for managing the dispreferred action of challenging a membership categorization that has been proposed by others." Higgins' research provides support for the view that identity is locally occasioned in the dynamic, unanticipated flow of talk.

Identity Work in an Educational Context

While identity in an L2 may be problematic for learners of the L2, even in the foreign language learning environment, it complicates more explicitly the lives of migrants, immigrants, and short- and long-term sojourners within the target language community. Radio talk shows are full of programs based on discussions, opinion sharing, and interviews with international residents of the United States about issues of local concern such as the building of a mosque near the grounds of the 9/11 disaster; the role of Hispanic parents in communities of practice involving bilingual education of their children; and the circumcision of female children of immigrants to the U.S. from Somalia. The word "identity" does not commonly come into the media talk, yet it is clearly part of the discourse, unexamined though it may be even by the participants. The discourse about the building of a mosque involves the identity of the U.S. as a whole, and of individuals and groups concerning how they want to be viewed and how they view themselves regarding aspects such as freedom of religion in society. Are they conservative or liberal or inclusive of all people, all religions? Regarding the maintenance of bi- and multilingualism in the U.S., studies by Schecter and Bayley (2002) and Perez (2004) cannot be understood without taking into consideration the participants' concerns about their own and their children's identities as residents of the United States. It is such populations, of international or nonnative speakers as residents within the receiving country/culture, particularly if the language is that of a high prestige country, that experience the most problems revolving around the notion of identity and accommodation or acculturation to the local context.

One group that may be particularly vulnerable to these issues is children in the K-12 school system in the U.S. Talmy (2009) engaged in a two-and-a-half-year critical ethnographic study of ESL students in the public school system in Honolulu, Hawaii. There was the official sanctioned view of the children and then the children's view of themselves that placed them in an "oppositional" stance *vis-à-vis* the view of the school.

Talmy (2009) carried out the ethnography study in a class of local ESL students at a high school in Hawaii, focusing on how the students created membership categories in the course of their talk with each other and their teacher. Specifically, he studied the category of "ESL student" in the context of lessons involving assignments with novels for third to fifth grades. Their teacher provided worksheets on vocabulary and grammar. In the class he observed, there were four students in one group, doing their "bookwork." Two of the students, Jennie and Computer, interact with their teacher in the excerpt below (p. 187).

1.	Mr. Day	Jennie where's your work?
2.		(0.9)
3.	Jennie	I don't know
4.		(2.5)
5.	Jennie	I've been <u>doing</u> it
6.	Mr. Day	where's your <u>book</u>
7.		(1.1)
8.	Jennie	at home
9.		(2.0)
10.	Mr. Day	what do you expect to do in class
11.	Jennie	No[thing
12.	Computer	[play

Source: Talmy 2009: 187

Jennie clearly takes an oppositional stance towards Mr. Day in her responses to his questions. She is not alone in her perspective on what is happening in the class: Computer adds his own point of view – negative – that class time or bookwork was a time to play, not do school work.

The talk with Mr. Day occasions their positioning themselves as "bad" students, one of the two "cultural productions" of ESL students at the school: "good" and "bad" students. The bad students portray themselves through their talk as being oppositional to the "good" student category. Jennie had not done the assignment nor brought her book to class; she responds along with Computer to Mr. Day's questions in a challenging manner. Her responses are "disaffiliative," that is, not in alignment with expectations of how students, specifically good students, act in Mr. Day's class. She uses her linguistic resources to demonstrate her lack of investment in the school, its curriculum, and the local

ESL student identity. Jennie does not wish to be a "good" ESL student. Talmy (2004, 2009) labels newly arrived ESL students as "FOBs", in other words, "fresh off the boats." The local ESL students, like Jennie and Computer, did not want to be put in the same category as the FOBs, whom they view as foreigners, having external markers such as hairstyles and clothing that were different, "from another country."

Talmy explains some of the background, for this modified CA methodology, that makes Jennie's and Computer's behavior more transparent. Jennie, originally from Korea, is a ninth-grader who had been in the U.S. for two-and-a-half years; Computer, also Korean, had lived in the U.S. for six years. They and many of their ESL peers had levels of proficiency in spoken English and comprehension that contrasted with those of the more typical ESL students, newly arrived in the local community. The curriculum for the school had been developed for the FOBs; it was not based on age or grade levels, previous schooling experience, or proficiency levels, but rather how long the students had been at the school. Thus, the undifferentiated curriculum and placement policy placed all of the students in one category: they were all positioned as "co-members" of the same class where they studied with materials for third- to fifth-grade learners. Their ages and cognitive development capacities were ignored. In sum, Jennie and Computer, as well as many similar ESL students in U.S. programs, were different from the newly arrived ESLers. Jennie and Computer constructed themselves as "bad" students in opposition to the system and learning environments presumed to be helpful for all of the students. Talmy's (2009) critical analysis of their identity constructions depicts them as disliking ESL, believing they did not need it, and being aware of the low prestige attached to it. Further, he notes that they had sufficient L2 competence to signal their lack of alignment with the general perception of "ESL student" while at the same time contributing or reproducing the negative views of ESL, the ESL students, and the stigmatized ESL programs in the educational system.

Application to Classrooms

Talmy's study provides a lead-in for discussion regarding the relevance of identity studies for language educators. It depicts the learning environment of ESL students at a Honolulu high school, but the situation is by no means unique to that school. The curriculum development team ignored the complexities of the student population, where students enrolled in the system a number of years were put in the same class, with the same materials, as newly arrived learners. Many K-12 and state university branches along the Mexican–U.S. border and urban school systems confront similar learning environments and the result is inadequate language proficiency development and a low motivational level due to learners' identity issues. Menard-Warwick (2009) states that resistance to learning develops when educational systems fail to take into account identity.

The issue of identity is not limited to minority groups in such countries as the U.S., Canada, or France, seeking better employment opportunities and educational advancement, where accommodation to local pragmatic norms may be an important aspect of their repertoire of linguistic skills. The desire to belong to the "right" group also influences foreign language learners of Swahili, motivated by family background factors and a deep interest in Afropop music. Students who devote themselves to learning Russian out of a love of Russian literature may find their motivation cut in classes organized for learners who only want to pass the required language courses for graduation. Language educators can facilitate linguistic and pragmatic competence development of such students by going beyond the regular curriculum to promote motivation and encouraging further learning of a language. A conversational or pen pal, or online exchanges, where the learners exchange lessons in English for lessons in Russian, for example, may go far in addressing the important question of identity in an instructed learning environment. Teachers may function as role models and encourage outside of the classroom activities to foster learners' ongoing L2 identity construction.

Conclusions

The discussion of identity has occupied Chapter 7. It has provided background and research results that inform this very important feature of human communication. Mostly out of awareness, choice of formulaic expression and communication strategy signals pragmatic meanings that not only, for instance, display politic behavior, but also perform something of the speaker's identity. It is arguably impossible to interact with others and not simultaneously display identity. Chapter 8 takes up the topic of institutional talk and provides examples of where identity is very much involved in this category of interactional discourse.

Suggested Readings

Anataki, C. and Widdicombe, S. (Eds.) (1998). *Identities in talk*. London: Sage.
Auer, P. (Ed.) (1998). *Codeswitching in conversation: Language, interaction, and identity*. New York: Routledge.
Block, D. (2009). *Second language identities*. London: Continuum.
Duff, P. (2011). Identity, agency, and second language acquisition. In A. Mackey and S. Gass (Eds.), *Handbook of Second Language Acquisition* (in press). London: Routledge.
Pavlenko, A. and Blackledge, A. (Eds.) (2004). *Negotiation of identities in multilingual settings*. Clevedon: Multilingual Matters.

Tasks

1. Generate a list of how people signal their identities through language and provide examples. Discuss your list with classmates.

2. Timothy Mo evokes the power of prosodic features for the heroine of his novel, *Soursweet* (1982: 135):

> She lacked not the vocabulary but the inflection which might request or admonish without causing offense. Her voice, so expressive and alive in her native Cantonese, became shrill, peremptory, and strangely lifeless in its level pitching when she spoke English. She would have sounded hostile and nervous; a cross between a petulant child and a nagging old shrew, neither of which descriptions adequately fitted the mature and outward-going young woman who was Lily Chen.

What is Mo saying about Lily Chen? Relate this passage to this chapter's content.

3. In LoCastro's (1996) study of group interactions in an advanced English language class at a Japanese university, the students were asked to organize their discussion of a reading they had been assigned for homework. The following list summarizes the themes they discussed concerning the task; LoCastro had asked them to make sure everyone had a turn at talking.

   1. This is a group interaction; we have to do this together and agree on our answers.
   2. This is a classroom task; follow the teacher's directions to record our discussion.
   3. We are learners of English: use the language correctly so we can practice using English.
   4. We have a worksheet with questions to be answered.
   5. You have to be the group leader when it's your turn; elicit talk from the other group members.
   6. We are having a discussion; disagree sometimes, but keep the discussion going.
   7. We must have the discussion in English; that is, don't use Japanese.
   8. But we can use Japanese sometimes; we're Japanese and this is Japan.

   Discuss with other classmates how these eight findings display identity work. Then generate a similar list of identity signals that would become part of the talk of a group discussion you were involved in. Push your thinking!.

4. Some people feel that speaking another language and adopting its pragmatic norms is a chance to experience a different side of themselves. It can be liberating, in their view. How do you feel about this idea?

5. Discuss with classmates your own experiences with identity in your second/foreign language learning experiences. Or experiences your parents or other relatives have had.

Data Analysis

Recent studies in sociolinguistics have learned that the use of "be like" have spread across varieties of English (Meyerhoff 2006). In introducing a quote in spoken English, it was common in the past to find speakers using "say." For example, "Susie said she'd be happy to help me with the pies for the potluck." Many other quoting verbs were available, including *murmur, call, yell,* and *go* (Meyerhoff 2006: 241): "That's such a beautiful song," murmured Jill. Or "So, I went, get out of my room." These verbs introduce speech or speech presented as if it were being quoted. Within the past three decades, *be like* and *be all* are also found in many varieties of English and there is evidence that the equivalents in other languages, such as Scandinavian languages, have been added to local speech communities. Here are some examples from Meyerhoff (2006: 241).

1. A: I'll come back and she's *like,* "So Jason, how are things with Pearl?"
   B: Good.
   A: Am I still the number one woman in your life?
   (Tagliamonte and D'Arcy 2004)

2. But then I went and drove to L.A. during rush hour and I was *all,* "Hmm, Flagstaff traffic's not that bad."

3. I'm *like,* "Can I speak with Antonio?
   And his mom's *like,* "Oh, so sorry! He's not home."
   (Tagliamonte and D'Arcy 2004)

4. Lena is *like,* "You haven't done a studio film in a year."
   (Mead 2003: 97)

You can do some background reading on this fairly recent introduction of these quotative verbs. You can also study the data and use the knowledge you have acquired in this chapter and any anecdotal evidence you may have to provide an interpretation of the function of these forms and the construction of identity.

8
INSTITUTIONAL TALK

Introduction

This chapter considers a particular genre or type of everyday language in use that is as ubiquitous as conversation, yet different. Often, out of awareness, participants engage in interactions constrained by norms of institutional settings, such as classrooms, job interviews, and doctor–patient sessions, where the talk has, in fact, consequences beyond simply conveying information or achieving comity in human relations. Take, for example, the process of obtaining a driver's license in an eastern U.S. state; it goes something like this (S = Motor Vehicle Agency staff; A = applicant):

1. S: Can I have your papers and application?
2. A: Yes
3. S: (looks through the papers) OK. Move the chair against the wall . . . there (points)
4. A: Should I leave my glasses on?
5. S: You can (silence – takes the photo with the machine on the opposite wall) OK.
6. S: Move up close to the machine (for the eye test)
7. A: OK
8. S: Read the letters at the bottom
9. A: (reads the letters and hesitates between a C and an O)
10. S: Read them again

There are noticeable features of this reconstructed talk between the Motor Vehicle Agency staff member and the applicant. In the context of processing the applicant's request for a driver's license, there is minimal use of language, consisting of short phrases, few markers of politeness (line 1 has a question rather than a command form), and deictic cues (line 3: "there;" and "the letters at the bottom" for the eye exam) that are ambiguous without the physical context of the cubicle and the eye exam machine. Further, the applicant provides minimal responses; the only elaboration – line 4 concerning her glasses for the photo – was to avoid having to repeat the photo step in the process. In some countries, Mexico being one, all official government photos prohibit glasses and one's hair has to be pulled back so that the full face is visible.

This example is one of the many contexts in everyday life where the talk, which may look like "normal" conversation, is in fact constrained by the norms and expectations of this genre of institutional talk. Some language-in-use strategies are allowable; others are not. The staff at the Motor Vehicle Agency only used the applicant's first name to let her know that her new license was ready, after she asked if she could use the restroom while she was waiting. Responding to a telephone customer survey about reasons for dropping one's cell phone service also involves the same, basic norm of institutional talk: answer the questions and politely. A common saying of using wisdom in dealing with bureaucracy reflects this norm: "Say only what you have to say – don't elaborate on reasons or you could get yourself into trouble."

Chapter 8 reviews, first, the notion of activity type, a useful framework to increase understanding of institutional talk. Then, examples of this genre of talk raise awareness of the creation of sociopragmatic meanings and emphasize, in particular, the enactment of bias and disadvantage in gate-keeping encounters. It becomes clear that differences are found both in intercultural as well as intracultural workplace settings. Macro, extralinguistic, or sociolinguistic dimensions intersect in interactional discourse and contribute to both the interpretation and production of pragmatic meanings that require micro linguistic analysis.

Activity Type

Contextual features are without exception significant in any instance of language in use. In institutional talk, what is allowable, what is constrained, even prohibited, develops over time according to such dimensions as the goals that are relevant for the particular institution. For example, any enterprise that sells goods to customers, from Selfridges on Oxford Street in London to the local 24-hour convenience shop, uses phrases such as "how can I help you?" to send the pragmatic message that the institution cares about its customers and, of course, wants to achieve its goal of making money! A question in a courtroom trial in the U.S., posed by the plaintiff's lawyer to the defendant, is likely to be designed strategically to convince the jury members to infer the defendant committed the crime. Each institutional context – from the Motor Vehicle Agency to the British Parliament – entails allowances and constraints regarding the use of language that occurs.

The theoretical basis for this approach to analyzing talk in institutional settings derives from the work of a famous contributor to pragmatics, specifically regarding how humans interpret meaning of utterances: Wittgenstein. He is known for introducing the concept of "language games" (1958) in his philosophy of language writings. His view emphasizes that language is embedded in human activities of all sorts and his intuitions reflect an effort to view speech acts and speech events as inseparable. His insights were valuable at a time when some scholars were challenging the insistence of others, such as Searle (1969), for focusing exclusively on speech acts. Levinson (1992: 68) explains that Wittgenstein was attempting to account for a very noticeable feature of talk, that "understanding of what is said depends on understanding the 'language game' in which it is embedded over and beyond whatever meaning the words or sentences may have *in vacuo*." From a sociopragmatic perspective, no word or sentence could have any meaning whatsoever in a vacuum, as there is always a context, even if only in the mind of the speaker.

Rather than the term "language game," Levinson (1992) introduced the notion of "activity type" to refer to "any culturally recognized activity, whether or not that activity is co-extensive with a period of speech or indeed whether any talk takes place in it at all" (1992: 69). Some characteristics of activity types that Levinson highlights are:

- Focal members who are goal-oriented and socially constituted;
- Events that are bounded, imposing *constraints* on participants and the setting.

Prototype examples would be a job or immigration interview, an oral academic presentation, workplace staff meetings, trials, and doctor–patient sessions. The explosion of paperless procedures or communication has presented new examples.

Getting a driver's license, as mentioned above, entails an interview with the applicant while the Motor Vehicle Agency staff member completes the application online, asking the applicant to check the information on a computer screen in front of the applicant, and adding information, such as height, weight, and date of birth. The two individuals interactively fill out the form with language and two computer screens. The questions by the staff may be functioning to detect, as well, possible fraud and invalid information (the person who physically is present to obtain a license may not be the person who is wanting to get a license). Levinson admits that "activity type" is a fuzzy category as none of the examples are completely static, pre-planned interactions. Further, there is the issue of how one knows an activity has started and finished. Levinson comments on changes in the style of talk from formal to informal language use or vice versa that could signal that a different genre of talk is beginning. However, any assumption that the informality in an academic advisement session with a faculty member and student in the U.S. implied that the student may use the faculty member's first name would be incorrect. Finally, Levinson (1992: 70) argues that it is difficult to account for the extent to which speech is embedded in a particular activity type. A fairly ritualized activity type, such as playing bridge or bingo or a wedding ceremony encompasses many nonverbal moves, whereas a telephone conversation is mostly about language: word choice, turn taking, speech acts, and prosodic features. A slight change in the tone of voice in a phone conversation triggers inferential schemata that a face-to-face interaction may not register as noticeable, where eye contact, posture, and head nods can override what might otherwise have been interpreted as conveying negative or unwelcome pragmatic meaning.

Activity type serves as the framework for the analysis of the talk in the examples that follow. The focus is on interactional discourse and the pragmatic meanings that are enacted in the context of the activity type in question. Levinson's categorization provides a means to assess the data and achieve insights regarding sociopragmatic meanings at the micro discourse level as well as at the more macro strata of meanings beyond the instance of talk.

Oral Examinations

This section presents studies of Japanese students who faced situations where their pragmatic competence in English was inadequate. They had demonstrated sufficient competence (on a TOEFL or the Cambridge First Certificate exam) to be enrolled in content or writing courses at a university; in other words, they were not in a class to learn English. However, high test scores do not necessarily indicate advanced academic literacy skills required for spoken and written assignments in the oral examination genre.

The first study (Mori 1996) examined tutorials in which Japanese first-year university students discussed their essay drafts in one-on-one conferences with their writing teachers, who were native speakers of English. The focus was on students' strategies to (1) signal non-understanding, (2) confirm information, and (3) request clarification. The talk between the teachers and learners was audiotaped and analyzed for linguistic and nonlinguistic cues related to the three research points of interest. The analysis highlighted how the learners enacted the three types of action in the context of a writing tutorial in the L2.

1. S: em I . . . my topic is m . . . recent education should change . . . should change
2. T: current, you mean education the way it is now? the way people are educated now in Japan should be changed?
3. S: yes
4. T: so current education
5. S: current?
6. T: current . . . world is happening now current education should be
7. S: Oh, I see . . . changed the (method of) current education should be changed okay

Source: Mori 1996: 73

The teacher's contribution in line 2 suggests that the student needed help with vocabulary. Then the student made a clarification request in line 5 by repeating the word "current" using rising intonation, implying the word was unfamiliar to her. However, it is possible that the student was doing a confirmation check; that is, trying to make sure she had heard the word correctly. If this was the student's intent, then there was an instance of pragmatic failure in conveying her intended meaning. Here is another example.

1. T: all right so what are your important words in this sentence?
2. S: m . . . important?
3. T: Noriko, that's a question, in this sentence what are the important words? what are the key words?
4. S: ah!
5. S: key words a (*jaa*) democracy and critical mind
6. T: yeah yeah okay

Source: Mori 1996: 74

In this case, the student first did not understand what the teacher was trying to have her discuss, despite class discussions about "important" or "key words." The student's repetition of the word "important" in line 2 was ambiguous; it may have been a confirmation check, as the teacher interpreted it in line 3, or an indication of lack of understanding of what the teacher meant by "important."

Another instance of ambiguity regarding the pragmatic meaning conveyed by the learner is as follows:

1. T: descriptive words? are talking about descriptive words?
2. S: description? No em . . .
3. T: detail? To give more detail?
4. S: detail? no
5. T: is that what you mean? Hirono? is that what you mean words that that give lots of detail?
6. S: ah, yes
7. T: okay, but show me . . .

Source: Mori 1996: 88

In this exchange, the student seems to have given up attempting to convey her own intended meaning and just accepted the teacher's interpretation. However, because the student's response in line 6 is ambiguous in propositional content and in intonation, the teacher asked the student in line 7 to show in her draft what her concern is. The learner was apparently unable to pose questions to the teacher or to comprehend the pragmatic norms for a writing tutorial with a native speaker teacher. The ability to benefit from tutorial sessions with instructors entails higher level, academic vocabulary, question strategies to elicit help, and pragmatic competence in the L2 to gauge instructors' meanings.

Hiraga and Turner (1995, 1996; Turner and Hiraga 1996) studied interactions of Japanese students in fine arts tutorials with their professors in British academic settings. They were interested in the differing perceptions of allowable content in British academic, one-on-one sessions where British tutors assess students' abilities to describe and discuss their own work, for the purpose of awarding final grades for the academic year. As can be observed in the examples above, the Japanese students tended to have unelaborated responses, which is contrary to the British expectations regarding this institutional setting. Here is one example:

1.	British tutor:	what kind of music do you like best?
2.	Japanese student:	minimalism
3.	BT:	I wonder what it is about minimalism that you like so much?
4.	JS:	em . . . this has a feeling . . . of em, er, techniques of Nihonga
5.	JS:	ah [after a noticeable pause, the tutor went on to elaborate]

Source: Turner and Hiraga 1996: 132

The British tutor was attempting to get the Japanese student to explain more explicitly her artwork, which the two of them were viewing in a studio. This example illustrates a mismatch between expectations about oral final examinations. The sociopragmatic mismatch may be due to the Japanese student's inability to process and respond to the tutor's use of what are called "leading questions," where elaboration concerning rationales for creating the work, making connections with the student's other artistic interests, such as music, and with a traditional artistic style of her home country were expected. These leading questions were to give the student the floor to develop extended talk. The student's perceptions, influenced by practices in Japan in the same kind of context, may have led her to avoid speaking about her work in an elaborated way. Cultural beliefs vary, not only with Japanese students, influencing the extent to which students feel comfortable in oral speech contexts, in particular discussing their own work. It is also possible that the student did not yet possess the proficiency level in English to use her L2 in this context despite this examination event having occurred at the end of a year of art school classes. The student and teacher have different expectations about not only what is allowable – to talk explicitly about one's work – but also what was dispreferred – unelaborated, vague or overly flowery responses, lacking in specifics. In Mexican Spanish academic discourse, such as at thesis defenses, a style called *rollo* is valued and considered more polite and more appropriate for the students' defending their theses than the highly organized, carefully timed events observed at U.S. institutions.

Yet another context where international students at tertiary institutions experience demands that entail learning sociopragmatic norms concerns oral academic presentations (OAP). This academic literacy hurdle must be overcome to become members of the discourse community of their targeted professions.

Morita (2000) studied the processes students in a graduate TESL program in Canada went through to become socialized to perform this speech event. In particular, she examined how the nonnative speaker students learned to produce a good OAP through discourse socialization. Morita used an ethnographic approach and collected data that consisted of classroom observations, video recordings and transcriptions, interviews with teachers and students, questionnaires, and relevant documents from the course. The course required every student to present a research article, assigned on the syllabus, and lead the class discussion on the article. Difficulties arose, however, because the teacher expected the presenters to avoid simply repeating the content in the article. Rather they were expected to provide their own analysis and critique the article, what Ohta (1991) labeled "epistemic stance." Epistemic stance "is an important aspect of language socialization because novices must learn how to display their knowledge (or lack thereof) in a way that demonstrates their competence as members of the social group" (Ochs, cited in Morita, 2000: 89). In carrying out this function of explicitly stating their own epistemic stance regarding the article, the presenters were expected to trigger a discussion that would engage all members of the seminar. In so doing, the presenter would attempt to act as the "expert" on the article and related content areas. The "performance was socially and collaboratively constructed" (Morita 2000: 89).

For the international students in Morita's study, the OAP proved to be problematic (as it was for at least some of the native English speakers in the course). Morita states that there were three reasons the international students in her study (N = 6) had problems with the OAP format: linguistic, sociocultural, and psychological. The linguistic reasons included their concerns about their proficiency levels in English. Morita claims that difficulties in the classroom discourse arose primarily because of their lack of communication skills. They had problems taking turns in discussions, for example, which caused them to feel uncomfortable. Another source of insecurity was their perceived lack of training in critical thinking and other intellectual skills. The psychological difficulties grew out of their lack of confidence, often the result of linguistic and sociocultural gaps and pressures they experienced.

To address those insecurities, experienced by both the international students and native English speakers, teachers modeled OAPs to provide a baseline norm for the activity, thereby demonstrating their expectations, in effect, role playing the activity. The six international students in Morita's study developed a variety of strategies to overcome their perceived limitations: (1) rehearse the OAP multiple times; (2) prepare clear handouts and outlines; (3) prepare careful notes in English for themselves; (4) choose an article on a topic on which they already had some expertise; and (5) use audiovisual aids skillfully. Both the teachers and students involved viewed the OAP not so much as a problem due to less than native speaker-like language proficiency in English, but rather as part of their acculturation into the academic discourse community. The students, both international and native English speakers, needed to be guided or socialized to participate and to become proficient members of the new discourse community.

Oral examination contexts are institutional sites where differing expectations concerning allowances and constraints become salient and the stakes high if the student does not display knowledge in the anticipated manner. In an oral exam event in France, when asked about Napoleon I and his contribution to the history of France and Europe, the test-taker attempted to explain his role by categorizing his life events in terms of social, economic, and political contributions. However, the tester for the exam came from a different perspective, prevalent in that cultural and institutional context, that expected the student to present the names of the wars with dates, of Napoleon's wives and dates, and, in general, facts and dates. The international student did not pass that part of the general exam!

Doctor–Patient Discourse

This type of institutional talk has been of interest to researchers for several decades and more recently has been a concern of not only doctors and other health care professionals, but also the whole industry that has developed around the provision of medical services and products to increasingly diverse populations; for example in areas of the United States where local demographic statistics did not previously include Somali immigrants, as in Minneapolis, Minnesota. The main focus of the research earlier comprised concern for the communication strategies used by doctors and patients in consultation sessions and the potential for misunderstanding and bias due to inappropriate or inadequate conversational moves in the interactions. Now, major pharmaceutical companies study doctor–patient discourse to learn how they can increase their sales figures and in particular persuade patients to comply with doctors' prescriptions for medications. Others study the various paper documents, such as the required flyer that pharmacies must distribute along with the prescription to patients. The flyers explain the contents of the drugs, the side effects, and other information that may prevent such behaviors as drug overdose or extreme reactions that lead to hospitalization. Connor *et al.* (2008) have assessed this type of institutional talk, in written form, to learn whether or not the recipients actually read the flyers and, further, how the pharmaceutical companies could improve their efforts to communicate important information to the patients. Still another interesting example of research (Schwabe *et al.* 2008) on language and doctor–patient discourse concerns the use of linguistic analysis, specifically conversation analysis, to assess doctors' listening skills to distinguish patients who present with different types of seizures. It has been found that patients with epileptic seizures provide a coherent account or narrative of their experiences, whereas patients with non-epileptic seizures give inconsistent and difficult to understand accounts. The different types of seizures require different medications and treatments. Thus, neurologists can improve their diagnoses and avoid misdiagnoses through careful attention to patients' communication behaviors.

Not only do doctors and other medical personnel seek to improve their communication with patients and their families, but so also do industries related to health care. They are all motivated to learn by studying discourse in a variety of settings to provide more "customer friendly" services. For patients themselves, medical personnel who have more receptive modes of communication and good listening skills empower patients, increase the level of satisfaction, and improve treatment outcomes. An important focus of research on interactional discourse in this institutional context is, thus, medical professionals' communicative competence.

Roberts and Sarangi (2001) researched medical students' styles of interaction with patients, in the context of a training program for medical students in the U.K., specifically the assessment procedure that was part of their final exam. The exam consisted of 25 simulated consultations where trained actors played the roles of the patients and students played the medical doctors. The interactional skills of the student doctors in videotaped role plays were assessed by the researchers and the examiners at the medical school. They evaluated the students on their ability to carry out the medical interview as well as their capacity to establish a relationship with potential patients. Roberts and Sarangi focused on evidence of attempts to create a more patient-centered consultation through the students' conversational skills. In particular, they looked for evidence of what they labeled as "empathetic" and "retractive" involvement styles. Empathy, or rapport, commonly refers to the ability to identify with the addressee and is manifested in a variety of ways, including the use of phrases such as "I know how you feel," or "I can understand your concerns." The researchers note, further, that "trained empathy," where the speaker may overuse these formulaic routines, can have the opposite effect and derail efforts to show empathy to a patient. The notion of a "retractive" style, the opposite of empathy, was coined to label behaviors that expressed detachment.

One example of empathetic style from Roberts and Sarangi (2001: 105–6) involves the use of tropes or metaphorical language to shorten the distance between the doctor in training and the actor-patient:

1. Medical student [MS]		what's happening is that you're drinking more than you should (. . .) and your stomach doesn't like it
2. Actor-patient [AP]		ah [overlapping speech]
3. MS		[overlapping speech] and your liver doesn't like it either
4. AP		mm (short pause) mm (overlapping speech)

The assumption is that metaphorical speech, where the doctor candidate anthropomorphizes the human body – "your stomach doesn't like it . . . and your liver doesn't like it either" – increases the closeness of the two participants. This strategy does entail that the patient shares the same understanding or it may lead to confusion. Patients who may be uncomfortable with medical terminology or talking about parts of their bodies may be less intimidated by the medical setting and personnel through this form of personalization of the consultation.

This lessening of the distance between the professional – the doctor – and the patient contrasts with what Roberts and Sarangi (2001: 107) call the "schema-driven progression and patient labeling" that typifies the retractive styles. It is characterized by rapid questions, topic shifts, and lack of any perceived effort to get the patient involved:

1.	MS	any rashes or
2.	AP	no don' think so
3.	MS	discharge (short pause) have you yourself had any discharges at all
4.	AP	no
5.	MS	any erm (short pause) irritation down there
6.	AP	no
7.	MS	any pain when you're passing water
8.	AP	no
9.	MS	erm (short pause) any blood in your urine
10.	AP	no

In this excerpt from the medical history and review of the current patient complaint, the medical student communicated to the patient a lack of interest in her/his situation through the sequence of questioning in a bald, interrogatory style, as if the only important aspect of the consultation was the diagnosis rather than displaying empathy or making efforts to build rapport. It is as if the more social dimensions, enacted through pragmatic meanings of solidarity, compassion, and a joint problem-solving frame (Roberts and Sarangi 2001), and deemed to be increasingly important in modern medical practices, are subordinated or virtually absent from the discourse of the doctor.

Other research on doctor–patient discourse concerns the asymmetrical relationship between doctors and patients. Needless to say, doctors throughout the world are viewed as in possession of expertise and knowledge that patients or laypersons do not have access to. Despite this clear, unequal situation, Heath

(1992) points out that the patient does have a certain degree of power; a doctor cannot begin a medical exam and then provide a diagnosis without relevant information that only the patient or a guardian can present. The consequence of this asymmetry is at times a delicate management issue, particularly if the patient has considerable lay expertise in the illness.

Heath (1992) carried out conversation analysis of naturally occurring doctor–patient talk to assess the ways in which doctors and patients handled the issue of asymmetry in the context of the diagnosis of illness. He found that patients generally subordinated themselves to the medical professionals even in cases where the doctor may present a medical assessment very briefly and without discussion. Heath concludes that "both doctors and patients contribute to (the) brevity" (1992: 260). At times a patient may try to elicit information of the sort seen in the following example:

1. Patient: What is it doctor if yer (don't) think that's a rude question, is it?
2. Doctor: Wehhhllh huh I don't think it's a ru:de question I mean I think it's jus:t (.) you know (.) (t) I think it is:: probably pai:n from your hear::t

Source: Heath 1992: 265

The patient mitigates her/his attempt to elicit the doctor's opinion in several ways: interrogative form; "yer," a dialectal form, instead of "your," a negative verb form in the first part of the conditional structure, taking the possible blame for the question by labeling it "rude" and then a tag form. The doctor's response is full of signals of discomfort: preface of hesitation markers at the start; elongating the vowels on five of the words; short pauses (.); the phrase "you know" the word "probably" and the repetition of "I think." These verbal strategies not only obfuscate the response, but also suggest an underlying anger with the patient. The patient is hesitant, perhaps embarrassed to make the request, and the doctor is also hesitant, reluctant to give a response, likely sensing at an unconscious level that the asymmetric relationship is being challenged.

Anecdotal evidence in Western nations that have experienced movements supporting the empowerment of women is abundant concerning the management of the relationships between patient and doctor. The sociopragmatic norms of talk in medical consultations of all sorts have been changing as society recognizes the rights of all patients, not just women, to ask questions, obtain all relevant information in diagnoses, and expect appropriate care, while at the same time having their needs respected. Medical practitioners who have not changed their patient care routines and developed communication strategies that are patient centered find patients do not return to them for care. Another recent change has been the increasing interest in preventive medicine and alternative and complementary medicines, as well as the massive amounts of information on health and medicine available on the Internet. Patients no longer defer exclusively to doctors and the relationship with patients has begun to shift towards a partnership, where the patients are actively involved in their own care.

U.S. Courtroom Trial Discourse

As was mentioned earlier in this book, attorneys in courtroom trials expect to ask questions and the witnesses to answer the questions. The first part of any adjacency pair entails that the second pair part be an answer. The strong expectation in American culture is that the addressee responds with some sort of response: "I'm just fine, how about you?" or "Where have you been, haven't see you for ages." The added dimension in courtroom trials is undeniably power as without the attorneys, the trial cannot proceed and the defendants and plaintiffs have hired attorneys to use their power within the U.S. legal system to win the case for them.

The power of the attorneys to coerce testimony from the person on the witness stand is particularly salient in the case of rape trials. In a rape case, typically the plaintiff is a female who has suffered a gross attack on her self, physically and emotionally. The defendant, most likely to be male, seeks to have the case thrown out of court, typically claiming lack of clear evidence and that the woman involved was "asking for it." In the example below, the lawyer (L) is questioning the plaintiff in a rape case (Levinson 1992: 83):

1.	L:	... You have had sexual intercourse on a previous occasion, haven't you?
2.	P:	Yes
3.	L:	On many previous occasions?
4.	P:	Not many
5.	L:	Several?
6.	P:	Yes
7.	L:	With several men?
8.	P:	No
9.	L:	Just one?
10.	P:	Two
11.	L:	Two. And you are seventeen and a half?
12.	P:	Yes

This example demonstrates how the attorney uses his power to ask questions of the plaintiff where, following the expectation that she merely answer the questions, she is led to construct herself as a "loose woman." The pragmatic meaning is derived from the inferences of the adjacency pairs as well as the societal context information that judges women as likely to entice men to carry out behaviors they would not normally engage in. The only allowable contribution for the female plaintiff is to respond. It is noticeable that the lawyer uses a negative tag question in line 1, which leads the witness to give the preferred response, that is, a positive answer. In line 9, no surface-level question is asked, but the lawyer's intonation is likely to make the word "just" prominent and to add a slight note of a rising tone at the end of the utterance, which implies some doubt or suspicion in her/his mind. Finally, the confirmatory question in line 11 again implies that the addressee is to give a positive response. These are all allowable contributions in the context of this activity type. The result is the construction of negative, derogatory views of women, at least in rape cases, which are created and amplified by the power of this attorney.

This courtroom construction of women came to the attention of feminists and the U.S. legal system during the 1980s and 1990s, leading to changes in U.S. laws regarding the use of language to create derogatory implicatures merely through the juxtaposition of one utterance, a question, and its response. Matoesian (2001) emphasizes the value of a microanalysis of courtroom discourse to highlight these contemporary issues in this genre of institutional discourse (LoCastro 2006). In particular, Matoesian describes and explains rape shield legislation, i.e. statutes that prevent the making of references to a victim's sexual history, which have been law since the early 1990s, both at the state and federal levels. Matoesian uses extracts from a case involving William Kennedy Smith to illustrate that, despite the changes in the definition of rape and allowable trial questioning, there are still linguistic mechanisms used by the attorneys to introduce the victim's sexual history. Attorneys used language in culturally approved ways to convey implicatures that were detrimental to the victim's case.

Here is an excerpt from the discourse of the William Kennedy Smith trial. The lawyer [L] for Kennedy Smith is cross-examining the plaintiff [V]:

1. L: You told us yesterday that Will invites you into the house, is that correct?
2. V: Yes, sir
3. L: You want to see the house?
4. V: Yes, sir
5. L: Cause you wanted to see what it looked like?
6. V: It's a landmark home it had some interest
7. L: Even though it was late you wanted to see the house?
8. V: I was uncomfortable about that . . .
9. L: So even though it was early in the morning you wanted to see the house?
10. V: It didn't appear to pose any problems for Mr. Smith
11. L: My question is even though it was early in the morning you wanted to see the house?
12. V: Yes
13. L: All right even though you were concerned for example about your child you still wanted to see the house?
14. V: Yes
15. L: Even though you had to get up early in the next morning to take care of her you still wanted to see the house?
16. V: I wasn't planning on spending any extended amount of time in the house
17. L: Now you wouldn't take off your pantyhose just to see the house would you?
18. V: No

Source: Matoesian 2001: 216

Notice that there is no explicit reference to the sexual history of the victim. Nevertheless, the attorney consistently questioned her that in a way that triggered pragmatic inferences constructing her as a woman who behaved in a manner that the sociocultural context of the U.S. would view as making herself available to Mr. Smith for sexual activity. In lines 3, 5, 7, 9, 11, 13, 15, and 17, the lawyer repeated essentially the same question, signaling to the audience in the courtroom, in particular the jury, that V's wanting to see the house very late at night was suspect, especially with a sick child at home. When the victim tried to deflect his questioning and bring in Mr. Smith in line 10, the attorney ignored her attempt and metacommunicated about his question in line 11, as if he were reprimanding her for not following the expected question–response adjacency pair. It is not until line 17 that the lawyer explicitly made a reference (taking off her pantyhose) that could be construed as making a link between that behavior and the actual sexual activity that occurred later that same night.

In sum, pragmatic inferences that get woven discursively into the discourse can be very poignant, especially when used by someone with socially recognized power. The lawyer's interrogation strategies made salient gender relations in a manner that disempowered one of the participants, in this case the female. This courtroom discourse provides a vivid example of how institutional talk constrains allowable talk and, consequently, may construct inferences detrimental to participants.

The next section looks into job interviews, a type of institutional talk of considerable interest. As globalization becomes a commonplace fact of everyday life, interethnic and intercultural dimensions of the workplace draw the attention of enterprises, government agencies, and universities as they seek to employ personnel from many parts of the world.

Job Interviews

As a site of interethnic and intercultural discourse, job interviews have experienced a spike of interest in the last decade (Kusmierczyk 2010, personal communication) in terms of scholarly articles, government research reports (Roberts and Campbell 2006), and pedagogical intervention (Louw, Derwing, and Abbott 2010). Even native speakers of the language of the job interview are not necessarily well prepared to present themselves in ways to become attractive job candidates. A job interview entails adoption of sociopragmatic norms for this talk type by applicants. All employers utilize both explicit criteria, such as candidates' being personable and friendly, self-aware, and flexible; and implicit criteria, which includes concerns about personality type, honesty, and language proficiency level (Roberts and Campbell 2006).

What is important to the employer may appear to be a quagmire to the prospective employee, particular when there are ethnic and sociocultural differences. Interviewers' criteria include nonverbal aspects such as clothing, shoes, hairstyle, make-up (for women), posture, gaze, and other features of a person's demeanor. Very importantly, the applicant needs not only to answer a variety of questions appropriately, but also to answer them in a way that meets the expectations of the potential employer. In other words, there are sociopragmatic meanings that are conveyed through the interactional use of language during the interview.

A seminal work on job interview discourse is the work of Gumperz (1982) regarding the use of contextualization cues that may contrast in interethnic communication such as job interviews. Contextualization cues comprise a large variety of linguistic forms that enable the listener to interpret pragmatic meaning. For example, a tag question at the end of a statement can invite the listener to take a turn at talk: "Lovely weather we're having, isn't it?" The expected response would be "Yes, isn't it?" Mismatches, however, can occur as seen in the example above from Turner and Hiraga (1996) where the Japanese art students did not realize that the British tutor's question was really an invitation to elaborate about their work, their attitudes and feelings, and in general demonstrate what they had learned during the academic year at the school.

In the following example from Gumperz's research, a British female speaker interacts with an Indian male speaker in the context of an interview-counseling session where the goal is to help the Indian man sort out problems related to employment. While both understand at a general level the purpose of the session, there are linguistic and sociocultural differences that become transparent in the discourse.

1. A: exactly the same way as you, as you would like to put on
2. B: (overlapping talk) oh no, no
3. A: there will be some of the things you would like to
4. B: (overlapping talk) yes
5. A: write it down
6. B: that's right, that's right (laughs)
7. A: but, uh . . . anyway it's up to you (pause about 1 second)
8. B: um (high pitch) . . . well . . . I I Miss C
9. A: (overlapping talk) first of all
10. B: hasn't said anything to me you see (pause, about 2 seconds)
11. A: I am very sorry if she hasn't spoken anything
12. B: (softly) doesn't matter (overlapping talk)
13. A: on the telephone at least
14. B: doesn't matter
15. A: but ah . . . it was very important uh thing for me
16. B: ye:s. Tell, tell me what it is you want
17. A: (overlapping talk) umm um, may I first of all request for the introduction please
18. B: oh yes sorry
19. A: I am sorry (pause about 1 second)

20.	B:	I am E.
21.	A:	oh yes (breathy) I see . . . oh yes . . . very nice
22.	B:	and I am a teacher here at the Center
23.	A:	very nice (overlapping talk)
24.	B:	and we run
25.	A:	(overlapping talk) pleased to meet you (laughs)
26.	B:	different courses (A laughs) yes, and you are, Mr. A?
27.	A:	N.A.
28.	B:	N.A. yes, yes, I see (laughs) OK, that's the introduction (laughs)
29.	A:	would it be enough introduction?

Source: Gumperz 1982: 175 (slightly modified by author to save space)

The clash of the sociopragmatic norms for this genre of institutional talk is clear. As Gumperz argues, the two interactants do not seem to reach any mutual understanding of what the job-counseling interview is about. B, the British female professional person, appears to want to get down to business quickly by referring in line 8 to a colleague who had apparently had some contact with Mr. N.A., A in the data, regarding the analysis of problems he was having obtaining and maintaining a job as a mathematics teacher in England. He was born in Pakistan, and attended secondary school in England. Thus, both A and B are educated speakers of British English. While B's orientation in this interview was to get on with the purpose, A provided evidence that he had other expectations regarding the interview. Lines 3, 17, and 29 suggest he believed that some preliminaries, such as the possible need to write down points from the interview, and then introductions, were necessary. Further, in his comments while B was introducing herself, he used a translation in Urdu "very nice" as a listener or back channel cue. Here this contextualization cue as well as the "breathy" intonation could imply sexual inferences. Further, A's word choice results in a mixed message; it is not clear if A is commenting on her personally or her position at the Center, or perhaps the Center itself.

What jumps out of the data very noticeably is the lack of synchronicity of the interactional contributions of the two speakers. The cues of discord or nervousness on the part of both A and B, which appear in the almost constant overlapping, the unexpected pitch changes (a high pitch on "oh well" in line 8), bursts of laughter, and awkward placing of listener markers, as well as the lack of agreement on what the interview was about, evidence asynchronous talk. This display of mismatched expectations derives from both linguistic differences and sociocultural knowledge. Part of the knowledge base that clashes in this instance concerns the roles of A and B and the gender difference. In A's view of the world, it may be highly unusual for a woman to be in a position of power over a man, especially one who is perhaps older than B. Further, interviews for jobs may be merely a perfunctory procedure such that

A may see the speech event in the example as unimportant and believe that B simply has to sign a paper relieving him of the need to take a course on communication skills, as recommended by another staff member of the Center.

Recent work on interethnic and intercultural job interviews has drawn considerable attention, in particular in the U.K. and Australia. Campbell and Roberts have co-authored several reports on this topic; one of particular interest in the context of this chapter concerns how institutional or work-based aspects and personal identities of interviewees are synthesized by foreign-born applicants for employment in the U.K. In Campbell and Roberts (2007), they described the critical situation for migrants in the preceding five years: 90 percent of "the lowest paid and least visible jobs in London are migrant workers . . . over 50 per cent of these migrants have tertiary-level qualifications and many are highly experienced" (p. 244). This state of affairs regarding migrant workers is not unique to the U.K. An Iranian emigrated to the U.S. several decades ago, with a Ph.D. in physics, and was unable to find a suitable job, given his education and previous work experience, in the Los Angeles area of California. The researchers looked into "the increasing demands placed on candidates in British job interviews for specific kinds of 'discursive' skill" (Campbell and Roberts 2007: 244). Iedema (2003) found that one discursive skill required the ability to synthesize personal and institutional features "to produce an acceptable identity" (p. 244). Campbell and Roberts focus on isolating the reasons interviewers reject candidates, in particular concerning personality features and stereotypes of members of the ethnic groups of interviewees. They concluded that at issue is the impression that candidates did not synthesize their work-based and personal identities to convince interviewers of their trustworthiness and consistency. For example, some interviewees, particularly after receiving advice on how to do interviews, would try to use certain key words, such as "teamwork" or "customer service," to impress the potential employer. However, their style of presentation of self was informal, personal, and viewed as unprofessional.

Campbell and Roberts' data set comprised 40 hours of recordings of 60 naturally occurring job interviews in the U.K., many at recruitment fairs of large companies, of interviewers with candidates, and retrospective interviews with interviewers as they reviewed selected videotaped interview sessions. The interviewees were white British, ethnic minority British, and others who were born abroad and thus second language speakers of English. The results provide a telling picture: the British and British ethnic minority candidates were equally successful in securing jobs, but those who were born abroad had a 21 percent lower success rate than either of the first two groups. Furthermore, there were more noticeable interactional weaknesses of the Born Abroad group than the other two groups.

The question now is to review explanations for this situation. First of all, interviewers need to develop awareness that there are undoubtedly cultural differences in how trust is enacted in a variety of contexts. Further, Campbell and Roberts cite the changing discourse requirements of workplace environments where "employees are increasingly expected to identify and conceive of their interests in terms of [the organization's] words and images" (Halford and Leonard 1999, cited in Campbell and Roberts 2007: 246). It seems that interviewers are more interested in assessing a candidate's attitudes, personality traits, and affective self than the individual's abilities to do the work for the open position. The job interview, in this changed institutional context, is more for the purpose of evaluating how candidates can portray themselves as solid representatives of "the organizational ideals of empowered individualism while making their responses fit the institutional framework" (Campbell and Roberts 2007: 247).

Candidates' failures to produce the expected synthesis are attributed to several factors. The unsuccessful candidates were viewed as being "untrustworthy" (see also Kerekes 2003), due to their mixing in their responses to interviewers' questions "rehearsed" talk and informal talk while changing topics frequently. Campbell and Roberts point out that such candidates did not have opportunities to be exposed to native speakers of British English or their communities. Given that they worked in low-paid jobs or were unemployed, they were marginalized in several ways that did not enable them to acquire the discourse skills to articulate the kind of talk expected by the interviewers. Further, and due partly to the same factors, they were unable to move in the direction of becoming bicultural individuals, particularly the homogenized self – including the personal and the institutional – that is required in the "new work order" (Campbell and Roberts 2007: 253). Here is an example of the mixing that characterizes the Born Abroad candidates' style of interviewing:

---

1. C: you can (.) I wouldn't have discussed with anybody had he not given his permission (.) so I contacted my friend in social services I mean she (.). hhh (slight laugh) contacted (.) {[ac] [lowers tone] I gave her a ring that night (.) and said look this situation's going on he knows I am talking to you about it what can he do} (.) she s- she said well I can't tell you give me his number or {[ac] here's my number tell him to ring me} (.) so fine and I had a discussion with my brother about it and er my brother said well give him my number and I'll talk to him so although they both put me out of the loop so [to speak
2. I: Yeah]
3. C: I expected [that
4. I: you] you'd sort of facilitated it (begins writing)

C = candidate, Sara, Maltese, unsuccessful; I = interviewer
[ ] overlapped talk
Source: Campbell and Roberts 2007: 258

In the context of a formal interview, Sara switched from institutional style (she uses terms such as "permission" and "contacted" and refers to the social services office) to a very personal style where it becomes difficult to follow her talk, with indeterminate pronoun referents and verb forms such as "gave her a ring." Sara uses direct speech, a lower tone of voice, and rapid speech – all markers of a personal style between friends – about helping a colleague with his childcare problems. Such talk is not convincing for the interviewer and the expectations of employees' having a "homogenized, synthetic self" (Campbell and Roberts 2007: 265) valued for employment as an "ideal worker" (p. 267) are not met.

Another researcher on job interview discourse, Kerekes, took a perspective on job interviews that includes analysis of interviewees' linguistic and nonlinguistic behaviors, including attention to sociopragmatic dimensions that led to successful outcomes. In her 2003 paper, she stated that interviewees must also trust the potential employer, a point of view which entails the co-construction of the interaction where the behaviors of the interviewers are important in leading the candidates to present themselves in a positive light and not create mutual distrust. Then, in 2006, Kerekes studied interview data where trust was established through the talk in the local context. Her study involved data from five successful job interviews; she examined both linguistic and nonlinguistic features. Kerekes collected the data sets during a fourteen-month period of participant observation at a branch of a national employment agency in California, FastEmp (a pseudonym). She participated in daily activities, including sitting in on job interviews where she video- and audiotaped them with the candidates' consent. Following those interviews, she collected reactions to the process with them. The ethnographic study comprised a variety of other forms of data to enable her to develop a grounded, rich picture of the dimensions of the research project.

Here is an example from one of the successful interviews (Kerekes 2006: 38; modified to save space):

Peter, the Candidate, and Amy, the Interviewer at Fastemp

1.	Amy	Great you saw our ad in Employment Weekly? uhu
2.	Peter	uhuh
3.	Amy	Wonderful. And um . . . you're in Burlingame so, um'd South San Francisco be a good location for you? =
4.	Peter	= definitely [within] my commuting range.
5.	Amy	[OK] Great. And you're looking for customer service?
6.	Peter	Right. That's what I seem to excel in and really enjoy
7.	Amy	Wonderful. (2) And you're available to start on the twenty-*third* which is . . . Friday?
8.	Peter	See. *yes*

= means overlapping talk; italics is for emphasis; (2) pause of about 2 seconds; [ ] simultaneous talk

In this interview, Amy sets a positive tone by using such words as "great" and "wonderful", all signaling a high involvement style. Peter responds in kind by (1) using a strong word ("definitely") to express his positive approach and enthusiasm; (2) he not only answers the questions, but also elaborates, giving some details about himself and his professional expertise and interests. This start of the longer interview suggests a level of rapport is being established which enabled Peter to feel confident; he elaborated about such factors as an employment gap on his resumé, and in turn Amy was inspired to see him as a strong candidate for the open position.

Regarding evaluations of linguistic competence of candidates, in 2007, Kerekes provided an inventory of the language use, mostly of nonnative speakers, where the baseline was their abilities to answer telephone calls and follow written instructions. That inventory includes the following items (Kerekes 2007: 1947–8):

Non-standard grammatical forms, such as "ain't"
Enunciation
Ease others had to understand the candidate
Ability to comprehend, explain clearly, and answer questions
Writing ability
Ability to understand such topics as safety rules and to follow instructions

In addition to these linguistic features, one that is more specifically sociopragmatic concerns the use of directness vs. indirectness (Kerekes 2007: 1950). Appropriate use of directness requires advanced language skills and intercultural awareness that many L2 users find difficult. Still another language feature is informal or casual communication styles. Kerekes found that less successful candidates tended to use more casual or "lax" speaking styles. This example clarifies this notion of "lax" talk (p. 1951):

Julie: when you say "lax," can you explain more?
Renata: In comparison to other interviews, body language, grammar, actually his grammar was fine just, very, almost laid back. Which is fine, which is fine, it's a norm for that type of position.

Renata claims that a lax style is fine for some jobs. Her pragmatic meaning communicates that, however, that style may not be appreciated for other types of jobs.

Note that nonnative speakers are not the only job candidates who find themselves disadvantaged due to language use that does not meet the expectations of the institutions. Undoubtedly, the findings of these research studies may apply to many, if not all, gate-keeping situations. The next section looks at another institutional context, the workplace itself, and the discourse requirements of that environment.

Workplace Communication

During the last several decades, an interest in workplace literacy and institutional talk and the communication strategies that are entailed has grown and arguably must develop even more as the multilingualism and globalization of business continues. The workplace may be a context where more is at stake and more tensions may arise due to the diversity of employers and employees even within one sector of business. Small towns in Minnesota and North Carolina in the U.S. suddenly find growing populations of speakers of several languages previously foreign to those communities. Migration across borders is commonplace worldwide as individuals and their families seek employment and a better life as economic migrants. Miscommunication in the workplace would not be unusual as these populations interact with each other as well as local groups, as they deal with the situated, institutional discourse of work environments. Researchers seek to understand the sources of the problems of communication to give advice and develop programs that are effective in meeting the needs of all concerned towards amelioration of the issues and the creation of effective spoken literacy skills in using the expected institutional forms of talk. The following examples illustrate how sociopragmatics is involved in workplace environments.

At issue in Katz's (2000) study is the extent to which proficiency in the language of the workplace, i.e. linguistically correct grammar, pronunciation, and lexis, is the locus of the problem, or the discursive creation regarding values, roles, and identities by the populations involved. Katz looked into workplace or vocational ESL classes offered by a California company to its employees where 90 percent of the workers on the production line were immigrants from Michoacán, Mexico, who all spoke Spanish. The fact that a high percentage of the workers were from the same area of Mexico led to an almost familial atmosphere at the company, a dimension that made it more difficult to work for change amongst the workers.

Most of the managers were males of European-American background. Some mid-level managers were of Mexican origin and some of the lower level managers were women. The goal of the language program was to help the employees become more fluent in English and to enable them to better understand and use workplace discourse, placing emphasis on language skills to deal with the problems experienced as "cultural differences between workers and managers." The managers saw the root of the tensions as "language" problems. In addition, they wanted the language program to put emphasis on the workers' personal and professional growth within the workplace.

Katz observed classes and interviewed teachers, managers, and workers who participated in the non-compulsory program. She also studied the various teaching and curriculum materials, employee handbooks, and internal memos. Katz's findings highlight an underlying model of competence promoted by the management that differed from that of the workers. The managers expected the employees to "speak their minds, step forward with new ideas and ways to solve problems, and show what they know by sharing that knowledge with co-workers" (Katz 2000: 152). In contrast, the participants in her study demonstrated that a valued worker in Mexican culture was likely to work hard and in behind-the-scenes contexts be helpful to her fellow employees. They prefer not to stand out in a crowd and draw attention to themselves, at the production floor or at group meetings, despite repeated attempts by the managers. The fact that a high percentage of the workers came from the same area of Mexico led them to view the workplace as an extension of their strong familial and community ties. Thus, their notion of identity brought their place of work into their conceptions of self, very much anchored in their home values regarding gender roles, group membership, and unequal status relationships. These more collectivist notions contrasted with the assumptions of the managers, who put value on independence, low social distance, speaking out, and allegiance to the company. By not speaking out, by remaining silent even when invited to talk, the workers were viewed as "pulling rank." It was interpreted as a move to create more social distance between themselves and the managers.

Here is an example from an employee's classroom discussion where the learners and the teacher reviewed a story about promoting one female character or another.

1.	Sarah	Jessica
2.	Jeanine	Juan? Jessica or Susanna?
3.	Juan	Jessica
4.	Jose	Jessica
5.	Jeanine	OK all of you would do Jessica why?
6.	Juan	'cause you know, she stay quiet and work always
7.	Jeanine	But Susanna's a good worker, she . . . learned quickly. And Susanna's she's not afraid to talk about to XX. Why do you want Jessica and not Susanna?
8.	Jose	No like (laughs) [lines deleted]
9.	Marianna	I prefer Jessica (said with a rising intonation)
10.	Jeanine	because
11.	Marianna	Because you know she always work? She no talking too much.

Source: Katz 2000: 153–4

This simulated discussion in class with Jeanine, the literacy teacher, provides evidence of the thinking and beliefs of the employees that contrast with the type of employee who usually gets recognition in workplaces in the U.S. Jeanine had written the story for class discussion to make visible the invisible so that the workers at the company would notice the differences between styles of communication and the preferred style of the management. While the issues were simplified in the story, as Katz explains, Jeanine's attempt produced a revealing view of the underlying fault lines in that workplace. Clearly, the models of competence and the underlying sociocultural values embedded in the discourse resulted in mismatches that occurred at this company. The management's articulated concern about increasing productivity led them to engage in efforts to improve and change the situation at the local site, whereas the predominantly Mexican workers preferred, as evidenced in their language behaviors, to remain loyal to the cultural model of their home community, transported in a sense to California from Michoacán.

In another part of the world, New Zealand, Schnurr, Marra and Holmes (2007) carried out two case studies of leaders, one from a Pakeha (New Zealanders of mostly European origin) workplace and the other, a Maori or indigenous workplace. They analyzed business meeting openings and the use of humor to look into leadership behaviors and adherence to politeness norms of the two culturally different environments. At issue is the ability to carry out behaviors that enact both their professional and ethnic identities as well as evidence respect for socially appropriate interactional norms of each workplace. The researchers' data in these two case studies came from the Wellington Language in the Workplace project.

The sociopragmatic norms concerning the management of meetings and use of verbal strategies in disagreement situations in the two workplaces contrasted, causing discomfort in the following two ways:

1. The tendency on the part of the Pakeha leaders to "dispense with formalities" at the start of meetings to save time suggested a disrespect for formalities viewed as important in welcoming the members attending the meeting.
2. Maori employees experienced humiliation when Pakeha members openly and directly criticized individuals for behavior they considered to be unacceptable.

(Schnurr et al. *2007: 726)*

Further, the use of humor served to illustrate the clash between the two styles. Humor serves several functions, such as signaling group, perhaps ethnic, identity; building social solidarity; maintaining or enhancing face; and mitigating damage to face. It can also legitimize face attack, a form of "contestive humor," used to criticize other members of the workplace group. As might be expected, the mismatch of humor in the two different workplaces was noticeable. In one example given in Schnurr *et al.* (2007), a complaint about an unnamed employee who had not cleaned the microwave shared by the staff and left it in a very dirty state resulted in a "respected leader" performing a humorous skit. The Maori style used indirectness to bring the issue to light, without naming any individual. A Pakeha office would be more likely to circulate a written memo concerning the etiquette of cleaning the microwave after using it. What is considered amusing in one sociocultural context reflects the cultural values of that particular speech community. Despite the vast changes that are occurring regarding alignment with international business models, local practices reflecting local beliefs and expectations are still prevalent.

The expectations of being a professional person and enacting leadership goals while at the same time taking into account situated interactional language use, which reflect the dominant sociocultural norms, is as much of a challenge in the New Zealand context as it is on the production line in the California company.

Applications to the Classroom

Development of pragmatic competence to function successfully in institutional contexts requires, first, recognition of the importance both for educators and students of the role of pragmatics in the world of work. The most highly educated individual, with multilingual proficiency in several languages, may not pass muster if the person is unaware of the various communication skills discussed in this chapter or they are ignored.

The studies and excerpts discussed point to several commonalities that cut across the varieties of institutional talk:

- Each activity type has norms regarding language use.
- Listening skills are as important as speaking skills.
- Language proficiency includes accuracy.
- Formal and informal use of language is required.

These four generalizations from the studies provide a baseline of features of institutional discourse for development of programs to train job seekers, management personnel, and new employees in need of further on the job training. More specific details of a program would include such items on a syllabus as learning how to elaborate on one's skills and competencies, use indirect rather than direct speech in formal contexts, or improve one's speech style and accent to achieve intelligibility. Lessons on questions would be wise so that participants can understand the functions of that language form from a pragmatic perspective. Doctor–patient discourse entails awareness raising concerning language skills to increase patients' sense of success in getting needed information and help. In general, a solid English for specific purposes course, for example, would seek to empower the students through knowledge of the connections between language, use of power, and achievement of communicative goals. Individuals or groups who may attribute their lack of success in functioning in institutional contexts to lack of language proficiency may come to realize the complexities and yet work towards overcoming the difficulties.

Conclusions

Chapter 8 has reviewed institutional talk as a topic within pragmatics that has become important to support concerns about the enactment of discrimination in interactional discourse. With the greater diversity in the workplace and international enterprises, both due to the transnational migration of people worldwide, research in this area has provided useful input for educational and training institutions. The next chapter addresses the related topic of language, gender, and power and overlaps with this chapter on institutional talk. Similar issues regarding discrimination arise with power and gender. Indeed, power and gender displays pervade social environments where language, again, plays a major role.

Suggested Readings

Bhatia, V. K., Candlin, C. N., and Allori, P. E. (Eds). (2008). *Language, culture and the law: The formulation of legal concepts across systems and cultures*. New York: Peter Lang.

Drew, P. and Heritage, J. (Eds.) (1992). *Talk at work: Interaction in institutional settings*. Cambridge: Cambridge University Press.

Heritage, J. and Clayman, S. (2010) *Talk in action: Interactions, identities, and institutions*. Oxford: Wiley-Blackwell.

Koester, A. (2004). *The language of work*. London: Routledge.

Matoesian, G. M. (2001). *Law and the language of identity: Discourse in the William Kennedy Smith rape trial*. Oxford: Oxford University Press.

Tasks

1. Why is the ability to use formal and informal language an important factor in many institutional contexts? Explain and give supporting examples.
2. What is an activity type? Why is it a useful concept when studying language in use? Provide at least one example.
3. Discuss how cultural norms become transparent in an activity type you are familiar with. Elaborate.
4. What is the role of questions in two of the types of institutional talk discussed in the chapter? How can a person, expected to respond only, deal with this type of preference organization?
5. What are contextualization cues? How does being a good listener help, especially in intercultural contexts?
6. How do you feel about being expected to elaborate on your own skills and competencies? Discuss this communication strategy with others in your group.

7. What advice would you give to someone who is nervous about going to a doctor's appointment? Your friend complained that the doctor does not give her the advice she needs.
8. Collect some data of you and your friends telling stories. Look at how often direct or indirect speech is used. When is one style more likely to occur in the flow of the talk?
9. Are you aware of any negative stereotypes connected in the U.S. with the use of direct speech in formal environments? Interview some older people about this and prepare to report back in class.

Data Analysis

The following excerpt is from Kerekes' (2006) study of successful job interviews. Maria is originally from El Salvador, where she did assembly work in a toy factory. She has had no formal training in English. She has, however, good listening comprehension and she wants to study and develop her skills to integrate into a new life in the U.S. eventually.

Analyze the data and discuss some qualities of Maria that resulted in this interview being successful. Note that Carol is the interviewer.

1.	Carol:	And what are your long-term goals?
2.	Maria:	Hm?
3.	Carol:	What are your long-term goals?
4.	Maria:	What is what is that?
5.	Carol:	Uh: do you know what a goal is?
6.	Maria:	Go oh goals my goals?
7.	Carol:	yes
8.	Maria:	Oh yeah yeah yeah I understand you. You know my goal is . . . try to fi fi find something good in my life for my future
9.	Carol:	Great!
10.	Maria:	Yeah I have a have a good job maybe try to make a career something for my yeah because it's terrible when you try to find something and nobody help you (laughs)

Source: Kerekes 2006: 52

9

LANGUAGE, GENDER, AND POWER

Introduction

In the 2008 U.S. presidential primaries for the nominee of the Democratic party, one question batted about below the radar of the media was: which is more important, gender or race, in the minds of the public in the privacy of the voting booth? In other words, is sexism surrounding Hillary Rodham Clinton stronger than racism *vis-à-vis* Barack Hussein Obama for the voting American public? A related issue arose once Sarah Palin became the running mate for Senator John McCain on the Republican ticket. She suddenly became the center of constant media attention on how she dressed, her style of talking, and her self-construction as a "hockey mom." Her own gendered presentation of self drew the attention of the media and the public even in the debate with Joe Biden, Obama's running mate. Race had been put on the back burner of the stove, while sexism and gendered behaviors were front and center.

While no studies, to my knowledge, have been carried out on this complex, but empirical question of the relative importance of race and gender, much anecdotal evidence supports the view that sexism is more salient than racism in the contemporary U.S. Despite strong beliefs on the part of younger women that the U.S. has become a post-racist, post-feminist society, there is still discrimination on the basis of gender in society. Women still only earn 67 cents to the $1.00 men earn.

This chapter focuses on the intersection of language, gender, and power in the comprehension and production of pragmatic meaning in interactional discourse.

Clearly, there are other social variables that are cited in the analysis of how power is enacted in talk: race, age, ethnicity, nonnative speaker identity, and educational background, to name several. In many gate-keeping situations, such as at border crossings with government agents, more than one variable or feature of an individual may be made salient and becomes noticeable for the individuals in the interaction. Gender may or may not be highlighted. Gender has received much attention in the past several decades and serves here as an example of how one aspect of identity is worthy of study in the context of pragmatics. Ortner (1974: 67) makes the claim that the secondary status of women in society is "one of the true universals, a pan-cultural fact," although the actual treatment of women and their relative power may vary enormously.' Indeed, one aim of this chapter is to shed light on gender in non-Western societies.

The chapter first takes up the topic of gender, in particular the various means that enact that aspect of identity in language use. The following sections review definitions related to the topic before taking a look at seminal work on gender in the West.

Enactment of Gender in Language Use

Evidence of what seems to be a universal treatment of females abounds, at least in parts of the world where research has been carried out. Sociolinguists such as Holmes (2008) and Meyerhoff (2006) discuss the distinction between "gender exclusive speech difference" and "gender preferential speech features" (Holmes 2008: 157–60) and support this notion of gender exclusive language use with examples from Japanese women's and men's forms for some lexical items. For example, a woman addresses her father by calling him *otoosan* and a man, *oyaji*. From Yana, a North American Indian language, females call a deer *ba* and males, *ba-na*. Such gender-exclusive forms correlate with very fixed social roles of women and men in communities that tend to be highly structured. With regards to linguistic forms that signal gender preferential features, they are found in situations where the social structures are more fluid, in the process of changing, and where the features are not constitutive of a person's identity, but rather suggest membership in a social category. An important variable is the frequency of a form in an individual's speech. Women may drop their h's (a speech variable found in Australia and the U.K.) in some communities more than the men to signal membership in lower, working-class areas. The practice of h-dropping occurs in everyday words like 'ouse (house), 'ome (home), and 'arverford (Haverford) and is associated with lower, working-class male speech. In another community where the women have been able to move outside their working-class communities to secure employment in more middle-class areas, they are less likely to drop their h's and indeed provide evidence of change towards the middle-class speech norms (see research by Trudgill 1972 and Milroy 1989). Studies have shown the intersections of gender, sociolinguistic context, and identity issues, in particular the desire to be viewed as a member of a group.

Further evidence of the universality of the use of gendered language comes up with the depiction of women as lesser members of society. The "dumb blonde" or bimbo jokes may seem like a thing of the past, but, in fact, a quick study of advertisements in mass media magazines still communicate to the readers the notion that purchase of a high-end luxury car entitles the male customer access to beautiful, blonde women. While the language used in the ad may not explicitly make the connections between the car and the woman, it is predictable that, at a subliminal level, the mental connection is made.

In addition to the standard jokes and manipulation of the mass media audience, lexical items can still be cited, despite earlier campaigns in Western countries to do away with sexist language use ("chairwoman" or "chair," rather than "chairman," as the default term), to show that sexist language is still very much present. Here is an example of this phenomenon from Holmes (2008: 318):

> The chicken metaphor tells the whole story of a girl's life. In her youth, she is a *chick*, then she marries and begins feeling *cooped up*, so she goes to *hen parties* where she *cackles* with her friends. Then she has her *brood* and begins to *hen-peck* her husband. Finally she turns into an *old biddy*.

All of the italicized items refer to animal imagery. This metaphorical language constructs women in a negative way, as similar to a chicken, as feather-brained and incapable of intellectual activities. Whole books have been written on the sexist language in English, and derogatory views of women are so commonplace that they remain below the radar and out of awareness in most communities.

Gender is also signaled in non-linguistic features. Particularly salient aspects comprise such dimensions of everyday discourse as topic uptake, silence, styles of talk, requesting information, and functions of tag questions. Certain uses of language from word choice to speaking styles are still linked negatively to female gender and serve to construct and reinforce social differences. Cultural differences abound in this regard as well, resulting in markers of being female as highly valued and therefore desirable. Newham (2005) reported on the Chinese practice of foot binding, a distinctly graphic practice as a marker of beauty and femininity, that communicated a message to the wider society that the woman came from a family that did not require her to work in the fields, that she accepted the traditional Chinese passive role for women, and that she was willing to undertake self-cultivation in all areas of life. Newham makes a connection between this practice, which dates back to before the tenth century, and the modern desire to be attractive to find a suitable husband. The significance of the foot binding thus communicates features about the woman's gender identity, at least for members of the social classes that engaged in gender work. One topic of study would be the language use of women who regarded foot binding as signal of their femininity; it is likely their language use was characterized by particular ways of speaking, tone of voice, and perhaps also vocabulary.

Needless to say, given the proliferation of research on gender and related constructs – power and identity – it would be impossible to provide a comprehensive review of the topic here. The goal of this chapter is to make a complicated area more compelling and more transparent for the non-specialist. The first section provides an overview of relevant definitions and terminology.

Definitions

It is well known that the word "gender" has replaced "sex" in not only academic fields, such as literature studies and sociolinguistics, but also in mass media and popular culture, with "sex" being reserved for use when referring to biological differences. "Gender" encompasses what Meyerhoff labels "a social property: something acquired or constructed through … relationships with others and through an individual's adherence to certain cultural norms and proscriptions" (2006: 202). The word "gendered" occurs with great frequency in the recent literature on language and gender studies, a term that clearly communicates the notion that gender is an action, something that one does. Sunderland (2004: 20–23) reviews ways in which the word is used. "Gendered discourse" is used to refer to interactional discourse of mixed-sex groups which provides evidence of dominance by one sex, by talking more, interrupting more, ignoring topics introduced by an opposite sex participant, and engaging in overt in-group comments about a topic that excludes others. It is possible for female participants to exclude the men from the conversation by bringing up topics related to child rearing, colors of lipstick, or personal feelings. However, stereotypically, it is men who are viewed as being more likely to dominate in mixed-sex groupings in Western cultural contexts.

"Gendered" can also refer to occupations, articles in popular magazines, an article of clothing, comments, certain subjects in school, or even an exercise class. "Gender" as communicating differences is, as Sunderland claims, ubiquitous. Regional or local community newspapers have whole sections devoted to fashion, food, volunteer activities, and children, directed mostly at the presumed audience of women. And academic courses include topics such as gender in the media, in the workplace, in religion, and in the family.

Research in gender studies has focused on both theoretical and methodological issues. For example, theorizing gender may seek to understand how children acquire at a very early age awareness of gender despite efforts on the part of parents to bring up their children in a more neutral home environment. Yet female children learn that pink is the color for girls. What starts as nonverbal cues of femaleness translates into differences in language use. The notion that speech styles develop in relation to gender, race, class, and sexual orientation brings up the second concern of researchers: that is, how data can be collected and analyzed to lead to more valid and reliable results that can then be used in educational systems to address issues of access and equity for all members of a community. What follows is a brief historical overview of the various theoretical perspectives on gendered language use.

Sociohistorical Overview of Gender Studies in Relation to Language in Use

This section comprises a brief review of the development of interest in language and gender. It is difficult to understand current discussions of language and gender without some knowledge of the earlier approaches. This field is characterized by pendulum swings and controversies involving the issue of the extent to which gender entails difference between men and women or dominance of men over women.

One scholar who has contributed much thought to the questions of feminism, sexism, and gender is Deborah Cameron. In an attempt to clarify some of the terminology in this field, Cameron (2005a) claims that the view that gender is a social practice was first introduced by Simone de Beauvoir in her work *The Second Sex*, first published in French in 1949. Although the title includes the word "sex," now outmoded with the preference for "gender," de Beauvoir's work was clearly a seminal discussion of the subject. Since the 1980s, "gender" has replaced "sex" as a more appropriate label for the social identity human beings co-construct through social interaction. "Gender" is, in effect, similar to a cultural categorization acquired by human beings in the course of their socialization where they learn the local norms of their communities (Meyerhoff 2006).

Note that although it is generally assumed that "sex" is a biological categorization, something that one is born with, that designation is not unproblematic. A gold medal winning runner from South Africa, Caster Semenya, has been challenged regarding her sex and forced to undergo intrusive testing on more than one occasion by track and field authorities. Scientists claim that there is no means to demonstrate conclusively whether a particular human being is male or female on the basis of such testing. Semenya identifies herself as female, as do her family members (Levy 2009). This case suggests that "gender" as a sociocultural category may be more appropriate as a means to distinguish individuals, rather than the continued use of sex and gender.

Focusing on the development of attention to language and gender within linguistics, gender entered the consciousness of researchers, undoubtedly energized in tandem with the growth of the women's movement in the U.S., concerning the role of women in society. In efforts to describe and explain the discrimination against women in U.S. society, one focus was women's use of language. Robin Lakoff's *Language and Woman's Place* of 1975 become a linguistics best seller and still remains a source to cite on the current topic. Lakoff had become increasingly drawn to consider the role of context in studying how language is used, despite her original grounding in the Chomskian approach to language. Lakoff used her own intuitions and anecdotal evidence to make claims about a set of features she viewed as characteristics of women's speech style in English. The list of characteristics that women use more than men includes (Lakoff 1990: 204):

1. more forms that convey impreciseness: *so, such*;
2. hedges of all kinds: *perhaps, maybe, kind of, sort of*;
3. intonation patterns that resemble questions, indicating uncertainty or the need for approval;
4. more indirectness and politeness; and
5. a communicative style that tends to be more collaborative than competitive.

These five characteristics (out of 14) are particularly relevant in the expression of pragmatic meaning. Lakoff does state that not all women use these features, that men may also use them for specific purposes, and gay men may adopt them (Lakoff 1990: 204). Despite empirical research that raises questions as to the validity of Lakoff's assertions, this attempt to designate a women's speech style has not been fully discredited.

The next milestone in perspectives on gender and language that grew out of Lakoff's work was the difference view that Tannen (1990) took up in publications where she claimed that differences in female and male speech are similar to sociocultural differences between ethnic or cultural groups. Tannen saw the differences arising from the way female and male children are raised and socialized in their local communities. The underlying issue that had become transparent was how differences in socialization of children contributed to male dominance in society in many areas of life. Efforts to explain how difference resulted in dominance proliferated.

One strand of research in Western societies focused on documenting the differences in female/male behavior, both verbal and nonverbal, such as interactional and communication strategies and the use of power in the workplace. One marker of the lower status of women has been their use of language, such as the tentativeness Lakoff claimed signaled uncertainty and the need for approval, both pragmatic meanings that are inferred from interactions.

Tannen published in 1993 on the need to rethink previous analyses of the characterization of such linguistic strategies and forms as "female." She claimed that, though there is no question that dominance by men of women exists, it is not possible to attribute the cause of the enactment of dominance to specific linguistic realizations of, for example, indirectness, interruptions, or topic shifts. A linguistic strategy may be ambiguous with regards to functional purpose. For example, overlapping in conversational talk or at informal meetings is not perceived universally as an effort on the part of the speakers to dominate the other participants' talk. Cooperative overlapping (Tannen 1993: 176) may carry a pragmatic meaning of displaying solidarity or camaraderie. If the interactants do not share cultural background knowledge or interactional style, the overlaps may be viewed as interruptions and attempts to control the floor. Women are as likely to overlap others' talk and steal turns at meetings as men. Tannen cites other linguistic strategies – silence vs. talkativeness, topic raising, and assertiveness – where "the impression of dominance might simply result from style difference" (1993: 179). In Tannen's view, multiple contextual variables, interactional styles, and mismatches of those styles need to be taken into consideration regarding the creation of perceived dominance in discourse.

Language and Gender

There have been several challenges to both the difference (Tannen) and dominance (Lakoff) views of language and gender over the last couple of decades. Cameron (2005a) states that the "post-modern" turn in feminist studies suggests a shift towards viewing gender as another manifestation of social diversity with "no assumption that the same patterns will be found universally" (2005a: 484–5). Particularly in the context of cross-cultural and intercultural pragmatics, it makes sense to recognize that gender may vary as an issue. Students of Japanese as a second language residing in Japan may balk at the local expectations concerning the use of language to signal femininity or gender, whereas Japanese women of any age take pleasure in using "beautification" forms (Ide 2005). Cameron (2005a: 488) points out that "cultural contrast might well be far more salient . . . than anything they share simply by virtue of being women." In other words, gender may disappear as, for instance, cultural practices become more dominant as a salient feature of an interaction. The postmodern stance sees gender not as a static, unchanging characteristic, but rather as "performed" (Butler 1990) in local contexts.

Butler's comment reflects her interest in social constructionism, perhaps the most recognized perspective currently on the enactment of power, identity, and gender. Social constructionism is based on the assumption that gender, like identity, is not a fixed characteristic of human beings. Rather, it is created in the context of everyday talk and interaction. De Fina, Schiffrin, and Bamberg (2006: 2) summarize the main tenants of this perspective.

1. Gender is a "process that ... takes place in concrete and specific interactional occasions;"
2. it forms "constellations of identities" rather than "individual" features;
3. it results from social negotiation processes; and
4. it involves doing "discursive work."

An important development of the social constructionist approach is the problematizing of assigning gender on the basis of sex and stereotypical characteristics of what it means to be female or male. It targets the folk linguistic value of labeling swearing as a practice only appropriate for men, for instance.

However, social constructionism does not address, Cameron claims (2005b), the real worldview of gender/sex, nor the institutionalized support for discrimination on the basis of gender. Cameron challenges the "relativism" of gender researchers who continue to maintain that gender is locally constructed in interactions only "when participants in an interaction explicitly make it relevant," and that an adequate analysis "should not need to import from outside the data more general ... assumptions about gender as a macro-social category" (pp. 323–4). She contrasts the "relativists" with the "realists" who argue that analysis of discourse has the goal of explaining how gender relations in society are "(re)produced" in talk. The essential issue for Cameron revolves around the question of the extent to which there are a priori assumptions about gender, power, and language use. Social constructionism, she claims, has not resolved that question by focusing only on the local, moment-by-moment participant relationships in instances of discourse. Cameron includes herself with the "realists" in seeking to explain "gender differentiation/inequality as an overarching principle of social organization" (2005b: 323). Social constructionism, in other words, ignores the taken-for-granted, outside-the-text meanings that get into talk, stemming from out of awareness values and beliefs by participants.

Address practices in many languages provide evidence of the ubiquitous concern for gender and even marital status. Until somewhat recently, women in the U.S. experienced the binary choice between being addressed by either Mrs. or Miss plus their family name. Mexican Spanish has a more neutral form, *seño* instead of using *señora* or *señorita*. Most of the time, these choices are made outside of awareness. The issue still remains, however, that gender and marital status are marked within those two cultures.

Cameron makes several points regarding the analysis of gender relations in discourse. First, she argues "the alleged problem of male–female misunderstanding appears to be common in societies where the influence of feminism has made gender relations a matter of contestation" (2005b: 328). It would be useful to compare the extent of misunderstandings in the talk of cultures where gender segregation is the unquestioned norm. Second, Cameron further questions the possibility of the microanalysis of discourse without going outside the text itself. Inferences based on shared knowledge and sociocultural background within the pragmatic framework would appear to be relevant for a satisfactory interpretation of a text. Third, related to the second point concerning the role of "beyond the data" features, Cameron notes that gender is "not only performed by speakers but also ascribed to them by the recipients of their discourse" (2005b: 330). Women in positions of power and authority experience numerous examples of such inferences, as evidenced in the 2008 media reports on Hillary Clinton during the primary race and Sarah Palin as the vice-presidential candidate.

In sum, such variables as gender, age, social class, and race cannot be ignored, even if they are not explicitly brought up in the course of a conversation. To ignore these features as constituents in discourse is to be blind to global socio-historical dimensions that play roles in local contexts. Cameron concludes by calling for pragmatic analysis that recognizes the use of inferences presupposing other information in communication from what is said or written by participants to make sense of each other's contributions.

Clearly, individuals cannot be free of the wider social, political, and economic pressures from dominant beliefs and practices that continue to stereotype one gender as, for example, women as being more polite than men, or associate an aggressive speech style as typical only of men. In contrast to what Mills (2003) calls a "utopian view of gender," in the sense that "one can perform as one wishes," she argues that gender is performed "within constraints established by communities of practice and our perceptions of what is appropriate within those ... communities" (p. 5). Clearly, some countries or societies have undergone social changes that have made identity work and gender salient dimensions. However, not all societies have had the same experiences in the past several decades and, as a result, gender may not be as highlighted as race, class, ethnicity, and religious backgrounds, for example, in choosing a political candidate to run for office. These other features may in effect be more important than gender. This description may apply as well to subcultures in the U.S., such as in speech communities of immigrant groups. The following section considers how gender is regarded outside the Western paradigm.

Non-Western Perspectives

Both of the perspectives on women's language – i.e. difference versus dominance – have been supported and challenged by research on putative women's language in sociocultural contexts outside the U.S. and U.K. One such culture, known even in folk linguistic circles in the West for its "women's" language, is Japan. Centuries ago, literate women of elite families were expected to write using the syllabary of *hiragana*; women were not expected to use Chinese characters, reserved for literate men. If they used *kanji*, i.e. Chinese characters, they were regarded as flaunting their erudition, their writings viewed as too "masculine." One famous novel of that period, *The Tale of Genji* (*Genji monogatari*), written by Murasaki Shikibu ca. 1011, was written predominantly in *hiragana*.

More contemporary discussions of Japanese women's speech style list such features as greater use of honorifics, different interactional particles, and of a high, soft pitch, especially in formal social contexts. Maynard (1990: 139–40) categorized the honorific markers as "respectful prefixes" these are more likely to be used by women:

osushi/sushi	sushi
otoomodachi/toomodachi	friend
obenkyoo/benkyoo	study

A particularly noticeable feature of everyday talk in contemporary Japan, noticeable even to visitors with basic Japanese language competence, is the affixing of honorific particles to lexical items of frequent, everyday use.

> O ohashi, omizu   (chopsticks, water)
> Go gohan, gozunji desu-ka?   (Would you like rice?)

Folk beliefs describe this practice of adding the honorific particles as solely found in women's speech. Further, the Japanese sociolinguist, Ide (2005) argues that the practice involves a Japanese tradition she labels "beautification" honorifics, a form of gendered language use that, in her view, does not correlate with dominance.

Ide explains the connection between high social status and the use of particularly "high" or elaborated linguistic forms; it is not the forms themselves that have "elegance" and "dignity," but rather the speaker of such speech. "In this way, speakers are able to index their identity as persons of dignity and elegance" (2005: 62). Common practice assigns that identity to women. In sum, Ide's stance positions honorifics as having two functions: to signal politeness, and further, to index the speaker as displaying particular qualities. According to Ide and Inoue (1991), women of higher social status tend to use more elaborated honorifics to signal beauty, grace, and dignity. It seems that, due to changes in Japanese society as a result of post World War II democratization and lessening of overt attention to social strata, women of all social levels have tended to engage in hypercorrection of their speech styles towards greater honorific use to index attributes of themselves by means of "beautification" linguistic forms.

Just as certain hand movements, styles of sitting on cushions or chairs, and positions of holding a bowl, hands, and chopsticks can communicate formality, deference, and femininity as well as respect for others and oneself, so do such forms of speech in Japanese.

While women are more likely to use the honorific prefixes, given the norms of traditional Japanese culture, men may use them. In a neighborhood sushi restaurant in Tokyo, the waiters may query customers about what they would like to drink, saying "*obiru, itadakimasen-ka?*" Rather than a more common word, *biru?* the men had accommodated to reported language change in the Kansai area of Japan where forms of female language use have become less gender specific.

Keating (1998) is another scholar who challenges the Western male dominance view on the basis of her own studies of the relationships between gender and honorific use in Pohnpei, Micronesia. She explains that in Pohnpei, it is only terms of address that index gender, with one pronoun used for both genders. This contrasts with gender being indexed in English by both referential pronouns and address terms. Further, Keating notes that "forms of address signal not only gender differences, but also relations of status" in Micronesia (1998: 123). With regards to interactional styles, research in American contexts has, for example, constructed male conversational style as being competitive in comparison to the more cooperative style of women (Tannen 1990). Yet it must be acknowledged that the data for such studies come from a white, middle and upper class, educated population. Keating contrasts this view of female/male speech of the dominant U.S. culture with findings from studies of speech in Mexico, Samoa, Japan, Madagascar, and New Guinea. She concludes by claiming that it is not possible to generate a list of linguistic features of speech that correlate with either female or male talk. She argues that status may be more important, where status is also defined or constituted according to local, situated norms (Keating 1998: 124–5).

Atkinson and Errington's (1990) work on *Power and Difference: Gender in Island Southeast Asia* includes several studies on the linkage of gender and status. The studies focus on Southeast Asian cultures, specifically Island Southeast Asia: Central Sulawesi, Eastern Indonesia, and Sumatra. Errington's remarks that Western researchers tend to consider Southeast Asian women as having "high status," as the women usually deal with household finances, often becoming traders and small shop owners. Errington problematizes such generalizations by Westerners by pointing out that "status" is constructed differently across cultures and, further, researchers working within Western frameworks may not be able to observe differences or lack of differences in other cultures due to their inability to transcend their own perspectives. Words like "equality," "power," and "woman" are all socioculturally defined and enacted. The languages of Island Southeast Asia are of the Austronesian group. Errington states that these languages are "gender-neutral." Examples of the gender-neutral features are the lack of gender marking with articles, or morphemes on nouns; specific lexemes like "human" or "person" are not marked for feminine or masculine. The local greeting is how many "older and younger siblings do you have" rather than how many "brothers and sisters do you have" (Atkinson and Errington 1990: 50). These are examples of the differences in how female and male identity is treated in this culture, in contrast to the contemporary dominant American view. Errington's work illustrates that it is important to consider the culturally embedded perspectives on gender and in particular the intersection of gender, status, and power.

Gender and Power

At this point in the chapter, it is time to introduce the elephant in the room, so to speak: power. It has a role to play in any consideration of gender, race, ethnicity, and class. Just as gender cannot be viewed as only a local, situated construction in the course of a specific instance of talk, the study of power in discourse is part of the "woodwork," as it is embedded in the practices, values, and worldviews of the participants and cannot therefore be ignored in the pragmatic meaning-makings of talk. "There are surely supra-local patterns in the way gender is enacted and talked about, which cannot be accounted for using a purely 'local' analytic approach" (Cameron 2005b: 329). The same perspective is taken in this chapter on the analysis of power in assessing speakers' intended meanings. As with gender, participants enact their background knowledge and beliefs about power and further attach features to others in the situation that entail attention to power even though there is no explicit mention of it. In the sections that follow, power as an object of study in pragmatics is considered.

Language and Power

This field of study within sociolinguistics is basically concerned with the role language plays in producing and reproducing the underlying structures of power and control in a society. Keating (2009: 997) defines power "as the ability or capacity to perform or act effectively, ... to exert control over others." The influence power affords an individual can be political, social, and/or economic and may occur in multiple situations (one neighborhood in a community gets its streets cleaned of snow first because of the affluent people living there) and in systems (the military functions on the basis of the hierarchical system that constrains how a private may address a sergeant). The enactment of power is ubiquitous. The emperor of Japan cannot apologize to China and Korea because doing so would communicate the inference that he was humbling himself to those two nations, something that an emperor in power does not do. The speech of a president of a country not only communicates content concerning a vital issue, but also maintains the face of the speaker as the main governmental leader of the country. Thus, in addition to describing and analyzing linguistic structures, the study of power also looks into how they create reality, a reality that maintains and extends power relations in society. Here are some ways power is visible in everyday language use:

- Nurses, medical personnel, and patients address medical doctors by formal terms of address, such as Dr. Murphy or Dr. Patel.
- Students in educational contexts do call their teachers by their first names in many parts of the world, but can do so with an honorific: Miss Virginia, Miss Kathie, Sir Geoff.
- Police detectives ask questions of witnesses or alleged criminals, even personal ones, when investigating a crime, but the individuals being questioned cannot inquire about the police officer's work or place of residence.

- People in high social positions may dominate others in interactions through the use of direct imperatives ("Close the door") and tag questions ("You will come on time for the next session, won't you?").
- Airport screening personnel control the language use and other behaviors of travelers at inspection points.

Once the average person becomes aware of the role power plays in everyday communicative activities, it may be difficult to ignore it as an important sociolinguistic topic in assigning speaker meaning. Power relations between and among interactants are embedded in the complex workings of cross-cultural pragmatics, displays of politeness, institutional talk, to name only a small number of domains, and this often taken-for-granted aspect of language use cannot be denied as an important factor in any discussion of language in use.

Frequently included in research on language and power is the word "critical." It reflects the view that researchers and average members of the public are aware that sociocultural issues cannot merely be described in the mass media, for example, in a neutral manner. Indeed, the study of language and power is often designated as Critical Discourse Analysis (CDA). Issues, such as the pros and cons of a new urban planning policy, are both explained and elaborated upon in the discourse of the speakers and simultaneously the discourse contributes to the embedding of the views expressed by the speakers as "normal" or "needed" for the community. There is always an ideology or point of view implicit in discourse. For instance, women in the northwestern part of England, Lancaster, may object to greetings by shopkeepers or post office personnel such as "How can I help you, luv?" or "Having a good day, ducks?" Is *luv* a sexist term? Or a display of friendliness, the interpretation usually applied to *ducks*? What may appear to be a simple greeting is viewed as sexist and a signal of male dominance and power in the greater British society. The pragmatic meaning in this example demonstrates the nonexistence of value-free, neutral language in use, reflecting and embodying bias. Within CDA and in general language and power research, "language thus becomes a part of social practice, a tool for preserving the prevailing order. It does this not only through propaganda ..." (Clark 2007: 142).

However, change is possible; human agency is potentially available and can bring about language change in social structures. Clark (2007: 142) gives the word "gay" as an example of how the term rarely means "happy" or "glad" as it did four decades ago, but rather has come to be a symbol of change within society, indeed in the international world, regarding the greater acceptance of the homosexual community for both sexes.

There are numerous ways in which power is enacted in discourse: doctor–patient interactions, courtroom trials, immigration checkpoints, and political campaigns. It can be observed in entire speech events. For instance, when the former President Clinton, a very powerful person with high international status, went to North Korea to negotiate the release of two Christian aid workers, the North Korean leader, also a very powerful person, presumably wanted his face needs met through negotiations only with someone at his perceived level of international status. Regular American government personnel were not able to achieve the success that Clinton did by having dinner with Kim.

Power relations are also played out at the micro level in discourse: the use of tag questions, turn taking, adjacency pairs, introduction and uptake of topics, politeness strategies, and choice of formal or informal speaking styles. These interactional features as well as many others may all reflect unequal power among the participants.

As is clear in the various examples, the exercise of power, like identity and gender, can be studied in naturalist linguistic data. Basic assumptions about how power and language intersect are captured in this checklist by Locher (2004: 321–2), who studied disagreement and power:

- Power is (often) expressed through language.
- Power cannot be explained without contextualization.
- Power is relational, dynamic, and contestable.
- The interconnectedness of language and society can also be seen in the display of power.
- [items deleted]
- The exercise of power involves a latent conflict and clash of interest, which can be obscured because of society's ideologies.

The final item on Locher's list refers specifically to disagreements, for instance, between a renter and a landlord. The disagreement may be current and explicit, over a noisy tenant who stays up late every evening, playing loud music that wakes up the neighbors. However, there is an element of latency involved as the landlord, due to many previous experiences with similar tenant problems, exercises her/his power through a legal document, the lease, which would support actually evicting the tenant, typically after three notices.

The following section presents examples of the complex working of language and power. The first entails a study of political discourse in Senegal and the second comprises a report on the need to assess the role communicative function in the context of gender and power factors. The uses of language exemplify the power relations in these societies.

Senegal Political Discourse

Political discourse is a genre of language in use which is often viewed as a transparent vehicle used by politicians to preserve or to seek to create their own power. The implied pragmatic meanings or implicatures function in the local context of the former Senegalese Prime Minister Idrissa Seck addressing citizens in his country about the formation of a new political party in September, 2006. The data set includes two speeches, one in Wolof, the second in French. Wolof is the main indigenous language of Senegal, whereas French is the language of the former colonial power and of the educated sector of contemporary Senegalese society. The researcher, M. Seck (forthcoming) examined these two speeches to find answers to the following research questions: Why are the two language versions different in content and style? How are they different linguistically?

The Wolof- and French-speaking communities constitute two different audiences for the speaker. The majority of Senegalese do not speak French and those that do comprise a minority; the social network that reads French newspapers and orients itself to France is likely to be composed of more educated citizens. Consequently, the former prime minister presents a different self to the two audiences as he displays his power as a former leader and in his mind a new leader.

One feature of the French speech is his use of the counterfactual conditional to gain support for his contention that he lost his position and was singled out even by the international press because he was a "yes" man whereas, in his view, he had only the best of intentions for his compatriots.

> *Il m'aurait suffi de dire oui à tout, de n'exprimer aucun désaccord, ... pour conserver tous les privilèges attachés à ma position d'alors, de quasi président de la République.*
>
> [I had only to have said "yes" to everything, to express no disagreement ... to have kept all of the privileges of my previous position as almost President of the Republic.]

A second noticeable feature is that the French speech is more elaborated, full of details about his efforts to found his own, new political party. The researcher M. Seck sites his use of verbs with what are assumed to connote positive meanings about the former Prime Minister Seck, as a man who listens and acts to bring about peace in their country.

> *Un homme qui écoute plus qu'il ne parle ... qui lorsqu'il consulte, se renseigne plus qu'il n'enseigne ... qui apaise, pacifie, harmonise, réconcilie et rassemble les différentes composantes de la Nation ...*
>
> [He is a man who listens more than he speaks, who, as he consults others, learns rather than teaches, who brings calm, harmony, reconciliation, and brings together all of the different parts of the Nation.]

Third, he includes in the French version the program for the new party: he seeks to provide security, electricity, health care, enough food, training, and employment for all citizens of Senegal.

In contrast, the Wolof version has more symbols or metaphors and jokes rather than outlines of his political platform. For example, one symbol is the *lëk* or hare, a metaphor in Wolof of intelligence, unlike the U.S. meaning where the hare connotes stupidity. Further, the former prime minister makes local references, and engages in attacks on his rival, the current president of Senegal. In addition, he adopts the local prosody while telling a narrative about the hare, of the Serer ethnic group, which enables him to make fun of the group and construct himself as a clever joker, as humorous person.

Another example of accommodation in Wolof is the use of exophoric references to demonstrate his connections with the local context that he shares with the listeners. This type of social deixis occurs in his use of the story about the hare. The hare is fast, but he cannot carry heavy things. The local pragmatic meaning is that cleverness may be important, but is not the most or only important feature. Rather endurance, energy to get things done, and the ability to do "heavy" things also must be considered. This metaphorical language serves to deride the current president, who is older (80), in comparison to the former prime minister (47), and thus less able to run the country.

The differences in the two speeches clearly demonstrate audience accommodation on the part of the former prime minister. The lack of details in the Wolof version, according to M. Seck, seems to support the view that the less educated Wolof listeners are less interested in the program for the new party than they are in the leader. The political leader's attitudes, personality, and beliefs count more and the former prime minister not only uses Wolof to appeal to those citizens, but also to construct himself as a powerful leader who addresses their needs, who is honest, truthful, and a member of their community. Language and the will to power interweave in this enactment of the former prime minister's identity construction.

Power and Communicative Function

Analysis of the communicative function of utterances illustrates the role of a variety of factors, including gender, but not exclusively gender, in a speaker's decision-making about signaling pragmatic meaning. A frequently cited stereotype of women's talk across languages is that the speakers sound tentative and seeking approval. Originally a characteristic cited by Lakoff (1975), it has been studied in data on the use of tag questions. However, empirical case studies of Cameron, McAlinden, and O'Leary (1988) demonstrate a classic example of confusion of form and function in the interpretation of data. In other words, a tag question does not always communicate hesitation and the seeking of agreement from the addressee. Cameron *et al.*'s study on women's language and tag questions brings out the importance of attending to the speech function in context to arrive at a better understanding of features of language use.

First of all, Cameron *et al.* cite the work of Holmes (1984) where she distinguishes two functions of tag questions: (1) modal and (2) affective. Modal tags are speaker-oriented, where the speaker uses a tag to express uncertainty, thus requesting information or confirmation of the information.

> You'll be home by five, right?
> The *Times* has arrived, hasn't it?

Affective tags are addressee-oriented, expressing attention to the addressee, acting as a form of mitigation or politeness.

> You're rather tired today, aren't you?
> Momo is such a beautiful cat, isn't she?

Further, affective tags can function as invitations for the addressee to participate in the talk.

> So, José, you've just come back from Peru, haven't you?
> What do you think, Henry? Not a bad painting, no?

Holmes labels this second affective type as "facilitative" tags. A typical example would seek agreement with assessments:

> What wonderful weather for sailing, isn't it?
> I think she did a good job with the painting, don't you?

Facilitative tags perform an interactional function, even if the addressee only responds with listener cues.

Then Cameron *et al.* (1988) applied Holmes' framework to two data sets: one is of casual conversation from a small corpus, part of the Survey of English Usage (SEU) from University College London, and the second, tag questions in data of unequal encounters, specifically broadcast talk where there were clear status differences in the participant roles, such as with a radio call-in program with a doctor and callers. The use of tags in the unequal encounters data was evaluated at two levels: (1) female/male and (2) women/powerful vs. women/powerless and male/powerful vs. male/powerless. The women and men who were powerful were the medical doctors while those coded as powerless were callers.

Type of tag	Women Powerful	Women Powerless	Men Powerful	Men Powerless
Modal	3 (5%)	9 (15%)	10 (18%)	16 (29%)
Affective: Facilitative	**43 (70%)**	0	**25 (45%)**	0
Affective: Mitigators	6 (10%)	0	4 (7%)	0

The differences are striking: it is the powerful speakers, both female and male, who use the tags most frequently; in particular, they used the facilitative tags. Here is an example from the study (Cameron *et al.* 1988: 90):

> I shouldn't have bothered my GP with it, should I?

The researchers explain that their research is supported by discourse analysis studies of naturally occurring talk which have found tags to be associated with the rights and obligations of the more powerful interlocutors to invite talk and keep a conversation going, at least on talk shows and during interviews. Gender is not the most salient feature here. Facilitative tags can also be interpreted as having a coercive pragmatic function:

> You'll put out the trash tomorrow morning, won't you?
> Sasha's going to do the laundry, right?

It is one of the more powerful members of a household who will use these utterances! It is noticeable in the results of the Cameron *et al.* (1988) study that the powerless participants, whether female or male, used no affective tags, and modal tags were used, irrespective of gender, by the less powerful participants.

While the findings of one study cannot be generalized easily to other contexts, it is clear that communicative function is an important feature of language use to consider when exploring the role of gender and power in language use. The next sections provide examples of recent research on how they are enacted in interactional settings.

Gender and Power in Interactions

Being a Man

Much research on gender and language prioritizes women's role and the co-construction of their identities in everyday talk. De Fina *et al.* (2006) include a section on "Becoming and being a man," with three contributions specifically concerned with the identity construction of American men where narratives-in-interaction constitute the databases. In what follows, I review one of the studies (Kiesling 2006) where the researcher, SK, interviews Mick, a white male who had just been elected as president of his fraternity at the time of the data collection. Note that SK, the interviewer/researcher, who had asked Mick to comment on the reasons he thought he had been elected, sets up the occasion; that is, provides the opportunity for Mick to discuss his identity as a powerful male in a self-report within the metapragmatic frame. The interviewer contributes to the talk on the basis of background knowledge which he shares with the speaker and which enables him to make sense of Mick's talk. This excerpt is a modified selection of Kiesling's data (2006: 271–2).

(a)	Mick	I:'m just a very:
(b)		Tha- the type of person that's goin' somewhere and and uh, whatever I mean
(f)		I mean I have I have *not* watched television in I couldn't tell you how long
(g)		I mean just don't do things that aren't very productive at all.
(i)	Mick	I don't No I don't you're right I don't ha:ng out.
(k)	Mick	No even if I go to the townhouse I'll sit there for a while
(o)	Mick	It's like. I just can't- I can't just do *n*othing.
(p)	SK	Yeah
(s)	Mick	I tore down, wa- we had a chicken coop?
(v)		It wasn't really our farm it was the closest- our closest neighbor.
(w)		But ah, it was huge.
(y)		It took me a whole summer to tear it down.
(aa)		Brick by brick I tore the damn thing down
(cc)		Like, if- I'd come in yeah, What's takin' so long?

Mick explains that he sees himself as the "type of person that's goin' somewhere." The fact that he was elected president suggests that not only is Mick this kind of person, but also that the fraternity places value on this aspect of his identity. As further evidence of this feature, he elaborates on his seriousness by not watching television or hanging out, activities that he views as wasting time. In interactions with his housemates, he comments on how focused he is in wanting to be active and not just spend time doing "nothing." Further, he had suggested to SK that his father has something to do with who Mick is, and then elaborates with anecdotal information about how he learned to work hard through his father's example and his pushing him to complete a task on the grandfather's farm. The final line in this excerpt is Mick mimicking what his father might have said, asking him why it took so long to break down the chicken coop. Mick constructs himself as a hard-working male person by narrating events to support his argument about his identity. Further, he speaks as an "explainer", communicating as well cooperativeness and a style of speech that is informal (he drops the final "g" on doing, going, bitching) and in-group (he uses words like "hang out," double negatives like "I can't just do nothing", and "damn" in (aa)). In sum, this example illustrates an instance of co-construction of masculine gender. This analysis pulls out of the naturally occurring talk micro features such as word choice, markers of informal American English style, and a grammatical non-standard form, as well as more macro pragmatic aspects. By answering the interviewer's question concerning his being elected president of a fraternity on a university campus, Mick externalizes his view of himself as a male with features he believes to be attractive for the position.

Contemporary theorists and researchers on gender and power insist on the need to go beyond individuals or even groups to look at language use in context, which includes extra-textual variables such as age, socioeconomic background, and social status as well as gender.

Imperatives in the Workplace

The next example comprises a study of the use of directives or imperatives in the workplace, specifically two government departments in New Zealand. Note that directives are speech acts that tend to correlate with enactments of power. Vine (2009) focused on the role of the social and discourse contexts on the speech acts expressed by three managers, one male and two females. Earlier research on male managers has promoted the view that they are likely to be more direct in asking subordinates to carry out activities in the workplace. However, Vine's study, which carefully considered contextual factors, questions that view. First of all, she looked at the purpose of each interaction regarding the effects on the participants as well as the frequency and choice of speech act. The purpose of the interaction was found to influence the frequency of directives. They were much more frequent with problem-solving and task allocation meetings.

Second, Vine examined the discourse context of the speech act and the more general interactional environment. With regards to the purpose of the speech act, Vine lists such activities as problem-solving, assigning tasks, and requests for weekly updates. The data she collected provided evidence that directives in the form of imperatives occurred "at the end of a long discussion of a topic and acted as a summary and clarification of the required actions" (Vine 2009: 1400). A possible explanation is that the preceding discourse "softened" the imperatives. Here are two examples from this discourse context (Vine 2009: 1400):

   a. you finish doing it and make some notes
   b. well um put a real- a really simple brief what we need to know er in order to respond to that

Participants in the interaction tolerated these direct imperatives in the context of a high-involvement, long planning meeting where they summarized actions to be taken to solve an urgent problem.

Other contexts that were conducive to directives were: (1) when multiple tasks were discussed; (2) response to questions that had been elicited by co-workers; and (3) when an immediate action was required, called a NOW directive by Vine (2009: 1401). Mitigated directives were found in the data when a topic had only been briefly discussed, the level of imposition was high, and the manager wanted a task done in a different manner.

Now, regarding the role gender played in the use of directives, Vine's data showed that "whereas fifty-one percent of all directives to men were imperative, only thirty-nine percent of the ones to women were" (p. 1403).

This is the data set from the male manager; it is close to the figure for the women managers who used directives 33 percent of the time with women. Vine suggests that an appropriate interpretation of the results indicates that the male manager demonstrated awareness of gender differences as much as the women managers. In sum, when considering both social factors and the discourse context, the male manager expressed directives with a variety of linguistic forms and strategies such that the variation was very similar to the language use of the female managers. Gender does appear to play a role, although there are other complicating factors, such as the status of Vine's participants as managers.

Apologies in Russian and English

A third study looks at the effect of culture and gender in English and Russian apologies. One of the goals of Ogiermann (2008) is to problematize the role of culture in analyzing the differences of female and male contributions in conversational discourse and the attitudes towards those differences. She compares language use for apologies in Britain and Russia in data from these communities collected by means of a Discourse Completion Task (DCT). It consisted of ten scenarios with eight targeted situations that would predictably elicit apologies. The sample size reached 1,600 responses from universities in London, Cardiff, and Swansea – where an English version was used – and from two universities in Moscow for the Russian version. There was an equal number of female and male informants.

The results of the comparison demonstrated the marked preferences for a particular illocutionary force-indicating device (IFID), expressions of regret in the English data, and requests for forgiveness with Russian informants. Ogiermann also looked at mitigation and intensification, indirectness, accounts or explanations for the offensive act, and combinations of strategies. The Russian informants apologized more without using any specific IFIDs, while the British respondents used more face-saving strategies as well as more IFIDs. The Russian speakers apologized when material damage occurred by offering to repair the offense by saying, "I will buy you new fish," rather than using a phrase such as "I apologize."

The statistical analysis of the data presented more significant differences across languages than across genders. Within each language, gender was slightly significant in Russian, but not as significant as in the British data. Ogiermann claims that the results lend support for the view that men and women do not constitute separate speech communities.

Rather than assume universal status for gender differences as a strong feature of language use, more research is needed to establish the role of other aspects of social identity in a variety of cultures outside the dominant Western perspective and research base. Further, socioeconomic changes in Russia, such that women during the previous communist regime were not able to stay at home with their children, contrasts with the contemporary Russian society where they are more likely to spend time at home as "housewives," entailing new social roles and thus new conversational styles. She also considers the status of the participants; a manager interacted differently with both temporary and permanent executive assistants than with other lower status staff. Here is an example (Ogiermann 2008: 1397):

Manager: I think it'll be too tight for this (rising intonation) (pause)
Exec. Asst: yeah
Manager: although we could wait a bit

In this example, the rising intonation on the manager's first line suggests an invitation for the executive assistant to provide her/his opinion, rather than the manager using a directive to achieve a work-related goal or task.

Conclusions

This chapter has focused on how gender and power become salient features of interactional discourse and communicate pragmatic meanings beyond the words of the human actors. A brief history of the field of gender studies in the U.S. and the U.K. provided background knowledge and concluded with a claim that lack of attention to gender or power in the context of talk-in-interaction does not mean the two sociolinguistic variables are without importance. Indeed, one task of sociolinguistics and pragmatics is to account for the role of the often unexamined, out-of-awareness enactment of gender and power, as well as race, ethnicity, and country of origin factors, in language in use. This is controversial territory, particularly for language educators, who struggle with decisions concerning teaching a second/foreign language as simply an object of study or as a means of communication, embedded in sociocultural contexts. In addition, learners from many parts of the world experience this complex area of language use in classrooms, having their L1 beliefs and practices challenged in unexpected ways. This volume's underlying intention to raise awareness and increase readers' knowledge base and understanding forms a start to come to terms with this contentious topic for teachers, materials writers, and students.

The final chapter of Part II reviews another topic of interest, particularly for language learners and educators: pragmatic competence development in instructed settings. Second language acquisition research evidences a lack of attention to just how learners can improve their competence to interact in pragmatically appropriate and successful ways to achieve their communicative goals. Chapter 10 is devoted to taking a look at what has been done and learned about this topic.

Suggested Readings

Cameron, D. (2005). Relativity and its discontents: Language, gender, and pragmatics. *Intercultural Pragmatics*, *2*, 3, 321–334.
Holmes, J. and Meyerhoff, M. (Eds.) (2005). *The handbook on language and gender*. Oxford: Blackwell.
Lakoff, R. T. (1975). *Language and woman's place*. New York: Harper & Row.
Tannen, D. (Ed.) (1993). *Gender and conversational interaction*. New York: Oxford University Press.
Weatherall, A. (2002). *Gender, language, and discourse*. London: Routledge.

Tasks

1. Provide examples in languages you know of how gender is performed in talk.
2. Review the definitions of terminology associated with gender studies.
3. Outline the sociohistorical overview provided in this chapter.
4. What are the current views of gender in language? Compare and contrast them.
5. What did you learn about non-Western perspectives?
6. How do language, gender, and power come together and interact? Give examples.
7. Why is language such an important tool for politicians anywhere in the world? Review the example of the former prime minister of Senegal.
8. Summarize the main points of the section on power and communicative function. How does power enter into this topic?
9. Review the main points of the studies in the section on power and communicative function. Make relevant generalizations across the studies that are helpful to you.
10. The conclusion refers to the often heated debate and controversies concerning the topics of gender and power. Do you agree with the point of view expressed in that section? Can you offer any explanations for the contentious nature of talk about gender and power?
11. Further, it is noted in the conclusions that learners in language classrooms may be uncomfortable with lessons on gender differences in particular. How would you handle situations that may arise in the context of discussion about gender issues?

Data Analysis

A. Study the example below of what Sunderland calls "gendered" discourse. It is an indirect way to construct gender (Sunderland 2004: 181). Explain how it can be described in that way. Discuss the evidence in the data to support your analysis and include text external features that allow for your interpretation.

1.	Romeo:	our house was a complete shithole (.) we had like um a family of slugs (.) and we used to sort of like
2.	Annie:	ahh that's gross (sneeze) I heard stories about that but I never ever met anyone that actually had slugs
3.	Romeo:	well you didn't ever see them but you saw the trails on the lino
4.	May:	yeah
5.	Romeo:	you know (?) as they were going round
6.	May:	my sister had that as well in her house in Exeter they h in their kitchen (.) when they first moved in all the snail (.) tracks everywhere
7.	Romeo:	yeah
8.	Annie:	there's ants in our kitchen it's terrible
9.	James:	um you know you know you don't want to go anywhere tropical Annie you think ants are (.) a problem (.) don't go anywhere south maybe of France
10.	Annie:	hh
11.	Romeo:	cockroaches I can't be doing with cockroaches
12.	Annie:	I hate them they're scary
13.	James:	(.) you can have the exterminator out to your house every day (.) you'll still have cockroaches
14:	Romeo:	especially the flying ones
15:	May:	that's disgusting

Source: Sunderland 2004: 181–2 (excerpt modified to fit space requirement)

B. Now, it is time to collect some data of gender and power in language use in everyday contexts. Be prepared to give a short oral presentation about your mini project. You will need the collected data in audio and/or written form and your interpretation of it. Note that data from a public source, such as radio, TV, or movie is best as there is no need to get permission to use it for your talk.

10
CLASSROOM PRAGMATIC DEVELOPMENT

Introduction

For language educators and learners, pragmatic competence development involves the issue of how they can develop that competence in instructional settings. This topic is of particular concern when teaching a foreign language, that is, outside the target language community, where there may be virtually no opportunities for contact with speakers of the foreign languages or exposure through local media sources such as newspapers, radio, and TV programs. Some argue that the Internet has solved that problem for anyone who makes the effort to search for, say, Arabic news broadcasts or other broadcasts, such as Spanish *teledramas*. However, those sources lack the important dimension of learners actually producing talk in interactional contexts.

Second language learners such as immigrants to the U.S. surely have an easier time, surrounded by the bath of American English in all areas of their lives. Yet that superficial picture of society in the U.S. may camouflage the actual lack of opportunities to become aware of the pragmatics of contemporary and regional American English in use, and the negotiation of everyday encounters. Activities such as finding and renting an apartment, negotiating accounts at banks, and dealing with medical care service personnel, themselves with origins in a variety of countries, may take place in isolated communities. Everyday life in mainstream American society provides much positive evidence on how to enact social rules of speaking and what inferences are drawn. However, negative evidence, i.e. about the glitches, or infelicities that occur, may have uncomfortable, even rather unpleasant consequences, and wind up reinforcing negative stereotypes.

This chapter addresses a variety of issues involved in the development of pragmatic competence. It focuses on instructional settings, primarily classrooms, for second/foreign language learners. The discussion is organized around a series of questions: why is pragmatic competence important for second/foreign language learners; can it be taught and learned in instructional contexts; what gets in the way of developing pragmatic competence in a classroom environment; and what other factors play a role. Finally, the chapter addresses what might be done to facilitate development of learners' ability to function in the L2. None of these questions have straightforward answers as multiple contextual factors are implicated. Much of the teaching of pragmatics may in fact depend on the creativity of individual instructors.

Why is Pragmatic Competence Important for Second/Foreign Language Learners?

Hopefully, the content of the first nine chapters of this volume has provided ample support for the conclusion that pragmatic competence for second/foreign language learners has importance even beyond acquiring high linguistic proficiency in the L2. Learning the social rules of speaking, as noted in the introductory chapter, opens doors to the community of the L2, serves to smooth entry into speech events and other occasions, and helps to break down stereotypes about the language learners and their L1 sociocultural backgrounds. Stereotypes develop and often resulting acts of discrimination occur – for example, on an uptown bus in New York City where drivers are much less willing to listen to and help someone who is obviously from elsewhere. A well-phrased question, asking for information about what bus to take, not only goes far to obtain the correct information, but also can help to break down barriers. Tips for travelers going to countries where they do not know the language advise them to learn basic phrases in that language to greet, thank, ask basic questions, and say goodbye. These phrases can smooth the social waters and present a positive image of the travelers and their country of origin and a willingness to get to know the local people.

Doing pragmatics as a second/foreign language speaker also works wonders for making people aware of the need to use socially appropriate language in their own L1 cultural environment. There is much anecdotal evidence that learning another language to a high level fosters a deeper learning of the person's L1: the vocabulary, grammar, morphology, and even pronunciation differences. This generalization holds true for the pragmatics of the L1 as well. Understanding the social rules of speaking, the role of contextual features, especially the sociocultural dimensions, and the importance attached to appropriacy and expected norms, improves for languages in general for those who have acquired a rich knowledge of another language and developed a degree of expertise in the pragmatics of that language. Note, further, that just as the linguistic systems of a language cannot be learned to any measurable point of excellence, so too does becoming pragmatic proficient in a language, even one's

L1, require a commitment over years and regular exposure to that speech community.

Development of communicative abilities and the use of appropriate language is not a topic of relevance only to learners seeking some basic proficiency in a foreign language to travel abroad. Many work environments require even native speakers of a language to be trained in speaking skills that are needed for particular job categories, such as receptionists answering phones at IBM or sales personnel in exclusive department stores who learn how to make customers feel welcome and that their emotional needs are taken into consideration in their purchase of everything from perfumes and colognes to bathroom fixtures (see Cameron 2000). Japanese young people receive training in the use of the honorific language of the business and professional world of Tokyo to prepare them for jobs upon graduation from university.

Thus, it seems to be a no-brainer that learning to be pragmatically proficient in the first/second/foreign language is worth devoting time and energy to. Lessons in language classrooms on, for instance, how to carry out speech acts in the L2, tend to be popular, where learners can more easily bring in personal experience and make connections with the real world of conversational interactions. However, the actual teaching of pragmatic competence is by no means straightforward. The next section takes up that topic and looks specifically at what researchers have contributed to this discussion.

Can Pragmatic Competence be Taught and Learned in Instructed Contexts?

This section reviews what researchers on pragmatic development have learned from their studies. The focus is on *instructed* development, that is, in classrooms, or other contexts organized for learning, as the acquisition of pragmatic competence in a naturalistic environment would involve other variables and require an entire book of its own!

Researchers who have spent a lot of time on the topic, Kasper and Rose (2002) argue that not only can L2 pragmatics be taught, but more importantly, it has to be explicitly taught. They take that stance on the basis of research that can be summarized in the following four points:

1. Research on L2 pragmatics acquisition where it has not been the focus of classroom activities results in unsuccessful outcomes.
2. Schmidt's (1993) noticing hypothesis emphasizes the need for attention to linguistic forms for learning to occur. If this research-based premise is true for grammatical items, it is highly likely it is also true for language functions.
3. Children do not typically learn the pragmatics of their L1 without adult intervention. Mere exposure is not sufficient.

4. There is little, if any, negative feedback for adult learners in communicative contexts as to what pragmatic glitches they may have enacted. Classrooms where L2 pragmatics is explicitly addressed can provide the required corrective advice.

These data-based generalizations are both intuitively meaningful to teachers and have been supported by several decades of second language acquisition research, in particular the work of Schmidt (1993) and colleagues, which has emphasized the value of the focus on form approach to teaching grammatical competence. This section provides a sampling of research-based studies relevant to the claims of Kasper and Rose regarding pragmatic competence development.

The first point from Kasper and Rose (2002) regards the requirement of explicit attention to L2 pragmatics in instruction. For example, lessons on such speech acts as requesting should highlight its function and relevant sociocultural information. Then the grammatical forms to enact requests are presented and practiced. Kerekes (1992) addressed the first stage of raising awareness by studying how learners evaluated the assertiveness signaled by native speakers of English using the following linguistic devices:

1. Qualifiers such as "It's *kind of* frustrating," "I can't seem, *y' know* . . ."
2. Tag questions using *isn't it* as "It's on reserve, *isn't it?*"
3. Neutral statements: On Thursday, at 4 o'clock.
4. Strong assertions with *definitely* or *I'm sure*.

(Kerekes 1992: 19)

The data comprise her nonnative English speaker informants reacting to short dialogues read by native English speakers with these target items. Kerekes's participants were at three proficiency levels; in addition, the researcher also looked at possible gender differences. The informants rated the native speakers for assertiveness of their speech. The learners categorized the four devices in order of salience: strong assertions, neutral statements, tag questions, and qualifiers. That is, they noticed that the native speakers used more strong assertions than neutral statements, more neutral statements than tag questions, and more tag questions than qualifiers. Further, the female native speakers were rated as less assertive. Proficiency level was a factor in the ratings of qualifiers, more so with the tag questions. There is a suggestion of sequences and, presumably as learners of the L2 improve their proficiency, their pragmatic comprehension will move closer to the ability level of native speakers of the L2.

L2 pragmatic comprehension remains an area for more research as it is possible that without adequate understanding of a co-participant's pragmatic meanings in the course of a conversation, the listener will not be able to contribute to successful communication. In addition, a commonsense rule of thumb in language acquisition is that comprehension precedes production. Studying the phonological system of a second/foreign language to become proficient in making meaningful, phonemic distinctions of the language entails being able to hear first the phonetic differences between, for example, a /b/ and /v/ in English, an important distinction for Spanish speakers whose L1 does not distinguish those sounds as meaningful phones. Appropriate production follows understanding and knowledge.

Nevertheless, most of the research carried out regarding the teachability of L2 pragmatics involves production, that is, the ability to interact in spoken discourse in the L2. Studies have focused on formulaic routines, conversational strategies, and speech acts. While many early studies on production involved international students, typically studying English in English Language Institutes at U.S. institutions, more recently, researchers have become interested in such groups as English-speaking kindergartners in immersion programs to acquire Japanese within the U.S. (Kanagy 1999). The children learn not only the language, but also the cultural practices and the pragmatic meanings of the routines of kindergartens in Japan with a native Japanese speaker teacher through observing and participating in classroom interaction patterns, including nonverbal behaviors that accompany the spoken language. Here is an example from Kanagy's study of the discourse of an immersion program (1999: 1472–3); this is the morning greeting routine – the *aisatsu* – with the whole class and the teacher:

1. T: *shusseki o torimasu. hai, ja shi . . .*
2. T: *hai, te wa ohiza. tatte*
3. S: *tatte*
4. S: *tatte*
5. T: *tatte kudasai, ne. ne. hai, ja ki o tsuke*
6. T: *kakato o tsukete yo, kakato o, kakato o tsukete*
7. T: *a: TY, oshiri wa te : buru ni tsukemasen*
8. T: *hai, koo ne. koo. ko ne. koo*
9. T: *oshiri w ate : buru ni tsukenai, ne. tsukenai, ne.*
10. T: *hai, ja moo ikkai nite yo, kotchi o mite yo.*
    (line deleted)
11. T: *supe : su o akete. Ne, hai. J no, hai, ne.*
12. T: *hai, jaa ki o tsuke – : shisei*
13. T: *A, poketto ni w ate o irenai de kudasai*
14. T: *hai, ja asa no aisatsu o shimasu*

T: we will do the attendance. *hai, ja shi*
T: OK, hands in your lap. stand up
S: stand up
S: stand up
T: stand up, OK? OK? OK? at attention
T: put your heels together, your heels, your heels together

T:	oh, TY, don't put your behind against the table
T:	OK, like this, OK. like this, like this, OK. like this
	[line deleted]
T:	leave a space, OK? J, too, OK?
T:	OK, heels together, posture
T:	A, don't put your hands in your pocket
T:	OK, we will have our morning greeting

Note that the single, capital letters are used to refer to individual students in the class.

Body posture is an inherent feature of the daily Japanese routine in primary schools; it signals attention and respect to the other participants, in particular the teacher. Deviant posture or physical stance is noticeable behavior and is regarded negatively, as impolite. This excerpt from Kanagy's primary school data vividly demonstrates the extent of the teacher's corrections of the pupils' nonlinguistic behavior at the start of the *aisatsu* that takes place every school morning at all levels of the educational system. She reminds them to put their hands in their laps, or in front of their bodies, then to stand up, and to use an *at attention* posture. Their heels have to be together, they should not lean against a wall or chair, their gaze is towards the teacher with their hands outside of their pockets, and they stand with a space between themselves, next to their desks or tables. The actual language greeting itself is short; the teacher wanted to ascertain that all of the pupils could verbalize the greeting correctly in Japanese.

S:	*asa no*
T:	*Ohayoo gozaimasu*
CLA:	*ohayoo gozaimasu, M sensei*
T:	*hai, ohayoo gozaimasu. jaa, suwatte*
S:	*suwatte*

[S: today; T: good morning; CLA: good morning, Ms. T; T: yes, good morning, sit down; S: sit down]

One student (S), usually the appointed class "manager" or leader, prompts the start of the greeting, by saying "this morning. . . ." Then the teacher greets the pupils with "good morning." The whole class in unison greets her in return, with "good morning, M teacher," using her name and the honorific marker "*sensei*." She returns the greeting and tells them to sit down, which is then echoed by the class leader. The verbal and nonverbal behaviors enact and reinforce each other to help these American pupils learn not only language, but most importantly, the pragmatic, formulaic routines that are found throughout daily life even for adults. They also learn the values embedded in daily practice in Japanese society. This routine is in fact training for adult life in Japan as offices and companies often start the work day with very similar verbal routines. Further, the nonlinguistic posture positions depicted in this excerpt are also found in numerous contexts, from tea ceremony etiquette to business meetings, dinners with higher status individuals, and job interviews. In sum, the explicit teaching of these routines, composed of language and nonlanguage behaviors, pushes learners' L2 pragmatic competence development.

Micro distinctions may be missed unless instruction focuses on awareness, illustrated with examples of pragmatic competence. Kasper and Rose's second point is illustrated by the research of Schmidt and colleagues. A basic premise is that training in language instruction starts with noticing. Since his famous study of learning Brazilian Portuguese through private lessons and interactions with native speakers while living in Brazil, Schmidt (Schmidt and Frota 1986) has been an important supporter of the need to engage the explicit attention of the learner to linguistic forms and pragmatic routines to push learning. Research on Schmidt's (1993) noticing hypothesis has emphasized that attention to linguistic forms is necessary for learning to occur. Attention that involves short-term memory processing is not sufficient. Studies have shown that the learner must *notice* in such a way that cognitive activity occurs, and presumably the features of, say, a particular verb form and its use in a formulaic expression (*Podrías ayudarme?*) to signal a polite request in Spanish are added to the long-term memory and made available for future use. If this research-based premise is true for grammatical items, it is likely to be true as well for language functions. The consequence of this statement involves explicit teaching of L2 pragmatics to promote the learning of both forms and conventions of meaning.

In their third point, Kasper and Rose (2002) draw a parallel between L1 and L2 acquisition of pragmatics. Children do not typically learn the pragmatics of their L1 without adult intervention. L1 acquisition studies demonstrate the role of caregiver intervention in the language socialization of children from the early stages of development. Children don't learn to say "thank you" without an adult in their immediate environment instructing them about the phrase and its context of use. Mere exposure is not sufficient. Thus, unlike other forms of the L1 language system that are acquired by children without instruction, the social use of language to convey interactional meanings requires a degree of explicit focus on form and context.

The fourth point of Kasper and Rose concerns one of the general characteristics of L2 acquisition that researchers have addressed. There is generally little, if any, negative feedback for adult learners in communicative contexts as to what pragmatic glitches they may have enacted. There is a noticeable lack of effort, remarked upon by students of the relevant languages, to teach local pragmatic norms to nonnative speakers. Native speakers of the target language may shy away from making learners aware of miscommunication due to local sociocultural influences. Further, research on the frequency of self-repair and other-repair sequences with native speakers of English (see Sacks, Schegloff, and Jefferson 1978) suggests that self-repair is certainly preferred. In some cultures, such as in France, corrections may be more likely to occur. However, when one student of French noticed she got corrected often while others didn't, her home stay mother commented that was because her French was good enough and could get better! Native speakers may not wish to provide corrective evidence to beginning, struggling learners.

Thus, international students with the best of intentions may be left knowing they have caused some communicative discomfort in the course of an interaction with native speakers of the L2, without any ready source of help that enables them to learn and avoid future problems. Consequently, classrooms where L2 pragmatics is explicitly addressed can provide needed corrective advice.

Clearly there are pedagogical implications of the large body of research regarding the teaching of pragmatic competence. Curriculums for language instruction require a focus on pragmatic development at all levels and awareness training about the importance of pragmatics. Actual lessons need to consist of explicit teaching of formulaic routines and the grammatical intricacies of linguistic forms in communicating pragmatic meaning as well as situational interactional opportunities for practice. Instruction is enhanced by the use of role plays and mini dramas that allow students to use a wide range of pragmatic roles and sociolinguistic abilities. Finally, the related fields of testing and assessment can, by testing for pragmatic competence, have a washback effect on curriculums and classroom activities.

The next section addresses the actual physical and interactional environment of conventional instructional contexts and some of the problems even the teacher with the best intentions may confront. The context of language teaching and learning plays a major role in pragmatic development.

What Gets in the Way of Developing Pragmatic Competence in a Classroom Environment?

This section of the discussion on pragmatic competence development addresses some of the factors that negatively affect the potential for teachers and learners to make progress within the institutional environment of classrooms. In addition, the discussion includes variables such as the ubiquitous pragmatic transfer from learners' L1, which would be present even in naturalistic environments as well. The following part takes up the issue of L1 transfer with a sampling of evidence from studies.

Transfer

One issue related to pragmatic transfer relates directly to the teaching of L2 pragmatics. Proficiency level in the second language was an early target of inquiry. It was argued that a higher level of L2 grammatical competence would result in less transfer from the L1. However, the evidence was mixed and motivated a study in 1987 by Takahashi and Beebe (1987). They looked at possible correlations between proficiency level and the extent of L1 transfer and found that lower level learners were *less* likely to transfer from their L1 as they lacked the linguistic means to enact the pragmatic meanings. The more advanced learners engaged in more L1 transfer, precisely because they could, i.e. they had the linguistic resources to do so. However, Maeshiba *et al.* (1996) found that transfer of apology strategies from their informants' L1, Japanese, was more or less likely to occur depending on the similarities of the speech act strategies and various contextual features. Positive or facilitative transfer, as well as negative transfer, took place with their informants due to those factors and not their proficiency level.

Early studies of L1 influence on L2 pragmatics were also motivated by researchers interested mostly in the problems or pragmatic failures learners of English experienced by mismatches of conventions of meaning and form across two languages. The emphasis was on helping teachers and learners themselves avoid miscommunication that arose as a result of mismatches of interpretation. For example, compliments carry different pragmatic meanings across cultures. In the U.S., they are often used as icebreakers, to initiate conversation with classmates and co-workers over the morning coffee break. Generalizations indicated that women were more likely than men to use compliments to signal attention to the co-participants' face needs as well as a desire to be friendly. However, in Asian cultures, compliments are not pragmatically appropriate and denials or deflection of compliments are likely. Despite language use changes as a result of globalization, compliments may still be frowned upon outside the world of young people. Compliments may seem harmless conversational routines; yet mixed-gender compliments may still carry pragmatic meanings that nonnative speakers of the language may not welcome.

Research results enable language teachers to understand and develop their knowledge bases in the pragmatics of the language they are teaching. The most commonly researched speech acts have been requests, refusals, compliments, greetings, apologies, and agreements/disagreements, where English is one of the languages of the study. More recently, there has been a noticeable expansion of data collection and findings regarding other languages and in research sites where those languages are used for daily interactions.

Smouse (2005) looked into the way requests are made in Xhosa, a main language of South Africa. She focused on several points. First, she assessed the grammatical competence required to formulate Xhosa requests – they require knowledge of the modal system of that language – and then the extent to which grammatical knowledge influenced the enactment of pragmatic competence. The results of her study were predictable: knowledge of the modal system was required in order to carry out requests in pragmatically appropriate ways.

Smouse added a new dimension of concern: the learners in the Xhosa as a foreign language classroom context were sensitive to the language socialization environment. In other words, learners are more likely to participate and attempt to acquire appropriate language forms and paralinguistic behaviors if they are explicitly socialized into the local practices for Xhosa.

Flores-Salgado's (2008) study of the developmental patterns for requests and apologies is helpful as she collected baseline data from thirty-six Mexican Spanish native speakers for these two speech acts using cartoon oral production tasks. The data were collected in central Mexico. The results confirm that there are two essential conditions for performing a speech act: the speakers need to have knowledge of the linguistic forms and knowledge of how and when to use them in a target-like manner. Even advanced learners of Mexican Spanish in her study need to learn the specific L2 pragmatic conventions to communicate successfully in the target language culture.

Finally, the ability to use the L2 pragmatics of a second/foreign language may have an influence on a learner's other languages. For example, an American studying Japanese in Japan finds that her second language, French, influences her pronunciation of Japanese rather than her first language, American English. Moreover, recent studies of the influence of English on the Hmong language in Wisconsin (Burt 2010) show that contact with English has changed how native speakers of the immigrant group make requests, thank, and perform interpersonal verbal tasks. In this case, the constant contact with English, their L2, resulted in transfer to their L1.

Transfer between languages, consequently, is a feature of language teaching and learning and part of awareness-raising and other learning activities. A recognition of this aspect of human language use can be dealt with positively and be valued as a communication strategy to aid achievement of interactional goals.

Classroom Input

For learners in foreign language environments, classrooms may be the only source of input on the language. However, it would be incorrect to assume that any ESL context, such as in a study abroad period, would enable learners to "pick up" the local pragmatics for requests, compliments, and apologies, particularly for adult learners. Input is necessary, but not sufficient to learn to communicate effectively in any language, even one's L1. Classrooms thus become the focus of attention regarding L2 pragmatic development. One dimension of those classrooms in this regard that is of particular interest is the need for interactional discourse between and among teachers and students. Language practice is the core environment to experience and experiment with interactional routines, discourse markers, and turn taking. However, can classrooms provide the environment for such practice?

Classroom research on interaction patterns is probably as old as the teaching profession itself, starting with the first teacher who asked, "What can I do to help the students learn more?" Or "Is there something in my way of organizing the class that influences how well the students succeed?" Probably the first known evidence of teachers' adjusting their practices to foster learning in the West is found in Plato. The so-called Socratic method, which involves the creation of dialogue between the teacher and students, with the teacher playing the devil's advocate by asking difficult, probing questions, exemplifies one teacher's solution to the age-old problem of getting students to think and talk. This approach to teaching has until recently been viewed as a Western practice. However, Jin and Cortazzi (2006) have studied Chinese "cultures of learning" and found teaching strategies in the Confucian heritage similar to those in educational environments in the West. The thinking of a famous Chinese scholar of the twelfth century, Zhu Xi, is clear in the following excerpt:

> I have observed that the sages and worthies of antiquity taught people to pursue learning with one intention only, which is to make students understand the meaning of moral principle through discussion . . . not [to] wish them to engage in memorizing texts.
> *(Gardner 1990: 31, cited in Jin and Cortazzi 2006: 14)*

Lin and Cortazzi also cite another pre-Confucian scholar, Li Ji, who describes a "good teacher" as capable of "guiding students to think for themselves" (2006: 14). Pratt (1992: 314–15) states that the teacher and learner are viewed as being part of a collective. Words such as "caring," "helping," and "guiding" are used in Chinese by his informants to explain desirable teacher behavior *vis-à-vis* learners and suggest a classroom where debate and active participation are the norm.

Classroom-centered research on interactional discourse in the U.S. has predated SLA-oriented studies. For example, scaffolding was described by Bruner, a cognitive psychologist interested in learning, in 1978, and Barnes produced his influential book on small groups and language learning in content subjects in 1976. It is important for SLA professionals to keep in mind that the field of education – in particular, educational psychology and teacher development – has contributed immensely to our knowledge of classroom discourse and learning (see Cazden 2001).

Research on language learning classrooms and the potential of interactional discourse to promote learning became noticed in the 1980s, specifically with qualitative design studies to examine teacher–student interaction patterns. Nevertheless, a discourse analytic perspective moved to the forefront of research with a book on teacher talk by Sinclair and Brazil (1982). It introduced a coding scheme for teacher–student discourse and elaborated on the role of prosodic features, such as intonation and stress patterns, in interpreting pragmatic meanings. However, few studies until recently have attempted to explain the processes – social, cognitive, and interactional – that foster pragmatic development. Recent attention to the work of a Soviet psychologist, Vygotsky (1978), has had a strong influence on primary school education. His theory emphasizes the influence of social environment in early childhood learning and the role of experts in guiding the learning of less competent pupils in the context of interactional discourse.

In the 1990s, SLA research shifted to the appropriateness of the input and facilitating learners' use of language to negotiate meaning in interactions. Studies looked at the language addressed to learners, the questions used to elicit talk, and teacher's feedback. Studies continue on learning outcomes, particularly with regard to development of pragmatic competence. K. E. Johnson's *Understanding Communication in Second Language Classrooms* (1995) is a useful recent contribution as the author uses data from a variety of classrooms to examine the moment-by-moment behaviors in teacher–student interactions. Lightbown and Spada (1999) have also looked into the effects of group work, NNS–NNS (nonnative speaker) interactions, proficiency levels, recasts, and communicative practice on learners' development.

Despite the lack of clear answers, the studies do elaborate on some of the variables in the classroom that influence second/foreign language pragmatic development. Input has been recognized as a vital dimension of the instructional environment and language educators promote appropriate language samples and activities to use the L2 in meaningful contexts by both teachers and learners.

Teachers

In addition to the opportunities to engage in interactions with others using the target language, there are other dimensions of the classroom discourse that also influence the potential for facilitative talk that promotes or compromises learning. Ever since Krashen (1982) first proposed the notion of comprehensible input, second language teachers and teachers in training have been aware of the importance of providing appropriate, adequate, and rich input to foster learners' pragmatic development. One main source of input is the teachers themselves. They provide a wide range of language input regarding L2 pragmatics, from content such as the basic rules of politeness, the need to be aware of social markers, and what to say to whom in which contexts. At the same time, they model the appropriate formulaic expressions and explain the differences in the variety of linguistic forms that can be used. The assumption is that the teacher knows the L2 code well and has studied pragmatics. In other words, the teacher has knowledge of social appropriateness in language use and can act as an informed role model for learners. However, without experience in the target language culture, the teacher may lack such knowledge.

Further, another dimension of the classroom environment often left below the radar is the multifaceted features of the teacher as a human being, a representative of a particular sociocultural and historical background, to name the arguably most important features of any teacher. They are treated as neutral beings, teaching linguistic features of a target language from a neutered second language acquisition perspective without overly engaging in inclusion of sociocultural information in lessons. This scenario is, of course, not possible, as any human activity, including teaching, has some underlying point of view or perspective that filters through the activities.

Here is an example from B. Johnson (2003) that illustrates how a teacher's values can be inferred from a short exchange with an international student:

Teacher: Guys? Do you want your wife to work?
Student 2: If she wants a job, I'll allow her to work.
Teacher: You'll ALLOW her to work?

Posing this question and the stressed intonation contour of the word *allow* communicate beyond the words used a distinct perspective about women working outside the home to the student.

Nonnative speaker teachers of the L2 are likely to be challenged at times as well, given their own perhaps conflicting identities, operating in third or hybrid spaces of L1 and L2 dimensions. A *third space* is used to explain the lives of many bilingual individuals who have lived in, for example, both France and the Philippines, and function successfully in both languages and cultures. Their identities that developed from such experience enable them to feel comfortable in both environments – or perhaps not comfortable in either. They are in neither one particular cultural and language context nor the other, but rather in a hybrid or third space that entails pragmatic competence in both languages.

Anecdotal evidence suggests that teachers are the most important factor in language classrooms as representatives of the particular L2 culture and for the influence they can exert on learners' motivation to make progress in achieving high levels of proficiency in the L2. They do not just teach a language as an object of study, but also the L2 as a means for communication with others, a responsibility that entails embedding work on pragmatic competence in their lessons and curriculums.

Materials

A third source of input in the learning environment is the materials: textbooks, dictionaries, videos, multimedia, and tests. Unfortunately, the materials may misrepresent the target language culture and its social rules of speaking. All too often they are not based on naturally occurring language research on everyday talk. Consequently, the rules of speaking, in particular politeness norms, may be distorted. Stereotypes may be reinforced or created, for example, about the level of directness used by Americans (LoCastro 1997; Robinson 1992; N. Tanaka 1988). The following example of artificial talk comes from a textbook used in junior high school English classes in Japan:

Student: For my generation, life is so difficult.
Teacher: Huh? Why?
Student: It's so difficult to be original. Lindbergh crossed the Atlantic. Others have climbed Mount Everest and gone to the moon. What's new?
Teacher: How about a cure for cancer? Could you find one?
Student: *Who, me? You must be kidding.* But I'd like to be in the famous Book of Records.

(Cited in LoCastro 1997: 252)

Perhaps this conversation could take place, but most native speakers of English would consider the student's responses in italics inappropriate. Certainly it would not be typical of talk between teacher and student and thus is arguably inappropriate in a textbook for the teaching of the English language. Thus, the cultural content of teaching materials – that is, the language examples as well as personas of the human beings in the lessons – needs to facilitate language learning.

As well as avoiding inaccurate representations of pragmatic knowledge and practices, materials should also be accessible to learners. Accessibility means that the lessons and practice sessions are connected to their daily lives in and outside the classroom. Just as language at the appropriate level is required to teach science to adolescents – not the language of academic publications such as *Nature* – so must the various discourse levels of adolescents, young adults, and older adults be recognized by teachers (Brown and Yule 1983). Language tests require passages that are accessible to test takers as well. The English language part of a Japanese university entrance examination supplies the following example of what not to do (LoCastro 1990: 351).

Boy: How about coming out with me tomorrow night? We can go somewhere . . . to eat together.
Girl: Well, actually, as it happens, *I am a little short of cash just at the moment.*
Boy: Oh, don't worry. . . . Of course, *I'll take care of the expenses.*
Girl: Well, . . . As a matter of fact, I don't eat supper because I want to lose some weight.
Boy: Oh, I can't believe that. *It seems to me that you've got a great figure.* But anyway, let's skip eating; er, how about going roller skating together?
Girl: Oh, that's impossible. *I haven't a clue about skating* and . . . I don't have any skates.
Boy: It's easy, you can get some there. . . . I'll be happy to show you how.

Girl: Well, maybe. . . . oh, I've just remembered: I'm going out with one of my school friends. . . .
Boy: *Oh heck*. Why don't you ask her if she can't come another day?
Girl: Yes, but, actually, she's leaving for home the day after, and *I shan't see her again for months*, so . . . I can't let her down. . . .
Boy: Yes, I see. Well, there's always another day. I'll be free on Friday. And *I had thought about taking in a ball game*. . . ?
Girl: . . . I've got a sociology quiz on Saturday, so I've just got to stay home on Friday and study.
Boy: Me, too, but I'm not going *to stick at home* studying just for some crummy old test.
Girl: *What a pity*! I do like intellectual boys. Bye-bye.

While there is much to be objected to in this dialogue (including the sexism of mentioning the "girl's" figure), the main point here is its dated language. It is a mixture of American and British conversational routines that does not fit the speakers, adolescents or university students. The italicized portions are the most salient instances of the sort of language that would more commonly come from the parents or grandparents of the test takers!

Learners

Still another source of input in the classroom is what the learners bring, their sociocultural backgrounds and expectations. According to Gillette (1994), learners' goals for learning an L2 are primarily a function of the social environment in which they grew up, their experiences with the world at large, and the value they attach to becoming a proficient user of the L2. A correlation between a positive level of motivation for learning an L2 and the willingness to develop their pragmatic abilities in it seems likely, although it has not been corroborated by research (but see LoCastro 2000). Further, since individual learners do live in the wider social and cultural environments, they take on board the attitudes of the speech communities towards the status of the L2. For example, in the U.S. today, Peninsula Spanish is still the status variety of that language rather than the varieties of Latin American countries. Thus, most language programs in American higher education institutions favor Peninsula Spanish, with study abroad programs in Spain. These broader societal and even global geopolitical movements and attitudes influence learners in their motivation to become pragmatically proficient in the L2.

In addition, learners also bring sociocultural expectations, embedded in the worldview they absorbed during the socialization process with their parents and community. Their attention to speech acts, degrees of (in)directness, and redressive action in the L2 are influenced by transfer from their L1 language use and norms.

Learners' social history has wider effects. Much has been done to raise the awareness of teachers about the existence of different expectations, learning and cognitive styles, discourse patterns, and communication styles in classrooms with a heterogeneous group of students (see early studies by Labov 1972). The same approach would benefit learners of any target language. Their first-language patterns and expectations have a strong influence on their behaviors in the language classroom. Consequently, teaching the linguistic forms and pragmatic realization strategies to signal such meanings as mitigation or hesitations may be easier with explicit discussion of the differences.

Another concern comes up regarding the extent to which learners can acquire accurate and appropriate language use by interacting with only other learners. Even more critical is the potential for learners to receive corrective feedback from each other, a function most learners assume is the responsibility of the teacher. It seems counter-intuitive to believe learners in groups can replace the teacher in promoting higher levels of proficiency regarding both linguistic forms and pragmatic appropriacy. Researchers have indeed looked into this topic and while earlier studies tended to find support for the stance that learners can receive corrective feedback and their development can be pushed by other learners, more recently (see Saville-Troike 2005) SLA scholars have been less positive about learners helping each other. Particularly regarding goals of high expectations of proficiency in the L2, other forms of input are viewed as necessary.

Finally, learner identities may erect obstacles to acquiring knowledge of pragmatic norms of U.S. English. Research has found that learners do not always enact or employ pragmatic norms in conversational interactions with native speakers (see Bouton's studies: 1988, 1994). Bouton's informants evidenced the ability to interpret or comprehend implicatures in English. That is, they had a knowledge base in their L2 English pragmatics. However, they did not always try to use that knowledge and, furthermore, learned it slowly when they were not explicitly taught. How should such results be interpreted? Among the many possible explanations would be the extent to which the learners are willing to compromise their own L1 strategies to communicate pragmatic meaning in favor of adopting native American English speakers' routines. Particularly international students who do not intend to remain in the U.S. after completion of their degrees may prefer to diverge from the American norms or not consider it worth the effort given their motivation to return to their countries of origin. In sum, learner identity is an issue regarding in particular production of L2 pragmatics.

What Other Factors Play a Role?

Discussions on the teaching and learning of pragmatic competence often cite individual differences, that is, factors that learners themselves bring to the learning context that may facilitate learning of the L2. Those differences relate to age, gender, socioeconomic background, learning strategies, aptitude, and attitudes, among other features. Needless to say, one or more of these features may actually impede learning. The following sections address two areas – sociocultural dimensions and decisions on whose pragmatic norms – that go beyond individual differences to consider the classroom environment and the sociocultural and institutional environments surrounding the instructional unit. This more macro level analysis of factors examines dimensions that play a role in facilitating pragmatic competence development.

Sociocultural Dimensions

Classrooms and educational systems as a whole are not without an underlying belief system, developed over many years and influenced by local philosophies of the nature of knowledge and learning. As such, language instructional contexts involve sociocultural dimensions that may or may not facilitate the goals of teachers and learners. This section looks briefly at some of those factors that play a role in language education.

Sociocultural values that are generally implicit in classroom activities include testing. Discrete-point test items that focus on pronunciation, grammatical items, and vocabulary communicate a very different approach to assessment than a test that seeks to evaluate learners' communicative competence, a form of assessment that has cloze passages, translation of discourse, and completing spoken discourse simulations. These two approaches to testing relate to teachers' theories of learning, of teaching, and of general philosophies about what constitutes knowledge of another language. The form of testing is particularly consequential regarding pragmatics. The first type is not likely to assess interactional competence. The second can. If the second type tests for pragmatic knowledge and competence, it results in students' paying attention to and recognizing the importance of developing their ability to use pragmatically appropriate language and strategies.

Professional activities such as testing and classroom practices are enacted in the broader, macro level aspects of the historical and sociocultural context where teachers function daily. Nations may impose constraints, for example, on pictures and examples of texts in textbooks; another requirement is that only female teachers can teach female students in some parts of the Muslim world. Publishers in the West require individuals in their textbooks to be representative of the population that constitutes their audience: people with glasses, those who are disabled and must use a wheelchair; older as well as young people; and males and females depicted in a variety of couplings and professional contexts. Perspectives on what constitutes appropriate materials and teaching situations interact with individual teachers and their values and classroom practices.

Another consideration is the politics of language teaching, specifically English language teaching (ELT). B. Johnson (2003) and Edge (2003) both address this issue involving questions of neo-colonialism, the decline of minority languages, the difficulties in maintaining bi- or multilingualism of immigrant groups and refugees, and the dominance of English in the globalization of business and the media. Sociolinguistic research provides numerous examples of the decision-making in Africa, for instance, concerning the language of instruction, the extent to which indigenous languages rather than English should be taught in schools, and the attempts to revive and maintain indigenous languages. Similar issues arise in former French-speaking colonies. Immigrant receiving countries, such as Australia, the U.K., the U.S., and France, struggle with the tensions over how to facilitate integration of the immigrant populations in the local communities while still helping them maintain their home languages.

Learners' local educational practices may influence efforts on the part of teachers to promote interactional talk opportunities to practice the L2 in meaningful contexts. One noticeable sociocultural feature is the extent to which learners are willing to participate actively in class activities. During observations of classroom practices and code-switching behaviors in both Japan and Mexico (LoCastro 1996), one noticeable feature was the more frequent attention the female teachers gave to the male students. The female students were relatively quiet and were not called upon to participate as much. When the researcher commented on this feature during critiquing sessions after the observations, the teachers claimed that they felt they had to give the boys more opportunities to talk to keep them from disrupting the class. In the case of the Mexican and Japanese teachers, they explained their practice as a means to keep order. It is not clear if the girls wanted to participate.

Losey (1995) found that, in her classroom-centered research on bilingual Mexican American students in a mixed class with monolingual English and bilingual Spanish/English students in California, Mexican American students spoke less frequently and, in particular, the female students spoke half as much. Her research found that all of her Mexican American informants in the study preferred more cooperative structures, rather than the more competitive one of the whole-class discussions in the American context. Further, the female students were more likely to prefer a supportive environment in peer groups and one-on-one interactions. In this case, sociocultural values supporting more cooperative interactions, especially for female students, resulted in less talk in the interactional contexts.

From an educational perspective, it is an important issue to determine if the silences result from institutional forces or policies, if there are underlying practices that serve to protect some in the school context, and whether the "muting of the students" (Losey 1995: 654–5) undermines the goal of promoting equity in learning opportunities. A cultural explanation may be particularly valid in the context of contemporary U.S. societal norms and views of Mexican Americans in general and in particular women, who within their own culture have low status.

Nakane's (2006) analysis of silence in Japanese classrooms, both in Japan and elsewhere, takes a different approach. She examined university seminar interactions in Australia composed of both Japanese-origin and Australian students to assess the two variables: participation levels and silence. In the specific discourse context of having to respond to teacher solicits, Japanese students used silence as a face-saving strategy whereas Australian students gave verbal responses. In interview data with her informants, Nakane found that they tended to cite the following reasons for practicing silence in class: (1) second language anxiety and (2) concern about producing only "correct" responses. Thus, they used silence as a means to maintain their own positive face and to avoid expressing any kind of disagreement with the instructor. The first strategy takes place when the instructor nominates them to participate in the class interactions. These strategies are not only found in Japanese students' behaviors when they study abroad, but also are common behaviors through all stages of the Japanese educational system. Japanese students use the strategies to avoid threats to their own faces and to avoid threatening the faces of their instructors.

Thus, the larger sociocultural context, now arguably at a global level, is implicated in local decisions about which language to use, whose norms to employ, and what sociopragmatic meanings are derived from interactional talk.

Whose Norms?

One of the issues addressed earlier concerns Mey's (1993) fundamental question regarding "whose norms" need to be taught and acquired by nonnative speakers of a language. There is no transparent or ready answer to this question.

Everyday life in most large cities of the world raises awareness of the diversity of peoples and the variety of accents of speakers of English, French, Spanish, and Arabic, to name only some examples, as both native speakers and nonnative speakers of those languages mix in many settings. Urban areas are plurilingual environments par excellence, leading students of, say, French to wonder just which variety of that language, with distinctive accents and stress and intonation contours, they should study. Senegalese speakers of French at a local Trader Joe's in the U.S. clearly speak differently from Parisian speakers and, given they speak English at the check-out counters, their accent in American English reflects the pronunciation of one of their native languages, perhaps Wolof, rather than that of a Parisian speaker of English. Regarding their interaction patterns, where the communication of pragmatic meanings becomes essential, Senegalese speakers of English may also use communication patterns more commonly found in their original or primary culture, of Senegal, rather than those of French-origin users of English.

French, Arabic, and Spanish are languages commonly studied in U.S. institutions where the local varieties of Arabic of Lebanon, Egypt, or Morocco become an issue in decision-making regarding which variety to teach, learn, and adopt for use in work and government positions. The complexity in language classrooms can be daunting. The diverse language backgrounds of the students and of the teachers reflect the globalized world. However, despite the linguistic diversity (Kleifgen and Bond 2009) and the rich verbal repertoire of many learners, the stated premise within linguistics is that all languages are equal in value, although they may serve different functions. Creole speakers in the Caribbean use their resource of speaking in the local creole while in that geographical area and in communities of Haitian immigrants in the U.S. Little value is attached, however, to that language in the U.S. educational system. Indeed, it is not recognized as a language, even though it has been codified and has a written literature, grammar books and dictionaries.

Thus, one fault line in sociolinguistcs and in pragmatic competence development forms along the fuzzy boundary of tension regarding language use in the real world, particularly urban environments of linguistic diversity and uneven proficiency levels of multiple languages with embedded cultural value systems. The tensions are acted out in the language classroom, the site of efforts to help learners become successful users of a target language and its resources to understand and communicate pragmatic meanings. A further complication is the attention to learner and teacher identities and the education models of the particular pedagogical contexts.

Another issue regarding norms for teaching and learning English is McKay's (2002) *Teaching English as an International Language*. In this book, McKay provides an overview of the changing situation in ELT that has evolved as English has become an international language in many sectors of nations, resulting in further questioning of the goals of teaching, learning, and materials. Citing Smith (1976), McKay (2002: 12) lists three reasons the ELT field has had to revise its goals and teachers their practices:

1. Learners of English as a second/foreign language do not have to also learn the cultures of native speakers of English;
2. English is not "owned" by native speakers; and
3. The main goal of learners is to communicate their own ideas and cultures to others, not become native speakers of the language.

While these features of English as an International Language (EIL) may seem obvious in the contemporary world, there are concerns, particularly when it comes to teaching the language systems. A debate has been ongoing concerning standards in English between Quirk and Kachru (Quirk and Widdowson 1985), who represent two opposing points of view on, in particular, the value of standards in educational contexts. Quirk argues that a standard of use is needed, rather than promoting tolerance for variation in language usage and use. Kachru, however, takes the stance that "traditional notions of standardization and models" (McKay 2002: 50) require revision. Note that Kachru refers specifically to Outer Circle countries (see Chapter 4) such as India, Pakistan, and South Africa, where educated, local varieties of English have developed that do not impede intelligibility among the varieties. The author of an earlier study, Shaw (1983), proposes a continuum of varieties of English in the following example of Singapore, an attempt to account for the use of English by individuals and at the national level:

Singlish: used with family and friends
Standard Singapore English: used for primary education and local news
Standard English: used for wider communication and official purposes

The debate continues as countries such as Singapore and Hong Kong push for projects to promote grammatical correctness in their educational system (McKay 2002) in contrast with India, which has preferred to support the development of local varieties. The discussion of varieties of English entails issues of identity, communication with the outside world, educational opportunities for advanced degrees at universities in primarily Anglophone countries, and publications in international journals in English. Thus, from the point of view of teachers of EIL, even English as a Foreign Language (EFL) or English as a Second Language (ESL), the dilemma as to what to teach, what language standard to prioritize, is far-reaching. One possible distinction to be made would entail different norms depending on the mode of the language, i.e. spoken vs. written discourse. It is, however, beyond the scope of this book to delve further into this topic.

What can be done to Facilitate the Teaching and Learning of Pragmatic Competence?

Teachers confront the reality of helping learners develop their pragmatic competence in a foreign language context. It is particularly difficult when they themselves are nonnative speakers of the language. They may have had no experience abroad in the target language environment.

It is a pressing issue when their students may even state that their goal in learning English is solely to be able to go backpacking through Europe, staying in student hostels, where "international" English is the language of communication. Clearly, they do not need English in Japan for most everyday purposes! They need English to do relational work with fellow travelers whose L1s come from many parts of the world.

Awareness Raising

What then can the best-intentioned teacher do who lives and works in an EFL sierra area of central Mexico? There is a lack of adequate teaching materials, and teacher training often focuses on ESL contexts where an underlying assumption that the learners will "pick up" the local pragmatic competence supports the lack of attention to principled attention to pragmatic development. First and foremost, the teacher from central Mexico needs to engage in activities, perhaps those she has created herself, to help her students become aware that doing pragmatics is not an unusual or foreign activity. They do pragmatics every day in their first or primary language of communication. Human beings constantly send pragmatic meanings through their use of language and language-related behaviors, such as intonation contours, tone of voice, and head movements, as well as linguistic phrases. Those behaviors are all part and parcel of human communication. Once learners develop an awareness regarding what pragmatics is and how they and their friends do it in their first-language culture, the first step is accomplished. Awareness training gives equal value to their L1 and the L2. Their language teacher can build their awareness and skills in the primary language and culture to help them become more capable of understanding and enacting pragmatic meanings in the target language.

Eslami-Rasekh (2005b: 200) states that students need information about pragmatics:

> ... what strategies are used for apologizing in their first language (L1) and second language (L2), what is considered an offence in their culture compared to the target culture, what are different degrees of offence for different situations in the two languages, and how the nature of the relationship between the participants affects the use of apologies.

Unless their attention is drawn to the L1/L2 differences, the learners may not attach any importance to them. Teachers can organize interactive presentations and discussion sessions about the differences and the language forms as well as the importance of pragmatics as a vital tool of human communication. Further, lessons can be built on student-collected data, where the learners function as ethnographers. In an FL context, they can find examples of apologizing on TV programs or feature-length movies. With awareness and lots of everyday examples from their home culture and primary language, the teacher can help the learners become ready for the next stage of pragmatic competence development.

The following suggestions can help foreign language teachers develop their students' pragmatic competence (LoCastro 2010a) through awareness-raising activities.

First, the instructor can teach about communication in general and the use of formulaic routines, speech acts, and social dimensions in the L1 about the L1. Examples are added from everyday life, such as how shopkeepers and medical personnel use language in their work to develop their businesses and communicate care and help to patients. Young people taking on new jobs are often not fully aware that they must learn how to use appropriate language to do their jobs successfully, depending on whether they are working for a law firm or an international restaurant.

The teacher can engage the learners in doing fieldwork in their own communities, so that they become ethnographers of their own lives. They can collect data by writing down informal family talk at the dinner table, or at other events by making field notes or diary entries they can share in class. For example, shops in Pakistan that sell rugs greet potential customers with cold drinks and persuasive language as they roll out many examples of the rugs they have for purchase; their language use is full of examples of pragmatic meanings. The flirtatious language of merchants at open-air markets is full of examples of persuasion. Women selling fruit and vegetables in market towns in the sierra areas of Central Mexico enact levels of politeness or lack thereof depending on whether the potential customer is interested in papayas or roasted meat.

Teachers and students can promote discussion of diversity, difference, and tolerance towards language use variation as well as nonlinguistic behaviors to create mindfulness regarding a non-deficit view of self and others. Teachers can make efforts to deemphasize the discrimination towards people who speak nonstandard dialects and who may signal different pragmatic meanings in their talk even within communities. One strategy to engage the learners is to seek out evidence of diversity in the local L1 community, have them collect data, and then develop lessons to continue to raise awareness of pragmatic meanings. The students can also collect examples in the public mass media.

The learners can develop materials for teaching people who are learning their L1 as a foreign or second language. For example, they could create a lesson to teach how to apologize in various situations for minor and more serious acts.

Once awareness is raised to make pragmatics less of a mysterious "thing," that only concerns them when they are using the target language, to make pragmatics more real for them, learners assume a different attitude and feel more engaged in their own learning to become better users of any and all languages. They are more likely to take on board the content of the lessons.

Eslami-Rasekh (2005b) suggests a particularly valuable use of translation of speech acts from the L1 to the L2 based on discourse completion tasks (DCTs). As she remarks, there are a number of published DCT-based studies that provide example of cross-cultural data for use in translation activities. By asking the learners to translate directly a speech act from their L1 into the L2, they become very aware of the difficulties of providing a "translation equivalent" that will carry the same or similar pragmatic meaning. Further, cross-cultural values and practices become more transparent in the course of such activities. Eslami-Rasekh suggests a variation of this activity where students complete a DCT using their L1 and then asking them to translate it into the L2. Here is an example of one item from Persian (2005b: 202):

> Instructions
>
> Please write in the provided spaces whatever you would say in the following conversational situations:
>
> You forget a meeting with a friend; this is the second time that the same thing has happened with the same person. At the end of the day, your friend phones you and says: "I waited for you for more than twenty minutes! What happened?"
> You:

Example responses in Persian:
> *Ei dad, agha ma baz sharmande shodim, joone to aslan nemidoonam chera*
> [Oh my gosh. Mr. We became ashamed again, to your soul I don't know at all why]
> *hamchin shod. Agha sharmandeh, feshare zendegi havasi bara ma nazashte!*
> [It happened. Mr. I'm ashamed, pressure of life has not left any attention to me]
> *Yadam raft*
> [I forgot]

Example of a response in American English:
> Oh, my gosh! I'm so sorry. I completely forgot. Can we schedule another time to meet?

The Persian responses came from Eslami-Rasekh's Persian students while the American English one was from a native English speaker. This activity can provide data for discussion of the production of pragmatic meanings in the two languages.

Another example from Persian clearly shows the difficulty of translation from a common conventional routine in that language into English:

> *Khahesh mikonam befarmaeed, ghabele shoma ra nadare*
> [Please, help yourself; it is not of value compared to your value]

In Iran, food is offered ritually and in very direct ways in comparison to the indirectness of American English speech acts to convince guests to eat and drink more at the dinner table. This ritual (*taarof*) in Persian is only with difficulty translated into English (Eslami-Rasekh 2005b: 203). Nevertheless, learners become intrigued by such activities and learn to be good observers, which will help them in their own language and culture as well as that of the target language and culture.

Variation in Classroom Interactional Patterns

The discussion earlier in this chapter noted that classroom input has a definite role to play in the pragmatic development of learners. Teachers' modeling and feedback of learners' production, such as in Kanagy's (1999) study of a Japanese–English bilingual primary school, can facilitate learning of L2 pragmatics. However, changes in classroom interaction patterns can also improve the input, particularly in the context of teacher–student interactions. Too often classroom interaction has been left out of view, possibly on the assumption that it is a form of institutional discourse that, like many others, is resistant to change. This unfortunate view greatly disadvantages the learning opportunities for students. Although pair and group work has been studied in the context of encouraging more interactional discourse, this section focuses on the teacher-fronted classroom.

The traditional IRE pattern (i.e. the teacher initiates, a student responds, and the teacher evaluates) continues to be a useful practice of discourse for many activities that involve review of assignments to check for learning. Another perspective on teachers' questioning strategies, for instance, prefers an alternative format that enables students to ask questions and provide elaborated responses, thereby fostering their pragmatic development in the L2. Here is an excerpt from K. E. Johnson's (1995: 101–2) work on variability in teacher–student classroom discourse.

1.	T:	So, what other questions do you have about this (the article) or Gay Pride Week in general?
2.	Stan:	What is this pin?
3.	Rosa:	Oh, I saw that too
4.	Stan:	I saw this on some people, but I didn't know. I thought it some politics or something
5.	T:	OK, it says, "Straight, Secure, Supportive." Do you know what that means?
6.	Stan:	Maybe some politics
7.	T:	You thought it had to do with politics? Well, you are sort of right . . . (deleted lines) do you have any ideas about what "straight" means in reference to what we have been talking about, in terms of Gay Pride Week?
8.	Rosa:	Opposite, no gay
9.	T:	The opposite of gay, or the opposite of homosexual
10.	Rosa:	Not gay
11.	T:	Right, the opposite of gay or heterosexual
12.	Stan:	Straight is not gay, OK, OK

In this excerpt, the ESL students are reviewing a recent event on the campus concerning Gay Pride Week with their teacher. At this point in the lesson, the teacher elicits talk with an open-ended strategy to learn from the learners themselves what questions they have and, in that context, the teacher embeds vocabulary they need to learn. The learners ask questions and produce more than one-word examples. They also practice turn taking and other skills in the L2 as they initiate talk and the teacher cedes control over the patterns of communication.

In this more interactive context, students can negotiate meaning with the teacher and each other, requiring that they comprehend pragmatic meanings, and then enact appropriately their own communicative goals. They can establish their own legitimacy as L2 speakers. Given that pragmatics is inherently woven together with social dimensions, becoming competent in the interactional rules of speaking entails a learning environment that reflects the world outside the traditional classroom.

Training in Pragmatics Outside the Traditional Language Classroom

Teaching to develop pragmatic competence does not end for L2 learners in language-focused classrooms and indeed there exist advanced communicative needs of both native and nonnative speakers of a target language, particularly regarding workplace literacy skills, job interviews, and business letter writing tasks, to name only a few areas. Chapter 8 on institutional talk reviewed studies of successful and unsuccessful job candidates, where it was clear that such factors as self-presentation, grammatical and lexical accuracy and appropriacy, and the ability to produce synthesized talk about personal and professional experiences and interests were highly important in succeeding in finding a job.

Louw, Derwing, and Abbott (2010) developed a research-based pedagogical process to help L2 learners improve their job-interviewing skills. A combination of videos of simulated job interviews, critiquing by experts on the needed skills, and trial runs by students led to improvement in their skills. They were rated on such variables as small talk, enthusiasm, body language, evidence of cross-cultural misunderstanding, intelligibility, and positive demeanor. The instructional process comprised three phases: students would (1) observe native speaker discourse for job interviews; (2) become aware of differences and salient features; and (3) have lots of practice using new discourse and sociopragmatic strategies.

Training for the workplace context is not a new challenge for employers or new employees. Japanese university students who are fortunate enough to be hired during their final year at university not uncommonly find they have to start on-the-job training in sociopragmatics before they actually start working in April, just after they graduate. Young women who have been hired as receptionists, secretaries, and other positions dealing with customers and the general public attend language classes so that they learn the proper use of formal Japanese – the honorifics – to cue status differences and what Ide (2005) calls beautification language. Note that this form of training in language use is not an exotic characteristic of Japan only. Cameron (2000), in her book entitled *Good to Talk?* looks into how the U.K. has changed practices regarding language use in contemporary consumer society. Sales clerks are expected to use language to make the prospective customer feel welcome. Their needs must appear to be attended to, and shopping becomes a pleasant experience rather than something to be gotten over with as quickly as possible.

Conclusions

Chapter 10 has included a brief overview of topics that are important for any discussion of classroom pragmatic competence development: the possibility of instructed L2 pragmatics and the variables that tend to get in the way of activating that possibility, such as L1 transfer, classroom input, and sociocultural dimensions. Thus, there are variables internal to the learner and the learning processes as well as factors that are external: the features of the classroom environment and features completely outside the learner and the classroom, involving international politics.

Part II has attempted to build an inclusive view of pragmatics and the instructional context brings together many of the dimensions elaborated on in the previous chapters. Part III prioritizes the need for research in multiple contexts on pragmatics and the various topic areas within the domain of sociopragmatics. Chapter 11 is intended to help students design and conduct pragmatics projects, in particular for those who need to complete end-of-semester research reports using naturally occurring talk data.

Suggested Readings

Duff, P. A. (2011). Identity, agency, and second language acquisition. In A. Mackey and S. Gass (Eds.) *Handbook of second language acquisition* (in press). London: Routledge.

Johnson, K. E. (1995). *Understanding communication in second language classrooms.* Cambridge: Cambridge University Press.

Kasper, G. and Rose, K. R. (2002). *Pragmatic development in a second language.* Oxford: Blackwell.

Kasper, G. and Roever, C. (2005). Pragmatics in second language learning. In E. Hinkel (Ed.), *Handbook of research in second language teaching and learning* (pp. 317–34). Mahwah, NJ: Lawrence Erlbaum.

McKay, S. L. (2002). *Teaching English as an international language.* Oxford: Oxford University Press.

Tatsuki, D. H. and Houck, N. R. (Eds.) (2010). *Pragmatics: Teaching speech acts.* Alexandra, VA: Teachers of English to Speakers of Other Languages, Inc.

Tudini, V. (2010). *Online second language acquisition: Conversational analysis of online chat*. London: Continuum.

Discussion Questions

1. Give an example of how you would use the Socratic method in teaching a second/foreign language.
2. In the following example of teacher–learner discourse, what is happening? How useful is such talk to the learner's development of (Mori 1996: 60) competence ?

    S: ah um . . . how many papers can . . . mm . . . should I . . . write?
    T: you mean how many drafts should you write?
    S: yeah

3. Give an example of how you would teach a lesson on social rules of speaking in a second/foreign language. Choose a situation, decide what the rules of social appropriateness would be, and develop a lesson plan.
4. Find examples in materials you use for teaching that represent or misrepresent social variables and language use in a second/foreign language.
5. Generate examples of where your L1 influences your pragmatic competence when you are using another language or variety of the standard language you regularly use.
6. In the following dialogue, learners did not take the opportunity to practice using the L2. Why didn't they? What could the teacher do differently in the interaction pattern so as to enable the learners to do so?

    T: OK, what have we been looking at in the past unit? What were you reading yesterday?
    S: (. . .)
    T: So what have we been looking at in this unit?
    S: (. . .)
    T: What?
    S: (. . .)
    T: OK, remember? Time clauses? What tense? Past?
    S: present
    T: present time clauses. What are the (. . .) time phrases that we have been looking at? What are they?
    S: (. . .)
    T: (. . .) match the two clauses with what? What do we do?
    S: um
    T: Put the clauses together. Before one, right?
    S: After
    T: After, what?

    (Benson 2000: 86)

7. How do you feel about working in groups? Generate a list of the positive and not so positive effects of group work. Then discuss your list and reasons for your reactions with some classmates.
8. "It is sometimes necessary to become conscious of the forms of social behavior in order to bring about a more serviceable adaptation to changed situations" (Sapir 1951, cited in Cazden 2001). Do you agree or disagree with the point of view expressed? Explain and support your view with examples.
9. Generate a list of ways you would try to help learners in a teaching context to improve their pragmatic competence.
10. Discuss your identities as teachers and/or students in language education contexts. How are they manifested? What is your point of view on enacting identity when you use the L2? How about for teachers?

Data Analysis

1. Videotape a language lesson, transcribe an interesting ten-minute segment, and analyze it for some of the aspects of classroom language learning discussed in this chapter. If you are working with a conversational language partner, you could video or audiotape one session and analyze that data.
2. The accompanying table presents a segment from a lesson on English as a foreign language at a Mexican university taught by a native speaker of English. Study carefully the kinds of questions the teacher is asking.

1.	Student:	Arrangement?
2.	Teacher:	What are the arrangements?
3.	S:	(. . .) [Silence]
4.	T:	Check or review all the arrangements. The marriage license to get married. Need a special license, a special paper
5.	S:	Acta?
6.	T:	Well, this is the United States, isn't it the same in Mexico?
7.	S:	Like church? Or the government?
8.	T:	The government. The license is something civil. You do, no?
9.	S:	No
10.	T:	Yes, OK, so let's listen to this exercise, let's hear the instructions (plays tape instructions)
11.	T:	OK, so you're going to organize in January what would be the action January?
12.	S:	Talk to the
13.	T:	Talk to the minister, OK? (plays the taped exercise)
14.	T:	OK, what happens in February?
15.	Ss:	Reception
16.	S:	Restaurant
17.	T:	The reception. OK, a place for the reception. Where? Where can you have a reception?

18.	S:	(. . .) (silence)
19.	T:	What? So where? They mentioned two, a restaurant. They said it could be a restaurant or a hall. What would be a hall?
20.	Ss:	Salon
21.	T:	Uh huh, like a big room special for parties, that would be a hall. For a reception that's February. Let's listen for March (plays tape)
22.	T:	In March, what?
23.	Ss:	Choose a gown
24.	T:	The wedding gown, the special dress (plays tape)
25.	T:	For April?
26.	Ss:	Wedding ring.

Source: Benson 2000: 60–1

Some questions are "real," that is, the teacher does not already know the answer. Some comprise a strategy the teacher uses to go over the content of the lesson. Are both present in this lesson? Which type is more like the kinds of questions found in the real world? What effect may the different questions have with regard to the learner's pragmatic development?

PART III
Research in Sociopragmatics

11
GUIDELINES FOR SMALL SOCIOPRAGMATICS PROJECTS

Introduction

Ideally, students interested in carrying out projects for courses should read all of the chapters of this book before they begin work on their projects. However, realistically, teachers make assignments at the beginning of the semester course as the collection of data, transcription, and analysis takes several weeks or months to complete. Consequently, this chapter provides important guidelines for the projects that can be addressed before all of the chapters on pragmatics are read. Nevertheless, teachers can encourage students to read through those content chapters to get a quick overview of possible topics for their data-based studies.

Sociopragmatics is a vast field of study, covering topics of great importance such as how embassy staff handle angry visa applicants to negotiations regarding car accidents to chat between two friends, one of whom has just suffered a severe loss in her family. This chapter limits the discussion to small pragmatics, specifically to studies of second language acquisition within – instructed learning – and outside classrooms – in naturalistic environments, such as learning how to cook Mexican food in a private class where Spanish is the language of communication. It reviews important issues and procedures involved in the process of setting up a study and carrying it out to the final stage of producing oral academic presentations as well as written reports about the study. For further information about research in this field, the Suggested Readings section at the end of the chapter points to several sources among many that can be found.

The chapter includes sections about developing projects, step by step, addressing concerns and issues, and offering examples and suggestions along the way. These guidelines are not inclusive of all relevant details and readers of this book should consult the Suggested Readings section for other materials to help them with their projects.

Setting up a Study

One of the most difficult and important steps in setting up a study in sociopragmatics is finding a topic that is both interesting – even exciting – and feasible. For example, doctor–patient discourse is fascinating and contributing to a better understanding about this genre of institutional talk is valuable for society. However, it is not generally feasible to engage in a study that depends on data collection in this context as this doctor–patient setting directly concerns privacy laws; it is very difficult to get permission from patients and doctors to use their private consultations for research purposes. A setting where privacy laws are not at issue is family dinner table conversation. Nevertheless, family members may not be comfortable and may question the value of studying their interaction patterns. In addition, the cultural background of the potential participants may caution them about the wisdom of "airing the dirty laundry" for a research project. Feasibility concerns go beyond content issues as well; inexperienced researchers may underestimate the amount of time it takes to collect naturally occurring talk data and transcribe them. Participants in a study may become busy and unavailable and equipment may break down or get locked in a closet for which there is no available key. Brainstorming with an experienced researcher helps to develop awareness of the various factors that may derail even the best-planned project.

Here is a short list of suggestions (see Clark 2007; Cameron 2001) that will help with developing ideas for studies:

- Replicate a study that has already been done, collecting different data.
- Compare and contrast talk in two different settings, such as from a group task in a classroom with a group discussing the same topic outside of a classroom
- Compare and contrast talk in the target language in an all-male group, an all-female group, and then a mixed-sex group
- Challenge a previous claim and demonstrate with data the reasons for questioning previous claims
- Describe talk in a new context, even a new location, such as code switching in an online chat site or a popular magazine such as *Latina*.

Once the general plan for the project is decided, then framing a research question is a useful step as it focuses attention on a problem that the study may be able to shed light on. For instance, collecting talk in the three groups mentioned in the third suggestion above while the individuals are using the target language may sound interesting; however, articulating an actual research question addresses the need to focus on a feasible project. Here is an example: In which group(s) are the third-year students of French more likely to continue to speak in French, despite the fact that they all speak the same first language, English? This research question concerns variables such as identity and the students' motivation to use the target language with other nonnative speakers in a context where they might be more concerned with their self-presentation with members of the same sex or opposite sex. It is particularly useful to frame the research as an actual question, with an interrogative marker at the end. Along with the question, generating at least one rationale for the study also helps to focus the mind. Why do you want to do this study now in this context? Meeting the requirements for a course may not be the only reason. Here is an example: one student in a sociolinguistics class who was curious about how men and women in a mixed group used informal language, in particular swear words, organized his male roommates to invite three women they all knew from the apartment building to have supper together in their apartment. He got all of them to agree to allow him to tape record their talk "for a course." He did not tell the participants the goal of the study. The study not only got him an A for the course, but he also made friends with his neighbors.

The next step happens almost automatically; as a question is developed, possible answers develop. For students who have had some training in research methods, they may think about a hypothesis: Men are more likely to be unwilling to use the target language with other men due to their identity concerns, rather than women or than in a mixed-sex group. This hypothesis is simply a claim about what are likely to be the results. However, formulating a hypothesis is more typically a step in positivist research approaches, where statistical analysis is used to "prove" results. Whereas in fields like physics or biochemistry, proof of a behavior between two physical substances is possible, in sociopragmatics, where human behavior is the center of attention, proof is not likely. Cause and effect in the physical sciences gives way to finding correlations between, for instance, men talking only with men and the lack of motivation to use the target language. That is a correlation only; the generalization does not explain the behavior.

At this point, a very important step is learning the ins and outs of the library and then reading, reading, and reading about the topic. Ideally, it is best to read "around," that is, the background literature on the topic of the project as well as recent studies published by researchers. By doing so, the student learns about the field of inquiry – language and gender studies for the project mentioned above – and theories, as well as some of the history of the field and the changes that have taken place in the last decade or so. Note that, while searching online (e.g. Google Scholar) may be useful, consulting published articles in academic databases leads to more suitable sources of information. In addition, more focused reading, on mixed-sex and same-sex studies, will present ideas about the possible research questions, methodologies, and results, plus what researchers have learned and see as gaps for studies in the future. Keeping a list of the publications that are consulted means that writing up the study is easier once that stage arrives. Reading previous research helps in refining the generated research question, suggests gaps in the already existing knowledge base, and gives a rich picture of others' projects, even how they then wrote up the project for publication. It is an indispensable stage in the management of the project.

Research Design

This section outlines the very important stage of designing the project. At this stage of the project development, all of what may be called the mechanics or organizational matters are worked out. An outline, mental map, or flow chart may help with the organization and management of the project, especially if more than one researcher is involved. The research design calls for lots of small tasks and decisions. The following chart maps out the parts of a study in chronological order, that is, the order in which brainstorming and decision-making about the project take place. Note, however, that this chart is only a heuristic device to promote ordered thinking, similar to a flow chart for computer programmers, as many aspects of planning for a project entail interactions between and among sections. It is difficult to develop a clear goal or objective without an awareness of what is possible in terms of participants, data collection equipment, and the time available for the project. One semester goes very quickly!

Part I Introduction
   Goals and rationales
   Background
   Research questions
Part II Research design
   Setting
   Participants
   Ethics
   Researcher
     Emic/etic perspective
     Observer's paradox
     Identity of researcher
   Data
     Types of data
     Quantity and quality concerns
     Transcription
   Instruments
   Data collection procedures

> Part III Data analysis and methodologies
> Part IV Presentation of findings
> Part V Discussion and analysis of findings

Note that all decisions about the research design for a project depend on the research questions. In other words, what the researcher wants to study structures the project and is the locus of the decision-making. Here is an example from a data-based study of interactional discourse of a small business meeting with five men: three Japanese and two Americans. They were discussing a matter of some import for a joint Japanese–American educational program. The researcher noticed that there were what seemed to be a large number of interruptions and wanted to assess the possible significance of those interruptions for the immediate decision making and for the educational program as a whole. The motivation or rationales for the study provide the frame and basis for research questions. Thus, in the case of a study of interruptions in a single-sex group of all men, it may be important to do several forms of analysis: count the number of interruptions, count who interrupts whom, and count whether or not the interruption ended in the interrupter taking over the floor. In addition, engaging in a detailed analysis of some representative examples of the interruptions in the data contributes to assessing contextual features that may explain the interruption pattern. That analysis made it clear that the two men who interrupted each other and stole the floor from the other were those with the most power of the five men in the group. In fact, they were the directors of the two parts of the program, one in New York, the other in Tokyo. The data gave further evidence that the less powerful of the five men did not interrupt each other or the powerful participants (LoCastro 1990). This synopsis of the study suggests some of the decisions that the research design entailed: obtaining permission to use the data; transcribing the collected data; reviewing the audio tape and transcription of the discourse repeatedly to assess salient features for deeper analysis; deciding on the best forms of analysis (both quantitative and qualitative) and the theoretical framework (critical discourse analysis); carrying out the analysis; and formulating the discussion and the interpretation of the findings.

Setting

Another step in the process of developing a study is selecting the setting where the data are collected. The data of sociopragmatics studies commonly consist of naturally occurring speech or, if the study involves collecting data in classrooms, authentic discourse in that environment, where the focus of the interaction can be on a variety of features such as the teacher–student interactions where the discourse may or may facilitate learning, equal opportunities to talk, or development of higher level, critical thinking. The setting is an important factor as it influences the talk and interaction patterns. People speak differently – or should – depending on whether or not they are having dinner with friends at a posh restaurant or a friendly local bar or coffee shop. The participants in a study find their speech constrained by the setting if the researcher is present, collecting data, particularly with an obvious or noticeable form of electronic equipment. It is then that the Observer's Paradox occurs. This phenomenon entails the participants, whose speech is being collected and observed, behaving less than naturally due, at some subconscious level, to an awareness resulting in their monitoring their speech. They may monitor their speech even if they suspect that an overhearer might hear them; bilingual people react by switching languages, if the conversational partner also has competence in the other language. Nonbilinguals may use more hesitations or become silent, expressing a discomfort that their talk is being observed.

The choice of the setting may also involve other concerns; videotaping or audio-recording classroom interactions may require permission from not only the teacher who is cooperating on the study, but also school authorities and the parents of children being observed. Permission is required; see below for a discussion on the ethics of such research.

Participants

In addition, carrying out a project with participants or informants requires not only official permission and consent, but also finding individuals or groups who are willing to cooperate and ideally are interested in the study. Further, another point to consider is the issue of comparable data. For example, to study successful acquisition of sociopragmatic formulaic routines of a target language, there is a whole range of factors that must be taken into consideration in the selection of participants; here are some of them: age, first language, any other second language they know, socioeconomic background, level of formal education, time spent abroad in the target language community, exposure to that community. Finding informants who are comparable on a high number of variables is not easy. An early study on agreement/disagreement (LoCastro 1987) compared the form of assessments of Japanese speakers of English in Japan with those of native speakers of English who also resided in Japan. The Japanese informants were students at a university whereas the native English speakers were older and were not students, but rather teachers of English. This study was flawed due to the differences in age and the backgrounds of the participants. Residence in Japan by the native English speakers for a number of years could have influenced their agreement/disagreement strategies; in other words, they may not have been good representatives of how native speakers of English enacted those speech acts. The study would need to be replicated with more comparable informants to obtain higher validity and reliability of the findings.

Careful selection of the participants, so that all of the factors match, provides more comparable data; the study compares apples with apples and not apples with kiwis.

Ethics and Obtaining Consent

To protect participants from misuse of the data they provide to a researcher, it is absolutely necessary to obtain consent in writing from them. The participants are sources of data for a study and it is necessary to obtain consent either before the data collection starts or after that step has taken place. Obtaining consent involves laws and ethical behavior norms regarding use of people's voices only with their permission. Most U.S. universities have websites, called Institutional Review Boards (IRB) that outline the requirements and provide guidelines and sample forms for the IRB process. While the norms of other countries may differ from those found in the Anglophone parts of the world, the consent rules apply to most research projects carried on at universities and at other institution and companies that engage in data collection activities. In addition, publication of findings requires that the researcher has obtained consent. Failure to carry through with this requirement can result in no credit being given for any report or presentation and rejection of manuscripts.

There are many pros and cons about obtaining consent before the data collection starts. It is easy to argue that the informants will monitor their talk if they know their voices are being recorded. While this point of view is valid, the research boards still require that permission be obtained. Recording data without telling the participants beforehand may not cause problems. However, should any of the informants object, perhaps become angry, then the data must be destroyed. Generally, the researcher communicates the overall outline of the project to the participants, i.e. everyone involved, such as both the cooperating teacher and any students involved, if it is a classroom-centered study. The rule of thumb is, however, to avoid telling exactly the purpose of the study. In a study of praise used by teachers in a primary school, the researcher does not tell the teacher about recording her praising patterns with her students. Rather the researcher can give a different reason, such as observing her use of Spanish with the children, for example, so that she won't modify her speech for the specific variable being studied.

Further, regarding privacy issues, the general practice is to use pseudonyms for each participant in the analysis of the data and publication; informants may volunteer to allow the researcher to use their real names. It may also be necessary to negotiate the use of electronic recording equipment as some participants may be sensitive to the actual recording processes, what is recorded, and disposal of cassette tapes and videos once the researcher has completed the project.

Researcher

Given that all aspects of the context of a study influence and constrain the interactions between and among the participants, the researcher must also take into consideration her role as one feature of the context. Many studies have demonstrated that gender, age, style of dress, race, ethnicity, perceived level of education, and certainly use of speech (formal/informal, use of slang or colloquialisms) all have an effect on how the participants will interact with each other and with the researcher. Labov (1972) found that in order to obtain the naturally occurring talk of groups of black adolescents in inner city neighborhoods, an interviewer from the same background, who would sit on the floor and drink pop and eat chips with the young people, was more successful than one who looked like an academic researcher from a different ethnic background. In a pilot study where the research question concerned standard use of a/an/the, the indefinite and definite article use in English, by international students from three Asian languages – Chinese, Japanese, and Korean – the informants spoke differently and had different rates of accuracy for article use when they were interviewed by a fellow Asian than a white graduate student in linguistics (Im 2010).

Changes in the neighboring field of anthropology require that the anthropologist offer information about any aspects of the researcher's professional background that may influence her epistemological approach to the study and other aspects of the project, in particular the analytical or theoretical approach for study and data analysis. The researcher's background is a concern in the analysis and interpretation of the data. If the researcher is from the same background, both linguistically and culturally, the study is called an emic study. If the researcher is not from the same sociocultural background, it is called an etic study. These two words derive from the dichotomy in phonology/phonetics between sounds that create meaning differences and those that don't:

English: r/l rice/lice → phon<u>emic</u> distinction
Spanish: b/v → phon<u>etic</u> distinction

In English, pronouncing r/l so that they are phonetically distinct makes a difference in meaning. The second sound difference in Spanish is not salient as both are used in spoken language. It is only in written Spanish that "cow" (*vaca*) is spelled with a "v." For speakers of Spanish who have weak spelling skills, they will sometimes spell "cow" or "vaca" with a "v" and sometimes with a "b."

An emic study takes the perspective of the local, situated culture, thus presumably providing more meaningful interpretations of local practices and language in use. An etic description of a community's language practices may be a valuable description, but at the level of interpretation, nuances and deeper meanings may not surface if the researcher is not a member of that community.

In sum, when an outsider carries out a pragmatics study, it is etic due to the difficulty the researcher may have in interpreting the data without close ties to the meanings members of that culture or speech community give. When the study is an emic or insider study, the assumption is that the interpretations of the findings are more likely to be more congruent with the local culture members. However, rather than one or the other, an ideal study would include researchers working together who can present both perspectives on the observed behaviors in the data. The outsider researcher may notice features of the talk, for example, that the insider may not notice due to preconceived expectations about her/his own culture. At times taboos may cause an insider to be unwilling to acknowledge meanings about some topics. After all, self-reports at any stage of a study are just that: individuals reporting on what they think rather than what may be the reality. Japanese personal pronouns in subject positions are used very differently from what textbooks for foreigners studying Japanese claim and what the average office worker believes! It takes observation on a daily basis over time to learn how people speak, rather than what they believe they say.

Data

Data for sociopragmatics studies may vary in form and comprise linguistic and nonlinguistic evidence to support the particular research questions and design. They may be observation notes written by a teacher about the language use of her students as they engage in a group activity. She wants them to practice working with each other on an assigned task after she has taught them phrases to organize their interactions so that every student had opportunities to contribute. Data may take the form of audiotaped interviews or focus groups where the language use has been transcribed. Another example is family talk that was audio or videotaped, where the researcher focuses on specific aspects of the talk at the dinner table involving requests and male and female contributions. Identity signals may be observed when a Hispanic worker on a building site refuses to speak Spanish with a non-Hispanic supervisor.

In addition to what kind of data is the "right" one to collect for a project, students carrying out a project for a course assignment often ask how much data they need to collect. Sometimes one dialogue of three to five minutes is enough to write a 30-page paper! The amount of data is often assessed only after at least a preliminary analysis is done for the study. Often, inexperienced researchers make the mistake of waiting to review the data until after the collection phrase, even after they have left the site for their study. Ideally, the researcher reviews what was collected daily, so as to be ready to make adjustments the next day in the procedures.

In terms of spoken language data, it may consist of monologues, dialogues, groups of people talking, radio or TV call-in and talk shows, movies or play scripts, or cartoons. An important distinction that needs to be made is whether or not the spoken discourse is planned or unplanned. Unplanned talk is generally spontaneous, what human beings do in conversation, the prototypical genre of talk, where the participants do not monitor what they say, or how they speak. It is unrehearsed talk and thus viewed as most "natural." Planned talk may be scripted, where the TV actors follow very closely a script written by a paid writer of the genre. The degree to which the actors follow the planned script can vary depending on the director of the drama. Thus, if a pragmatics project is based on TV or movie talk, the researcher explains the decision to use this variety of speech and the rationales for doing so. Note that, just as with printed and online material, citation information for the TV show and movie must be provided in both the text and the list of references. There may also be limitations on how much material can be cited directly from the language used; restrictions, as with online materials, need to be verified.

Corpus data from other researchers may be available at online sites, often at a cost for use by others. There are some advantages to using these sources: a written transcript is provided, although not the audio or video recordings; it is searchable for selected linguistic and nonlinguistic cues; and the corpus may include a million or more entries. Disadvantages may include a limited database derived only from printed media, rather than spoken talk; the need for manual coding of the data to set the tags; a lack of prosodic markings if the data are spoken items; and computer skills beyond the competence of researchers.

The researcher has to review the data that has been collected to select segments that relate to the research question asked at the first stage. Decisions about the data depend on what the researcher wants to study and learn. It is useful to listen and review the collected data multiple times as the first time or two it seems there is nothing that is useful in the data. However, with repeated listening details related to the study will "jump out" and become noticeable. Those are the bits to focus on, and the surrounding talk, depending on the objective of the study. It is like putting on a new pair of glasses, with new lenses, enabling one to see things from a different perspective.

Data for pragmatics studies are likely to be naturally occurring talk, rather than quantitative data that allow for statistical analysis. The quality of the data may present a problem once it is time to transcribe the talk. The researcher has to balance the need for good-quality recording and ethical questions of, for example, eavesdropping on a conversation and recording it without obtaining consent. Public domain data – that is, what is obtained from sources that are available to the general population – are a source of instances of sociopragmatic strategies that do not require permission. An example of this data collection procedure typically involves taking down in a field notebook how sales or bank clerks respond to common requests for service, to assess how the personnel handle inquiries. Labov (1972) is famous for his department store survey of New York City English; he was studying contextual features that correlated with the dropping of the postvocalic /r/. He asked clerks on the first floor of targeted New York department stores where the shoe department was to elicit the response: "On the fourth floor." Labov knew where the shoe department was; he wanted to hear whether or not the sales clerk pronounced the two /r/s: fourth, floor. In this study, he noted in IPA symbols the responses. (At the time of the study, in fact, the equipment we have today to record such data didn't exist!) A similar study today would be carried out the same way, where the data are collected in field notes constituting "public domain" data.

Further, the quality of the equipment may also enter into the picture, as well as such factors as the placement of the microphones; use of microphones in the tape or video recorders that pick up the sounds of the machine rather than the voices of the participants; and participants speaking into the microphone as if they were on YouTube.

A debate within areas of research based on naturally occurring talk raises the question of just what "natural" means. Sociolinguists would argue that natural talk is the most casual, vernacular style of speaking, when there is the least amount of monitoring of their speech by the participants. Another way of thinking about "natural" is to argue that it is the style of speaking that is normal for a particular setting. Thus, what is natural in a family and a casual friendship group setting is not what is natural in an institutional context. In the same vein, classroom-centered research, which depends on collecting data in that environment, is an appropriate context to obtain "natural" data for studies about teacher–student discourse. Context shapes all talk and, thus, the researcher must collect data in contexts that support the particular objective of the study. The disadvantage of classroom data for sociopragmatic research centers on a legitimate concern for the development of pragmatic competence. A basic example of the limitations of classroom interactional opportunities is the pattern of teachers asking questions and students answering them. Clearly students need to learn how to ask a variety of types of questions in the target language, and a good teacher makes that happen at least some of the time. Another example concerns opportunities for students to practice extended talk in the target language in instructional learning contexts. In sum, the research design of a project needs to take into consideration all of these factors in selecting data collection sites.

Transcription

Excerpts selected from the collected data need to be transcribed. In fact, this is the first stage of the data analysis; it forces the researcher to engage with the data in a more intense way that goes beyond simply listening repeatedly to the recording (Cameron 2001). Thus, the effort to transcribe is not wasted time.

This necessary though time-consuming activity is a practical solution that enables the researcher to study the talk repeatedly in the way that a tape or video recording does not. Ideally the audio and visual text of a piece of talk supports the analysis of what is happening in the talk at a level that only an audio version can. Needless to say, field notes of quickly recorded instances of talk do not facilitate the required in-depth analysis for a solid study. It is not usually necessary to transcribe an entire data set of, say, ten hours of audio recording, unless it is a requirement set by a teacher or dissertation director. Nor is it necessary to use IPA symbols, that is, phonetic symbols from the International Phonetic Alphabet, for pragmatics studies, as the type of research questions for sociopragmatics is different from sociolinguistic research on variation in dialects. Orthographic script is adequate for pragmatics issues, such as sequences or turn taking in talk, or in general management of talk. IPA may be required if a study of language in use involves phonological and prosodic variables. A study of one phone – say, a final consonant – that correlates with careful speech in formal contexts in a speech community versus the dropping of that sound in casual speech would suggest a need for IPA transcription, at least of those targeted sounds.

Transcription is not simply a matter of writing down how people talk, however. While beginners to the task of transcribing data may think that it is possible to write down completely accurately how people speak, it cannot be done, as experience informs all efforts to do so. Any transcription, however carefully it is done, is essentially an interpretation of the collected data. Just as human beings are not able to talk without embedding a point of view, so too when listening to others' speech and then writing it down in the form of a transcription is there decision-making required that involves the transcriber's point of view.

Transcription conventions are readily available and it is useful to find a set of conventions used by another researcher in pragmatics. Generally, the transcriber writes down as accurately as possible what s/he hears, including hesitations, sounds, laughter, and any and all ungrammatical utterances. There is a temptation to modify the transcription and "correct" all of the ungrammatical parts. However, the purpose of transcribing is to present how the participants talked without any editing, including all the messiness of human communication. It should be the best effort to show what is going on, including relevant prosodic features, so that the reader of the transcript knows when a participant has used a loud voice to emphasize a word, an intonation contour to signal a question, pauses to communicate hesitations, or elongated vowels for emphasis. The overall format of the transcription, further, depicts all evidence of overlapping talk, interruptions, and simultaneous speech, as these features are important to give a full view of the interactions. It is not writing down individual words so much as the overall depiction of speech that is desired. All of these features noted here, and some left out for space reasons, are "sensitive," that is, aspects of talk that are particularly implicated in sociopragmatic meanings.

A special note is needed regarding transcribing recorded data where it is not possible to decipher every word or line. This problem arises in pragmatics studies where high-quality recording is not always possible for a variety of reasons. The guideline requires effort be made to transcribe as faithfully as possible what can be heard, and then all irrecoverable words and phrases be noted in the text, by signaling the unclear talk with parentheses or brackets.

Transcript conventions leave out punctuation and capital letters unless they are used (see below) for other functions. Capital letters are reserved for proper nouns, generally. All of the transcriptions in this book provide examples of the conventions adopted; here is an abbreviated, exemplary list from Clark (2007: 90–1):

- (.) – just noticeable pause
- (0.3) (2.3) – examples of exactly timed pauses, in seconds
- word. – full stop (period) after a word denotes the falling and end of an intonation [contour]
- word? – question mark after a word depicts a rising, questioning intonation
- wo:rd – a colon indicates stretching of the preceding sound
- (word) – transcriber's guess at an unclear word or words
- () – unclear talk
- word – underlined words are those which are spoken loudly
- WORD – capitals indicate even louder speech
- [overlap] – overlapping speech

One final note regarding transcription: it is often useful to do what is called "member checking." If I transcribe a piece of text into Spanish, I then ask a native speaker of Spanish (a colleague or friend) to listen to the tape or video and check my transcription. However, even when transcribing in one's first language, a second person reviewing a transcription often helps to iron out parts that are inaudible or difficult to figure out.

Instruments

The title of this section refers to such items as questionnaires, discourse completion tasks (DCTs), computer software for doing corpus linguistic analysis, or a standardized test to measure language proficiency. Some of the instruments are written by the researcher; a questionnaire or DCT based on the local research project context is created by researchers to learn about how a literacy skills program, for example, is implemented for newly arrived immigrants. Other instruments are from outside sources, often recognized nationally and internationally as valid and reliable for measuring such aspects as language proficiency, motivation and aptitude, and academic writing skills (e.g. TOEFL, IELTS).

Any electronic equipment required for carrying out the data collection needs to be as unobtrusive as possible as it becomes part of the physical context of the study. It can influence the participants and therefore the potential findings of the study. In some sociocultural contexts, the use of a video camera, for instance, may be less of a problem than others. Over time, a video camera, set up in a corner where data can be collected on a daily basis, is often forgotten about by the participants. However, this step in the process of carrying out the project is probably the most unpredictable and the researcher needs to be flexible and should anticipate having to move from "plan A to plan B," where repeating videotaping sessions may be necessary to obtain good data. The researcher introduces these concerns in the Instruments section.

Data Collection Procedures

Here, the researcher carefully enumerates all the steps involved in the data collection process so that readers of the study can understand exactly what was done and in what order, including explanations for the order of the steps. Other scholars who may want to replicate a study require this careful detailing of the plan for the data collection phase in particular.

Here is an example. A pre-test and post-test design for data collection typically involves administering a pre-test, i.e. before the actual data collection of discourse takes place, and then a post-test to assess the value of a pedagogical intervention. For instance, a teacher may wish to evaluate how effective explicit teaching about sociopragmatics is before lessons on a targeted speech act are carried out. The pre-test assesses the students' knowledge of sociopragmatics in general and perhaps also of the particular speech act. Once the series of lessons on that speech act has ended, a post-test measures how much they learned. Still another post-test, perhaps the exact same one, may be administered again after a six-week interval. The data collection procedures spell out these steps.

Data Collection Methodologies

Observation

A very basic, yet important method for collecting data is observation of language in use and accompanying nonverbal behaviors. Without a keen ability to look at and listen to what is happening in multiple environments or contexts, studying pragmatics is problematized. It takes an inquisitive mind about human beings to start the process of developing a research project in this field. So, starting with observations, in particular of the site or behavior that is a potential object of study, is wise. If there is interest in how teachers seek to develop learners' pragmatic competence in the classroom, observations of what happens in the classroom help the researcher understand the variables of that context and focus research questions. In naturalistic contexts, such as in cafés, or transactions at grocery stores, where immigrants to the U.S. interact with native speakers, observations in those environments to assess the extent to which they can acquire American English will also go a long way to help develop a project with that goal.

One strategy for the researcher to use in the course of observations of a local situation is to "misbehave" on purpose to learn what the reaction would be. In parts of the U.S., for instance, cashiers at supermarkets greet the customers with "Hi, how are you today?" "It is a blessed day today," or "Did you find everything you were looking for?" In other parts of the U.S., there may be no talk between the customer and cashier. A "test" of local norms by acting and using language from another geographical location either results in a silent response or similar talk, even a cashier commenting that the researcher must be from the South, where people are more "polite," because they greet people "down there." Misbehaving in a non-serious manner teaches about the local sociopragmatic norms for a variety of everyday talk situations.

In sum, researching sociopragmatics entails an active mind and a willingness to experiment with one's own behavior and language use to learn the norms of the local context. Good observation skills are indispensable.

Interviews

At first thought, interviewing informants to get their opinions on a topic or to find out what issues they are concerned about seems normal or natural in "the interview society." The so-called TV "talk shows" are essentially informal interviews where the host interviews the guests about their opinions, and as a means to gather information on a topic. Interviews are ubiquitous in numerous areas of life and they are carried out by just about anyone: children's homework can consist of having them interview their grandparents about their lives before they immigrated to the U.S. Marketers for consumer companies are constantly seeking the views of consumers on aspects of potential products ranging from the color of toilet paper to special license plates to commemorate race horses. Researchers, however, who depend on collecting valid and reliable data from informants follow recognized procedures and norms that have developed surrounding this means to reach informative results. It is not as easy as meets the eye and requires some practice and skill.

There are several types of interviews to consider regarding sociopragmatics studies: structured, group, and unstructured In the case of structured interviews, the researcher prepares a list of questions that are asked of each participant and often an answer sheet with a limited number of possible responses that the interviewer or informant circles or checks off. There is little flexibility in the way the answers can be coded and categorized, thus limiting the types of information that can be presented, often in graphs or tables in numerical form. It is an instrument to collect quantitative data for statistical processing. The questionnaire or survey, whether administered in person, over the phone, or on an Internet site, requires that the interviewer be a neutral, non-evaluative agent.

Group interviews, also called focus groups, are commonly used by marketing teams, political parties, candidates, and universities. In the competition for good students, universities seek the opinions of groups of already admitted students about their marketing, the image of the university, and procedures for admission, welcoming activities, and other variables to attract the best students away from competing institutions. They may be more or less structured depending on the purpose of the interview, and the interviewer is expected to be dynamic and capable of energizing all of the focus group members to participate to get full coverage of all of the participants' views. The goal may be to explore upcoming changes, not yet public, or to elicit unexamined beliefs of the group.

An unstructured interview is a qualitative instrument to elicit ethnographic types of information informally, with informants who are asked open-ended questions to understand the world from the informants' point of view. While it is still important not to impose the researcher's point of view, the researcher is involved as a human being, voicing her/his point of view and feelings. It is as if the participants and the researcher are having an in-depth discussion about often controversial topics. Structure is not totally absent as there is a definable setting, with pre-selected informants, and at least a list of topics or points to include in the interview, with the interviewer free to pose questions on the topics as they develop organically in the course of the interaction. The interviewer/researcher considers how to present her/himself and works at gaining trust and establishing a rapport with the participants.

A dimension of interviewing that needs to be taken into consideration is how the interviewer can influence a study and the contributions of the informants. The interviewer cannot escape playing an important role as a human being, where gender, race, class background, educational level, and physical presentation of self may be noticed. In addition, the interview as a discourse genre sets up expectations that the interviewer asks the questions and the interviewee gives responses. This norm appears in all interviews as, try as hard as the interviewer may, the result is that the interviewee is influenced and constrained by the questions, particularly in a structured format. In unstructured ones, or informal group discussions, alternative roles for both interviewer and interviewee may be constructed in the course of the interactions, where a group leader or facilitator may interact with the other participants to soften the powerful role found in structured interviews. Here is where the rigor required for research design is observed.

Another procedure to elicit informants' attitudes and thinking processes is a retrospective interview of audio- or videotaped data. It entails structured or unstructured talk with participants as soon as possible after carrying out a task for the study, about what they were thinking when they spoke as they did or engaged in responding to a question as they did, to give two examples. Note that retrospective talk data are self-reported and thus potentially lacking in validity. However, it is considered a potentially valuable source of data for the purpose of triangulation of information from the informants.

If a researcher wants to conduct retrospective interviews with the participants in the study on the value of teaching a particular speech act, the timing of those interviews is vital. Ideally, such interviews are conducted immediately after the participants have finished, for instance, doing role plays to enact their knowledge of making requests of role-play partners and then either accepting the request or refusing it. Role plays are a possible post-test to assess how much they learned during the pedagogical intervention where the teacher explicitly taught those speech acts. Retrospective interviews can add further information by providing the participants with an opportunity to explain and metacommunicate about their role-play behaviors. It is another useful source of information for the study, which must be carefully organized and scheduled into the data collection process.

Data Analysis and Interpretation

The reading at the preparatory stage of the project development helps with the very important stage of data analysis. It is not uncommon for students to transcribe collected data and then seemingly to forget to provide a careful analysis and interpretation of the data. Yet, without analysis the study cannot contribute to furthering the knowledge base in pragmatics. Note also that the framework for the data analysis provides the base for the interpretation of the findings from the study. This section can only contribute an overview of some of the approaches for valid data analysis. The reader is referred to the Suggested Readings at the end of the chapter for more possibilities, as well as more in-depth information on the approaches.

The first step regarding data analysis involves a decision concerning the adoption of a theoretical framework or approach to the data. A study may be descriptive; that is, the researcher describes evidence in the form of general patterns in the data of participants' use of sociopragmatic strategies. Another type of study is an exploratory or pilot study to trial a particular design and data collection procedures for a more elaborated study at a future date. In fact, it is often wise to practice carrying out a study first for, as with reading in the topic area, it can inform the researcher about unpredicted aspects of a proposed study, help with generating appropriate research questions, and push for a tightening up of variables of the future study. The ideal type of study should seek to describe and explain the observed behavior.

Another consideration regarding data analysis is the issue of the use of quantitative and qualitative techniques. Pragmatics research generally involves qualitative studies, where there is a small sample of data collected of naturally occurring speech from a small number of informants. The purpose is to carry out a detailed analysis of the data to find patterns in the talk and learn about how human beings use speech every day in particular contexts (Clark 2007). Thus, a qualitative approach is preferred to quantitative techniques that focus on larger amounts of data and utilize such instruments as questionnaires to make generalizations. When a quantitative research design is chosen, the statistical analysis of collected data tends to consist of such procedures as Chi-square and t-tests. The sample sizes are small and thus do not support more advanced means to look for statistical significance.

Nevertheless, a mixed-methods research design is considered acceptable or desirable, depending on the research questions. It involves both quantitative and qualitative techniques in a single study, with the goal of triangulating the sources of information to reach more reliable and valid results. Triangulation came into linguistics research from the social sciences to provide "multiple perspectives on a phenomenon" (Dornyei 2007: 167). A common research design in pragmatics that utilizes this approach is bringing together videotaped data of a teacher's classroom practices when teaching sociopragmatics of requesting and refusing, and retrospective accounts of the video data from both the teacher and the students, separately, who are asked to discuss the teacher's strategies. This research design would provide three to four data sets or sources.

Another example is the use of a standardized proficiency test of language proficiency levels in the target language along with teacher-prepared and administered tests, with both discrete point and discourse items on the test. The two sources of information facilitate achieving findings that are more reliable, valid, and transparent for teachers and other educationalists who have practical concerns about the applications of studies to everyday classroom contexts.

A popular instrument used in pragmatics studies within the quantitative paradigm is questionnaires or surveys. They seem to be ubiquitous in marketing and preferences studies, in particular in online surveys of consumers' concerns. They can be useful for pragmatics studies as a means to get data quickly and to focus on particular speech acts, for example. To collect data of requests and refusals in daily transactions at markets in Uruguay, a researcher may wish to use a questionnaire or DCT first to find out how those two speech acts are enacted by a population before eliciting them at open-air markets on the streets of the capital city. A DCT is a means to obtain samples of the kind of data a researcher wants to study and quickly. The caveat is that the data are self-reported; in other words, the informants' responses are what they think they would say. Another weakness of DCTs is that they take the speech acts out of any kind of normal context that usually accompanies speech; and, further, the researcher has to develop the DCT carefully so that the informants are asked to respond in the way they would talk in a situation similar to events they had actually experienced. A person who has never had to negotiate a rental agreement with the owner of an apartment complex could not produce language from personal experience and, thus, would not be a desirable informant for a study on that topic.

Discourse analysis is certainly a well-known approach to language analysis and is commonly used in pragmatics studies. In fact, it is a basic requirement for conducting pragmatics studies that the researcher be able to analyze the discourse in the data set first, which may include lexical, syntactic, and phonological analysis of the talk. This stage constitutes part of what is called a microanalysis of data. The researcher in pragmatics has to first of all be a linguist.

In addition to the linguistic analysis, microanalysis includes such features as selection of the next speaker, overlapping and interrupting talk, and cooperative vs. competitive talk. At the microanalysis level, features of the data under analysis are studied for patterns that are in evidence through an extended piece of data, such as negotiation of a disagreement or explanations for missing a meeting. It can also consist of reviewing interview talk shows of politicians running for election, which may lead to an awareness of how they tend not to answer the interviewer's questions, but rather address everything they say to make them appear to be attractive candidates for the voters in the TV audience. Links between the data and the larger society become transparent in the course of the analysis and constitute a particular form of discourse analysis, critical discourse analysis, where the goal is to make transparent the dynamics between language use and the local societal context. Chapter 9 on language, gender, and power discusses more extensively this approach to discourse analysis.

Another approach to the analysis of data comes from the work of M. A. K. Halliday (Eggins 1994) and his colleagues; it is called systemic functional linguistics. A full introduction to this linguistic paradigm is beyond the scope of this book. A basic review of the main premise of this perspective on language and its value for discourse analysis is offered. A systemic functional, or simply functional, approach to the study of language use prioritizes the purpose or goal of communication. Using language entails a communicative goal or function the speaker wishes to enact. A greeting, one function of language, is communicated in American English commonly by friends as "Hi, how are you doing?" in the course of walking through campus or entering a popular café. Or it can be more elaborated: "Oh hi, how ARE you? I haven't seen you in a long time," inviting more than a conventional response. Or more formal: "Good afternoon, nice to meet you." The function or purpose is the same in all cases, but the way in which the language is used is not. Essentially, the functional approach works from function to language, rather than the more typical linguistic analysis that starts with syntactic, lexical, and phonological analysis. Looking first at the function of an instance of language use is an effective perspective to take in pragmatics research as it is a field that is by definition interested in the enactment of intentional language use, how human beings understand and produce language with meaning beyond the words that are used. Variation in requests in the context of use is a topic of interest for sociopragmatics; a functional study of that topic would start with what requests are, the purposes of requests (we can ask someone to loan us a pen and we can ask for a hug when we feel down: the first is more transactional and the second more related to affective dimensions of life), how they are commonly rendered in, say, English, and then move on to looking at requests in different contexts to find relationships between how the function is carried out depending on such contextual factors as gender, age, and object or service being requested, among others.

An ethnography of communication makes connections between human behavior, both linguistic and nonlinguistic, and cultural beliefs and practices. Ethnographic studies examine the role of situated, local context factors on talk, specifically the influence of sociocultural shaping. Although all talk is shaped by the context, this approach prioritizes the effect on interactions of participants. A small town car repair shop in the southern part of the U.S. invites informal chat and joking between the repair persons and the customers. An urban repair store in the North is noticeably more businesslike, with the focus on transactional talk. Everyday interactions provide evidence for the effect of context on talk.

A more elaborated example is how listener behavior in one cultural context may occur more frequently than in another due to local cultural expectations about the role of the listener in conversation interactions. If there are no norms for a particular culture on turn taking, one person could dominate and others would have a difficult time getting a word in edgewise, that is, getting a turn at talk. While it is difficult to imagine a culture that did not have such norms, there are certainly cultures that, in formal contexts, do have expectations where the age, gender, and socioeconomic background of the group members influence who talks first, for how long, and who should remain silent. Turn taking is an occasion where status and power differences can become noticeable.

Situated, local studies of talk emphasize a dimension of ethnographies. Specifically, the claim is made that, rather than the researcher's interpretations, the local participants' understandings of their language behaviors is the goal. A famous example of a situated, local study is Shirley Brice Heath's *Ways with Words: Language, Life, and Work in Communities and Classrooms* (1983). Heath taught in three different school systems in the Piedmont area of Virginia, where she was able to look at classroom interaction patterns to compare and contrast how teachers asked questions in classes with mostly white, middle-class students with those in schools that had a black/African-American, working-class population. This brief description provides details of the local situation or context of the study. Her observations led her to discover that, due to the students' sociocultural backgrounds, the white children responded readily to the teachers' questions, whereas the black children did not. They came from families where adults did not ask questions in the same way as the middle-class, white teacher. This local difference in the questioning strategies of parents and teachers affected the children, disadvantaging them in their progress through the educational system. By engaging in participant observations as a teacher, and then interviewing both parents and children, Heath made a significant contribution to knowledge about the effect of classroom interaction patterns on the education success of students.

Interactional sociolinguistics, an approach to the analysis of talk, was reviewed in Chapter 3. It overlaps with discourse analysis and conversation analysis, and aims to make transparent such features as contextualization cues, discourse markers, and other features important in institutional talk situations.

Another theoretical approach that has found acceptance recently is conversation analysis. It is a form of linguistic analysis of talk that draws from a view of structure of human interaction that prioritizes sequences in talk. For example, one problem Sacks, Schegloff, and Jefferson (1978) studied in the structure of talk concerned the cues that enter into signaling when another person could have a turn at talking. Participation in conversation entails the ability to figure out when a contribution or a turn at talk is possible. Sometimes the speaker will select the next person to speak by means of a head nod, or gazing directly at the person. However, sometimes the speaker ceases talking. In cross-cultural contexts, the silence can be confusing to the participants. How long should one wait at the pause before entering the conversation? Conversation analysts may study such topics, along with many others that focus in particular on sequences in spoken data. They attempt to explain mechanisms involved in the ongoing stream of talk. Research has shown that there are multiple cues that participate in managing turn-taking repairs, adjacency pairs, and repeated questions in the flow of discourse.

Corpus linguistics is a relatively recent addition to the approaches to linguistic analysis due to two events: (1) the greater availability of software to engage in this form of analysis of very large databases; and (2) the need to have more informed sources of information for the creation of dictionaries and educational materials. One major contribution of this form of analysis is concordancing. Computer programs scan large databases to provide linguistic contexts for individual words, such as prepositions, phrasal verbs, and collocations, greatly facilitating specialists in lexicography who are working currently on developing a dictionary of Mexican Spanish. Of interest to scholars in pragmatics, specifically sociopragmatics, is the capacity of the same concordancing function to provide evidence for the use of words like "please," "well," and "like (you know)," all of which contribute to pragmatic meaning creation. These and other pragmatic markers are frequent linguistic cues that are multi-functional. For example, "you know" is commonly heard in everyday talk in English, from a speech by Michelle Obama to the local teenagers talking with their friends. Pragmatics leads to an understanding of the functions of this marker, specifically that it is a strategy to mitigate what the speaker is saying, and simultaneously to invite the listeners to give their opinions or at least respond nonverbally with head nods, smiles, and soft "uhuhs."

Access to corpora may require payment for that service of those readily available, particularly the large ones (over a million words) such as the famous London–Lund corpus, compiled by the Survey of English Usage at University College London, and a smaller one, MICASE, the Michigan Corpus of Academic Spoken English. Others are the property of individuals or groups of researchers who work with spoken English data, such as CANCODE, the Cambridge–Nottingham Corpus of Discourse of English (McCarthy 1998). There has been an expansion of studies using corpora, despite disadvantages involving having to code and tag prosodic features manually and to find comparable data across the corpora, as well as when comparing the corpus data with data collected in everyday talk contexts (LoCastro 2011).

Presentation of Findings

As with transcriptions, research results or findings are based on interpretations of the collected data. Reality is not found in the findings, but rather it is the researchers' interpretations of what was going on in the talk that are presented in the report or article on the study. This fact is still another reason for both extensive and intensive reading before starting a study, to learn what others have written about the project about to be considered. Knowledge and interpretations are built upon earlier fonts of knowledge and others' work.

A caveat in the context of presenting findings is to mitigate any tendency to make overly direct or confident generalizations. It is best to be "modest," as Cameron states (2001: 190), and to view your project as a small contribution to the knowledge base in the field of pragmatics. It is as if researchers are hacking away at a big iceberg to lead towards a genuine theory of human communication at some future time. Cameron suggests that in writing up a report on a project it is best to state explicitly that the findings only apply to the particular group of informants in the study. Due to the complexity of studies in pragmatics, it is not possible to control for all of the variables that may influence the data collection and thus the results. Even with corpus studies in this field, where large amounts of data are available theoretically, the actual analysis requires editing of data by human beings.

Writing up Findings

Writing up the project and findings is an important requirement in academic, business, and institutional settings, both in oral presentations and for reports and publications. Modern society depends on making decisions on the basis of research findings from all fields of study, the hard sciences as well as the social sciences. In addition, students practice preparing themselves for those real-world responsibilities by presenting their findings in oral academic presentations and written reports. It is a valuable opportunity to develop skills needed to join discourse communities, which can include local community networks as well as those of professional contexts. Neighborhood projects to study the quality of the local water supply system entail the same skills to gain support for initiatives as those to improve community services at meetings and city council debates.

The format for the write-up should include all of the steps outlined in the list at the beginning of this chapter, from the introduction, where the goals and rationales for the study are introduced, to the interpretation of the data. In addition, these two sections follow, before a conclusion:

VI   Limitations of the study
VII   Future research
VIII Conclusion

It is not possible to complete a study without recognizing that there are limitations to the study. Research on human behavior in general, in particular on language in use, is complex, presenting issues related to control and predictions of the variables or factors involved such as collection of high-quality, relevant data, the role of identity regarding interactions, and participant cooperation. Obvious limitations include small sample size, which leads to two concerns: it precludes generalizations across populations and the use of statistical analysis to support qualitative analysis.

Recommendations for future studies answer the question: if it were possible to do the study again, how and what could be done differently? Critical thinking comes into play here as this section provides an opportunity to evaluate objectively the project and make suggestions for future studies on the same topic. For instance, a data-based study of the use of verb tenses and other forms of language to show respect or politeness in Mexican Spanish, where the data were collected at an elite, private university in Mexico, would only give a picture of how students from elite, upper socioeconomic groups signaled politeness. Given the social class structure of Mexican society, a more valid view of language use for respect would have to include data from an urban, public university and, ideally, from an open-air market in a local community. Anecdotal evidence of transactions in such environments sheds light on a large, Mexican subculture that communicates respect rather differently from the two other groups.

The final section of the written report or oral presentation draft forms the conclusion. Typically the conclusion includes a brief summary of the findings and interpretations of the collected data. The second requirement of a conclusion involves a review of what the study taught the researcher about the topic, about the research methods used, difficulties in carrying out the study, and contributions to the field of pragmatics. The conclusion content varies and may even be an opportunity to encourage more future research.

Conclusions

Chapter 11 is like a primer, a short text designed to teach novices about a complex topic. It reviews the main topics and issues of carrying out pragmatics projects and provides, in order, the steps for designing and implementing those steps in the course of developing a research study in this field. Important terminology and references to exemplary studies are included to help the inexperienced student of pragmatics. Needless to say, this primer is only a brief introduction and outside reading of other sources of information and advice is a wise extra step. If this chapter has motivated students of pragmatics to get their hands dirty by engaging in real-world data collection and interpretation, it has been successful.

In tandem with this chapter, the final one, Chapter 12, introduces four topics as examples of interesting research questions and studies, to further motivate and encourage students who need to complete end-of-semester projects. The very best way to acquire a deeper knowledge of pragmatics, of one's first or any second languages, is to observe and experiment in everyday interactions. Holding the door open when entering a building for others can, just by itself, communicate pragmatic meaning.

Suggested Readings

Books

Cameron, D. (2001). *Working with spoken discourse*. London: Sage.
Carter, R. and McCarthy, M. (1997). *Exploring spoken English*. Cambridge: Cambridge University Press.
Denzin, N. K. and Lincoln, Y. S. (Eds.) (2005). *Handbook of qualitative research*. 3rd edition. Thousand Oaks: Sage.
Gee, J. P. (2005). *An introduction to discourse analysis: Theory and method* 2nd edition. London: Routledge.
Spradley, J. P. (1979). *The ethnographic interview*. New York: Holt, Rinehart, & Winston.

Journals

The following databases are the best sources of information on articles in journals. The first two require access to a research library. The third is online and free.

LLBA : Linguistics and Language Behavior Index
Social Sciences Index
Google Scholar

12

IDEAS FOR RESEARCH PROJECTS IN SOCIOPRAGMATICS

Introduction

In this chapter, exemplary studies in areas of interest take a primary place to illustrate possible small, even doctoral dissertation research projects in the field of sociopragmatics. The purpose is to spark brainstorming, reading on the topics, and discussion with teachers and fellow students to move in the direction of setting up and designing appropriate studies based on the previous chapters of this book. The topics are discussed to raise issues that may be taken up as suitable for further study. Four areas are discussed in the following sections: questions; requests and refusals; pragmatic glitches and misfires; and bilingual political discourse.

Questions

Questions are so ubiquitous in everyday life that little attention is paid to them unless personal experience leads to the awareness that they are not without problems, particularly in cross-cultural contexts. Learners of a target language may lack complete control regarding the grammatical formation of interrogatives as well as concerning the degrees of directness and indirectness in question use. Sites where questions may play a significant role in interpersonal relations are customer care encounters, classroom discourse, parental and child talk, and arguments with friends.

There are prototype questions that function in two ways: (1) to get information and (2) to communicate indirectness when asking for a favor or making a suggestion. Conventional requests range from "Could you pass me *The Times*?" to "Would the Senator entertain addressing the topic introduced by the committee?" These two types of questions have been documented extensively in pragmatics research. Yet one issue that remains problematic in interactional discourse, particularly across cultures and languages, is how listeners know whether a speaker is asking type 1 or type 2. The common customer care question in the U.S. is "How can I help you?" Depending on the listener's background and experience with this genre of spoken language, an appropriate response is not immediately clear. Is it asking for information about the customer's efforts to find a particular item in a supermarket? Or is the question designed to elicit more interpersonal concerns?

Other types of questions can be heard in different types of talk. Kasper (2004) studied "question substitutes" in the context of oral proficiency interviews (OPIs), a form of test to assess a nonnative speaker's proficiency in a target language. It is a gate-keeping, interactional site where what appear syntactically to be requests are question substitutes. Here is an edited excerpt (Kasper 2004: 128) from an oral proficiency interview to highlight the role of questions in this instance:

1.	I:	Mm can you tell me about – what – you did over Golden Week?
2.	C:	Pardon?
3.	I:	Tell me what you did for Golden Week over Golden Week.

Line 1 illustrates the question substitute, while line 2 suggests that C was unclear about how to interpret I's request in line 1. The interviewer essentially repeats the question for information in line 1, with a direct request, indeed in command form. The "direct" Wh-question form and question substitutes that are in the form of requests – that is, prefaced with phrases like "can you tell me?" and "tell me" – may not be transparent to the testee. These questions, presumably designed to elicit an extended period of talk so that the tester can evaluate C's proficiency in English, may lead to confusion and C then may not do her best on the OPI.

Questions may also function as a means to challenge another person in a situation where the speaker seeks to convey a negative assessment of the person who is addressed. Koshik (2003) labels these "challenge questions." Koshik used a conversation analysis approach to study the occurrence of these challenges in sequences of talk, typically in the context of disagreement, argument, and accusation. She argues that the targeted questions could only be interpreted as challenges due to the existence of prior claim or actions in the talk. Further, the addressee of the challenge orients or reacts to the speaker's talk as a challenge. Here is an example from Koshik's research (2003: 70):

1.	Kathy:	It wove itself once it was set up. =
2.	Freda:	= It's woo:l?
3.	Kathy:	It's wool.
4.		(0.8)

5.	Rubin:	Whaddyou mean it wove itself once it w's set up.=
6.		=[What d's that] mean.=
7.	Kathy:	=[oh i-]
8.	Kathy:	= well I mean it's ve:ry simple,

In this excerpt, three participants are discussing a piece of work that Kathy had made. This challenge, from Rubin, does not necessarily imply a strong negative assertion about Kathy's work, but rather seeks to clarify the phrasing of her talk in line 1. Koshik's point is to demonstrate that, within the sequence of the talk excerpt, the context is necessary to infer the meaning of Rubin's contribution in line 5. His Wh-question in line 6 may not be a preferred response; however, it is in alignment with the others' talk and is relevant. A researchable topic related to Koshik's study is the underlying purposes of using Wh-questions to make challenges.

Finally, one more possible topic related to the use of questions in talk involves cross-cultural differences regarding the extent to which they can function to show disagreement and criticism of a speaker. For instance, a presenter of an invited talk found that one audience member used up the entire question and answer session to barrage the speaker with one Wh-question after another. The speaker tried to provide adequate responses to all of the questions, and only concluded after the presentation that the attendee was using the questions to indirectly express his negative assessment of the content of the talk and/or of the speaker. The presenter and the attendee were from two different cultural backgrounds, and the talk took place at a conference in the country of the attendee. Questions may signal a variety of functions, as Kasper states (1995: 63), and are likely to be universal strategies. Yet the exact force of questions as a means to give a warning or make a suggestion is often only weakly conventionalized and leads to miscommunication cross-culturally. There are some well-known examples in the research literature. Beebe and Takahashi's 1989 paper, "Do you have a bag?" recounts how a Japanese waiter in a sushi bar in New York asked a female American customer if she had a bag. What she understood to be an information question was actually a warning that her bag was about to be stolen as he spoke. In the same paper, Beebe and Takahashi reported that the use of a series of questions, as in the Q and A session remarked upon above, by Japanese international students in Beebe's seminars, provided the professor with a "self-discovery" means to convey that she had made a mistake in her lecture. What was a status and face-saving strategy for the Japanese students, a convention in their culture, created more of a face-threatening environment for the American professor, who would have preferred to be informed more directly of her mistake, even during the seminar.

Bouton (1988) reports that what he called "The Pope Question" can certainly require more processing time in order to understand the question's inference. Here is an example:

A: How about going downtown for some ice cream?
B: Is the Pope Catholic?

B responds positively to A's question: "Of course, I'll go downtown to get some ice cream – you know I love ice cream." The question response is likely designed to be humorous in addition. This style of indirectness, an example of irony, seems to be common in the U.K. as well as the U.S. and may not be easily understood by nonnative speakers from different sociocultural backgrounds.

The use of questions to avoid direct disapproval of a speaker's talk appeared in a study by Bardovi-Harlig and Hartford (1991) of academic advisor–student interactions. There were instances in the collected data illustrating how a student showed disagreement with a recommendation by an advisor (1991: 47):

Advisor: you will need to take, uh, after you take L503
Student: ah, excuse me, what was the name?

In the subsequent exchanges of talk, the student avoided any direct indication of disagreement by asking information questions. Bardovi-Harlig and Hartford state that it was not just the nonnative speakers who used this questioning strategy.

In sum, questions are a rich area for study for both small and more elaborated projects. In particular, more knowledge would be valuable about cross-cultural differences and the processes of both comprehending and producing language in use regarding the indirectness of questions.

Apologies and Refusals in Latin American Spanish

Carrying out studies of speech acts in context can be very useful for preparing for a language-teaching career. Not only does a study in an environment where native speakers use the language in multiple everyday interactions provide linguistic information, but also contextual features often not found in textbooks for teaching the language. Such a project develops general pragmatic awareness and the confidence of the teacher as a result. Kaiser (forthcoming) collected data for a study on refusals and apologies in Uruguayan Spanish. One of her main goals was to study the linguistic strategies that these speakers use to manage uncomfortable or offensive situations.

Kaiser focused on apologies and refusals in quotidian interactions from the perspective of Uruguayan women, from both lower and middle socioeconomic sectors of the city of Rosario, Uruguay. Using equipment to collect recorded speech, and field notes as she observed many of the interactions, Kaiser asked twelve Rosarian women to wear a lapel microphone as they went about their everyday lives, engaging family, friends, work peers and others in talk. While the study might have asked the native speaker informants to make, for example, a request that would be likely to get a refusal as a response, Kaiser's primary aim was to collect data that could serve as a baseline of native speaker norms – that is, data that would reflect what these speakers really say and do. Therefore, she sacrificed some efficiency in data collection for more naturalness.

The payoffs were well worth the wait. Below is an example from the apology data, illustrating different verbal phrase choices for offering a condolence as opposed to an apology. Whereas a speaker of American English could very acceptably employ a variant of "I am sorry" for both situations, the Spanish speakers clearly display a preference for *"lo siento"* as a condolence and a form of *perdonar* for apologies. Names have been changed to protect the privacy of the speakers.

The situation involves a wake and Moqui, 35, arrives alone and greets a series of people, both family members and friends of the deceased, most many years her senior. Without her mother present, the people she greets have trouble recognizing her.

1.	Moqui:	*(beso de saludo) lo siento mucho*
2.	Hombre 1:	*quién es?*
3.	Moqui:	*Moqui, la hija de Juliana*
4.	Hombre 1:	*ah Moqui, mirá perdón no te conocía (.) gracias*
5.	Moqui:	*Bianca, (beso de saludo) lo siento mucho*
6.	Bianca:	*Muchas gracias mi amor*
7.	Moqui:	*Moqui, la hija de Juliana*
8.	Bianca:	*ah no te conocía corazón ésta es mi hermana*
9.	Moqui:	*(a la hermana) ay, lo siento mucho*
10.	…	…
11.	Mujer 2:	*sabé quién es ella? La hija de Juliana, Moqui Bertolli*
12.	Hombre 2:	*Ah! la vecina de Carla!*
13:	Mujer 2:	*seguro, la persona que tenía*
14.	Hombre 2:	*Perdoná! (beso de saludo) perdoná (se ríe)*
15.	Moqui:	*no pasa nada (se ríe)*

Source: Kaiser (Forthcoming)

English Translation

Moqui:	(greets with kiss) I'm so sorry.
First man:	who are you?
Moqui:	Moqui, Juliana's daughter.
First Man:	oh Moqui, well I'll be, I'm sorry. I didn't recognize you. Thank you.
Moqui:	Bianca, (greets with kiss) I'm so sorry.
Bianca:	thank you very much, my dear.
Moqui:	Moqui, Juliana's daughter.
Bianca:	oh, I didn't recognize you, dear. This is my sister.
Moqui:	(to her sister) I'm so sorry.
Woman 2:	d'you know who she is? Juliana's daughter, Moqui Bertolli.

Man 2: ah, Carla's neighbor!
Woman 2: right, the person who had . . .
Man 2: my apologies (greets with kiss) my apologies (laughter).
Moqui: oh, that's quite all right (laughter).

In this data excerpt, the two speech acts, expressing condolences and apologies, are performed by the participants. The Spanish speakers use different verbs to show respect for the family and to apologize for not recognizing Moqui, Juliana's daughter and an intimate member of the community, as evidenced in the family members' use of *perdonar* with her. They are embarrassed that they do not recognize her without her mother. What is one speech act where one phrase can be used for both situations in English, i.e. "I'm sorry," is rendered by different verbs in Spanish. Note that the *beso de saludo* is a kiss on the left cheek of the person being greeted.

The goal of Kaiser's study was to learn about not only how speakers in this community made apologies, but also how they negotiated situations in which they felt they must refuse, for instance, a suggestion, request, or invitation. These two speech acts are often linked, with apologies commonly figuring as part of the refusal sequence. A refusal tends to be a dispreferred response and thus more problematic for the speaker to negotiate so as not to threaten the face of the requester. Local sociopragmatic norms may prefer avoidance of refusals, or use of indirectness to mitigate a refusal depending on sociocultural features, such as age, gender, and social class. Refusals are also more dispreferred depending on what the interaction is about.

Kaiser recorded several refusal sequences in the context of service encounters. Here is an example from her data where the speaker, a middle-class female shop owner, refuses a female customer's request. Note the directness on the part of the shop owner, the client's insistence, and the solidarity that both demonstrate toward each other in the end.

Rena, 47, owns and runs a small clothing boutique on the town square where she sells children's and women's garments. It's winter and a customer in her late twenties of middle-class appearance enters the shop looking to buy a man's scarf. Rena has none in stock.

1.	Rena:	*hola cómo andás?*
2.	Clienta:	*andás bien?*
3.	Rena:	*bien, vos?*
4.	Clienta:	*bien*
5.	Rena:	*qué puede ser?*
6.	Clienta:	*alguna bufanda de hombre o que pueda usar un hombre una negra o algo?*
7.	Rena:	*ay, no, creo que no me queda nada . . . había una negra ahi . . . ah pero capaz que para hombre no, no, no, no ésa no es para hombre.*
8.	Rena:	*no [no me queda*
9.	Clienta:	*[marrón o algo . . .*

10.	Rena:	*ningun – ninguna, ninguna, ninguna*
11.	Clienta:	*ay, no, en ningún lado*
12.	Rena:	*ahh*
13.	Clienta:	*bueno, [gracias*
14.	Rena:	*[yo tengo que ir a Montevideo pero hace mucho frío*
15.	Clienta:	*y bueno. chau, no dan ganas de ir tampoco*
16:	Rena:	*(risita) chau*
17:	Clienta:	*que pases bien*

English Translation

Rena:	hi how are you?
Customer:	doing well?
Rena:	fine, you?
Customer:	fine.
Rena:	what'll it be?
Customer:	a scarf for a man or one that a man could wear, a black one or something?
Rena:	ay no, I don't think I've got anything left, there was a black one over there . . . ah but perhaps not for a man no. no, no, no. no.
Rena: no.	[not a thing
Customer:	[brown or something xxx
Rena:	not- not one, not one, not one.
Customer:	ay no, nowhere.
Rena:	ahh! ((sympathizing))
Customer:	well, [thanks.
Rena:	[I've gotta go to Montevideo but it's so cold.
Customer:	I know. bye, it makes you just not even feel like going.
Rena:	(chuckles) bye.
Customer:	have a good day.

Rena, the shop owner, uses the second person singular verb form and local colloquialisms such as *andar* and *chau*, signaling directness and a lessening of social distance between herself and the customer. The client is insistent about purchasing a man's scarf and Rena spends some time looking in her shop for something that might serve. Rena does not want to refuse the customer and wants to appear to be doing her best, possibly so that the woman will return to her shop in the future. So she at least pretends to search more in the shop to see what she might have that could serve as a man's scarf. At the end of the interaction, the two women display solidarity by commenting that making a trip to Montevideo, the capital, would be wise, and they would be likely to find more merchandise, but it is winter and the cold weather doesn't make them feel like traveling. When the customer leaves, they are on good terms and display friendliness to each other.

Pragmatic Glitches and Misfires

The chapter on cross-cultural pragmatics (Chapter 4) discussed the notion of pragmatic failure and the recent challenges to the view that nonnative speakers' pragmatic competence is insufficient to avoid miscommunication with native speakers of the target language. In the real world of everyday talk, with the great diversity of speakers as nonnative users of the local language that is found in urban environments in particular, it is still commonplace for what are called misfires to occur. A typical example arises when a nonnative speaker of French mistakenly says "*Je suis plein*," thinking it is a polite phrase to use to refuse any more food at the dinner table. In fact, the transfer from English, "I am full," is not the translation equivalent as the French phrase means "I am pregnant." These failures or glitches are even used as examples on public radio of how one must be careful when in a "foreign" restaurant in Washington, D.C., famous for its French restaurants.

A project was assigned to students in an undergraduate second language acquisition course to work with a conversational partner who did not speak English as a first or primary language (they could also work with a nonstandard speaker of English). Many international students on the campus, even if they are enrolled in graduate-level programs, are happy to work with a native speaker of English not only to get help with particular linguistic needs, but also to have someone they can talk, socialize, and study with outside of their own specializations. So a conversational partner provides benefits to them. The students in the SLA course negotiated with their partners to find if they had any particular concerns. In addition, they worked with their partners on pragmatic misfires, i.e. "times when they felt uncomfortable and realized they must have said something wrong." Very often they did not know what exactly had happened or how the uncomfortable situation arose. The students explained that they would be writing a report for their final grade in the SLA course and, moreover, that they would contribute their papers to the faculty member in charge of the course. Thus, permission to use the data was secured and neither the students' nor the partners' names would be used. The following are examples of some misfires that have been edited (LoCastro 2010b: 12–15):

1. Marie presents her friend, Fatimah, with a CD of English music as a gift. Fatimah says: "Oh, I don't know what I can give you in return for your kindness."

A simple "thank you" would be preferred in American English, rather than a response that implies gift-giving requires something be presented in return.

2. Mario asks Ivan, a fellow graduate student, "Do you mind if I borrow your dictionary?" Ivan answers: "No."

In the U.S., a dictionary may be passed around amongst students readily. It is likely that in his country of origin, Ivan apparently has a different attitude, possibly due to the economic situation where a dictionary may be worth a considerable sum of money. A response like "not at all," would be preferred.

> 3. In this "nonverbal" speech act, a nonnative English speaker female, upon being introduced to a native English speaker, ran up to the person and hugged her.

Gestures and other nonverbal forms of communication can also lead to misfires, as in this case. A stereotype of Americans' friendliness may suggest that hugging is a norm, even for greeting a new person. A more appropriate return greeting for the young woman would have been to offer her right hand to shake and to say "It's nice to meet you." Even though some Americans may seem to greet anyone with a hug, in fact it is rare among strangers to do so and, as a nonnative to the culture, it is safer to use a more neutral response.

Conversational partners provide an opportunity for both participants to exchange language lessons and learn about each others' cultural beliefs and practices, as well as engage in small projects on a variety of topics. A joint project could develop so that both participants benefit from working together and developing their language and interactional skills.

Bilingual Political Discourse

Studies of language use in African countries have become more and more of interest for several reasons. A primary impetus for those interested in sociopragmatics is the fact that African cities are increasingly plurilingual, with rural populations migrating within countries and across borders in pursuit of jobs, better educational opportunities, and modernity, with access to technology and IT. Plurilinguism is, however, not a new phenomenon, but has become arguably more complex as a result of the globalization of English as a language of international commerce, government, and education. Urban areas in Africa are sites of great diversity on several levels, in particular the mixing of languages, and the sociopragmatic norms of discourse experience implicit pressures to converge to take in new expectations and diverge to signal nationalism and new local identities.

Bwenge (2010) studied one local situation in his native Tanzania: the national legislative body, or parliament, is called the Bunge in Swahili. In the 1960s, when Tanzania had gained independence from Great Britain, it adopted one national language, Swahili, and then both Swahili and English as official languages. Swahili is an African language that serves as the primary lingua franca of East Africa, and the former colonial power's language was adopted as a language of liberation and representative of the new country, with its eyes on the future of international contacts and opportunities. Consequently, it is not surprising that the code switching or mixing of those two languages would become a norm in some contexts. Bwenge focused on the parliament, where elite, highly educated members of Tanzanian society are elected to that body and use what Bwenge has labeled ES (Elite Swahili), that is, the Swahili–English mixed code of this socioeconomic class. His study documents how this "communicative innovation" and symbol of "the society's linguistic culture" comprises not only a distinct code, but also how this particular language choice is "pragmatically and symbolically motivated" (2010: ii). Bwenge looked into the use of this mixed code by members of parliament, by the government, and in society, before narrowing his focus to formal parliamentary debates in the Bunge. The coming together of social and political dimensions is exemplified in this case of linguistic resources in this mixed code. Here is an example from a parliamentary debate (Bwenge 2010: 48):

> *Je, haoni bado ni muhimu ku*-invest *katika kiwanja cha Namfua badala ya kutawanya fedha ndogo ambayo tunayo?*
>
> [Doesn't he/she see it's still important to invest in the Namfua stadium instead of spreading that little money we have?]

Bwenge explains that the phrase "*ku*-invest" is linguistically and semantically the core of the question during the Q and A session, and it signals the speaker's motivation to use the mixed code, i.e. ES, to self-identify as an educated, cosmopolitan Tanzanian. However, it simultaneously expresses the modern identity of Tanzania, embracing English as a language of international communication. They have moved away from the past of being a colonial nation, rejecting any symbol of that unfortunate period in their history.

Information about when standard Swahili (SS) and ES are used in the Parliament gives a synopsis of when the mixed code is used (Bwenge 2010: 49):

Opening prayer: standard Swahili (written)
Question and answer hour: elite Swahili [supplementary question, spontaneous]
Presentation of budget speech: standard Swahili (written)
Debating the budget speech on the floor: elite Swahili [spoken spontaneously]
Presenter's closing remarks: elite Swahili [spoken spontaneously]

This picture of when ES is used, i.e. three times out of five, suggests that it is the more dominant choice and that is most likely to be the choice when spontaneous, spoken language is the norm. Further study could look into the motivations for the use of standard Swahili with regard to written documents where historic background may add information on this feature of multilingualism in a country such as Tanzania.

Bwenge's study is a good example of how combining microanalysis of language use in a targeted environment and macroanalysis of sociocultural influences and constraints in the same environment provides information on the sociopragmatic rules of speaking. His study goes into more depth for, as Bwenge points out, the educated elite of Tanzania use ES in informal, social interactions as well as in the very formal contexts of Parliamentary business. Although non-elites, who are likely to be uneducated and monolingual, view ES as a symbol of *"usomi"* or Tanzanian identity in a very positive way, the use of this mixed code is contested (Bwenge 2010: 78) by other sectors of society who challenge that view and the degree to which the current members of parliament are representative of Tanzania.

Conclusions

This chapter has aimed to provide a sample of studies as examples of topics that have been pursued and have resulted in publications and doctoral dissertations. Readers of this book who need to do projects for course credit in the space of one fifteen-week semester can read these examples for ideas and to spark lateral thinking. For the most part, these could not be carried out within a short period of time. One exception is the third one, pragmatic misfires and glitches, and the first section on questions clearly has several ideas, any of which can be developed into small projects. The hope is that this chapter encourages the readers to get into brainstorming, testing out ideas by doing the opposite of what seems to be expected, and generally putting on a new pair of glasses to become an astute observer of people and our behaviors to come up with topics for projects. Doing the opposite can also be fun: try teaching a class only from the back of a classroom for an hour or saying hello to everyone you pass in your office one day. And then observe what happens with the interactions and patterns of ingrained language behaviors.

Tasks

1. Review your answers to the awareness-raising tasks you completed at the end of Chapter 1. Consider what you have learned and how you can apply what you learned to your everyday life, education, and professional development.
2. Discuss the examples of studies in this chapter in depth with peers and your teacher. How would you go about doing a study related to one of those above?
3. Brainstorm with your classmates similar studies you could do in your environment.
4. Then seek out, usually at a university library, more information about your topic and studies that may have been done on it or that are related in some way to your possible study.

PART IV
Conclusion

13
PRAGMATIC COMPETENCE IN OUR DIVERSE WORLD

Introduction

This final chapter brings together themes that have been woven through the book. Both the creation of a book and then readers' processing and thinking about the content require a linear perspective. That's how our brains work. One starts at the first page and continues to the end. The book introduces and elaborates on principles, concepts, and research methodologies as if each topic was a separate entity. However, in fact, the topics and concepts are all intertwined and have a dynamic and interactive relationship to each other. There are layers of meaning from the micro, linguistic level to the macro, sociocultural level that can only be separated for heuristic purposes. In the real world, in real time, it is difficult to isolate one feature from others in the miniseconds of interactions. This chapter focuses on consolidating the dimensions of pragmatics relevant for achieving situationally appropriate language use and, ideally, comity in interactions.

The goal of this volume has been to make pragmatics accessible to a wide range of learners and teachers: (1) to raise their language awareness regarding the real, ubiquitous situations of social action; (2) to develop the ability to think critically about interactional discourse; and (3) to acquire knowledge about pragmatics and skills to do pragmatics. These three objectives become inseparable in pursuing a deeper goal of applying the knowledge and skills of pragmatics to improving communication, particularly intergroup and intercultural interactions in our increasingly global world. While the multiple sources of news media report ceaselessly on different forms of "interconnectivity" from new technologies, the instances of discrimination, discord in governmental contexts, and unwillingness to talk and work with others who are "different" suggest the importance of understanding the role of pragmatics as a minimum requirement for engagement in any field involving communication between and among people.

An Inclusive Approach to Pragmatics

Since the 1960s, pragmatics has developed from a form of solely linguistic analysis of isolated instances of speech to inclusion of sociocultural dimensions, both linguistic and nonlinguistic, in interactional discourse. The semantic view of pragmatics still attaches importance to word meaning and truth conditions of sentences. Austin (1962) and others increasingly emphasized the need to study language in use, as a form of social action, i.e. in its social context, requiring attention to the communicative function or force of utterances. The intention of the speaker of a speech act took priority over word meaning. Subsequently, Hymes (1972) introduced an elaborated view of the linguistic competence of Chomsky, which he called "communicative competence." His approach recognized the reality of human interactions and opened the field of study to research that would account for people's use of language in contexts in socially appropriate ways. Sociolinguistic researchers sought to learn how social factors influence speech behavior, in particular the "social rules of speaking." Further development in this area acknowledged that there were no "rules," hard and fast prescriptions about what to say and when, but rather patterns of behavior, some of which were more likely to be used in formal situations and others, in other contexts.

On a parallel track within linguistics, pragmatics was developing. Rather than focusing on individual speech acts by the speaker, researchers and theorists began to push beyond to concentrate on naturally occurring interactional discourse, to observe how speakers *and* hearers took turns in talk. Arguments for inclusion of nonverbal aspects were finally taken on board and cognitive linguists pursued the goal of explaining the dynamic, mental processing that underlies the comprehension and production of pragmatic meaning in talk-in-interaction. As a consequence of those developments, pragmatics has become a form of language analysis that works at understanding the core factors of human interactional communication.

This book has brought together sociolinguistics and pragmatics in an explicit way. While sociolinguistics generally links linguistic cues – such as phonological or syntactic variations – to social groups in a particular speech community, pragmatics stays at the local, micro level of analysis, seeking to understand the linguistic organization of meaning creation. For instance, the choice of an imperative instead of a mitigated request communicates something about the participants in an interaction. A speaker's intended meaning in context is the starting point. However, the intended meaning interacts with features beyond the linguistic forms. A sociolinguistic perspective in pragmatics adds the recognition, often left unexamined, that the participants in the interaction make linguistic choices on the basis of such variables as their identities, gender, sociocultural background, previous experiences, and world knowledge. In other words, many factors can play a role in speakers' choices, linguistic, microsociolinguistic, and macrosociolinguistic. In sum, this volume offers a more inclusive view of what is entailed in performing pragmatic meanings and in understanding those meanings.

Pragmatic Competence

The knowledge that influences and constrains speakers' choices regarding use of language in socially appropriate ways is called pragmatic competence. As was pointed out in earlier chapters, this underlying knowledge informs pragmatic meaning creation in an individual's first or primary language as well as other languages the person may use. Research has tended to concentrate on second language pragmatic competence, however. There are undoubtedly universal or core features of the knowledge base. The fact that people traveling to a country where they do not know the language try to learn basic speech acts and phrases, such as thanking, greetings, and asking directions, suggests an awareness of the role of language in achieving successful interactions. Generally, people want to be perceived as polite, at the very least.

Indeed, development of pragmatic competence is a complex undertaking that involves experience, world knowledge, certain personality traits, and general language awareness. It entails as well good listening and observation skills to comprehend others' signals of pragmatic meaning, and good language learning strategies to observe, internalize, and then use vocabulary, formulaic language, and strategies in context. Even with our own L1 speech communities, pragmatics requires recognition of group differences related to regional, ethnic, age, and educational backgrounds.

For second or foreign language learners, the task is even more complex, as transfer from the L1 and sociocultural factors play greater roles. An additional burden is the issue regarding how and when to learn how to use pragmatically appropriate speech. The most obvious environment is in classrooms or other instructional environments. Yet, limitations seem to loom large for teachers and learners. Exposure to naturalistic environments would appear to be the answer. Yet, research on study abroad programs shows that the learners do not necessarily return to their home countries with increased fluency or improved pragmatic competence in the L2. Research is needed to understand the factors that interfere with pragmatic competence development.

Value of Research

To gain deeper knowledge, research – with a big R or a small r – is clearly a useful tool. This book has discussed many studies of scholars; this category is research with a big R. Not everyone can do – or wants to do – elaborate studies, which are often very time consuming and may require funding. Reading the studies, however, can be informative and can spark interest and motivation to engage in small studies, with a small r. Small studies can raise awareness and develop respect for the complexity of interactional discourse and for the participants. Even reflecting on one's own behavior can be enlightening. Experimenting with responses to greetings in grocery stores is a learning opportunity.

However, there is another reason for the book's emphasis on research. Doing even small research projects, and reading about others, small and large, develops an attitude of inquiry, questioning, and observation. Seeking evidence before making generalizations and judgments becomes a part of one's daily life. This attitude helps in new situations, with an L2 in the speech community in particular, to figure out the local pragmatic norms, to see the situated inferencing in real time, and to discover the role of identity in converging to or diverging from group members. One can "do an ethnography" of family interactions to learn how to handle discussions and use politeness to make an older family member feel valued. These examples are only some of the many instances in daily life which require sometimes fine tuning of one's communication skills.

Pragmatics in our Diverse World

Equipping oneself to be knowledgeable about pragmatic competence is as important as developing one's IT and technology skills. Both are indispensable tools for the world of today, irrespective of one's regional or geographical location. This volume has focused on the social dimensions of language in use in a wide variety of everyday contexts in an effort to help readers recognize the variation in language to signal meanings beyond those that can be derived from formal linguistic analysis.

ESL/EFL teachers are on the frontlines regarding second language pragmatic development, particularly in environments where learners use the L2 on a daily basis to carry out tasks in institutional contexts. They also hold great responsibility for learners who intend to use the L2 for study or work abroad. Thus, teachers in particular need to pursue their own ability to think critically about language data and instances of use to prepare themselves. Their learners benefit from the explicit teaching of pragmatics by their teachers and ideally become autonomous learners, doing pragmatics to solve communication problems and pushing their competence level as successful participants in L2 interactions.

The acquisition of greater knowledge and skills to do pragmatics hopefully fosters the development of a non-deficit view of other participants and ourselves. An earlier chapter addressed the issue of "whose norms," by pointing out that both nonstandard speakers of the L1 and nonnative speakers of the L2 may have communication strategies that diverge from those of standard speakers of the languages. Difference is acknowledged. However, to label those speakers as deficient or rude, stereotyping and discriminating against them, is an unproductive means to achieve comity and better communication in general. A non-deficit stance is particularly important regarding nonnative speakers of English; they outnumber native English speakers in most parts of the world. With knowledge and skills for doing pragmatics, educators as well as other readers of this book can work towards developing their own communicative competence and contribute to raising the awareness of others to move beyond the deficit view.

A Final Note: Doing Pragmatics can be Fun!

An undergraduate student, Kyle, in a sociolinguistics class decided to do a data-collection project on a pragmatics topic for his final paper for the semester. He explained in his proposal that he had been sharing an apartment with two other young men, all friends since their high school days. Studying pragmatics had sparked his curiosity about the extent to which the three apartment mates interacted differently when they were alone in comparison to their communication strategies in a mixed-sex group. So he persuaded his apartment mates to invite three women, other students who lived down the hall, for dinner one evening. Kyle did not tell the others exactly what he was interested in observing. However, to get their consent for audio-taping the dinner talk, he explained that he was doing a project on their topics of conversation. He transcribed parts of the collected data that were related to his study and wrote an excellent paper. Kyle explained that doing the project gave him a feeling of competence and helped him decide to specialize in sociolinguistics. Finally, last but not least, he and one of the women became friends.

NOTE

Chapter 4 Cross-cultural Pragmatics

1 It is difficult to avoid a monolithic view of "culture." Yet it is beyond the scope of this book to address this very controversial and contentious issue of defining what constitutes a culture. I use it as a means to categorize people and communities for the purpose of discussion, while being fully aware myself of the limitations of doing so. I use it to acknowledge differences between people from diverse language, ethnic, national, class, and regional backgrounds, all variables that may influence their language and nonverbal behaviors.

REFERENCES

Aijmer, K. and Simon-Vanderberger, A. M. (Eds.) (2006). *Pragmatic markers in contrast*. Amsterdam: Elsevier.

Al-Issa, A. (2003). Sociocultural transfer in L2 speech behaviors: evidence and motivating factors. *International Journal of Intercultural Relations*, 27, 581–601.

Alcón Soler, A. and Martínez-Flor, A. (Eds.) (2008). *Investigating pragmatics in foreign language learning, teaching, and testing*. Clevedon: Multilingual Matters.

Allwright, D. and Hanks, J. (2009). *The developing language learner: An introduction to exploratory practice*. Basingstoke: Palgrave Macmillan.

Anataki, C. and Widdicombe, S. (Eds.) (1998). *Identities in talk*. London: Sage.

Astley, H. and Hawkins, E. (1985). *Using language*. Cambridge: Cambridge University Press.

Atkinson, J. and Errington, S. (Eds.) (1990) *Power and difference: Gender in Island Southeast Asia*. Stanford, CA: Stanford University Press.

Auer, P. (Ed.) (1998). *Codeswitching in conversation: Language, interaction, and identity*. New York: Routledge

Austin, J. L. (1962). *How to do things with words*. Oxford: Clarendon Press.

Bardovi-Harlig, K. and Hartford, B. (1990). Congruence in native and nonnative conversations: Status balance in academic advising sessions. *Language Learning*, 40(4), 467–501.

Bardovi-Harlig, K. and Hartford, B. (1991). Saying "no" in English: Native and nonnative rejections. In L. F. Bouton and Y. Kachru (Eds.), *Pragmatics and language learning*, 2 (pp. 41–57). Urbana, IL: Division of English as an International Language, University of Illinois at Urbana-Champaign.

Bardovi-Harlig, K. and Hartford, B. (1993). Learning the rules of academic talk. *Studies in Second Language Acquisition*, 15, 279–304.

Barnes, D. (1976). *From communication to curriculum*. Middlesex, UK: Penguin.

Beebe, L. and Takahashi, T. (1989). Do you have a bag?: Social status and patterned variation in second language acquisition. In S. Gass, M. Madden, D. Preston, and L. Selinker, (Eds.), *Variation in second language acquisition: Discourse and pragmatics* (pp. 103–125). Clevedon: Multilingual Matters.

Benson, T. J. (2000). A study of target language use in the upper-beginning EFL university classroom. Unpublished M.A. thesis, Universidad de las Americas Puebla, Mexico.

Bergman, M. L. and Kasper, G. (1993). Perception and performance in native and nonnative apology. In G. Kasper and S. Blum-Kulka, (Eds.), *Interlanguage pragmatics* (pp. 82–107). Oxford: Oxford University Press.

Bhatia, V. K., Candlin, C. N., and Allori, P. E. (Eds.) (2008). *Language, culture, and the law: The formulation of legal concepts across systems and cultures.* New York: Peter Lang.

Bialystok, E. (1993). Symbolic representation and attentional control in pragmatic competence. In G. Kasper and S. Blum-Kulka (Eds.), *Interlanguage pragmatics* (pp. 43–58). Oxford: Oxford University Press.

Block, D. (2009). *Second language identities.* London: Continuum.

Blum-Kulka, S. (1983). Interpreting and performing speech acts in a second language: A cross cultural study of Hebrew and English. In N. Wolfson and E. Judd (Eds.), *Sociolinguistics and language acquisition* (pp. 36–55). Rowley, MA: Newbury House.

Blum-Kulka, S. (1991). Interlanguage pragmatics: The case of requests. In R. Phillipson, E. Kellerman, L. Selinker, M. Sharwood-Smith, and M. Swain (Eds.), *Foreign/second language pedagogy research* (pp. 255–272). Clevedon: Multilingual Matters.

Blum-Kulka, S., House, J., and Kasper, G. (Eds.) (1989). *Cross-cultural pragmatics: Requests and apologies.* Norwood, NJ: Ablex.

Bourdieu, P. (1990) *The logic of practice.* Cambridge: Polity Press.

Bousfield, D. and Locher, M.A. (Eds.) (2008). *Impoliteness in language: Studies on its interplay with power in theory and practice.* Berlin: Mouton de Gruyter.

Bouton, L. F. (1988). A crosscultural study of ability to interpret implicatives in English. *World Englishes,* 7, 183–197.

Bouton, L. F. (1994). Conversational implicature in the second language: Learned slowly when not deliberately taught. *Journal of Pragmatics,* 22, 157–167.

Bradford, B. (1988). *Intonation in context.* Cambridge: Cambridge University Press.

Brown, G. (1995). *Speakers, listeners, and communication: Explorations in discourse.* Cambridge: Cambridge University Press.

Brown, G. and Yule, G. (1983). *Discourse analysis.* Cambridge: Cambridge University Press.

Brown, P. and Levinson, S. (1987). *Politeness: Some universals in language usage.* Cambridge: Cambridge University Press.

Bruner, J. (1978). The role of dialogue in language acquisition. In A. Sinclair, R. Javella, and W. Levelt (Eds.), *The child's conception of language* (pp. 241–256). New York: Springer-Verlag.

Butler, J. (1990). *Gender trouble: Feminism and the subversion of identity.* New York: Routledge.

Burt, S. M. (2010). *The Hmong language in Wisconsin: Language shift and pragmatic change.* Lewiston, NY: The Edwin Mellen Press.

Bwenge, C. (2010). *The tongue between: Swahili and English in Tanzanian parliamentary discourse.* Munich: LINCOM.

Cameron, D. (1995). *Verbal hygiene.* London/New York: Routledge.

Cameron, D. (2000). *Good to talk? Living and working in a communication culture.* London: Sage.

Cameron, D. (2001). *Working with spoken discourse.* London: Sage.

Cameron, D. (2005a). Language, gender, and sexuality: Current issues and new directions. *Applied Linguistics,* 26/4, 482–502.

Cameron, D. (2005b). Relativity and its discontents: Language, gender, and pragmatics. *Intercultural Pragmatics 2–3*, 321–334.
Cameron, D., McAlinden, F., and O'Leary, K. (1988). Lakoff in context: The social and linguistic functions of tag questions. In J. Coates and D. Cameron (Eds.), *Women in their speech communities* (pp. 74–93). London/New York: Longman.
Campbell, S. and Roberts, C. (2007). Migration, ethnicity and competing discourses in the job interview: Synthesizing the institutional and personal. *Discourse and Society, 18*(3), 243–271.
Carter, R. and McCarthy, M. (1997). *Exploring spoken English*. Cambridge: Cambridge University Press.
Cashman, H. R. (2005). Identities at play: Language preference and group membership in bilingual talk in interaction. *Journal of Pragmatics, 37*, 301–315.
Cazden, C. B. (2001). *Classroom discourse: The language of teaching and learning*. 2nd edition. Portsmouth, NH: Heinemann.
Channell, J. (1994). *Vague language*. Oxford: Oxford University Press.
Chast, R. (2010). The G.P.S. for Conversations. Cartoon published in *The New Yorker*, Oct. 11, 2010, 83.
Chodorowska-Pilch, M. (2008). *Verás* in Peninsular Spanish as a grammaticalized discourse marker invoking positive and negative politeness. *Journal of Pragmatics, 40*, 1357–1372.
Clancy, P. M., Thompson, S. A., Suzuki, R. and Tao, H. (1996). The conversational use of reactive tokens in English, Japanese, and Mandarin. *Journal of Pragmatics, 26*, 355–387.
Clark, H. H. (1996). *Using language*. Cambridge: Cambridge University Press.
Clark, H. H. and Clark, E. V. (1977). *Psychology and language: An introduction to psycholinguistics*. New York: Harcourt Brace Jovanovich.
Clark, U. (2007). *Studying language: English in action*. Basingstoke, UK: Palgrave.
Cohen, A. D. (1996). Speech acts. In S. L. McKay and N. H. Hornberger (Eds.), *Sociolinguistics and language teaching* (pp. 383–420). Cambridge: Cambridge University Press.
Connor, U., Ruiz Garrido, M., Rozycki, W., Goering, B., Kinney, E., and Koehler, J. (2008). Intercultural study of patient-directed medicine labeling: Text differences between the United States and Spain. *Communication and Medicine, 5*, 117–132.
Cook, H. M. (2006). Japanese politeness as an interactional achievement: Academic consultation sessions in Japanese universities. *Multilingua, 25(3)*, 269–291.
Cook, V. (1992) Evidence of multicompetence. *Language Learning, 42(4)*, 557–591.
Cook, V. (Ed.) (2002). *Portrait of the L2 user*. Clevedon: Multilingual Matters.
Crystal, D. (1997). *English as a global language*. Cambridge: Cambridge University Press.
Crystal, D. (1985). *A dictionary of linguistics and phonetics*. 2nd edition. Oxford: Blackwell.
Dacey, J. (2009). Swiss seek multilingual equilibrium. *The Guardian Weekly*, Learning English, August 7, 2–3.
Davis, S. (Ed.) (1991). *Pragmatics: A reader*. New York: Oxford University Press.
De Fina, A., Schiffrin, D., and Bamberg, M. (Eds.) (2006a). *Discourse and identity*. Cambridge: Cambridge University Press.
De Fina, A., Schiffrin, D., and Bamberg, M. (2006b) Introduction. In A. De Fina, D. Schriffin and M. Bamberg (Eds.), *Discourse and identity* (pp. 1–23). Cambridge: Cambridge University Press.

Denzin, N. K. and Lincoln, Y. S. (Eds.) (2005). *Handbook of qualitative research.* 3rd edition. Thousand Oaks: Sage.

Dornyei, Z. (2007). *Research methods in applied linguistics.* Oxford: Oxford University Press.

Doughty, C. (1991). Second language instruction does make a difference: Evidence from an empirical study on SL relativization. *Studies in Second Language Acquisition, 13,* 431–469.

Drew, P. and Heritage, J. (Eds.) (1992). *Talk at work: Interaction in institutional settings.* Cambridge: Cambridge University Press.

Duff, P. A. (2011). Identity, agency, and second language acquisition. In A. Mackey and S. Gass (Eds.), *Handbook of second language acquisition,* in press. London: Routledge.

Dufon, M. (2000). The acquisition of negative responses to experience questions in Indonesian as a second language by sojourners in naturalistic interactions. In B. Swierzbin, F. Morris, M. Anderson, C. A. Klee, and E. Tarone (Eds.), *Social and cognitive factors in second language acquisition* (pp. 77–97). Somerville, CA: Cascadilla Press.

Edge, J. (2003). Imperial troopers and servants of the lord: A vision for TESOL for the 21st century. *TESOL Quarterly, 37* (4), 701–709.

Edmondson, W. and House, J. (1991). Do learners talk too much? The waffle phenomenon in interlanguage pragmatics. In R. Phillipson, E. Kellerman, L. Selinker, M. Sharwood-Smith, and M. Swain (Eds.), *Foreign/second language pedagogy research* (pp. 273–286). Clevedon: Multilingual Matters.

Eggins, S. (1994). *An introduction to systemic functional linguistics.* London: Pinter.

Egner, I. (2006). Intercultural aspects of the speech act of promising: Western and African practices. *Intercultural Pragmatics 3–4,* 443–464.

Ellis, R. (1994). *The study of second language acquisition.* Oxford: Oxford University Press.

Ellwood, C. and Nakane, I. (2009). Privileging speech in EAP and mainstream university classrooms: A critical evaluation of participation. *TESOL Quarterly, 43,* 2, 203–230.

Erickson, F. (1984). Rhetoric, anecdote, and rhapsody: Coherence strategies in a conversation among black American adolescents. In D. Tannen (Ed.), *Coherence in spoken and written discourse* (pp. 81–154). Norwood, NJ: Ablex.

Erickson, F. (2004). *Talk and social theory: Ecologies of speaking and listening in everyday life.* Cambridge: Polity Press.

Erickson, F. and Schultz, J. (1982). *The counselor as gatekeeper: Social interaction in interviews.* New York: Academic Press.

Errington, S. (1990). Recasting sex, gender, and power. In J. Atkinson and S. Errington, (Eds.), *Power and difference* (pp. 1–58). Stanford, CA: Stanford University Press.

Eslami-Rasekh, Z. (2004). Face-keeping strategies in reaction to complaints: English and Persian. *Journal of Asian Pacific Communication, 14,* 1, 181–197.

Eslami-Rasekh, Z. (2005a). Invitations in Persian and English: Ostensible or genuine? *Intercultural Pragmatics, 2–4,* 453–480.

Eslami-Rasekh, Z. (2005b). Raising the pragmatic awareness of language learners. *ELT Journal, 59/3,* 199–208.

Fairclough, N. (2001). *Language and power.* 2nd edition. Harlow: Pearson Education.

Ferrara, A. (1985). Pragmatics. *Handbook of discourse analysis, 2,* 137–157. London: Academic Press.

Flores-Salgado, E. (2008). Development patterns of requests and apologies. Unpublished doctoral dissertation, Macquarie University, Sydney, Australia.

Gardner, D. K. (1990). *Learning to be a sage*. Berkeley: University of California Press.
Gardner, R. C. (1985). *Social psychology and second language learning*. London: Arnold.
Gardner, R. C. and Lambert, W. E. (1972). *Attitudes and motivation in second language learning*. Rowley, MA: Newbury House.
Gee, J. P. (2005). *An introduction to discourse analysis: Theory and method* 2nd edition. New York/London: Routledge.
Gershenson, O. (2003). Misunderstanding between Israelis and Soviet immigrants: Linguistic and cultural factors. *Multilingua 22*, 275–290.
Gillette, B. (1994). The role of learner goals in L2 success. In J. P. Lantolf (Ed.), *Vygotskyan approaches to second language research* (pp. 195–231). Norwood, NJ: Ablex.
Goffman, E. (1963). *Behavior in public places: Notes on the social organization of gatherings*. New York: Free Press.
Goffman, E. (1971). *Relations in public*. Harmondsworth: Penguin.
Goodwin, C. (1981) Restarts, pauses, and the achievement of a state of mutual gaze at turn-beginning. In C. Goodwin (Ed.), *Conversational organization: Interaction between speakers and hearers* (pp. 272–302). New York: Academic Press.
Green, G. M. (1989). *Pragmatics and natural language understanding*. Mahwah, NJ: Lawrence Erlbaum.
Grice, H. P. (1975). Logic and conversation: A cognitive approach. In P. Cole and J. L. Morgan (Eds.), *Speech acts*, vol. 3 of *Syntax and semantics* (pp. 41–58). New York: Academic Press.
Grundy, P. (1995). *Doing pragmatics*. London: Edward Arnold.
Gu, Y. (1990). Politeness phenomena in modern Chinese. *Journal of Pragmatics, 14*, 237–257.
Gumperz, J. J. (1971). Dialect differences and social stratification in a North Indian village. In J. J. Gumperz (Ed.), *Language in Social Groups* (pp. 25–47). Stanford: Stanford University Press.
Gumperz, J. J. (1982). *Discourse strategies*. Cambridge: Cambridge University Press.
Halford, S. and Leonard, P. (1999). 'New identities? Professionalism, managerialism and construction of self. In M. Exworthy and S. Halford (Eds.), *Professionals and the new managerialism in the public sector*. Buckingham: Open University Press.
Hall, E. T. (1969). *Beyond culture*. New York: Anchor Books.
Halliday, M. A. K. (1978). *Language as a social semiotic: The social interpretation of language and meaning*. London: Edward Arnold.
Hanks, W. F., Ide, S., and Katagiri, Y. (2009). Towards an emancipatory pragmatics. *Journal of Pragmatics, 41*, 1–9.
Hasan, R. (1985). The structure of text. In M.A.K. Halliday and R. Hasan (Eds.), *Language, context, and text: Aspects of language in a social-semiotic perspective* (pp. 52–121). Oxford: Oxford University Press.
Hatch, E. (1992). *Discourse and language education*. Cambridge: Cambridge University Press.
Heath, C. (1992). The delivery and reception of diagnosis in the general-practice consultation. In P. Drew and J. Heritage (Eds.), *Talk at work: Interaction in institutional settings* (pp. 235–267). Cambridge: Cambridge University Press.
Heath, S. B. (1983). *Ways with words: Language, life and work in communities and classrooms*. Cambridge: Cambridge University Press.
Heritage, J. and Clayman, S. (2010). *Talk in action: Interactions, identities, and institutions*. London: Wiley-Blackwell.

Hickey, L. and Stewart, M. (Eds.) (2005). *Politeness in Europe*. Clevedon: Multilingual Matters.

Higgins, C. (2009). "Are you Hindu?": Resisting membership categorization through language alternation. In H. Nguyen and G. Kasper (Eds.), *Talk-in-interaction: Multilingual perspectives* (pp. 111–136). Honolulu: University of Hawaii, National Foreign Language Resource Center.

Hinkel, E. (1994). Pragmatics of interaction: Expressing thanks in a second language. *Applied Language Learning*, 5, 1, 73–91.

Hinkel, E. (1996). When in Rome: Evaluations of L2 pragmalinguistic behaviors. *Journal of Pragmatics*, 26, 51–70.

Hiraga, M. K. and Turner, J. M. (1995). What to say next? The sociopragmatic problem of elaboration for Japanese students of English in academic contexts. *JACET Bulletin*, 10, 13–30.

Hiraga, M. K. and Turner, J. M. (1996). Pragmatic difficulties in academic discourse: A case of Japanese students in English. *Journal of the University of the Air*, 14, 91–109.

Hofstede, G. (2001). *Culture's consequences: Comparing values, behaviors, institutions, and organizations across nations*. 2nd edition. Thousand Oaks: Sage.

Holland, D. and Quinn, N. (Eds.) (1987). *Cultural models in language and thought*. Cambridge: Cambridge University Press.

Holliday, A., Hyde, M., and Kullman, J. (2004). *Intercultural communication: An advanced resource book*. London/New York: Routledge.

Holmes, J. (1984). Hedging your bets and sitting on the fence: Some evidence of hedges as support structures. *Te Reo 27*, 47–62.

Holmes, J. (1992). *An introduction to sociolinguistics*. London: Longman.

Holmes, J. (2008). *An introduction to sociolinguistics*. 3rd edition. London: Pearson/Longman.

Holmes, J. and Meyerhoff, M. (Eds.) (2005). *The handbook on language and gender*. Oxford: Blackwell.

Huang, Y. (2007). *Pragmatics*. Oxford: Oxford University Press.

Hymes, D. (1972). "SPEAKING." In J. J. Gumperz and D. Hymes (Eds.), *Directions in sociolinguistics: The ethnography of communication*. Oxford: Blackwell.

Ide, S. (1989). Formal forms and discernment: Two neglected aspects of universals of linguistic politeness. *Multilingua*, 8, 2–3, 223–248.

Ide, S. (2005). How and why honorifics can signify dignity and elegance: The indexicality and reflexivity in linguistic rituals. In R. T. Lakoff and S. Ide (Eds.) *Broadening the horizon of linguistic politeness* (pp. 45–64). Philadelphia, PA: John Benjamins.

Ide, S. and Inoue, V. (1991). Onna kotoba ni miro aidentiti [Identity in women's language]. *Gekkan Gengo*, 11, 46–48.

Iedema, R. (2003). *Discourses of post-bureaucratic organization*. Amsterdam: Benjamins.

Im, H. S. (2010). The use of definite and indefinite articles in English by speakers of Chinese, Japanese and Korean. Unpublished M.A. thesis. University of Florida.

Isaacs, E. A. and Clark, H. H. (1990). Ostensible invitations. *Language in Society*, 1, 493–509.

Jackson, J. (2008). *Language, identity and study abroad: Sociocultural perspectives*. London: Equinox.

Jakobson, R. (1960). Linguistics and poetics. Cited in S. C. Levinson (1983). *Pragmatics* (p. 41). Cambridge: Cambridge University Press.

Jin, L. and Cortazzi, M. (2006). Changing practices in Chinese cultures of learning. *Language, Culture, and Curriculum*, 19, 1, 5–20.

Johnson, B. (2003). *Values in English language teaching.* Mahwah, NJ: Lawrence Erlbaum.
Johnson, K. E. (1995). *Understanding communication in second language classrooms.* Cambridge: Cambridge University Press.
Jorden, E. H., with Noda, M. (1987). *Japanese: The spoken language.* 3 parts. New Haven: Yale University Press.
Kachru, B. B. (1989). Teaching world Englishes. *Indian Journal of Applied Linguistics, 15/1,* 85–95.
Kaiser, H. R. (forthcoming, 2012). Apologies and refusals in Uruguayan Spanish. Doctoral dissertation, in progress. University of Florida, Gainesville, Florida.
Kanagy, R. (1999). Interactional routines as a mechanism for L2 acquisition and socialization in an immersion context. *Journal of Pragmatics, 31,* 1467–1492.
Kasanga, L. A. (2006). Requests in a South African variety of English. *World Englishes, 26,* 1, 65–89.
Kasper, G. (1984). Pragmatic competence in learner-native speaker discourse. *Language Learning, 34,* 1–20.
Kasper, G. (1992). Pragmatic transfer. *Second Language Research, 8,* 203–231.
Kasper, G. (1993). Routine and interaction in interlanguage pragmatics. In L. F. Bouton (Ed.), *Pragmatics and language learning 6* (pp. 59–78). Urbana, IL: Division of English as an International Language, University of Illinois at Urbana-Champaign.
Kasper, G. (1995). Interlanguage pragmatics. In J. Verschueren, J. O. Ostman, and J. Bloomaert (Eds.), *Handbook of pragmatics* (pp. 1–17). Amsterdam: John Benjamins.
Kasper, G. (2004). Speech acts in (inter)action: Repeated questions. *Intercultural Pragmatics, 1–1,* 125–133.
Kasper, G. and Blum-Kulka, S. (Eds.) (1993). *Interlanguage pragmatics.* New York: Oxford University Press.
Kasper, G. and Roever, C. (2005). Pragmatics in second language learning. In E. Hinkel (Ed.), *Handbook of research in second language teaching and learning* (pp. 317–334). Mahwah, NJ: Lawrence Erlbaum.
Kasper, G. and Rose, K. R. (1991). Pragmatics and SLA. *Annual Review of Applied Linguistics, 19,* 81–104.
Kasper, G. and Rose, K. (2002). *Pragmatic development in a second language.* Oxford: Blackwell.
Kasper, G. and Schmidt, R. (1996). Developmental issues in interlanguage pragmatics. *Studies in Second Language Acquisition, 18,* 149–169.
Katz, M. L. (2000). Workplace language teaching and the intercultural construction of ideologies of competence. *Canadian Modern Language Review, 57,* 1, 144–172.
Keating, E. (1998). *Power sharing: Language, rank, gender, and social space in Pohnpei, Micronesia.* New York: Oxford University Press.
Keating, E. (2009). Power and pragmatics. *Language and Linguistics Compass 3/4,* 996–1009.
Kecskes, I. and Horn, L. R. (Eds.) (2007). *Explorations in pragmatics: Linguistic, cognitive and intercultural aspects.* Berlin/New York: Mouton de Gruyter.
Kerbrat-Orecchioni, C. (1997). A multilevel approach to the study of talk-in-interaction. *Pragmatics, 7,* 1, 1–20.
Kerbrat-Orecchioni, C. (2005). Politeness in France: How to buy bread politely. In L. Hickey and M. Stewart (Eds.), *Politeness in Europe* (pp. 29–44). Clevedon: Multilingual Matters.
Kerbrat-Orecchioni, C. (2006). Politeness in small shops in France. *Journal of Politeness Research, 2,* 79–103.

Kerekes, J. (1992). Development in nonnative speakers' use and perception of assertiveness and supportiveness in mixed-sex conversations. *Occasional Paper No. 21*. Honolulu: University of Hawaii at Manoa, Department of English as a Second Language.

Kerekes, J. (2003). Distrust: A determining factor in the outcomes of gatekeeping encounters: Strategies of linguistically diverse speakers. Doctoral dissertation, Stanford University, 2001. *Dissertation Abstracts International, 62* (10), 3366.

Kerekes, J. (2006). Winning an interviewer's trust in a gatekeeping encounter. *Language in Society, 35,* 27–57.

Kerekes, J. (2007). The co-construction of a gatekeeping encounter: An inventory of verbal actions. *Journal of Pragmatics, 39,* 1942–1973.

Kiesling, S. F. (2006). Hegemonic identity-making in narrative. In A. De Fina, D. Schiffrin and M. Bamberg (Eds.), *Discourse and identity* (pp. 261–287). Cambridge: Cambridge University Press.

Kirkpatrick, A. (1991). Information sequencing in Mandarin letters of request. *Anthropological Linguistics, 33,* 2, 184–203.

Kleifgen, J. A. and Bond, G. C. (Eds.) (2009). *The languages of Africa and the diaspora: Educating for language awareness.* Bristol: Multilingual Matters.

Koester, A. (2004). *The language of work.* London: Routledge.

Koshik, I. (2003). *Wh*-questions used as challenges. *Discourse Studies* 5(1), 51–77.

Kramsch, C. (1993). *Context and culture in language teaching.* Oxford: Oxford University Press.

Krashen, S. (1982). *Principles and practice in second language learning.* Oxford: Oxford University Press.

Kress, G. and Fowler, R. (1979). Interviews. In R. Fowler, R. Hodge, G. Kress, and T. Trew (Eds.), *Language and control.* London: Routledge & Kegan Paul.

Kusmierczyk, E. (2010) Personal communication.

Labov, W. (1972). *Language in the inner city.* Philadelphia: University of Pennsylvania Press.

Labov, W. and Fanshel, D. (1977). *Therapeutic discourse: Psychotherapy as conversation.* New York: Academic Press.

Lakoff, G. (1987). *Women, fire, and dangerous things: What categories reveal about the mind.* Chicago: University of Chicago Press.

Lakoff, R. T. (1971). Language in context. *Language, 48,* 907–927.

Lakoff, R. T. (1975). *Language and woman's place.* New York: Harper & Row.

Lakoff, R. T. (1990). *Talking power: The politics of language.* New York: BasicBooks.

Lambert Graham, S. (2008). A manual for (im)politeness?: The impact of the FAQ in an electronic community of practice. In D. Bousfield and M. A. Locher (Eds.), *Impoliteness in language: Studies on its interplay with power in theory and practice* (pp. 281–304). Berlin/New York: Mouton de Gruyter.

Laphasradakul, D. (2006). Politeness in cross-cultural communication: A case study of a Thai TA and American students. Unpublished paper for LIN 7885: Discourse analysis and pragmatics course, fall, 2006. University of Florida, Gainesville.

Leech, G. N. (1983). *Principles of pragmatics.* London: Longman.

Levinson, S. C. (1983). *Pragmatics.* Cambridge: Cambridge University Press.

Levinson, S. C. (1992). Activity types and language. In P. Drew and J. Heritage (Eds.), *Talk at work: Interaction in institutional settings* (pp. 66–100). Cambridge: Cambridge University Press. Reprinted from 1979 *Linguistics, 17,* 356–399.

Levy, A. (2009). Either/Or: Sports, sex, and the caste of Caster Semenya. *The New Yorker,* Nov. 30, 46–59.

Li, C. and Thompson, S. (1976). Subject and topic: A new typology of language. In C. Li (Ed.), *Subject and topic*. New York: Academic Press.

Li Wei (1998). The "why" and "how" questions in the analysis of conversational code-switching. In P. Auer (Ed.), *Code-switching in conversation: Language, interaction, and identity* (pp. 156–176). London/New York: Routledge.

Lifesouth (2006). Unpublished data from a deposition for legal case. Gainesville, Florida.

Lightbown, P. M. and Spada, N. (1999). *How languages are learned*. 2nd edition. Oxford: Oxford University Press.

Lightbown, P. M. and Spada, N. (2006). *How languages are learned*. 3rd edition. Oxford: Oxford University Press.

Liu, B. M. (2009). Chinese discourse markers in oral speech of mainland Mandarin speakers. In X. Yun (Ed.), *Proceedings of the 21st North American Conference on Chinese Linguistics* (NACCL-21), 2: 358–374. Smithfield: Bryant University.

LoCastro, V. (1987). Yes, I agree with you, but . . .: Agreement and disagreement in Japanese and American English. *JACET Annual Bulletin*, 18, 71–87. ERIC Document ED 654321.

LoCastro, V. (1990). Intercultural pragmatics: A Japanese-American case study. Ph.D. dissertation, Lancaster University, U.K.

LoCastro, V. (1996). English language education in Japan. In H. Coleman (Ed.), *Society and the language classroom* (pp. 40–58). Cambridge: Cambridge University Press.

LoCastro, V. (1997) Politeness and pragmatic competence in foreign language education. *Language Teaching Research*, 1, 3, 239–267.

LoCastro, V. (1998). Learner subjectivity and pragmatic competence development. Paper presented at Pac SLRF Conference 1998, March 26–29, Tokyo. ERIC Document no. 420 201.

LoCastro, V. (1999). A sociocultural functional analysis of fragmentation in Japanese. *Multilingua*, 18, 4, 369–389.

LoCastro, V. (2000). Evidence to accommodation to L2 pragmatic norms in peer review tasks of Japanese learners of English. *JALT Journal* 22, 2, 245–270.

LoCastro, V. (2001). Individual differences in second language acquisition: Attitudes, learner subjectivity, and L2 pragmatic norms. *System*, 29, 69–89.

LoCastro, V. (2003). *An introduction to pragmatics: Social action for language teachers*. Ann Arbor: University of Michigan Press.

LoCastro, V. (2005). Unpublished data. Seminar at the University of Florida.

LoCastro, V. (2006). Law and the Language of Identity: Discourse in the William Kennedy Smith rape trial. Book Review. *Journal of Pragmatics*, 38, 1122–1125.

LoCastro, V. (2008a). Relational work in an ITA classroom: Building and maintaining rapport. Paper presented at the AAAL 2008 Annual Conference, March 29–April 1, 2008. Washington, D.C.

LoCastro V. (2008b). Long sentences and floating commas: Mexican students' rhetorical practices and the sociocultural context. In U. Connor, E. Nagelhout, and W. V. Rozycki (Eds.), *Contrastive rhetoric: Reaching to intercultural rhetoric* (pp. 195–218). Amsterdam/Philadelphia: John Benjamins.

LoCastro, V. (2009). The interview as site for doing teacher identity. Paper presented at the AAAL Annual Conference, Denver, Colorado, March 21–24, 2009.

LoCastro, V. (2010a). Pragmatic development through awareness raising. *SPELT Quarterly*, 24, 4, 2–9.

LoCastro, V. (2010b). Misunderstandings: Pragmatic glitches and misfires. In D. H. Tatsuki and N. R. Houck (Eds.), *Pragmatics from research to practice: Teaching speech acts* (pp. 7–16). Washington, D.C.: Teachers of English to Speakers of Other Languages.

LoCastro, V. (2011). Second language pragmatics. In E. Hinkel (Ed.), *Handbook of research in second language teaching and learning* (pp. 319–344). London: Routledge.

LoCastro, V. and Tapper, G. (2006). International teaching assistants and teacher Identity. *Journal of Applied Lingusitics, 3,* 2, 185–218.

Locher, M. A. (2004). *Power and politeness in action: Disagreements in oral communication.* Berlin: Mouton de Gruyter.

Locher, M. A. and Watts, R. (2005). Politeness theory and relational work. *Journal of Politeness Research, 1,* 1, 9–33.

Locher, M. A. and Watts, R. (2008). Relational work and impoliteness: Negotiating norms of linguistic behavior. In D. Bousfield and M. A. Locher (Eds.), *Impoliteness in language: Studies on its interplay with power in theory and practice* (pp. 77–100). Berlin/New York: Mouton de Gruyter.

Long, M. (1983). Does second language instruction make a difference? A review of the research. *TESOL Quarterly, 17,* 359–382.

Long, M. H. (1996). The role of the linguistic environment in second language acquisition. In W. C. Ritchie and T. K. Bahtia (Eds.), *Handbook of second language acquisition* (pp. 413–68). New York: Academic Press. Reprinted in L. Ortega (Ed.), *Second language acquisition: Critical concepts in linguistics.* London: Routledge, forthcoming.

Losey, K. K. (1995) Gender and ethnicity as factors in the development of verbal skills in bilingual Mexican American women. *TESOL Quarterly, 29,* 635–661.

Louw, K. J., Derwing, T. M., and Abbott, M. L. (2010). Teaching pragmatics to L2 learners for the workplace: The job interview. *The Canadian Modern Language Review/La Revue Canadienne des Language Vivantes, 66,* 5, 739–758.

McCarthy, M. (1998). *Spoken language and applied linguistics.* Cambridge: Cambridge University Press.

McKay, S. L. (2002). *Teaching English as an international language.* Oxford: Oxford University Press.

Maeshiba, N., Yoshinaga, N., Kasper, G., and Ross, S. (1996). Transfer and proficiency in interlanguage apologizing. In S. M. Gass and J. Neu (Eds.), *Speech acts across cultures: Challenges to communication in a second language* (pp. 155–187). Berlin: Mouton de Gruyter.

Mashiri, P. (2003). Managing "face" in urban public transport: Polite request strategies in commuter omnibus discourse in Harare. In S. Makoni, and U. H. Meinhof (Eds.), *Africa and applied linguistics.* AILA Review Volume 16 (pp. 120–126). Amsterdam/Philadelphia: John Benjamins.

Matoesian, G. M. (2001). *Law and the language of identity: Discourse in the William Kennedy Smith rape trial.* Oxford: Oxford University Press.

Matsumoto, Y. (1988). Reexamination of the universality of face: Politeness phenomena in Japanese. *Journal of Pragmatics, 12,* 403–426.

Maynard, S. K. (1986). On back-channel behavior in Japanese and English casual conversation. *Linguistics, 24,* 1079–1108.

Maynard, S. K. (1990). *An introduction to Japanese grammar and communication strategies.* Tokyo: The Japan Times.

Mead, R. (2003). The almost it girl. *The New Yorker,* October 20, 96–104.

Menard-Warwick, J. (2009). *Gendered identities and immigrant language learning.* Bristol, UK: Multilingual Matters.
Mey, J. (1993). *Pragmatics: An introduction.* Oxford: Blackwell.
Meyerhoff, M. (2006). *Introducing sociolinguistics.* London/New York: Routledge.
Miller, R. (1967). *The Japanese language.* Chicago: University of Chicago Press.
Mills, S. (2003). *Gender and politeness.* Cambridge: Cambridge University Press.
Milroy, L. (1989). Gender as a speaker variable: The interesting case of the glottalised stops in Tyneside. *York Papers in Linguistics, 13,* 227–236.
Mitchell-Keenan, C. (1972). Signifying, loud-talking, and marking. In T. Kochman (Ed.), *Rappin' an stylin' out: Communication in urban Black America* (pp. 315–335). Urbana: University of Illinois Press.
Mizutani, O. and Mizutani, N. (1987). *How to be polite in Japanese.* Tokyo: Japan Times.
Mo, T. (1982). *Soursweet.* London: Sphere Books Ltd (Abacus).
Moerman, M. (1988). *Talking culture: Ethnography and conversation analysis.* Philadelphia, PA: University of Pennsylvania.
Morgan, M. (1996). Conversational signifying: Grammar and indirectness among African American women. In E. Ochs, E. A. Schegloff, and S. A. Thompson (Eds.), *Interaction and grammar* (pp. 405–434). Cambridge: Cambridge University Press.
Mori, M. (1996). Conversational analysis of writing conferences between English-speaking teachers and Japanese EFL students. Master's thesis, International Christian University, Tokyo, Japan.
Morita, N. (2000). Discourse socialization through oral classroom activities in a TESL graduate program. *TESOL Quarterly, 34,* 2, 279–310.
Nakane, I. (2006). Silence and politeness in intercultural communication in university seminars. *Journal of Pragmatics, 38,* 1811–1835.
Netsu, M. and LoCastro, V. (1997). Opinion-giving and point of view in discussion tasks. In T. Fujimura, Y. Kato, M. Ahmed, and D. Fujimoto (Eds.), *Proceedings of the 8th Conference on Second Language Research in Japan* (pp. 136–153). Niigata, Japan: International University of Japan: Language Programs.
Newham, F. (2005). The painful ties that bind. *The Guardian Weekly* April 1–7, 19.
Norton, B. P. (1995). Social identity, investment, and language learning. *TESOL Quarterly, 29,* 9–31.
Ochs, E. (1992). Indexing gender. In A. Duranti and C. Goodwin (Eds.), *Rethinking context* (pp. 335–358). Cambridge: Cambridge University Press.
Ochs, E., Schegloff, E., and Thompson, S. A. (Eds.) (1996). *Interaction and grammar.* Cambridge: Cambridge University Press.
Ogiermann, E. (2008). On the culture-specificity of linguistic gender differences: The case of English and Russian apologies. *Intercultural Pragmatics, 5-3,* 259–286.
Ohta, A. S. (1991). Evidentiality and politeness in Japanese. *Issues in Applied Linguistics, 2*: 211–238.
Ohta, A. S. (2001). *Second language acquisition processes in the classroom: Learning Japanese.* Mahwah, NJ: Lawrence Erlbaum.
Okamoto, S. (1999). Situated politeness: Coordinating honorific and non-honorific expressions in Japanese conversation. *Pragmatics, 9,* 1, 51–74.
Olshtain, E. and Cohen, A. (1983). Apology: a speech act set. In N. Wolfson and E. Judd (Eds.), *Sociolinguistics and language acquisition* (pp. 18–35). Rowley, MA: Newbury House.

Ortner, S. H. (1974). Is female to male as nature is to culture? In M. Rosaldo and L. Lampere (Eds.), *Woman, culture, and society* (pp. 67–88). Stanford: Stanford University Press.
Partridge, B. (2007). *Discourse analysis: An introduction.* London/New York: Continuum.
Pavlenko, A. and Blackledge, A. (Eds.) (2004). *Negotiation of identities in multilingual settings.* Clevedon: Multilingual Matters.
Peirce, B. N. (1995). Language, identity, and the ownership of English. *TESOL Quarterly, 31,* 409–429.
Perez, B. (2004). *Becoming biliterate: A study in two-way bilingual immersion education.* Mahwah, NJ: Lawrence Erlbaum.
Philips, S. U. (1976). Some sources of cultural variability in the regulation of talk. *Language in Society, 5,* 81–95.
Pienemann, M., Johnson, M., and Brindley, G. (1988). Constructing an acquisition-based procedure for assessing second language acquisition. *Studies in Second Language Acquisition, 10,* 217–243.
Pomerantz, A. (1984). Agreeing and disagreeing with assessments: Some features of preferred/dispreferred turn shapes. In J. M. Atkinson and J. Heritage (Eds.), *Structures in social action: Studies in conversational analysis* (pp. 57–101). Cambridge: Cambridge University Press.
Pratt, D. (1992). Chinese conceptions of learning and teaching: A westerner's attempt at understanding. *International Journal of Lifelong Education, 11,* 4, 301–319.
Quirk, R. and Widdowson, H. (1985). *English in the world: Teaching and learning the language and literatures.* Cambridge: Cambridge University Press.
Ramirez Verdugo, D. and Romero Trillo, J. (2005). The pragmatic function of intonation in L2 discourse: English tag questions used by Spanish speakers. *Intercultural Pragmatics, 2,* 2, 151–168.
Rampton, B. (1990). Displacing the "native speaker:" Expertise, affiliation, and inheritance. *ELT Journal, 44,* 97–101.
Random House College Dictionary (1984). Revised edition. New York: Random House
Roberts, C. and Campbell, S. (2006). *Talk on trial: Job interviews, language, and ethnicity.* London: Department of Work and Pensions, Research Report 344.
Roberts, C. and Sarangi, S. (2001). Mapping and assessing medical students' interactional involvement styles with patients. In K. Spellman Miller and P. Thompson (Eds.), *Unity and diversity in language use* (pp. 99–117). London: Continuum.
Roberts, C., Davies, E., and Jupp, T. (1992). *Language and discrimination: A study of communication in multi-ethnic workplaces.* London: Longman.
Roberts, C., Byram, M., Barro, A., Jordan, S., and Street, B. (2001). *Language learners as ethnographers.* Clevedon: Multilingual Matters.
Robinson, M. A. (1992). Introspective methodology in interlanguage pragmatics research. In G. Kasper (Ed.), *Pragmatics of Japanese as a native and foreign language* (pp. 27–82). Technical Report No. 3. University of Hawaii at Manoa: Second Language Teaching and Curriculum Center.
Sacks, H., Schegloff, E. A., and Jefferson, G. (1978). A simplest systematics for the organization of turn-taking for conversation. *Language, 50,* 4, 696–735.
Salisbury, T. and Bardovi-Harlig, K. (2000). Oppositional talk and the acquisition of modality in L2 English. In B. Swierzbin, R. Morris, M. E Anderson, C. A. Klee, and E. Tarone (Eds.), *Social and cognitive factors in second language acquisition: Selected proceedings of the 1999 second language research forum* (pp. 57–69). Somerville, MA: Cascadilla Press.

Sapir, E. (1951). The unconscious patterning of behaviour in society. In D. G. Mandelbaum (Ed.), *Selected Writings of Edward Sapir*. Berkeley: University of California at Berkeley. Cited in C. B. Cazden (2001), *Classroom Discourse: The Languages of Teaching and Learning*. 2nd edition. Portsmouth, NH: Heinemann.

Sasaki, M. (1995). Unpublished data. Tokyo: National Language Research Institute.

Saville-Troike, M. (2005). *Introducing second language acquisition*. Cambridge: Cambridge University Press.

Schecter, S. R. and Bayley, R. (2002). *Language as cultural practice: Mexicanos en el norte*. Mahwah, NJ: Lawrence Erlbaum.

Schegloff, E. A. (1982). Discourse as an interactional achievement. In D. Tannen (Ed.), *Analyzing discourse: Text and talk* (pp. 71–93). Washington, D.C.: Georgetown University Press.

Schegloff, E. A. (1992). On talk and its institutional occasions. In P. Drew and J. Heritage (Eds.), *Talk at work: Interaction in institutional settings* (pp. 101–134). Cambridge: Cambridge University Press.

Schegloff, E. A., Ochs, E., and Thompson, S.A. (1996). Introduction. In E. Ochs, E. A. Schegloff, and S. A. Thompson (Eds.) (1996), *Interaction and grammar* (pp. 1–51). Cambridge: Cambridge University Press.

Schiffrin, D. (1988). *Discourse markers*. Cambridge: Cambridge University Press.

Schiffrin, D. (1994). *Approaches to discourse*. Oxford: Blackwell.

Schiffrin, D. (1996). Interactional sociolinguistics. In S. L. Mackay and N. H. Hornberger (Eds.), *Sociolinguistics and language teaching* (pp. 307–328). Cambridge: Cambridge University Press.

Schmidt, R. R. (1993). Consciousness, learning, and interlanguage pragmatics. In G. Kasper and S. Blum-Kulka (Eds.), *Interlanguage pragmatics* (pp. 21–42). Oxford: Oxford University Press.

Schmidt, R. W. and Frota, S. N. (1986). Developing basic conversational ability in a second language: A case study of an adult learner of Portuguese. In R. R. Day (Ed.), *Talking to learn: Conversation in second language acquisition* (pp. 237–326). Rowley, MA: Newbury House.

Schnurr, S., Marra, M., and Holmes, J. (2007). Being (im)polite in New Zealand workplaces: Maori and Pakeha leaders. *Journal of Pragmatics*, 39, 712–729.

Schumann, J. H. (1978). The acculturation model for second language acquisition. In R. C. Gringas (Ed.), *Second language acquisition and foreign language teaching*. Arlington, VA: Center for Applied Linguistics.

Schwabe, M., Reuber, M., Schöndienst, M. and Gülich, E. (2008). Listening to people with seizures: How can linguistic analysis help in the differential diagnosis of seizure disorders. *Communication and Medicine*, 5, 1, 53–66.

Scollon, R. and Scollon, S. B. K. (1983). Face in interethnic communication. In J. C. Richards and R. Schmidt (Eds.), *Language and Communication* (pp. 156–190). London: Longman.

Scollon, R. and Scollon, S. W. (1995). *Intercultural communication*. Oxford: Blackwell.

Searle, J. R. (1969). *Speech acts: An essay in the philosophy of language*. Cambridge: Cambridge University Press.

Seck, M. (forthcoming) A comparative analysis of Wolof and French discourse: The case of the Senegalese former Prime Minister Idrissa Seck addressing his compatriots.

Selinker, L. (1972). Interlanguage. *International Review of Applied Linguistics*, 10, 209–231.

Shaw, W. D. (1983). Asian student attitudes towards English. In L. Smith (Ed.), *Readings in English as an international language* (pp. 21–34). Oxford: Pergamon.

Shiraishi, T. (1997). Pragmatics of requests in Japanese: A look at V+*te kudasai*. Senior thesis, International Christian University, Tokyo.

Siegal, M. (1994). Looking East: Identity Construction and White Women learning Japanese. Ph.D. dissertation, University of California at Berkeley.

Simon, B. (2004). *Identity in modern society: A social psychological perspective.* Oxford: Blackwell.

Sinclair, J. M. and Coulthard, R. M. (1975). *Towards an analysis of discourse: The English used by teachers and pupils.* London: Oxford University Press.

Sinclair, J. M. and Brazil, D. (1982). *Teacher talk.* Oxford: Oxford University Press.

Smith, L. (1976). English as an international auxiliary language. *RELC Journal,* 7, 2, 38–43.

Smouse, M. R. (2005). Conveying requests in Xhousa as a foreign language. Paper presented at the International Conference of Pragmatics and Language Learning, Indiana University, Bloomington, IN, April 15, 2005.

Spencer-Oatey, H. (2007). Theories of identity and the analysis of face. *Journal of Pragmatics,* 39, 639–656.

Spencer-Oatey, H. and Franklin, P. (2009). *Intercultural communication: A multidisciplinary approach to intercultural communication.* London: Palgrave.

Sperber, D. and Wilson, D. (1986). *Relevance: Communication and cognition.* Oxford: Blackwell.

Spradley, J. P. (1979). *The ethnographic interview.* New York: Holt, Rinehart, and Winston.

Stilwell Peccei, J. (1999). *Pragmatics.* London: Routledge.

Sunderland, J. (2004). *Gendered discourses.* London/New York: Palgrave.

Tagliamonte, S. and D'Arcy, A. (2004). *He's like, she's like*: The quotative system in Canadian youth. *Journal of Sociolinguistics,* 8, 493–514.

Takahashi, T. and Beebe, L. M. (1987). The development of pragmatic competence by Japanese learners of English. *JALT Journal,* 8, 131–155.

Talmy, S. (2004). Forever FOB: The cultural production of ESL in a high school. *Pragmatics,* 14, (2/3), 149–172.

Talmy, S. (2009). Resisting ESL: Categories and sequence in a critically "motivated" analysis of classroom interaction. In H. Nguyen and G. Kasper (Eds.), *Talk-in-Interaction: Multilingual perspectives* (pp. 181–213). Honolulu: University of Hawaii, National Foreign Language Resource Center.

Talmy, S. (2010). The interview as collaborative achievement: Interaction, identity, and ideology in a speech event. *Applied Linguistics,* 31, 1–9.

Tanaka, M. (1997a). The acquisition of indirect-passive in Japanese as a foreign/second language. Paper presented at the Tenth Biennial Conference of the Japanese Studies Association of Australia. Japanese Studies Centre, Monash University, Melbourne, July 6–10.

Tanaka, M. (1997b) The acquisition of point of view and voice in Japanese as a second/foreign language: The influence of the linguistic and non-linguistic environment. Document No. 08680323. Tokyo: Ministry of Education.

Tanaka, N. (1988). Politeness: Some problems for Japanese speakers of English. *JALT Journal* 9, 81–102.

Tannen, D. (1986). *That's not what I meant: How conversational style makes or breaks relationships.* New York: Ballantine Books.

Tannen, D. (1990). *You just don't understand.* New York: Morrow.
Tannen, D. (1993). The relativity of linguistic strategies: Rethinking power and solidarity in gender and dominance. In D. Tannen (Ed.), *Gender and conversational interaction* (pp. 165–188). New York: Oxford University Press.
Tannen, D. (2005). *Conversational style: Analyzing talk among friends.* New edition. New York: Oxford University Press.
Tarone, E. (1980) Communication strategies, foreigner talk, and repair in interlanguage. *Language Learning, 30,* 417–431.
Tarone, E. and Swierzbin, B. (2009). *Exploring learner language.* Oxford: Oxford University Press.
Tatsuki, D. H. and Houck, N. R. (Eds.) (2010). *Pragmatics: Teaching speech acts.* Alexandra, VA: Teachers of English to Speakers of Other Languages, Inc.
Thomas, J. (1983). Cross-cultural pragmatic failure. *Applied Linguistics, 4,* 2, 91–112.
Thomas, J. (1995). *Meaning in interaction: An introduction to pragmatics.* London: Longman.
Traverso, V. (2006). Aspects of polite behavior in French and Syrian service encounters: A data-based comparative study. *Journal of Politeness Research, 2,* 105–122.
Trudgill, P. (1972). Sex, covert prestige and linguistic change in the urban British English of Norwich. *Language in Society, 1,* 2, 179–196.
Tudini, V. (2010). *Online second language acquisition*: Conversational analysis of online chat. London: Continuum.
Turner, J. M. and Hiraga, M. K. (1996). Elaborating elaboration in academic tutorials: Changing cultural assumptions. In H. Coleman and L. Cameron (Eds.), *Change and language* (pp. 131–140). Clevedon, UK: Multilingual Matters.
Van Ek, J. (1975). *The threshold level.* Strasbourg: Council of Europe and Oxford: Pergamon Press.
Vine, B. (2009). Directives at work: Exploring the contextual complexity of workplace directives. *Journal of Pragmatics, 41,* 1395–1405.
Vygotsky, L. (1978). *Mind in society.* Cambridge, MA: Harvard University Press.
Wall, A. P. (1987). *Say it naturally: Verbal strategies for authentic communication.* Orlando, FL: Harcourt Brace.
Watts, R. (2003). *Politeness.* Cambridge: Cambridge University Press.
Watts, R. J., Ide, S., and Ehlich, K. (Eds.) (2005). *Politeness in language: Studies in its history, theory and practice.* 2nd edition. Berlin/New York: Mouton de Gruyter.
Waugh, L. R., Fonseca-Greber, B., Vickers, C., and Eroz, B. (2007). Multiple empirical approaches to a complex analysis of discourse. In M. Gonzalez-Marquez, I. Mittelberg, S. Coulson, and M. J. Spivey (Eds.), *Methods in cognitive linguistics* (pp. 120–148). Amsterdam/Philadelphia: John Benjamins.
Weatherall, A. (2002). *Gender, language, and discourse.* London: Routledge.
Weizman, E. and Blum-Kulka, S. (1996). Requestive hints. In S. Blum-Kulka, J. House, and G. Kasper (Eds.), *Cross-cultural pragmatics* (pp. 71–95). Norwood, NJ: Ablex.
Wertsch, J. V. (1991). *Voices of the mind: A sociocultural approach to mediated action.* Cambridge, MA: Harvard University Press
White, R. (1993). Saying please: Pragmalinguistic failure in English interaction. *English Language Teaching Journal, 47,* 3, 193–202.
Wichmann, A. (2000). *Intonation in text and discourse.* London: Longman.
Wichmann, A. (2004). The intonation of please-requests: a corpus based study. *Journal of Pragmatics, 36,* 1521–1549.

Widdowson, H. G. (1978). *Teaching language as communication*. Oxford: Oxford University Press.
Wierzbicka, A. (1991). *Cross-cultural pragmatics: The semantics of human interaction*. Berlin: De Gruyter.
Wikipedia (2006). 'Respect'. Retrieved from http://en.wikipedia/org/wiki/Respect, May 15, 2006.
Wilkins, D. (1976). *Notional syllabuses: A taxonomy and its relevance to foreign language curriculum development*. Oxford: Oxford University Press.
Wittgenstein, L. (1958). *Philosophical investigations*. Oxford: Blackwell.
Yngve, V. (1970). On getting a word in edgewise. In *Papers from the Sixth Regional Meeting, The Chicago Linguistic Society* (pp. 567–577). Chicago: Chicago Linguistic Society.
Young, L. W. (1982). Inscrutability revisited. In J. J. Gumperz (Ed.), *Language and social identity* (pp. 72–84). Cambridge: Cambridge University Press.
Yule, G. (1996). *Pragmatics*. Oxford: Oxford University Press.
Yule, G. (1997). *Referential communication tasks*. Mahwah, NJ: Lawrence Erlbaum.

INDEX

academic speech event 124–6
action 19–21
action theory 166–9; action and activity 167–8; basic notions 166–7; coordination problem 168–9
"activity type" 186
adjacency pairs 56–7
aizuchi 97
anaphora 27–9
Anglo-American pragmatics 7
anthropological pragmatics 6
apologies 93, 294–7
Austin, J.L. 60

back channel cues 97
background knowledge 40–1
baited indirectness 89
bilingual political discourse 299–301

CA *see* conversation analysis
CANCODE 288
cataphora 28–9
CCCA *see* culturally contextualized conversation analysis
CCSARP *see* Cross-Cultural Speech Act Research Project
CDA *see* Critical Discourse Analysis
"challenge questions" 292
code switching 71, 178
"communicative competence" 306
communicative function 6, 225–7
concordancing 287

conditions of appropriateness *see* felicity conditions
consent 273
context 19–21
contextual meaning 39
Continental pragmatics 7
Contrastive Analysis 116
contrastive rhetoric 102
conversation analysis 13, 53–4, 170–1
Cooperative Principle 48
corpus linguistics 287–8
Critical Discourse Analysis 222
cross-cultural pragmatics 79–110; applications to language teaching 107; criticisms of pragmatic failure perspective 90–2; cross-cultural speech acts 92–4; defining 80–1; formal business letters **103–4**; intercultural rhetoric 102–7; listener behavior 96–9; non-English cross-cultural studies 99–102; pragmatic failure 83–90; sample of cross-cultural studies 94–9; values and beliefs 81–3; the verb *ask* in English and its semantic core meanings and functionally equivalent Walmatjari verb **95**
Cross-Cultural Speech Act Research Project 93–4
cross-cultural speech acts 92–4
culturally contextualized conversation analysis 171
culture 40–1

data 275–7
data collection procedures 280
DCT *see* discourse completion task
deixis 24–7 *see also* discourse deixis; social deixis; spatial deixis; temporal deixis
discourse analysis 13, 285
discourse completion task 93–4, 164, 230, 256–7, 284–5
discourse deixis 27
discourse markers 126
dispreferred responses 57–60
doctor–patient discourse 191–5
Dyirbal 82

Elite Swahili 300–1
emic study 274–5
endophoric reference 28
English as an International Language 253
English language teaching 253
entailment 29–31
epistemic stance 190
ethics 273
ethnography of speaking 13
ethnopragmatics 6
etic study 274–5
exophoric reference 28

"face" 137
face-enhancing acts 142
face-flattering acts 142
face-saving strategies 140–2
face-threatening acts 138–40
felicity conditions 63
focus groups *see* group interview
folk linguistic theory 9
force 21–2
functional linguistics 285–6

gender: communicative function 225–7; definitions 213–14; effect in English and Russian apologies 230–1; enactment in language use 211–16; identity construction of men 227–9; imperatives in the workplace 229–30; power 220–1; power in interactions 227–31; sociohistorical overview of Studies in relation to language in use 214–16
gender exclusive speech difference 211
gender preferential speech features 211
gendered 213
gendered discourse 213
grammaticalization 35–7

Grice, H.S. 47; contribution to pragmatics 47–53; four maxims 48–50; limitations to Grice's model of communication 50–3; regular flouting of CP and maxims **52**; role of maxims **50**; suspending of CP and maxims **52–3**
group interview 282
Gumperz, J. 69

habitus 150–1
Hindi-Punjabi code switching 69
How to Do Things with Words 21, 60

identity 160, 162–3; action theory 166–9; application to classrooms 180–1; conversation analysis 170–1; educational context 178–80; enactment 166–70; explanatory definitions 160–2; Hinduism 177–8; interactional construction 159–83; La Lotería 171–2; learning English 175–7; occasioning identity work 173–5; role of sociocultural factors 163–6; semantic formulas used by both Jordanian groups **165**; studies 171–80
illocutionary act 61
illocutionary force-indicating device 62, 230
implicature 39–40
impoliteness 149
inclusive approach 306–7
indeterminacy 98
indexicality 21–3
indexicals 23
inference 39–40
information structure 34–5
Institutional Review Boards 273
institutional talk 184–209; activity type 185–7; applications to the classroom 207–8; doctor–patient discourse 191–5; job interviews 197–203; oral examinations 187–91; U.S. courtroom trial discourse 195–7; workplace communication 204–7
intentionality 21–2
Interaction Hypothesis 117
interactional sociolinguistics 68–73, 287
intercultural communication 80–1
intercultural rhetoric 102–7
interlanguage pragmatics 80, 111–35; definitions 112–16; developmental

stages involving relative clauses **118**; developmental stages of pragmatic development 118–20; influence of third languages 129; interlanguage realization strategies 120–8; learner language 116–18; limiting factors on development 129–33; pragmatic transfer from L1 to L2 113–16
interlanguage realization strategies 120–8; academic speech event 124–6; pragmatic markers 126–8; referential communication 122–4
interpersonal markers 126
interviews 281–3; group interview 282; retrospective interview 282–3; structured interview 281–2; unstructured interview 282
IRE pattern 258

job interviews 197–203

La Lotería 171–2
Lakoff, G. 82
Lakoff, R. 214–15
language: functional view 37–8; gender 216–18; gender and communicative function 225–7; gender and power 210–31, 220–1; gender and power in interactions 227–31; gender enactment 211–16; non-Western perspectives 218–20; power 221–5; Senegal political discourse 223–5
Language Acquisition Device (LAD) 112
language analysis 12–14
Language and Woman's Place 214
language data 42
"language games" 186
learner language 116–18; history 116–17; study 117–18
listener behavior 96–9
listener cues *see* back channel cues
locutionary act 61
London-Lund corpus 288

MCA *see* membership categorization analysis
meaning: interactions 38–9
"member checking" 279
membership categorization analysis 178
MICASE 288
microanalysis 285
misunderstood intentions 85, 88–90

modality 120
Morris, C. 5

negative politeness 137–8; strategies 141

OAP *see* oral academic presentations
observation 280–1
Observer's Paradox 272
occasioning 13
oral academic presentations 190
oral examinations 187–91
oral proficiency interviews 292

participants 272–3
performance data 7
performative 60
perlocutionary act 62
personal deixis 24–5
phatic 8
planned talk 276
plurilingualism 299
pointed indirectness 89
politeness 136–58; applications to classroom 154–6; criticism of Brown and Levinson model 143–7; new perspective 147–51; relational work 149–51; showing respect 151–4; theory 137–43; Watts and Locher 147–9
politeness theory 137–43; cross-cultural differences 142–3; face-saving strategies 140–2; face-threatening acts 138–40; positive and negative face 137–8
politic behavior 149
political discourse 223–5
positive politeness 137–8; strategies 141–2
Post, E. 9
power: and gender 220–1; and language 221–5
Power and Difference: Gender in Island Southeast Asia 220
pragmalinguistic failure 84–5, 86
pragmatic competence 305–9; activities in local communities 256–8; awareness-raising 254–6; classroom input 243–5; development in classroom 234–63; diverse world 308–9; facilitation of teaching and learning 254–9; factors affecting development 241–9; inclusive approach 306–7; instructed contexts 236–41; learners 248–9; materials

246–8; norms 252–4; other factors 249–54; second/foreign language learners 235–6; sociocultural dimensions 250–2; teachers 245–6; training outside traditional language classroom 259–60; transfer 241–3; value of research 307–8; variation in classroom interactional patterns 258–9
pragmatic development 118–20
pragmatic failure 83–90; categories of 84–90; criticisms of 90–2; indirectness in a talk within a family **89–90**; misunderstood intentions 88–90; part of job interview in London **87**; pragmalinguistic failure 86; sociopragmatic failure 87–8
pragmatic markers 126–8
pragmatic meaning: anaphora 27–9; context and action 19–21; cultural and background knowledge 40–1; deixis 24–7; entailment and presupposition 29–31; functional view of language 37–8; grammaticalization 35–7; Grice's contribution to pragmatics 47–53; inference and implicature 39–40; information structure 34–5; intentionality and force 21–2; interactional sociolinguistics 68–73; language data 42; levels of addressee forms and verb endings **35**; meaning in interactions 38–9; preference organization 53–60; principles of 18–45; prosody 31–4; reference and indexicality 21–3; sentence and utterance meaning 18; sociolinguistic theories of 46–76; from speech acts to events to activities 60–8; use and usage 19
pragmatic misfires 298–9
pragmatics 3–17; definition of 5–7; difference from semantics 11–12; Grice's contribution 47–53; how does it study language 10–11; other related forms of language analysis 12–14; what does it study 7–10
preference organization 53–60; adjacency pairs 56–7; preferred and dispreferred responses 57–60; turn taking 54–6; types of preferred and dispreferred responses **58**
preferred responses 57–60
presupposition 29–31
prosody 31–4, 71
public domain data 276–7

"question substitutes" 292
questionnaires 284–5
questions 291–4

redressive action 139
reference 21–3, 29
referential communication 122–4
refusal 294–7
relational work 149–51; showing respect 151–4
Relevance Theory 9
research 307–8
research design 270–1
research projects: apologies and refusals in Latin American Spanish 294–7; bilingual political discourse 299–301; pragmatic glitches and misfires 298–9; questions 291–4; sociopragmatics 291–301
researcher 274–5
respect 151–4; case study participants 153; data analysis and findings 153–4
retrospective interview 282–3
reviewing vocabulary 67
rollo 189

second language acquisition 111, 162
"Self-Aspect Model of Identity" 160–1
semantics 11–12
sentence 18
sex 213, 214
signifying 89
SLA *see* second language acquisition
social action theory 166
social deixis 26–7
sociocultural values 250–2
sociolinguists 12; Grice's contribution to pragmatics; interactional sociolinguistics 68–73; preference organization 53–60; from speech acts to events to activities 60–8; theories of pragmatic meaning 46–76
sociopragmatic failure 85, 87–8
sociopragmatics 159; ideas for research projects 291–301
sociopragmatics project: data 275–7; data analysis and interpretation 283–8; data collection methodologies 280–3; data collection procedures 280; ethics and obtaining consent 273; guidelines 267–90; instruments 279–80; participants 272–3; presentation of findings 288; research design 270–1; researcher 274–5;

setting up a study 268–70; study setting 271–2; transcription 277–9; writing up findings 288–90
spatial deixis 25
speaker meaning *see utterance meaning*
SPEAKING taxonomy 20
speech act theory 21, 60–8; felicity conditions 63; form and function problem 64; illocutionary act 61; limitations of 64–5; locutionary act 61; perlocutionary act 62; recognition of intended force 62–3; research on classroom learning **67**; speech events and activities 65–8
speech acts 8, 13
speech event 13, 20
structured interview 281–2
Survey of English Usage (SEU) 226

Teaching English as an International Language 253
temporal deixis 25–6
That's Not What I Meant 88
"The Pope Question" 293–4
The Second Sex 214
The Tale of Genji 218

transcription 277–9
transition relevant place 55
trial discourse 195–7
Trillo, R. 32
turn taking 54–6

Understanding Communication in Second Language Classrooms 245
unmotivated looking 70
unplanned talk 276
unstructured interview 282
U.S. courtroom trial discourse 195–7
usage 19
use 19
"*usomi*" 301
utterance 18
utterance meaning 18, 39

Verbal Hygiene 147
Verdugo, R. 32

"waffling" 122
Wittgenstein 186
workplace communication 204–7

zero anaphora 29

WITHDRAWAL